Search Engine Optimization Bible

Second Edition

Jerri L. Ledford

WILEY

Wiley Publishing, Inc.

Search Engine Optimization Bible, Second Edition

Published by
Wiley Publishing, Inc.
10475 Crosspoint Boulevard
Indianapolis, IN 46256
www.wiley.com

Copyright © 2009 by Wiley Publishing, Inc., Indianapolis, Indiana

Published simultaneously in Canada

ISBN: 978-0-470-45264-6

Manufactured in the United States of America

10 9 8 7 6 5 4 3 2

Library of Congress Cataloging-in-Publication Data is available from the publisher.

Credits

Acquisitions Editor
Katie Mohr

Development Editor
William Bridges

Technical Editor
Andrew Edney

Production Editor
Melissa Lopez

Copy Editor
Luann Rouff

Editorial Manager
Mary Beth Wakefield

Production Manager
Tim Tate

Vice President and Executive Group Publisher
Richard Swadley

Vice President and Executive Publisher
Barry Pruett

Associate Publisher
Jim Minatel

Proofreader
Justin Neely and Todd Spencer, Word One

Indexer
Jack Lewis

Cover Image
Joyce Haughey

Cover Designer
Michael Trent

About the Author

Jerri Ledford has been a freelance business technology writer for more than 15 years. During that time, more than 700 of her articles, profiles, news stories, and reports have appeared online and in print. Her publishing credits include: *Intelligent Enterprise*, *Network World*, *Information Security* Magazine, *DCM* Magazine, *CRM* Magazine, and *IT Manager's* Journal.

She develops and teaches technology training courses for both consumer and business users, including courses on security, customer service, career skills, and various technologies for companies such as: ClipTraining, IBT Financial, Writer's Village University, You Don't Say, LLC., Hewlett-Packard, Sony, Gateway, Forbes and CNET. She is also the author of 15 books including *Google AdSense for Dummies and Google Analytics 2.0*.

When she's not buried in a writing project, Jerri spends all her time working in other creative pursuits or on the Alabama and Florida beaches with her children.

About the Technical Editor

Andrew Edney has been an IT professional for more than 12 years and has worked for a range of high-tech companies, including Microsoft, Hewlett-Packard, and Fujitsu Services. He is experienced in virtually all aspects of Microsoft computing solutions and has been a designer and architect of large-enterprise solutions for government and private-sector companies. He is currently involved in numerous Microsoft beta programs, including next-generation Windows operating systems and Microsoft Office products.

Acknowledgments

After having written more than a dozen books, there is one thing that I can say for sure: No book is written without a ton of helpful people guiding, pushing, and providing for the author. Before even acknowledging that team, though, I must say thanks to God for giving me a talent that few people possess and the means by which to use that talent.

There is an entire team at Wiley that I owe a huge thank-you to. These people — Katie Mohr, Mary Beth Wakefield, Tom Dinse, and a good dozen or so other people whom I never get to speak to — are responsible for making this book a reality. They handle the book from beginning to end, and without them, there would be no book.

My favorite development editor in the world is among those I owe thanks to as well. Bill Bridges has worked with me on several books now, including both editions of this one, and he's the reason that my words are spelled and ordered correctly and not full of clichés. Without Bill, the book would be only half the quality that it is now. Thanks, friend!

And then there's Andrew Edney. He put lots of hours into ensuring the technical accuracy of the text within these pages. His suggestions (and saves) have kept my facts true. Thanks, Andrew.

All the interviews included in Appendix B were also gifts to me. Thanks to each of you who took the time to talk to me, to answer my sometimes dumb questions, and to allow me to pass your wisdom on to our readers. Your help provided valuable insight for me, as I hope it will for the reader as well.

Thanks, too, to my Mobile family. Big Jennifer and Little Jennifer, Rick, and James — you're my support system. And you're there when I need you; you leave when I need space, and you understand that brain drain from writing is a temporary situation and love me still. Without you and our weekly dinners, I wouldn't be able to function nearly as effectively. Thanks, guys!

And thanks to you, the reader. I hope you find all the information here that you seek.

Contents at a Glance

Part V Appendices

Contents

Part II SEO Strategies

Contents

Contents

Part III Optimizing Search Strategies

Contents

Part IV Maintaining SEO

Part V Appendices

Introduction

Welcome to the second edition of the *Search Engine Optimization Bible*. Like all books in the Bible series, you can expect to find both hands-on tutorials and real-world practical-application information, as well as reference and background information that provide a context for what you are learning. This book is a comprehensive resource on search engine optimization. By the time you have completed the *SEO Bible*, you will be well prepared to optimize your web site or blog to achieve the best possible search engine rankings.

Search engine optimization means a lot of different things to a lot of different people. In the strictest sense, SEO is about the on-page and off-page design strategies you can use to improve your search engine ranking. This usually means tweaking your web site using design elements and content — and in most cases, it also means spending no money at all.

SEM, or search engine marketing, is not just SEO. More accurately, SEM includes PPC, or pay-per-click, advertising. Search engine marketing is about doing whatever you need to do to ensure that your web site ranks as high as possible in search engine results. This means not only that you make the needed changes to your web site design, but that you also employ other tactics, such as using a paid advertising program or investing in content strategies.

I lump all these efforts into one category. The ultimate goal of both SEO and SEM is to bring more people to your web site, and you can do that by improving your search engines results. You can also do that by taking advantage of a growing phenomenon on the Web — social media. Social media are a viral form of sharing information on the Web. You might think of this as a more sophisticated method of sharing your favorites or information that you think will interest other people. Using social media to improve the traffic to your web site is called *social media marketing*, or *SMM*.

I've covered social media in more depth in this second edition. I've also added information about mobile web site marketing, because the mobile Web is growing very quickly.

I vote we do away with the alphabet soup completely. All these marketing efforts have one thing in common: reaching your target audience. Today, anyone who is not an SEO purist places all these marketing methods under the SEM umbrella. All of them are methods for optimizing your web site for the audience that you're trying to reach, and as social media and the mobile Web grow in popularity, they're going to be affected by and included in search engine results as well.

Every now and then, you need to step away from the crowd and stop doing what everyone else is doing. In SEO, stepping out alone is usually rewarded with better traffic results. Everyone is doing the same thing. That doesn't mean that you shouldn't. What it means is that you should do the same thing in a different way, and that's where the *SEO Bible* comes in.

Throughout the pages that follow, I'll show you the best practices for search engine optimization and provide insight into the theory behind the strategies that you'll learn. These strategies are tested. They work. Use them to build on. Follow the best practices of search engine optimization but do it creatively. Try something different. That's how blogs became such a huge phenomenon. It's how social bookmarking and social communities caught on. Someone looked at marketing in a different way and came up with a new angle.

You'll find several new chapters in this edition of the *SEO Bible*. New information has been added about Long Tail search, how creating communities can improve your search results, monetizing your web site as an SEO tactic, and even some information on the available SEO plug-ins that you might find useful. I've also updated resources and added information about the phases of the buying process to help you understand where your site visitors are when they come to your site. It's through that understanding that you'll better be able to reach those visitors.

Use the information that you'll find in the following pages to improve your search engine ranking. Use it to improve the traffic to your web site. Most important, use it to reach highly targeted customers who will take the actions you desire them to take on your web site. That customer audience always comes first. Remember this as you market — keep the audience as your focus, and your efforts will be successful.

Who Should Read This Book

Search engine optimization is not for the faint of heart. It requires a lot of time and a lot of hard work. What it doesn't require is a professional. Anyone with time and the desire to do it can learn the most successful strategies of SEO. That's probably why there are so many SEO consultants in the world today.

Anyone can be an SEO consultant. No official certification programs exist, and no industry standards guide the development of an SEO consultant. On the one hand, that's good news for you. It means that you can become your own SEO consultant. And a good first step is to learn the information you'll find in the following pages.

On the other hand, not everyone wants to be an SEO consultant. Your goal in picking up this book might be simply to learn about the SEO process so that you can be certain your SEO consultant, or the SEO firm you're considering hiring, can do the job they should be doing to help your web site rank high. That's good.

Two types of people will get the most out of the *SEO Bible* — people who are interested in being their own SEO consultants and people who just want to know how SEO works. If you're already an SEO expert, then you'll likely already be familiar with the information contained in these pages. There might be a few new tidbits that are worth your while, though, so if you need a refresher course, keep reading.

For those of you who are new to SEO, you'll find the information you need to understand and begin implementing SEO strategies that will help improve your search engine rankings and drive better-targeted visitors to your site.

How This Book Is Organized

Search engine optimization can be a complex process, but there are distinct areas of the process that can be addressed on their own, and that's how you'll find this book divided. It has four parts, each of which represents a portion of the SEO process.

Within each part are chapters that address different pieces for that step in the SEO process; and within each chapter are sections to help you work through that piece of the process. You'll also find four separate appendices, which provide guidelines and support for the various strategies and actions that are recommended.

Part I assumes that you're faced with some kind of SEO task, whether it's creating SEO for your site or familiarizing yourself with SEO so that you'll know how to deal with a professional. In this part, you'll learn the following:

- What search engines are and how they work (Chapter 1)
- What Long Tail search is and how it affects SEO (Chapter 2)
- How to create an SEO plan (Chapter 3)

In Part II, you learn about different SEO strategies to use with your web site or blog. These strategies range from common strategies such as building an SEO-friendly site to more cutting-edge strategies such as using communities as an SEO tool. You'll learn to do the following:

- Build an SEO-friendly web site (Chapter 4)
- Use effective keywords (Chapter 5)
- Leverage pay-per-click (Chapter 6)
- Maximize pay-per-click advertising (Chapter 7)
- Use keywords to gather conversions (Chapter 8)
- Target PPC advertising properly (Chapter 9)
- Manage keyword campaigns (Chapter 10)
- Work with the three major PPC programs (Chapter 11)
- Tag your web site effectively (Chapter 12)
- Create great content (Chapter 13)
- Leverage communities as an SEO tool (Chapter 14)
- Create effective linking strategies (Chapter 15)

Once you understand the basics of search strategies, you can begin to improve upon those strategies to gain attention from people and from search engines.

In Part III you'll find six additional chapters that will help you hone your SEO efforts. You'll learn to do the following:

- Add your web site to directories (Chapter 16)
- Determine if pay-for-inclusion services are right for you (Chapter 17)
- Work with search engine crawlers (Chapter 18)
- Avoid SEO spam (Chapter 19)
- Add social media to your toolbox (Chapter 20)
- Optimize your site for mobile Web users (Chapter 21)
- Determine if web site monetization is the right strategy for your SEO plan (Chapter 22)
- Use SEO plug-ins to monitor your successes (Chapter 23)
- Automate optimization (Chapter 24)

Part IV is all about what needs to happen once you have your SEO plan and strategy in place. Your work doesn't end once all the tags are created, so in this part you'll learn how to do the following:

- Maintain SEO after the launch (Chapter 25)
- Analyze the success of your efforts (Chapter 26)

In addition to the chapters, four appendices include additional helpful information and resources that you can refer to as you work on your SEO. In these appendices, you'll find the following:

- Optimization tips for all three major search engines (Appendix A)
- Interviews with industry experts (Appendix B)
- SEO software, tools, and resources (Appendix C)
- SEO worksheets to help you stay on track (Appendix D)

Conventions and features

There are several different organizational and typographical features throughout this book designed to help you get the most from the information.

Tips, Notes, and Cautions

Whenever the authors want to bring something important to your attention, the information will appear in a Tip, Note, or Caution.

CAUTION This information is important and is set off in a separate paragraph with a special icon. Cautions provide information about things to watch out for, whether these are simply inconvenient or potentially hazardous to your data or systems.

TIP Tips are generally used to provide information that can make your work easier, such as special shortcuts or methods to do something easier than the traditional way.

NOTE Notes provide additional, ancillary information that is helpful, but perhaps somewhat outside the scope of the main material being presented.

Where to Go From Here

Before you even finish reading the *SEO Bible*, you'll be itching to start putting some of the strategies that are covered here into place. Go for it. Just keep the book handy to refer to — and remember to come back and finish reading the sections that you haven't completed.

In addition, remember that implementing SEO is an ongoing process. You can start immediately, but you have to keep it up, even once the desired increases are achieved. The effort you put into it will pay off in terms of the traffic increases to your site; and even better than the increased traffic is the improved conversion rate you should experience. In other words, more people will show up at your site and take the actions that you want them to take while they are there.

It's not easy to achieve, but if you work at it, you can expect to see major improvements over time.

Good luck!

Part I

Understanding SEO

Search engine optimization (SEO) is such a broad term. It can be quite overwhelming if you try to take the whole of it in a single bite. There are so many facets of search engine optimization, from how search engines work (and they all work a little differently) to how a web page is designed. There are enough elements to worry about that you could spend far more time than you can afford to invest in trying to achieve the SEO you have in mind. However, search engine optimization doesn't have to be such an onerous task that it can't be accomplished — not if you understand what it is and how it works.

Part I explains the basics of search engine optimization. This part includes an explanation of what search engines are and how they work. There is also an explanation of Long Tail search and the concept of an SEO plan. Together, these elements will have you up to speed and ready to begin implementing the right SEO strategies to build the web site traffic that you need.

Chapter 1

Search Engine Basics

What do you do when you need to find some bit of information — a fact, a statistic, a description, a product, or even just a phone number? In most cases, you bring up one of the major search engines and type in the term or phrase that you're looking for and then click through the results, right? Then, like magic, the information you were looking for is right at your fingertips, accessible in a fraction of the time it used to take. But of course search engines weren't always around.

In its infancy, the Internet wasn't what you think of when you use it now. In fact, it was nothing like the web of interconnected sites that has become one of the greatest business facilitators of our time. Instead, what was called the Internet was actually a collection of *FTP (File Transfer Protocol)* sites that users could access to download (or upload) files.

To find a specific file in that collection, users had to navigate through each file. Sure, there were shortcuts. If you knew the right people — that would be the people who knew the exact address of the file you were looking for — you could go straight to the file. That's assuming you knew exactly what you were looking for.

The whole process made finding files on the Internet a difficult, time-consuming exercise in patience; but that was before a student at McGill University in Montreal decided there had to be an easier way. In 1990, Alan Emtage created the first search tool used on the Internet. His creation, an index of files on the Internet, was called Archie.

If you're thinking Archie the comic book character created in 1941, you're a little off track (at least for now). The name Archie was used because the filename Archives was too long. Later, Archie's pals from the comic book series (Veronica and Jughead) came on to the search scene, too, but we'll get to that shortly.

Archie wasn't actually a *search engine* like those that you use today, but at the time it was a program many Internet users were happy to have. The program basically downloaded directory listings for all the files that were stored on *anonymous FTP* sites in a given network of computers. Those listings were then plugged in to a searchable database of web sites.

Archie's search capabilities weren't as fancy as the *natural language capabilities* you find in most common search engines today, but at the time it got the job done. Archie indexed computer files, making them easier to locate.

In 1991, however, another student named Mark McCahill, at the University of Minnesota, realized that if you could search for files on the Internet, then surely you could also search plain text for specific references in the files. Because no such application existed, he created Gopher, a program that indexed the plain-text documents that later became the first web sites on the public Internet.

With the creation of Gopher, there also needed to be programs that could find references within the indexes that Gopher created, and so Archie's pals finally rejoined him. Veronica (Very Easy Rodent-Oriented Net-wide Index to Computerized Archives) and Jughead (Jonzy's Universal Gopher Hierarchy Excavation and Display) were created to search the files that were stored in the Gopher Index System.

Both of these programs worked in essentially the same way, enabling users to search the indexed information by keyword. From there, search as you know it began to mature. The first *real* search engine, in the form that we know search engines today, didn't come into being until 1993. Developed by Matthew Gray, it was called Wandex. Wandex was the first program to both index and search the index of pages on the Web. This technology was the first program to *crawl* the Web, and later became the basis for all search crawlers. After that, search engines took on a life of their own. From 1993 to 1998, the major search engines that you're probably familiar with today were created:

- Excite — 1993
- Yahoo! — 1994
- Web Crawler — 1994
- Lycos — 1994
- Infoseek — 1995
- AltaVista — 1995
- Inktomi — 1996
- Ask Jeeves — 1997
- Google — 1997
- MSN Search — 1998

Today, search engines are sophisticated programs, many of which enable you to search all manner of files and documents using the same words and phrases you would use in everyday conversations. It's hard to believe that the concept of a search engine is just over 15 years old — especially considering what you can use one to find these days!

What Is a Search Engine?

Okay, so you know the basic concept of a search engine. Type a word or phrase into a search box and click a button. Wait a few seconds, and references to thousands (or hundreds of thousands) of pages will appear. Then all you have to do is click through those results to find what you want. But what exactly is a search engine, beyond this general concept of "seek and ye shall find"?

It's a little complicated. On the back end, a search engine is a piece of software that uses algorithms to find and collect information about web pages. The information collected is usually keywords or phrases that are possible indicators of what is contained on the web page as a whole, the URL of the page, the code that makes up the page, and links into and out of the page. That information is then indexed and stored in a database.

On the front end, the software has a user interface where users enter a search term — a word or phrase — in an attempt to find specific information. When the user clicks a search button, an algorithm then examines the information stored in the back-end database and retrieves links to web pages that appear to match the search term the user entered.

CROSS-REF You can find more information about web crawlers, spiders, and robots in Chapter 18.

The process of collecting information about web pages is performed by an agent called a *crawler, spider,* or *robot.* The crawler literally looks at every URL on the Web that's not blocked from it and collects key words and phrases on each page, which are then included in the database that powers a search engine. Considering that the number of sites on the Web exceeded 100 million some time ago and is increasing by more than 1.5 million sites each month, that's like your brain cataloging every single word you read, so that when you need to know something, you think of that word and every reference to it comes to mind.

In a word ... overwhelming.

Anatomy of a Search Engine

By now you probably have a fuzzy idea of how a search engine works, but there's much more to it than just the basic overview you've seen so far. In fact, search engines have several parts. Unfortunately, it's rare that you find an explanation describing just how a search engine is made — that's proprietary information that search companies hold very close to their vests — and that information is vitally important to succeeding with *search engine optimization (SEO)*.

Query interface

The query interface is what most people are familiar with, and it's probably what comes to mind when you hear the term "search engine." The query interface is the page, or user interface, that users see when they navigate to a search engine to enter a search term.

There was a time when the search engine interface looked very much like the Ask.com page shown in Figure 1-1. This interface was a simple page with a search box and a button to activate the search, and not much more.

FIGURE 1-1

The Ask.com search page shows how most search engine interfaces used to look.

Today, many search engines on the Web have added much more personalized content in an attempt to capitalize on the real estate available to them. For example, Yahoo! Search, shown in Figure 1-2, is just one of the search services that now enable users to personalize their pages with a free e-mail account, weather information, news, sports, and many other elements designed to make users want to return to that site to conduct their web searches.

One other option users have for customizing the interfaces of their search engines is a capability like the one Google offers. The Google search engine has a customizable interface to which users can add different *gadgets*. These gadgets enable users to add features to their customized Google search home page that meet their own personal needs or tastes.

FIGURE 1-2

Yahoo! Search enables users to make their search page more personal.

Search has even extended onto the desktop. Google and Microsoft both have search capabilities that, when installed on your computer, enable you to search your hard drive for documents and information in the same way you would search the Web. These capabilities aren't of any particular use to you where SEO is concerned, but they do illustrate the prevalence of search and the value that users place on being able to quickly find information using searching capabilities.

When it comes to search engine optimization, Google's user interface offers the most potential for you to reach your target audience, because it does more than just optimize your site for search: If a useful tool or feature is available on your site, you can enable users to have access to this tool or feature through the *Application Programming Interface (API)* made available by Google. Using the Google API, you can create a gadget that users can install on their Google Desktop, iGoogle page, or Firefox or Chrome browser. This enables you to have your name in front of users on a daily basis.

CROSS-REF You can find more information about Google APIs in Appendix A in the section "Optimization for Google."

For example, a company called PDF24.org offers a Google gadget that enables users to turn their documents into PDF files right from their Google home page once the gadget has been added. If the point of search engine optimization is ultimately to get your name in front of as many people as possible, as often as possible, then making a gadget available for addition to Google's personalized home page can only further that goal.

Search engine results pages

The other sides of the query interface, and the only other parts of a search engine that's visible to users, are the *search engine results pages (SERPs)*. This is the collection of pages that are returned with search results after a user enters a search term or phrase and clicks the Search button. This is also where you ultimately want to end up; and the higher you are in the search results, the more traffic you can expect to generate from search. Specifically, your goal is to end up on the first page of results — in the top 10 or 20 results that are returned for a given search term or phrase. Getting there can be a mystery, however. We'll decode the clues that lead you to that goal throughout the book, but right now you need to understand a bit about how users see SERPs.

Let's start with an understanding of how users view SERPs. Pretend you're the searcher. You go to your favorite search engine — we'll use Google for the purposes of illustration because that's everyone's favorite, isn't it? Type in the term you want to search for and click the Search button. What's the first thing you do when the page appears?

Most people begin reading the titles and descriptions of the top results. That's where you hook searchers and entice them to click through the links provided to your web page. But here's the catch: You have to be ranked close enough to the top for searchers to see those results page titles and descriptions and then click through them, which usually means you need to be in the top 10 or 20 results, which translates into the first page or two of results. It's a tough spot to hit.

There is no magic bullet or formula that will garner you those rankings every time. Instead, it takes hard work and consistent effort to push your site as high as possible in SERPs. At the risk of sounding repetitive, that's the information you'll find moving forward. There's a lot of it, though, and to truly understand how to land good placement in SERPs, you really need to understand how search engines work. There is much more to them than what users see.

Crawlers, spiders, and robots

The query interface and search results pages truly are the only parts of a search engine that the user ever sees. Every other part of the search engine is behind the scenes, out of view of the people who use it every day. That doesn't mean it's not important, however. In fact, what's in the back end is the most important part of the search engine, and it's what determines how you show up in the front end.

CROSS-REF You can find more in-depth information about crawlers, spiders, and robots in Chapter 18.

If you've spent any time on the Internet, you may have heard a little about spiders, crawlers, and robots. These little creatures are programs that literally crawl around the Web, cataloging data so that it can be searched. In the most basic sense, all three programs — crawlers, spiders, and robots — are essentially the same. They all *collect* information about each and every web URL.

This information is then cataloged according to the URL at which they're located and are stored in a database. Then, when a user uses a search engine to locate something on the Web, the references in the database are searched and the search results are returned.

Databases

Every search engine contains or is connected to a system of databases where data about each URL on the Web (collected by crawlers, spiders, or robots) is stored. These databases are massive storage areas that contain multiple data points about each URL.

The data might be arranged in any number of different ways and is ranked according to a method of ranking and retrieval that is usually proprietary to the company that owns the search engine.

You've probably heard of the method of ranking called *PageRank* (for Google) or even the more generic term *quality scoring*. This ranking or scoring determination is one of the most complex and secretive parts of SEO. How those scores are derived, exactly, is a closely guarded secret, in part because search engine companies change the weight of the elements used to arrive at the score according to usage patterns on the Web.

The idea is to score pages based on the quality that site visitors derive from the page, not on how well web site designers can manipulate the elements that make up the quality score. For example, there was a time when the keywords that were used to rank a page were one of the most important factors in obtaining a high-quality score.

A Little More About PageRank

PageRank is one of those mysteries that may never be completely unraveled. Volumes have been written about it, but probably the only two people in the world who understand it completely are Larry Page and Sergey Brin. That's because it was their brainchild.

PageRank actually started as part of a research project that Page and Brin were working on at Stanford University. The project involved creating a new search engine that ranked pages in a democratic fashion with a few weights and measures thrown in for accuracy. Hence, the term. (What else would you call a ranking system for web pages that was developed by Larry Page?)

The interesting thing about PageRank is that although Page and Brin conceived the idea and created the algorithm that arrives at a PageRank, it didn't belong to them. Stanford University actually owned the patent on the PageRank algorithm until Google purchased the exclusive right to use the algorithm for 1.8 million shares of the company (which were sold in 2005 for $336 million).

continued

continued

PageRank is a method by which web pages are ranked in Google search results. A combination of factors create the actual rank of a web page. Google explains it this way:

"PageRank relies on the uniquely democratic nature of the Web by using its vast link structure as an indicator of an individual page's value. In essence, Google interprets a link from page A to page B as a vote, by page A, for page B. But Google looks at more than the sheer volume of votes, or links a page receives; it also analyzes the page that casts the vote. Votes cast by pages that are themselves "important" weigh more heavily and help to make other pages "important.""

In other words, it's a mystery. A page that has more links (with equal votes) might rank lower than a page that has a single link that leads to a "more important" page. The lesson? Create pages for visitors, not for search engines.

That's no longer the case. Don't get me wrong. Keywords are still vitally important in web page ranking. However, they're just one of dozens of elements that are taken into consideration, which is why a large portion of Part II of this book is dedicated to using keywords to your advantage. They *do* have value; and more important, keywords can cause damage if not used properly — but we'll get to that.

Quality considerations

When you're considering the importance of databases, and by extension page quality measurements, in the mix of SEO, it might be helpful to equate it to something more familiar — customer service. What comprises good customer service is not any one thing. It's a conglomeration of different factors — greetings, attitude, helpfulness, and knowledge, just to name a few — that come together to create a pleasant experience. A web page quality score is the same.

The difference with a quality score is that you're measuring elements of design, rather than actions of an individual. For example, some of the elements that are known to be weighted to develop a quality score are as follows:

- Domain names and URLs
- Page content
- Link structure
- Usability and accessibility
- Meta tags
- Page structure

It's a melding of these and other factors — sometimes very carefully balanced factors — that are used to create the quality score. Exactly how much weight is given to each factor is known only to the mathematicians who create the algorithms that generate the quality score, but one thing is certain: The better quality score your site generates, the better your search engine results will be, which means the more traffic you will have coming from search engines.

Search algorithms

All the parts of the search engine are important, but the *search algorithm* is the cog that makes everything work. It might be more accurate to say that the search algorithm is the foundation on which everything else is built. How a search engine works is based on the search algorithm, which is closely related to the way that data is discovered by the user.

In very general terms, a search algorithm is a problem-solving procedure that takes a problem, evaluates a number of possible answers, and then returns the solution to that problem. A search algorithm for a search engine takes the problem (the word or phrase being searched for), sifts through a database that contains cataloged keywords and the URLs with which those words are associated, and then returns pages that contain the word or phrase that was searched for, either in the body of the page or in a URL that points to the page.

But it even goes one better than that. The search algorithm returns those results based on the *perceived quality* of the page, which is expressed in the quality score. How this neat little trick is accomplished varies according to the algorithm that's being used. There are several classifications of search algorithms, and each search engine uses algorithms that are slightly different. That's why a search for one word or phrase will yield different results from different search engines.

Search algorithms are generally divided into three broad categories: on-page algorithms, whole-site algorithms, and off-site algorithms. Each type of algorithm looks at different elements of a web page, yet all three types are generally part of a much larger algorithm.

On-page algorithms

Algorithms that measure on-page factors look at the elements of a page that would lead a user to think the page is worth browsing. This includes how keywords are used in content as well as how other words on the page relate. For example, for any given topic, some phrases are common, so if your web site is about beading, an on-page algorithm will determine that by the number of times the term "beading" is used, as well as by the number of related phrases and words that are also used on the page (e.g., wire, patterns, jump rings, string or stringing, etc.).

These word patterns are an indicator that the algorithm results — that beading is the topic of the page — are, in fact, correct. The alternative, no related patterns of words, suggests that keywords were entered randomly on a page, just for their value.

The algorithm will also likely look at the proximity of related words. This is just another element of the pattern that validates the algorithmic results, but these elements also contribute to the quality score of a page.

The on-page algorithm also looks at some elements that human visitors can't see. The back side of a web page contains special content designed specifically for web crawlers. This content is called *meta tags*. When a crawler examines your web site, it looks at these tags as definitions for *what you intend your site to be about*. It then weighs that against the other elements of on-site optimization, as well as whole-site and off-site optimization, too.

CROSS-REF   **You can find additional information about meta tags in Chapter 7.**

Whole-site algorithms

If on-site algorithms look at the relationship of words and content on a page, then whole-site algorithms look at the relationship of pages on a site. For example, does the home page content relate to the content on other pages? This is an important factor from a user's viewpoint, because if users come to your site expecting one thing and then click through a link and wind up in completely unrelated territory, they won't be happy.

To ensure that your web site is what it claims to be, the whole-site algorithm looks at the relationship of site elements, such as the architecture of pages, the use of *anchor text*, and how the pages on your site are linked together. This is one reason why it's best to have separate web sites if you have a site that covers multiple, unrelated topics or subjects.

How your site is architected — that is, how usable it is for a site visitor, based on the topic it appears to be about — is a determining factor in how useful web site visitors find your site. Understand that one of the most important concepts in SEO is how useful site visitors find your web site, and a recurring theme throughout this book is building sites that visitors want to spend time on. Do that and SEO will (usually) fall naturally into place.

Off-site algorithms

I can hear you already. "What does anything that's off my web site have to do with how my web page ranks in SERPs?" The answer is *incoming links*, which constitute an off-site factor that will affect your page ranking in sometimes dramatic ways. A *good incoming link* is the equivalent of a vote of confidence for your site, and a high level of confidence from surfers will also help boost your page ranking.

Notice the emphasis I placed on *good* incoming link? That's another of those vitally important things you should commit to memory. Good incoming links are those that users willingly provide because they found your site, or a page on your site, useful. These typically are not links that are paid for.

Let's go back to the concept that creating a site visitors will find useful is your best SEO tool. Good incoming links are how visitors show other visitors (and therefore web crawlers) the value they attach to your site. The number of good incoming links you have is directly proportionate to the amount of confidence and trust that visitors appear to have in your site.

In summary, the off-site algorithm adds yet another dimension to how the quality of your page is ranked. Like the other algorithms, it's not a stand-alone measurement, but a component of a larger algorithm that tries to extract the true value of the web page or web site.

 **CROSS-REF** You'll find much more detailed information about links and linking strategies in Chapter 15.

Additional algorithms

Phew, that was a lot of information about search algorithms to take in, and we're not done. Within those three main categories of algorithms are many other lesser algorithms that also contribute to the way your web site and web pages are ranked. Some of the most common types of search algorithms include the following:

- **List search:** A list-search algorithm searches through specified data looking for a single key. The data is searched in a very linear, list-style method. The result of a list search is usually a single element, which means that searching through billions of web sites could be very time-consuming, but yields a smaller search result.

- **Tree search:** Envision a tree. Now examine that tree either from the roots out or from the leaves in. This is how a tree-search algorithm works. The algorithm searches a data set from either the broadest to the most narrow or from the most narrow to the broadest. Data sets are like trees: A single piece of data can branch to many other pieces of data, which is very much how the Web is set up. Tree searches, then, are more useful when conducting searches on the Web, although they are not the only searches that can be successful.

- **SQL search:** One of the difficulties with a tree search is that it is conducted in a hierarchical manner, meaning it's conducted from one point to another, according to the ranking of the data being searched. A SQL (pronounced *see-quel*) search enables data to be searched in a nonhierarchical manner, which means that data can be searched from any *subset* of data.

- **Informed search:** An informed-search algorithm looks for a specific answer to a specific problem in a tree-like data set. The informed search, despite its name, is not always the best choice for web searches because of the general nature of the answers being sought. Instead, informed search is better used for specific queries in specific data sets.

- **Adversarial search:** An adversarial-search algorithm looks for all possible solutions to a problem, much like finding all the possible solutions in a game. This algorithm is difficult to use with web searches because the number of possible solutions to a word or phrase search is nearly infinite on the Web.

- **Constraint satisfaction search:** When you think of searching the Web for a word or phrase, the constraint-satisfaction-search algorithm is most likely to satisfy your need to find something. In this type of search algorithm, the solution is discovered by meeting a set of constraints, and the data set can be searched in a variety of different ways that do not have to be linear. Constraint satisfaction searches can be very useful for searching the Web.

These are only a few of the various types of search algorithms that are used when creating search engines; and frequently more than one type of search algorithm is used, or, as happens in most cases, some proprietary search algorithm is created. The key to maximizing your search engine results is to understand a little about how each search engine you're targeting works. Only when you understand this can you know how to maximize your exposure to meet the search requirements for that search engine.

Retrieval and ranking

For a web search engine, the retrieval of data is a combination activity of the crawler (or spider or robot), the database, and the search algorithm. These three elements work in concert to retrieve web pages that are related to the word or phrase that a user enters into the search engine's user interface. As noted earlier, how that works can be a proprietary combination of technologies, theories, and coding whizbangery.

The really tricky part is the results ranking. Ranking is also what you'll spend the most time and effort trying to affect. Your ranking in a search engine determines how often people see your page, which affects everything from revenue to your advertising budget. Unfortunately, how a search engine ranks your page or pages is a tough science to pin down.

The most that you can hope for, in most cases, is to make an educated guess as to how a search engine ranks its results, and then try to tailor your page to meet those results. But keep in mind that although retrieval and ranking are listed as separate subjects here, they're actually part of the search algorithm. The separation is to help you better understand how search engines work.

Ranking plays such a large part in search engine optimization that it appears frequently in this book. You'll look at ranking from every possible facet before you reach the last page; but for now, let's look at just what affects ranking. Keep in mind, however, that different search engines use different ranking criteria, so the importance each of these elements plays will vary.

- ■ **Location:** Location doesn't refer here to the location (as in the URL) of a web page. Instead, it refers to the location of keywords and phrases on a web page. For example, if a user searches for "puppies," some search engines will rank the results according to where on the page the word "puppies" appears. Obviously, the higher the word appears on the page, the higher the rank might be. Therefore, a web site that contains the word "puppies" in the *title tag* will likely appear higher than a web site that is about puppies but does not contain the word in the title tag. This means that a web site that's not designed with SEO in mind will likely not rank where you would expect it to rank. The site www.puppies.com is a good example of this. In a recent Google search, it ranked as the fifth item in the results, rather than first, potentially because it does not contain the keyword in the title tag.

- ■ **Frequency:** The frequency with which the search term appears on the page may also affect how a page is ranked in search results. For example, on a page about puppies, one that uses the word five times might be ranked higher than one that uses the word only two or three times. When word frequency became a well-known factor, some web site designers began using hidden words hundreds of times on pages, trying to artificially boost their page rankings. Most search engines now recognize this as *keyword spamming* and ignore or even refuse to list pages that use this technique.

- **Links:** One of the more recent ranking factors is the type and number of links on a web page. Links that come into the site, links that lead out of the site, and links within the site are all taken into consideration. It would follow, then, that the more links you have on your page or leading to your page, the higher your rank would be, right? Again, it doesn't necessarily work that way. More accurately, the number of relevant links coming into your page, versus the number of relevant links within the page, versus the number of relevant links leading off the page has a bearing on the rank that your page gets in the search results.

- **Click-throughs:** One last element that might determine how your site ranks against others in a search is the number of *click-throughs* your site has versus click-throughs for other pages that are shown in page rankings. Because a search engine cannot monitor site traffic for every site on the Web, some search engines monitor the number of clicks each search result receives. The rankings may then be repositioned in a future search, based on this interaction with users.

Page ranking is a very precise science. As previously mentioned, it's accomplished by assigning a quality score, based on numerous factors, to a web site; and it differs from search engine to search engine. To create the best possible SEO for your site, it's necessary to understand how these page rankings are made for the search engines you plan to target. Those factors can then be taken into consideration and used to your advantage when it is time to create, change, or update the web site that you want to optimize.

Understanding how a search engine ranks a web site is no easy task, and ultimately it ends with some educated guesswork. One way to become educated is to read what others have learned about how specific search engines rank web sites.

In Appendix A, I try to decode the mystery a little by providing some tips and information about the top three search engines — Google, Yahoo!, and MSN. But bear in mind that search engines change constantly based on how Internet users behave online. What's true of search engine ranking today may not be tomorrow. This is evidenced by the value placed on keywords today versus what it was just a few years ago.

Characteristics of Search

Understanding how a search engine works helps you to understand how your pages are ranked by the search engine, but how your pages are *found* is another story entirely. That's where the human element comes in. Search means different things to different people. For example, one of my colleagues searches the Internet using the same words and phrases he would use to tell someone about a topic or even using the exact question that he's trying to get answered. It's called *natural language*. Another colleague, however, was trained in search using *Boolean* search techniques. She uses a very different *syntax* when she's creating a search term. Each of these methods returns different search results, even when the same search engines are used.

The characteristics of search refer to how users search the Internet. This can be everything from the *heuristics* they use when creating a search term to the selection the user makes (and the way those selections are made) after the search results are returned. It is interesting to note that more than half of American adults search the Internet every time they go online; and in fact more people search the Internet than use the yellow pages when they're looking for phone numbers or the locations of local businesses.

This wealth of search engine users is fertile ground for SEO targeting, and the better you understand how and why users use search engines, and exactly how search engines work, the easier it will be to achieve the SEO you're pursuing.

Classifications of Search Engines

With a decent understanding of how search engines work and how people use those search engines, you can now concentrate on some more detailed information about these engines. For example, you already know that all search engines aren't created equal, but did you know that there are different types, or classifications, of search engines? Search engines can be broken down into three different types (in the broadest of terms): primary, secondary, and targeted.

Primary search engines

A *primary search engine* is the type you think of most often when search engines come to mind. Some index most or all sites on the Web. For example, Yahoo! Google, and MSN are primary (also called major) search engines.

Primary search engines generate the majority of the traffic to your web site, and as such they will be the primary focus of your SEO efforts. Each primary search engine differs slightly from the others. For example, Lycos has been around much longer than Google, yet Google is the most popular search engine on the Web. Why is that? Most likely, it's because people find that Google provides better search results.

The difference between those search results lies in the search algorithm used to create the search engine. Most primary search engines are also more than just search. Additional features such as e-mail, mapping, news, and different types of entertainment applications are also available from most of the primary search engine companies. These elements were added long after the search feature was established as a way to draw increasing numbers of users to the search engine. Although those features don't change the way people search, they might affect which search engine people choose.

Google Overview

Each of the major search engines differs in some small way. Google is the king of search engines, in part because of the accuracy with which it can pull the results from a search query. Sure, Google offers all kinds of extras like e-mail, a personalized home page, and even productivity applications, but those value-added services are not what made Google popular.

What turned Google into a household word is the accuracy with which the search engine can return search results. This accuracy was developed when the Google designers combined keyword searches with link popularity. The combination of keywords and the popularity of links to those pages yields a higher accuracy rank than just keywords alone. Of course, it also helps that Google places paid advertisements in a separate part of the page, as obvious ads, and not as part of the actual search results.

However, it's important to understand that link popularity and keywords are just two of dozens of different criteria that search engines can use in ranking the relevancy of web pages.

Yahoo! Overview

Most people know that Yahoo! is a search engine, but it's also a *web directory*, which basically means that it is a list of the different web pages available on the Internet, divided by category and subcategory. In fact, few people know that Yahoo! started as the favorites list of the two young men who founded it. Through the acquisition of companies like Inktomi, All the Web, AltaVista, and Overture, Yahoo! gradually gained market share as a search engine.

Yahoo!, which at one time used Google to search its directory of links, now ranks pages through a combination of the technologies that it acquired over time. However, Yahoo!'s link-ranking capability is not as accurate as Google's. In addition, Yahoo! has a paid-inclusion program, which some users think tends to skew search results in favor of the highest payer.

MSN Overview

MSN's search capabilities aren't quite as mature as those of Yahoo! or Google. As a result, MSN has not yet developed the in-depth link analysis capabilities of these other primary search engines. Instead, MSN relies heavily on web site content for ranking purposes. However, this may benefit new web sites that are trying to get listed in search engines.

The link-ranking capabilities of Google and Yahoo! can preclude new web sites from being listed for a period of time after they have been created. This is because (especially where Google is concerned) the quality of the link may be considered during ranking. New links are often ignored until they have been in place for a while.

Because MSN relies heavily on page content, a web site that is tagged properly and contains a good ratio of keywords will be more likely to be listed — and listed sooner — by the MSN search engine. Therefore, though it's not the most popular of search engines, MSN is one of the primaries, and being listed there sooner rather than later will help increase your site traffic.

Secondary search engines

Secondary search engines are targeted at smaller, more specific audiences, although the search engine's content itself is still general. They don't generate as much traffic as the primary search engines, but they're useful for regional and more narrowly focused searches. Examples of secondary search engines include Lycos, LookSmart, Miva, Ask.com, and Espotting.

Secondary search engines, just like the primary ones, vary in the way they rank search results. Some rely more heavily on keywords, whereas others rely on reciprocal links. Still others might rely on criteria such as meta tags or some proprietary criteria.

Secondary search engines should be included in any SEO plan. Though these search engines might not generate as much traffic as the primary search engines, they will still generate valuable traffic that should not be overlooked. Many users of secondary search engines are users because they have some loyalty to that specific search engine. For example, many former AOL users who have moved on to broadband Internet service providers still use the AOL search engine whenever possible because it's comfortable for them.

Targeted search engines

Targeted search engines — sometimes called *topical search engines* — are the most specific of them all. These search engines are very narrowly focused, usually to a general topic, such as medicine or branches of science, travel, sports, and so on. Examples of targeted search engines include CitySearch, Yahoo! Travel, and MusicSearch; and like other types of search engines, ranking criteria vary from one search engine to another.

When considering targeted search engines for SEO purposes, keep in mind that many of these search engines are much more narrowly focused than primary or secondary search engines. Look for the targeted search engines that are relevant to your specific topic (such as pets, sports, locations, and so on).

Putting Search Engines to Work for You

All this information about search engines has one purpose — to show you how they work so that you can put them to work for you. Throughout this book, you'll find various strategies for optimizing your web site so it appears high in search engine rankings when relevant searches are performed, but this requires that you know how to put search engines to work.

Search engine optimization is essentially the science of designing your web site to maximize your search engine rankings. This means that all of the elements of your web site are created with the goal of obtaining high search engine rankings. Those elements include the following:

- Entry and exit pages
- Page titles
- Site content
- Graphics
- Web site structure

In addition to these elements, however, you also have to consider things such as keywords, links, HTML, and meta-tagging. Even after you have all the elements of your page optimized for search engine friendliness, there are other things to consider. For example, you can have all the right design elements included in your web pages and still have a relatively low search engine ranking. Factors such as advertising campaigns and update frequency also affect your SEO efforts.

All of this means that you should understand that the concept of search engine optimization is not based on any single element. Instead, search engine optimization is based on a vast number of elements and strategies. It's also an ongoing process that doesn't end once your web site is live.

SEO is a living, breathing concept of maximizing the traffic that your web site generates, and as such it is a constantly moving target. If you've ever played a game of Whack-a-Mole, you can appreciate how difficult search engine optimization is to nail. In that game, a little mole pops up out of a hole. Your job is to whack the mole on top of the head before it disappears back down the hole and appears in another.

Search engine optimization operates on much the same concept. Search engines are constantly changing, so the methods and strategies used to achieve high search engine rankings must also change. As soon as that little mole pops up in one hole, it disappears and then reappears in another. It's a frustrating game, but given enough time and concentration, you can become very good at it.

Manipulating Search Engines

There's one more topic to touch on before this chapter is finished. SEO is about manipulating search engines — to an extent. Beyond that, the manipulation becomes something more sinister and you run the risk of having your web site removed from the search engine rankings completely. It's true. It happens.

What exactly can and can't you do? There's a list, and here is part of it.

You can:

- Create a web site that contains meta tags, content, graphics, and keywords that help improve your site ranking.
- Use keywords liberally on your site, so long as they are used in the correct context of your site topic and content.
- Include reciprocal links to your site from others as long as those links are legitimate and relevant.

- Encourage web site traffic through many venues, including keyword advertising, reciprocal links, and marketing campaigns.

- Submit your web site to search engines manually, rather than wait for them to pick up your site in the natural course of cataloging web sites.

You can't:

- Trick search engines by imbedding hidden keywords in your web site. This is a practice that will very likely get you banned from most search engines.

- Artificially generate links to your site from unrelated sites for the purpose of increasing your ranking based on link analysis. Most search engines have a built-in mechanism that detects this type of deceptive practice.

- Artificially generate traffic to your web site so that it appears more popular than it is. Again, there are safeguards in place to prevent this from happening; and if you trip those safeguards, you could end up on the banned list for many search engines.

- Force your web site to appear in search engine rankings by submitting the site repeatedly for inclusion in the rankings. A good general rule of thumb is that you should submit your site once and then wait at least six weeks before submitting it again. Submitting it repeatedly will, again, only lead to something nasty like being banned from the search engine.

- Expect search engines to automatically rank you at the top of your topic, category, or keyword as soon as the site is picked up. It can take a little time to build the *status* that you need to reach a high search engine ranking. Remember, SEO is a process.

These are just basic rules for putting search engines to work for you. There are many more, which you will discover in the coming chapters. As you get started, however, keep these in mind because you'll see them repeatedly throughout the course of this book and any other research that you might be doing on search engine optimization.

SEO is hard work

Something to remember as you embark on this journey toward SEO is that it is not going to be easy. Just when you think you have it figured out, the search ranking algorithm will change. If you're lucky, the change will only mildly affect your search rankings. However, if you build your site to please search engines, it's more likely that your search rankings will be turned on their head.

That's one reason why it's vitally important that you build your web site with users in mind first, and then search rankings. Ultimately, search engine designers take cues for the changes they may make from the behavior of searchers. Therefore, if you're constantly vigilant and attending to your visitors' needs, your web site won't be as affected by changes in the search engine algorithm.

It's still a lot of work to reach this level of user-friendly design. Some people assume a few tweaks here and there are all they need, but unless your site is very well designed to start with, tweaking just won't cut it. It's more realistic to understand that you'll end up putting dozens of hours into your separate SEO efforts.

Scheduling SEO efforts

Because SEO is so much work, a good way to manage it is to schedule daily time into your routine for SEO efforts. Of course, this is after the initial implementation of SEO. Initially, SEO should be done during the build of a new web site, or it can be built into existing sites if they are not new constructions. However, if you're building better SEO into an existing site that's poorly optimized, then be prepared for a major site redesign.

SEO is a holistic approach to improving your search engine rankings. As such, it requires attention to your whole site. It does little good to optimize portions of your site and leave other areas lacking the same attention to detail. If you're going to SEO your site, do it right and make sure you hit all of the elements as you go.

Chapter 2

The Theory of Long Tail Search

The counterpart to understanding how a search engine works is understanding how searching works. How do users *find* the products and information they are looking for when they go to a search engine? A lot of research has gone into answering that question, but it looks as if it always comes back to the same principles that are used in so many other areas — economics, science, mathematics, and even chaos theory.

As with everything in the universe, searching happens in patterns. Finding happens in patterns, too. Your job, as you optimize your web site, is to recognize and tap into those patterns. Fortunately, many have come before you and left behind information that makes your job much easier.

Let's define a few principles that explain how users search:

- **Zipf's Law:** Developed by the linguist George Kingsley Zipf, this essentially states that the specificity of any word is inversely proportional to its rank on a frequency table. In other words, a word used often is likely to be a broad, common word, whereas a word used less often is likely to be a narrower, more specific word.

- **Pareto's Principal:** Also known as the 80/20 Rule, this principle holds that for any given event, 80 percent of the results come from 20 percent of the activity. For example, if you subscribe to Pareto's Principle, then you probably believe that 80 percent of the work in any organization is performed by about 20 percent of the employees.

- **The Long Tail:** The Long Tail is a phrase coined by Chris Anderson in an October 2004 article in *Wired* magazine that essentially explained how a small portion of very popular products generate

23

a sizable income; however, a large portion of semipopular products generate small amounts of income that when added together can be equal to or larger than the income generated by the very popular products.

How do a linguistic principle and two economic principles come together to explain how users search? It's all explained in the theory of *Long Tail search*, which grew from Anderson's article on the Long Tail of economics.

Thoroughly confused? No need to be. This chapter explains Long Tail search in great detail. As with any buzzword, Long Tail is a term that caught the media's attention and has been thrown about until we're all pretty much sick of hearing it. No doubt you've heard the term before, but you may not have a clear idea of exactly what the Long Tail is and how it applies to search.

What Is Long Tail Search?

Long Tail wasn't coined to deal specifically with search. Anderson was originally trying to explain the difference between the success of e-commerce stores compared to that of brick-and-mortar stores. His theory was that because of space constraints, brick-and-mortar stores have to justify every item that's put on their shelves. This means the items have to "earn their keep," so to speak, which in turn means that an item found in a store needs to generate consistently high revenue.

E-commerce stores aren't beholden to the same rules. Theoretically, an e-commerce store doesn't have to pay for the actual shelf space to stock a store, which should reduce the cost of carrying items. In many cases, nor do e-commerce stores have to physically stock an item in a warehouse somewhere. They can (and very often do) use a method called *drop shipping*, whereby products are shipped directly from manufacturer to consumer. The e-commerce site is nothing more than an order-taking system. That reduces the cost of providing a wide selection of items to consumers, which in turn means that e-commerce stores can afford to stock less popular, but still wanted, items.

A commonly quoted example of this concept is a brick-and-mortar bookstore such as Barnes and Noble versus a pure e-commerce store such as Amazon.com. By most estimates, Barnes and Noble stocks an average of 300,000 books, and not all of those books appear in all stores. What all those books do have in common is that they sell a certain number of copies each month. They are items that have proven to be in demand, and therefore they earn the half inch or so that they occupy on the shelf.

Amazon.com stocks millions of books — many of them books that don't sell more than a copy or two each month. Nonetheless, Amazon is still a successful retail business because it costs much less to make those books available to customers. There's no shelf to pay for and not everything you find on the Amazon.com web site is stored in Amazon warehouses, which means Amazon can offer customers books that are less popular or are popular with only a niche segment of the population.

What really makes this concept interesting from both a retailing and a searching aspect is that studies show that around 20 percent of the revenue generated by a retailer is generated by the most popular items — those items that are most searched for and most in demand. The remaining 80 percent of revenue is generated by the less popular niche items that users are searching for.

The Long Tail in action

The Long Tail, then, is roughly the reverse of Pareto's Principle, which would hold that 20 percent of a company's products generate 80 percent of its sales. (Keep in mind that this is an estimate. The exact ratio of products to sales varies by company. You'll see estimates of everything from 20/80 to 50/50.) The important point of this Long Tail theory is that a large number of niche products can, and do, generate a huge volume of sales. Companies such as eBay prove it.

eBay is a niche product company. Search for products on eBay and you'll find all kinds of very obscure and yet in-demand products. The adage, "One man's junk is another man's treasure," applies, just as it applies to Long Tail search theories, too.

The Long Tail can be represented by a graph, where the vertical axis details the number of a particular product sold, and the horizontal axis illustrates the number of products that sell something each month.

The theory holds that the top-selling item for any given retailer sells nearly twice what the next-ranked item sells, and that each item after that progressively decreases. For example, a sample Long Tail graph for any given retail store might look something like the one shown in Figure 2-1. (How this model relates to search terms is indicated in parentheses on the figure.)

FIGURE 2-1

The Long Tail of search represents dozens of search terms that each generate a few clicks each month.

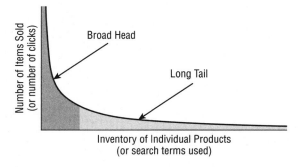

Notice the narrow spike at the beginning of the graph (illustrating the number of highly popular items) and the long tail of less popular items from the middle to the end of the graph. For example, consider an electronics store. The items that make up that spike are products such as the Nintendo Wii, the iPod Touch, and other wildly popular products that everyone thinks they must have. (The spike is called the *Broad Head*, a term that is discussed later in the chapter.)

The Long Tail theory that Anderson posited for e-commerce works for search behavior too, because what is the Internet but a giant conglomeration of both popular and obscure information and products? An illustration of the Long Tail will help you get the full picture.

For example, a computerized version of Herman Melville's classic *Moby Dick* was broken down by word, and each word was ranked according to the number of times it was used in the book. What researchers found was that the word "the" was the most frequently used word, at about 15,000 times.

Of course, the word "the" doesn't tell you anything at all about the content of the book. Conversely, the word "whale," which would seem to be more indicative of the novel's subject, was used only 2,000 times. It ranked twenty-first on the list of words included in the book by frequency.

Translating this example to search, you have to think in terms of keywords. Someone searching for the word "the" in the book would find many instances but not necessarily helpful ones in terms of a search for the book's topic. Switching to the term "whale" would show fewer search results, but better-targeted ones. A user would be able to gather more information from the results returned.

When you're considering keywords for your web site, therefore, you have to look at all the words that are indicative of your chosen topic. When you do, you'll find that only a small percentage of those words appear frequently, and these are usually very broad terms. They'll generate a lot of clicks, but if you concentrate only on them, you could miss out on a sizable number of clicks that are more narrowly focused.

Here's a real-world illustration from a web site for which I create content. Table 2-1 contains a list of search terms that were used to find articles on this site in a given day. The table indicates that the top three terms generated 285 clicks for the site. Those are pretty broad terms.

Dig deeper into the search terms, however, and you'll see that the remaining 29 terms generated almost half as many clicks, totaling 139. Notice, too, that the majority of the terms that have low click rates are very specific — those visitors were looking for something in particular.

Google is widely known for understanding the intricacies of search better than any other search engine company on the planet. And after studying search patterns, the gurus at Google estimate that about half of all searches through the Google search engine are one of a kind. That equals more than 100 million unique searches each day on Google alone. Add in all the other search engines out there, and the number of unique searches in a day's time is absolutely astronomical.

TABLE 2-1

Long Tail Keywords Add Up

Keyword	Number of Clicks
Identity theft	145
Identity theft articles	98
Identity theft statistics	42
Election scams	15
Steps to recover from identity theft	15
Identity theft methods	10
Reporting identity theft	8
Internet identity theft statistics	7
How to report identity theft	7
Ident	5
What is monitoring your credit	5
Top identity theft method	4
Idetit	4
Identity theft.com	4
Id theft	4
Tips for reporting identity theft	3
Lightyear wireless + scam	3
2006 identity theft statistics	3
Do my own credit check	3
How to use stolen identities	3
Email spoofing	3
Computer spyware	3
Definition of identity theft	3
Identity theft where to begin	3
Where is identity theft the most prevalent	3
How to know identity thief on credit card	3

continued

TABLE 2-1 (continued)	
Keyword	**Number of Clicks**
Identity theft information	3
How identity theft happens	3
Identi	3
Credit card protection	3
Signing president bush identity theft enforcement and restitution act of 2008	3
Dumpster diving identity theft	3

Characteristics of Long Tail keywords

Long Tail keywords are not actually keywords. They're more key phrases that are very specific; and all Long Tail search queries have a few things in common:

- Average 3–5 words in length
- Usually not competitive phrases
- Usually directly related to a product or specific bit of information
- Each phrase generates only a few clicks each month.

How do you know which Long Tail phrases are appropriate for your web site? To know that, you have to understand a little about how people search.

People rarely search for random information — they are usually looking for something specific. If you have an idea of what visitors might be searching for, then you know how to target each of those searches, using both broad terms and narrower Long Tail phrases. Here are some bits of information that people use search engines to find:

- Product names
- Product functionality
- Product appeal
- Product quality
- Product usefulness
- Uses of products
- Solutions to problems
- General industry terms
- Specific industry terms

- General terms and geographical locations
- Specific terms and geographical locations

These are pretty general, but if you begin to apply key terms from your web site topic to these bits of information, then you can see the different ways that you might apply both broad terms and Long Tail key phrases to your SEO efforts.

Clearly, Long Tail keywords can be a very important part of your SEO strategy. They can account for a sizable chunk of the clicks that are generated on your site each day. And that's to say nothing of the value of clicks that result from Long Tail keywords. There's more on that a little later in this chapter.

Long Tail vs. Broad Head

Going back to applying Long Tail to products rather than search, the items that make up the Long Tail of less popular products are things such as food, cleaning supplies, and some clothing items. These are the products that you actually must have on a weekly basis to survive.

For example, consider your own spending. Think of all the purchases that you make in a given month (we're taking bills out of the equation; it's too painful to think about those every month and they're only loosely classified as products, so worthless to us at the moment). Chances are good that you spend a certain amount of money every month on the essentials that it takes to survive and maintain a household. Those are the items that appear in the Long Tail theory that Anderson posited.

You may also spend a certain amount of your income each month on nonessential items. These are things (like the new iPod Touch) that you don't need but would really like to have. The products that fall into this "want" category are often referred to as being in the *Broad Head*. Now compare the two. Two things should stand out in this comparison. First, it's likely that your spending on the essentials is larger than your spending on the one or two want items that you've been eyeing. Second, you'll re-spend on essentials every month.

Is the picture becoming clearer? Translating this to search, it works about the same way. Searchers are going to search for those big, Broad Head search terms (the ones that are wildly popular) when they're at the beginning of a buying process. But as they narrow their buying process, they'll search for narrower terms — Long Tail search terms. These narrower terms are like the essential items that you pick up at Wal-Mart each week. They're not as popular as the more exciting terms, but people will keep searching for them.

CROSS-REF The buying process consists of four phases that potential customers go through, from hearing about a product to purchasing that product. You can learn more about the buying process in Chapter 13.

Here's the best part in all of this: Those searchers who are looking for the less common terms are also looking for more-targeted words and are in a more purchasing state of mind — they've worked through the buying process and are closer to making a purchase, which also means they're closer to reaching whatever goal conversion you've set up for them.

Working from the Bottom Up

Even though it now seems as if those Long Tail keywords are the most important ones, you shouldn't discount the value of Broad Head words either. When you're considering the keywords and phrases that you want to use to market your web site and to rank in search engines, you should be looking at both Broad Head and Long Tail terms.

The key is how you do it. You have broad, usually very popular terms that everyone is fighting for, and then you have narrow terms that are used by people who are more likely to reach a conversion goal on your site, whether it's to purchase a product or service, to fill out a form that generates a sales lead, or to sign up for a newsletter or other marketing-related service. Knowing this, your instinct is to go to the heart of the matter and shoot for the audience most likely to convert.

In doing so, however, you leave a large part of the audience out completely. The broad-term searchers may not be as likely to reach a conversion goal *right now*, but they might reach that goal in the future, so you also want to bring those searchers to your site. Finding the right balance of broad-term keywords and Long Tail keywords can be a little tricky, though.

So how do you handle it? I say start at the bottom and work your way up. Obviously, you want to generate a lot of traffic as quickly as possible, but you also need to prove that your efforts are working, so you need to reach people who are going to convert quickly. Each Long Tail keyword isn't going to generate a lot of traffic, but it will generate very specific traffic — people who have a goal in mind. Your job is to help them reach that goal. Understand that you're not going to optimize for one type of keyword over another. It's not Long Tail first and then Broad Head — the two really go hand-in-hand. You should focus on optimizing both. Many web site owners begin with the broad keywords that reach the largest audience and come back later to build pages that are more highly targeted.

That method works, albeit slowly. Instead, optimize for the broad terms, but also for the Long Tail terms. That means putting together pages as quickly as possible that target both broad terms and more specific terms. You can use multiple keywords per page, so a progression from broad to narrow on a single page works fine.

For example, if you own a web site that sells electronic gadgets, you'll need pages that target broad keywords such as electronics, cell phones, MP3 players, and whatever other categories of electronics you might offer; but you also need to include much more specific terms, such as iPhone, HTC G1, iPod, Zune, and Sandisk on those same pages.

The solution is to create content that is relevant to the narrower Long Tail keywords. In the process, however, it will be nearly impossible for you to create that content without including references to the Broad Head terms.

For example, the front page of your web site will likely introduce your company, show special offers and featured products, and perhaps have small articles or text-based snippets of information that are targeted to specific products. Each of those broader categories is going to lead to a page that's progressively more specific with each level of the site into which the user goes. Therefore, the next page might be slightly more detailed and narrow, and the next page more focused still. On each of these pages, you're targeting a couple of sets of keywords. The first will be the broad terms that apply to your site. On your electronics site, a second page might be related to MP3 players. On that page, you could create an article or even a chart that explains to the site visitor what features to look for in an MP3 player.

Each of those features will lead one page deeper to an explanation of the feature that you're highlighting, and from that page you could go even deeper (and narrower) to explain to the visitor what specific uses that feature has. Along the way, though, you'll probably refer to the term "MP3 player" several times on each page, so you're not only creating content that targets the Long Tail keywords and phrases; the same content also targets the broader terms.

It's in this melding of both broad terms and Long Tail terms that you'll find your most powerful keyword mixture.

Tying It All Together

Here's why using both Long Tail and Broad Head keywords works: The Long Tail keywords will likely generate the most traffic for you in the beginning — hence my advice to work from the bottom up. If you optimize your site for those Long Tail words, you should very quickly begin to see results from those efforts.

You're not going to debut your site and generate tons of traffic, no matter how well you optimize it; and Long Tail keywords aren't a magic solution ensuring that you automatically have a ton of converting traffic either. However, competition for Long Tail keywords isn't as tough as it is for the broader ones, so you should begin to see traffic more quickly than if you just target the broader words.

Cost is another consideration. Broad keywords tend to be far more expensive when you're using keyword-targeted ads than the keywords and phrases associated with Long Tail search terms. In fact, it's possible that you'll rank on the first page for some Long Tail words and phrases within a few days (and sometimes even just a few hours) of going live. Because these terms are narrow and more targeted, there's not as much competition. As soon as a search crawler examines your site and adds it to the results database, you should begin to see some kind of ranking. If the Long Tail terms you've selected are well targeted, then the site will likely be fairly high in the rankings. I've seen some web sites create pages that appeared in the top 10 on Google search results for their chosen term within four hours. It's rare, but it does happen.

In addition to your site showing up in rankings for Long Tail terms faster than for broad terms, you should see traffic that's converting at a reasonably steady rate as well. Remember that Long

Tail keywords tend to target visitors who are further along in the buying process, which means they're ready to make a commitment. Whether that's to sign up for your site newsletter or actually make a purchase from your site, if you're showing up high enough in search rankings to garner clicks, then it's likely that you're also going to reach goal conversions with those visitors who find you.

Of course, the Broad Head keywords will also generate some traffic. In the beginning, it will be slow; but over time (and that's the key with Broad Head words) the traction that you gain with your Long Tail keywords will contribute to traction for the broader words. Where broad terms with a lot of competition are concerned, numerous factors go into determining search ranking. One of those considerations is how long your web site has been around. Another is how much traffic is generated from other, more targeted searches. And if you've optimized your site well, for both Long Tail and broad terms, then you should begin to see your ranking for those broader words climb too.

Long Tail search terms are not an SEO panacea. Long Tail targeting is a strategy. It works well when done properly, but alone it won't guarantee you top ranking or high conversion rates. Moreover, Long Tail should be just one facet of a well-considered, well-planned, and well-executed SEO plan.

Chapter 3

Creating an SEO Plan

Before you can even begin to optimize your web site for search engines, you need to have a search engine optimization plan in place. This will help you create SEO goals and keep those goals in focus as the purpose of your site changes, and as the methods for search engine optimization change — and they will change.

Your SEO plan will help you see where you need to concentrate your efforts at any given time. This need will change. In the beginning, you're most likely to be focusing on getting started with SEO, which means you'll be wrestling keyword issues, adding metadata tags, and building content. However, after you've put all of your SEO strategies into place, the focus of your SEO activities should become more focused on maintaining and updating the elements of SEO that help you rank well.

Note that I said your efforts will change, not that they will end. Once you've started SEO, if you plan to continue using it, you'll need to constantly monitor and update your SEO plan, strategies, and activities. There was a time when the only thing you had to worry about was which keywords or links would be most effective for getting your site ranked high in relevant search results. Today, very few search engines focus on a single aspect of search engine optimization. This means that over time, those who focused only on keywords or only on links have found themselves with diminished SEO effectiveness.

Web sites today are — or should be — living organisms. A successful web site grows and changes constantly. From simply adding new content to something as drastic as complete site redesign, a good web site will look different from one year to the next, and sometimes from one month to the next.

33

Search engines also naturally change and mature, as the technologies and principles that enable SEO and the search engines themselves change. To keep pace, your SEO plan should be considered a dynamic, changing document. Your approach to SEO needs to evolve and change as well, and that's where your SEO plan will help you stay on track.

Using the SEO plan, you can quickly and easily tell where you are and where you need to be with your search engine optimization efforts.

Understanding Why You Need SEO

Before you can understand the reasons for using SEO, it might be good to have a definition of what SEO — search engine optimization — is. It's probably a safe assumption that if you've picked up this book, you have some understanding of SEO, so I'll keep it simple.

SEO is the science of customizing elements of your web site to achieve the best possible search engine ranking. That's really all there is to search engine optimization, but as simple as it sounds, don't let it fool you. Both internal and external elements of the site affect the way it's ranked in any given search engine, so all of these elements should be taken into consideration. Good SEO can be very difficult to achieve, and great SEO seems pretty well impossible at times.

Why is search engine optimization so important? Think of it this way: If you're standing in a crowd of a few thousand people and someone is looking for you, how will they find you? In a crowd that size, everyone blends together. Now suppose there is a system that separates groups of people. Maybe if you're a woman you're wearing red and if you're a man you're wearing blue. Now anyone looking for you will have to look through only half the people in the crowd. You can further narrow the group of people to be searched by adding additional differentiators until you have a small enough group that a *search query* can be executed and the desired person can be easily found.

Your web site is much like that one person in the huge crowd. In the larger picture your site is nearly invisible, even to the search engines that send crawlers out to catalog the Web. To get your site noticed, both by crawlers and visitors, certain elements must stand out. That's why you need search engine optimization — to help you focus on the *right* elements.

By accident, your site will surely land in a search engine; and it's likely to rank within the first few thousand results without any effort from you. A crawler will eventually find the site and bury it somewhere in the results with every other web site on the same topic. Clearly, that's not good enough. Being ranked on the ninth or tenth page of search results is tantamount to being invisible. To be noticed, your site should be ranked much higher.

Ideally, you want your site to be displayed somewhere on the first two to three pages of results. Most people won't look beyond the third page, if they get even that far. Indeed, it's the sites that land on the first page of results that get the most traffic, and traffic is translated into revenue, which is the ultimate goal of search engine optimization.

To achieve a high position in search results, your site must be more than simply recognizable by a search engine crawler. It must satisfy a set of criteria that not only gets the site cataloged, but can also get it cataloged above most (if not all) of the other sites that fall into that category or topic. This is no easy task.

Some of the criteria by which a search engine crawler determines your site's rank in a set of results include the following:

- Anchor text
- Site popularity
- Link context
- Topical links
- Title tags
- Keywords
- Site language
- Content
- Site maturity

It is estimated that there are at least several hundred other criteria that could also be examined before your site is ranked by a search engine. Some of the preceding criteria also have multiple points of view. For example, when looking at link context, a crawler might take into consideration where the link is located on the page, what text surrounds it, and where it leads to or from.

These criteria are also weighed differently. For some search engines, links are more important than site maturity; and for others, links have little importance. These weights and measures are constantly changing, so even trying to guess what is most important at any given time is a pointless exercise. Just as you figure it out, the criteria will shift or change completely.

Many of the elements used in search engine rankings are likely to have some impact on your site ranking, even when you do nothing to improve them. However, without your attention, you're leaving the search ranking of your site to chance. That's like opening a business without putting out a sign. You're sure to get some traffic, but because people don't know you're there, it won't be anything more than the curiosity of passersby.

Setting SEO Goals

Okay, so you understand how important it is to put time into SEO. How exactly do you go about it? One thing you *don't* do is begin trying to implement SEO strategies without defining some sort of goal you want to accomplish. One of the greatest failings of many SEO plans, like all technology plans, is the lack of a clearly defined goal.

The goal for your SEO plan should be built around your business needs, and it's not something every business requires at the same level. For example, if you run a simple blog, in-depth SEO might be more expense than it's worth; but if your plans for that blog are to turn it into a brand, then something a little more than the simplest of SEO strategies might be just what you need to build the traffic that begins to establish your brand.

If you have a larger business, say a web site that sells custom-made silk-flower arrangements, one way to increase your business (some estimate by more than 50 percent) is to invest time, money, and considerable effort into optimizing your site for search. Just don't do it without a goal in mind. In the case of a silk-flower web site, one goal might be to increase the amount of traffic your web site receives. Another might be to increase your exposure to potential customers outside your geographic region.

Those are both good reasons to implement an SEO plan. Another reason you might consider investing in SEO is to increase your revenues, which you can do by funneling site visitors through a sales transaction while they are visiting your web site. SEO can help with that, too.

In other words, before you even begin to put together an SEO plan, the first thing you need to do is determine what goal you want to achieve with that plan. Be sure it is a well-articulated and specifically defined goal, too. The more specific it is, the closer you will come to hitting it.

For example, a goal to "increase web-site traffic" is far too broad. Of course you want to increase your web-site traffic. That's the overarching goal of any SEO plan. However, if you change that goal to "increase the number of visitors who complete a transaction of at least $25," you are much more likely to implement the SEO that will indeed help you reach that goal.

Make sure the goal is specific and attainable. Otherwise, it's very easy to become unfocused with your SEO efforts. In some cases, you can spend all your time chasing SEO and never accomplish anything. As mentioned previously, search engines regularly change the criteria for ranking sites. They started doing this when internal, incoming, and external links became a factor in SEO. Suddenly, every webmaster was rushing to add as many additional links as possible, and often those links were completely unrelated to the site. That led to a sudden and often meaningless rise in page links. It wasn't long before the linking criteria had to be qualified with additional requirements.

Today, link strategies are quite complex and must abide by a set of rules or your web site could be banned from some search engines for what's called *SEO spam*, or the practice of targeting a specific element or criteria of search engine ranking with the intention of becoming one of the highest-ranked sites on the Web. If you establish an SEO goal, however, you're more likely to have a balanced traffic flow, which will improve your search engine ranking naturally.

In addition to well-focused goals, you should also consider how your SEO goals align with your business goals. Business goals should be the overall theme for everything you do with your web site, and if your SEO goals are not created with the intent of furthering those business goals, you'll find that the SEO goals ultimately fail. Make sure that any goal you set for optimizing your site for search is a goal that works well within the parameters that are set by your overall business goals.

Finally, remain flexible at all times. It's fine to set a goal, or even a set of goals, and hold tightly to them. Just don't hold so tightly that the goals get in the way of performing great SEO activities. SEO goals and plans, like any others, must be flexible and grow with your organization. For this reason, it's always a good idea to review your SEO goals and plans periodically — at least every six months, and quarterly is better.

Creating Your SEO Plan

Once you have a goal or set of goals in mind for your web site, it's time to create your SEO plan. The SEO plan is the document that you'll use to stay on track as you try to implement SEO strategies on your site.

For many people, the thought of implementing SEO on a web site that includes dozens or even hundreds of pages is overwhelming. It doesn't have to be, though.

Picky details

As you begin to consider what it is you're doing with SEO, keep something in mind: SEO is all in the details. You may have heard this tired phrase before, but don't discount it because it's no longer completely fresh and "buzzy." It's still true. SEO, especially organic SEO, is all about the little things you do that make a big difference over time, and sometimes even immediately.

For example, I work on a web site about identity theft, and one of the things I do is create content to help people avoid identity theft or recover from it if they have already been victimized. In the course of taking over this site from the person who worked on it last, I found myself fighting struggling page ranks on various search engines. One thing I did to combat this was some keyword research.

I looked into all the keywords that people were using to find my site, and then I began integrating those keywords into content that people are actually looking for. I still don't rank number one for my most desired keyword (identity theft), but I do rank on the first page for many of the Long Tail keyword phrases that my users search for (such as disaster identity theft, senior identity theft, and vacation identity theft).

It was a minor change in the larger picture. I was already creating content for the site, but by focusing on some of the terms that I learned visitors were using, I improved my web site's search rankings. In at least one case, that improvement happened on the same day!

In other words, don't discount the little things. Even minor details, such as refocusing your keyword efforts or adding the right tags in the right places, can make a major difference in the amount of traffic that your site receives.

Prioritizing pages

As you begin putting your SEO plan together, the whole task of SEO may seem a little over-whelming. Don't let it get the best of you. Look at SEO in small, bite-size pieces. For example, instead of looking at your site as a whole, look at each page on the site. Prioritize those pages, and then plan your SEO around each page's priority. Taking a single page into consideration helps to eliminate the "everything has to happen right now" issue and makes it possible for you to create an SEO plan that maximizes your web site's potential in the minimum amount of time.

Top-priority pages should be the ones that your visitors will most naturally gravitate to, such as your home page, or pages that will generate the most traffic or revenue. When prioritizing pages, you're also creating a road map for your marketing efforts. If three of the pages on your site are your top priority, those three will have the lion's share of time, capital, and effort when it comes to SEO and marketing.

Site assessment

After you have prioritized your site, you should assess where you stand and where you need to be with your current SEO efforts. Again, assess each page individually, rather than the site as a whole. In SEO, individual pages are equally important (if not more so) than the entire site. All of your efforts are designed to rank one page above all others in search results. Which page is the most important should be determined by your business needs.

Your SEO assessment should be a document that outlines the current standing of the main SEO elements of each page. It should contain columns for the element of the site you're assessing, the current status of that element, what needs to be improved in that element, and the deadline for improvement. It's also helpful to put a check box next to each item, which can be marked when improvements are completed, and a column for follow-up, because SEO is an ongoing process.

The elements that should be considered during an assessment include the following:

- **Site/page tagging:** The meta tags that are included in the coding of your web site are essential to having that site listed properly in a search engine. Tags to which you should pay specific attention are the title tags and the description tags, because these are the most important to a search engine.

- **Page content:** How fresh is your content? How relevant is it? How often is it updated? How much content is there? Content is still important when it comes to search results. After all, most people are looking for a specific piece of content, whether it's information or a product. If your content is stale, search engines might eventually begin to ignore your site in favor of a site with fresher content. There are exceptions to this generalization, however, and one exception is when your content is, by nature, very rich but not very dynamic. Because of the usefulness of the content, such a site will probably continue to rank well, but it's a difficult case to determine. In general, fresh content is better.

- **Site links:** Site links are essential in SEO. Crawlers and spiders look for the links into and out of your site in order to traverse it and collect data on each URL. However, they also look for those links to be *in context*, meaning the link must come from or lead to a site that is relevant to the page being indexed. Broken links tend to be a large problem when it comes to search engine ranking, so ensure that links are still working during the assessment process.

■ **Site map:** Believe it or not, a site map will help your web site be more accurately linked. This is not the ordinary site map that you include to help users quickly navigate through your site. This site map is an XML-based document, at the root of your HTML, that contains information (URL, last updated, relevance to surrounding pages, and so on) about each of the pages within the site. Using this XML site map helps to ensure that even the deep pages within your site are indexed by search engines. If you don't have a site map, you should create one. If you do have one, make sure it's accurate and up to date.

CROSS-REF You can find an example SEO assessment worksheet in Appendix D. Use this worksheet to create an accurate assessment of your web site.

Finishing the plan

With the site assessment out of the way, you should have a good idea of what areas need work and what areas are in good shape. Don't assume that the areas that don't currently need work will always be perfect, however. That's not how it works. At the very least, changes to the pages will require changes to the SEO efforts that you're putting forth; at most, they may require that you begin SEO efforts for that page all over again.

You can now take the time to put together all of the information that you've gathered into a cohesive picture of the SEO efforts you should be making. Your SEO plan is more than just a picture of what's there and what's not, however. This is the document that you use to tie everything together: current standing, marketing efforts, capital expenditures, time frames — all of it.

The document should look much like any other plan that you create, such as your business plan, which likely includes an area for background information, marketing information, plans for growing the business, and plans for managing problems that may arise.

An SEO plan is very similar. You'll have your current standings, the goals that you plan to hit, and the marketing efforts that you plan to make for each page (or for the site as a whole). You'll even include the capital expenditures that you anticipate as you implement your SEO plan.

You'll also want to include the strategies you plan to use. Those strategies can include efforts such as submitting your site or pages from your site to directories manually and planning the content you'll use to draw search crawlers, or they can be keyword marketing plans or pay-per-click programs you plan to use. In addition, be sure to include a time line for the testing and implementation of those efforts, as well as for regular follow-ups.

Follow-up

Follow-up is also an essential part of your SEO plan. Many people assume that they can develop and implement an SEO plan and then forget about it. The truth is, however, that SEO is not just a one-time event. It's an ongoing process that requires testing, monitoring, and often rebuilding.

A good plan for conducting follow-ups is to schedule them quarterly. Some companies choose to follow up and reassess their SEO biannually, but to be truly effective quarterly is much better. Conversely, following up on your SEO efforts too soon is nonproductive. In many cases, it takes at least three months to get a clear picture of how successful your efforts are. Conducting an evaluation before that three-month mark could have you chasing after an elusive SEO goal that doesn't really exist; or worse, it could lead you away from a successful strategy.

Give your plan at least three months but no more than six between check-ups. Once you create the habit of reevaluating your SEO efforts on that schedule, it will be much less time consuming than you might assume.

Understanding Organic SEO

All this talk about planning for SEO is great, but what about *organic SEO*. You don't have to put any efforts into that, do you? Don't go foolin' yourself. Organic SEO is just as much work as any other type of SEO. It's just a slightly different method of creating a site optimized for search ranking, without having to implement any new technologies or spend a lot of time submitting your site to different primary and secondary search engines. In fact, the distinction here is a very general one. Only SEO purists consider *real SEO* as being strictly organic — meaning you use no fee-based services whatever. Most people are happy with just *plain SEO*, which usually means a combination of organic and fee-based, which is often referred to as SEM, or search engine marketing. It's best if you think of SEO as just SEO; then you don't have to worry about distinctions that aren't really important in optimizing your web site.

The definitions of organic SEO vary a little, depending on whom you talk to. Some SEO experts think it's all about optimizing the content of your web site to catch the attention of the crawlers and spiders that index sites. Others think it's the number of quality links you can generate on your site. Organic SEO is actually a combination of those and other elements, such as site tagging, that will naturally place your web site in search engine rankings. How high in those rankings depends on how well you design your site.

Before you assume that organic SEO is just the solution you've been looking for, however, take a step back. Organic SEO is not an easy way to land in a search engine. Basically, if you put a web site online and spend a little time getting it ready for the world to see, you will have probably achieved some measure of organic SEO without really trying.

That's because your site will probably be listed in some search engine somewhere, without too much time and effort on your part. Elements that naturally occur on a web site — such as the title of the site, the URL, included web links, and even some of the content — will probably land you in a search engine (unless those elements are *black-hat SEO* efforts, in which case the engine could permanently exclude you). The question is *where* in the results will you land? Without attention from you, that might be on page 10,000 of the rankings — not high enough to gain any attention at all.

Organic SEO maximizes those naturally occurring elements, building upon each element to create a site that will naturally fall near the top of the search engine results pages (SERPs). One of the most attractive features of organic SEO is that the methods used to achieve high SERPs rankings are free — other than the time it takes to implement these ideas.

However, there is a trade-off. Achieving organic SEO can take anywhere from three to six months. For web site owners impatient to see results from their SEO efforts, this can seem like an eternity; but it's worth the extra time if the budget is an issue.

Achieving Organic SEO

Not only can achieving organic SEO take time, it also requires targeting the right elements of your web site. You can spend a lot of time tweaking aspects of your site only to find that it still ranks below the third page of search results. If your attention is focused on the right elements, however, you'll find that organic SEO can be a fairly effective method of achieving a higher search engine ranking.

Make no mistake, however: Organic SEO alone is not as effective as organic SEO combined with some form of *pay-per-click* or keyword advertising program. Though organic SEO is good, adding the extra, more costly programs can be what you need to push your site right to the top of the SERPs.

A good first step in search engine optimization is to ensure that the organic elements of your site are as optimized as possible, and then focus on search engine marketing elements such as keyword advertising. Although these elements are covered in detail in future chapters, the following sections look at some of the basics.

Web site content

Web site content is one of the most highly debated elements in search engine optimization, mostly because many rather unethical SEO users have turned to black-hat SEO techniques such as *keyword stuffing* in an attempt to artificially improve search engine ranking. Despite these dishonest approaches to search engine optimization, web site content is still an important part of any web site optimization strategy.

The content on your site is the main draw for visitors. Whether your site sells products or simply provides information about services, what brings visitors to your site are the words on the page. Product descriptions, articles, blog entries, and even advertisements are all scanned by spiders and crawlers as they work to index the Web.

One strategy of these crawlers and spiders is to examine just how the content of your page works with all of the other elements (such as links and meta tags) that are examined. To rank high in a selection of search results, your content must be relevant to those other elements.

Some search engines will delist your page or lower your page rank if the content of your site is not unique. Especially since the advent of blogs, search engines now examine how frequently the page content is updated, and look for content that appears only on your web site. This doesn't mean you can't have static content on your page. For e-commerce sites, the product descriptions may rarely change.

Including other elements on the page, however, such as reviews or product updates, will satisfy a crawler's requirement that content changes regularly. Content is an important part of your site and the ranking of your site in search engine results. To achieve organic SEO, take the time to develop a content plan that not only outlines what should be included on each page of your site, but also how often that content will be updated, and who will do the updates.

One other element you might want to consider when looking at your page content as part of SEO is the keywords that you plan to use. Ideally, your chosen words should appear on the page several times, but as mentioned previously, this is a balancing act that might take some time to accomplish.

CROSS-REF   Chapter 5 contains additional information about keywords and how to use them to improve your search engine ranking.

As part of your site content, keywords require special attention. In fact, selecting the right keywords is a bit of an art form that takes some time to master. For example, if your web site were dedicated to selling products for show dogs, you might assume that "show dogs" would be a perfect keyword, but selecting the right keywords requires a thorough understanding of your audience and what they *might* be looking for when they visit your web site. In the case of show dogs, people looking for products for show dogs might search for "grooming products," "pedigree training," or just "dog supplies." It could even be something entirely different, such as the name of a product that was featured at the most recent dog show.

Learning which keywords will be most effective for your site requires that you study your audience, but it also requires some trial and error. Try using different keywords each quarter to learn which ones work best.

It's also advised that you use a tracking program such as *Google Analytics* to monitor your web site traffic and track the keywords that most often lead users to your site.

Google Analytics

Google Analytics is a free web site statistics application that you can use to track your web site traffic. You can access Google Analytics by going to `www.google.com/analytics`. You must have a Google user name to access the program.

If you do not have a Google user name, you can create one when you sign up for the application. It's simple. Provide your e-mail address and a password, type the verification word from the graphic provided, and then read the Terms of Service and click "I accept. Create my account."

Once you've created your user name and password, accessing the tracking capabilities of Google is easy. You'll need to copy a snippet of text that Google provides into the coding of your web site. Once you've added the code to your site, it will take a few days for Google to gather enough information to provide reports about it, and as much as two months to gather enough data to give you real insight into your site. But once there is enough data, you'll have access to the keywords that most often lead visitors to your site.

Google Analytics can also be combined with Google's AdWords program to provide paid keyword tracking and information. To learn more about Google Analytics, check out *Google Analytics 2.0* by Mary Tyler and Jerri Ledford (Wiley, 2007). Note that Google Analytics doesn't currently track spiders and crawlers, however, so there may be some limitations to its SEO functionality. Still, if you need a (free) tool to help you examine some of the metrics surrounding your SEO efforts, Google Analytics is a good starting point.

Internal and external links

Another element of organic SEO that's just as important as your web site content is the links on your pages. Links can be incoming, outgoing, or internal — and where those links lead or come from is as important as the context in which the links are provided.

When links first became a criteria by which crawlers ranked web sites, many black-hat SEO users rushed to create *link farms*. These were pages full of nothing but web links, some of which led to relevant information and some of which led to sites in no way related to the topic of the web site. It didn't take long for search engine designers and programmers to catch on to these shady practices and change the way that crawlers use links to rank sites.

Today, links must usually be related to the content of the page, and they must link to something relevant to that content. In other words, if your links don't go to or lead in from pages that match the keywords that you're using, they will be of little value to you.

The balance of links that are included on your page is also relevant. Too many links and your site could be considered a link farm. Too few and you'll lose out to sites that have more and better-targeted links.

Your best option when including links on your web site is to link to the pages you are certain are relevant to your site content. Don't include a link unless you're sure it will have value to your visitors, and then take the time to pursue links into your site from them as well.

One other type of link, the *internal link*, is also important. This is a navigational link that leads visitors from one page to another on your site. The navigation of your site (which is what these links are, essentially) should be intuitive, and natural in progression.

CROSS-REF   You can find more information about links and linking in Chapter 11.

Finally, don't forget to include the site map. Your site map not only makes it easier for crawlers to index every page of your site, but it also makes it easier for users to find their way around in it. Ideally, users will never have to rely on the site map, but it's nice to include it in the event that they either need it or simply want to click directly to the page they're seeking.

How you design your site map is a matter of preference. Some organizations create site maps that include only the top two levels of pages. Others include maps that go three levels down or deeper. Whatever level of depth you think will be required by the majority of users is how deep your site map should go. Keep in mind, however, that site maps can become just as overwhelming as any other navigational structure if your site contains hundreds of pages. In short, design your site map so it's easy to decipher and takes users to the pages they are seeking without difficulty and confusion.

User experience

User experience is a little harder to quantify than other site-ranking elements. It's easy to claim that users will find your site simple to use, that they will find the information or products that they're seeking, or that they will have reason to return to your site. In practice, that's a little more difficult to achieve.

How in the world can a site gain search engine ranking by user experience? It's fairly simple really. Search engines today are smarter than ever. They may not be able to make you a grilled cheese sandwich, but they can certainly keep track of what results users click when they run a search. Those result selections are essential to the organic ranking of your site.

Here's a scenario. Suppose you search for something like health-insurance information. When the search results appear, how do you choose which results to look at? Most users read the small descriptive lines that are included with the search engine ranking and select according to those.

In most cases, the sites that are visited are those sites that are highest in the rankings, but search engines also monitor which sites are actually clicked on, so let's say you search through the results and click a link on the fifth page. Suppose several other people do so as well. That link on the fifth page is going to show more traffic than links that are higher in the results, so smart search engines will move that page higher in the rankings. It may not jump right up to the number one position, but it's entirely possible for the site to move from the fifth page of rankings to the second or third. This is part of the equation used when user experience is taken into consideration.

Another part of that experience might be how quickly the user jumps back to the search page. Maybe when you click that link on the fifth page, you can tell when you hit the site that it's not the page you were looking for, or doesn't contain the information or product that you were looking for. You click the back arrow and you're taken back to the page of search results.

This behavior is called *bounce*, and the rate at which users bounce off your site is an indicator of the site's usability in terms of how relevant it is to what users are searching for. This relates directly to the keywords the user searched, which relates directly to how your site matches those keywords. To maximize the usability of your site, make sure the keywords you choose and the description of your page are as accurate as possible.

It may take some time for you to learn how to make all of these elements work together, especially when it comes to elements such as descriptions and keywords. Be patient, and be willing to experiment with different combinations of words or descriptions until you hit on the ones that send your site rank closer to the top search results. Just remember that this is a process that's more of an art than a science, and it takes time (usually two to three months) to see the most accurate results.

Site interactivity

When the Internet first came into being, web sites were all about disclosing information. The only interaction between a web site and a user was the passive reading the user did while on the site. Today, reading is still important, as users search web sites to learn more about products, services, or topics, but there's much more to web sites now than just text on a screen.

We now live in an interactive age, and most of us want and expect to interact with the web sites we visit. That interaction might take the form of a poll, the capability to comment on a blog post, the downloading of a file, or even a game that relates to the site content. No matter what the type of interaction, users expect it, and search crawlers look for it.

Site interactivity is essential to achieving a high SEO ranking. Sure, you can garner a high ranking without interaction, but it won't happen nearly as fast, and the ranking will likely be lower than that of a site that does offer some form of interaction with the user.

Why is interaction so important? Simple. If you can influence a user to interact with your site, you have more of a chance of gaining a *goal conversion*. Goal conversions are the completion of some form of activity designed to gather further information about your user. A goal conversion can be something as simple as enticing users to sign up for a newsletter, or it can be more specific, such as persuading them to make a purchase.

No matter what goal conversion you're seeking, the way to achieve it is through interactivity; and the more frequently users interact with your site, the more likely it is that they will reach that goal conversion page you're monitoring so closely.

Goal conversion is the purpose of many web sites. For example, the target goal conversion for an e-commerce web site might be for the user to make a $25 purchase. If you can entice a user to purchase from your site — that is, meet the goal conversion — you have more of a chance of getting that user back to your site for a future purchase, to find additional information, or simply to interact with your site again.

All of these are important aspects of your web site's traffic patterns, and search engines look for elements of interactivity to judge the value of your site to users. One goal of search engines is to provide value to users. Those users turn to the search engine for help in finding something specific.

Just as it's important for your site to land high in the search results, it's important for the search engine to provide the information that a user seeks within the first page or two. Making the user happy is one way search companies make their money. Another way is through the fees that advertisers will pay to have their pages ranked high in the search results or their advertisements shown according to the keywords the user was searching by.

In other words, search engine optimization is a two-way street. It's also a business, and search engine companies are always trying to find ways to improve their business. For that reason, these elements, and many others, are an essential part of search engine optimization.

Organic SEO is certainly not easy to achieve, but you can improve your chances dramatically by having a solid SEO plan that outlines both where you are and what needs to be added to your site design or content to make it more visible to users. It also takes a lot of time and effort to create and implement the right SEO plan, but if you use your SEO plan as a stepping-stone, even for organic SEO, you'll stay focused and eventually achieve the search engine ranking that you are working toward.

Part II

SEO Strategies

SEO is hard work. It takes much effort to optimize just the right elements of your web site so search engines will not only find you, but will also index your site so that it appears high in search query results. And all that effort must be attended to by you. There are currently no tools that will put all the elements of SEO in place for you.

Instead, you have to build your web site with SEO in mind, choose all the right keywords, and use them in the right places and with the right balance on your site, determine if pay-per-click and paid-inclusion programs are for you, use the right meta tags in the right places, create great content, build and participate in communities, and add all the right links. Sounds like a lot of work, doesn't it?

It is. But don't let the amount of work overwhelm you. Consistent effort and the strategies included in this part of the book will have you working toward your SEO goals in no time. Each of the chapters in this section contains an explanation of how these elements affect SEO, and how you can create and implement strategies to help you leverage that element to reach your SEO goals.

Chapter 4

Building Your Site for SEO

Search engine optimization is a collection of strategies that improves the level at which your web site is ranked in the results returned when a user searches for a keyword or phrase.

By now, that's a definition you should be pretty familiar with. What you probably don't know (yet) is how to achieve SEO. You can't do it all at once. Instead, SEO has to happen in stages. If you try to implement too many strategies at one time, two things are going to happen:

- You won't be able to tell which of your strategies are successful. Implementing one strategy at a time makes it possible for you to pinpoint which strategies are working and which are not.

- When you try to implement too many strategies at one time, your efforts — even the successful ones — could be lost in the shuffle. It's like changing a recipe in multiple ways at once. Even if you like the result, you won't know which addition or deletion made the difference.

SEO is most successful when you concentrate on one effort at a time. A great place to start is on the way your site is built. One of the first things that attracts a search engine crawler is the actual design of your site. Tags, links, navigational structure, and content are just a few of the elements that catch a crawler's attention.

Before You Build Your Site

One of the most common misconceptions about SEO is that it is implemented after a web site has been built. It can be, but it's much harder to be successful when your site isn't built on a solid SEO foundation. A better option is to consider SEO before you begin to build your web site, if that's possible. It may not be; but if that's the case, you can still implement SEO strategies in the design of your site — it will just require a lot more work than building it in at the beginning.

Know your target

Before you even start contemplating how to build your web site, you should know in what types of search engines it's most important for your site to be ranked. Search engines are divided into several types beyond the primary, secondary, and targeted search engines that you learned about in Chapter 1. Search engine types are also determined by how information is entered into the index or catalog that's used to return search results. The three types of search engines are as follows:

- **Crawler-based engines:** Up until this point, the search engines discussed fall largely into this category. A crawler-based search engine (such as Google) uses an automated software agent (called a *crawler*) to visit, read, and index web sites. All the information collected by the crawler is returned to a central repository — a process called *indexing*. It is from this index that search engine results are pulled. Crawler-based search engines revisit web pages periodically in a time frame determined by the search engine administrator.

- **Human-powered engines:** Human-powered search engines rely on people to submit the information that is indexed and later returned as search results. Sometimes human-powered search engines are called *directories*. Yahoo! is a good example of what, at one time, was a human-powered search engine. Yahoo! started as a favorites list belonging to two people who needed an easier way to share their favorite web sites. Over time, Yahoo! took on a life of its own. It's no longer completely human controlled. Newer search engines such as Mahalo (www.mahalo.com) and Cuil (www.cuil.com) *are* entirely human powered, however, and this is creating a buzz on the Web. Human-powered search engines add an element of personalization to search that fits in with the current social nature of the Web.

- **Hybrid engines:** A hybrid search engine, as you might guess, is not entirely populated by a web crawler or by human submission. It is a combination of the two. In a hybrid engine, people can manually submit their web sites for inclusion in search results, but there is also a web crawler that monitors the Web for sites to include. Many search engines today fall into the hybrid category to at least some degree. Although the majority are populated mostly by crawlers, others offer some method by which people can enter their web site information.

It's important to understand these distinctions because how your site ends up indexed by a search engine may have some bearing on when it is indexed. For example, fully automated search engines that use web crawlers might index your site weeks (or even months) before a human-powered search engine. The reason is obvious: The web crawler is an automated application. The human-powered search engine may actually require that all entries be reviewed for accuracy before a site is included in search results, and that takes time.

In any case, the accuracy of search engine results varies according to the search query that is used. For example, entries in a human-powered search engine might be more technically accurate, but the search query that is used will determine whether the desired results are returned.

CROSS-REF More information about how search queries affect the results that are returned can be found in the section "Understanding Heuristics" in Chapter 5.

Page elements

Another facet of SEO to consider before you build your web site is the elements needed to ensure that your site is properly indexed by a search engine. Each search engine places different importance on different page elements. For example, Google is a very keyword-driven search engine, but it also looks at site popularity and the tags and links on any given page.

How well your site performs in a search engine is determined by how the elements of your page meet the engine's search criteria. Every search engine looks for the following main criteria:

- Text (meaning keywords)
- Tags — both HTML and meta tags
- Links
- Popularity

Text

Text is one of the most important elements of any web site. Of particular importance are the keywords within the text on a page, where those keywords appear, and how often they appear. This is why keyword marketing has become such a large industry in a relatively short time. Your keywords make all the difference when a search engine indexes your site and then serves it up in search results.

Keywords must match the words and phrases that potential visitors will use when searching for your site (or for the topic or product that's listed on your site). To ensure that your keywords are effective, you'll need to spend some time learning which keywords work best for your site. That means doing keyword research (which you learn more about in Chapter 5) and testing the keywords that you do select to see how effective they really are.

Tags

In search engine optimization, two kinds of tags are important on your web site: *meta tags* and *HTML tags*. Technically, meta tags *are* HTML tags; they just appear in very specific places. The two most important meta tags are the keyword tag and the description tag.

The keyword tag occurs at the point where you list the keywords that apply to your web site. A keyword tag on a search engine optimization page might look something like this:

```
<meta name="keywords" content="SEO, search engine optimization, page
rank">
```

The description tag provides a short description of your page. Such a tag for the search engine optimization page might look like this:

```
<meta name="description" content="The ultimate guide to
search engine optimization!">
```

Not all search engines take meta tags into consideration because in the past, these tags have been overloaded with keywords that were irrelevant or inaccurate. For that reason, your site should use both meta tags and other HTML tags. Some of the other HTML tags that you should include on your web site are the *title tag*, the top (or H1) *heading tags*, and the *anchor tags*.

The title tag is the tag that's used in the title of your web site. This tag will appear like the following:

```
<Title>Your Title Here</Title>
```

Once you've tagged your site with a title tag, when a user pulls the site up, the title that you entered will appear in the *reverse bar* at the very top of the page if the user is using an Internet Explorer (IE) browser earlier than IE7. In IE7 and the Firefox browser or Google Chrome, the title will appear on the browser tab, as shown in Figures 4-1, 4-2, and 4-3, respectively.

FIGURE 4-1

In IE 7 browsers, the HTML title tag you entered will appear on the browser tab.

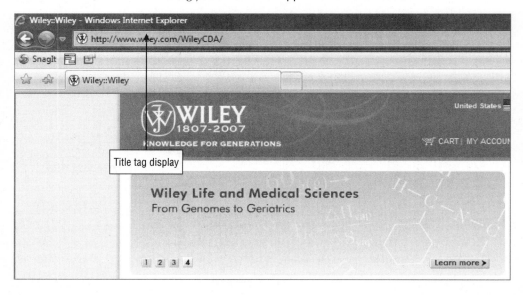

FIGURE 4-2

The Firefox browser shows the title tag in the browser tabs.

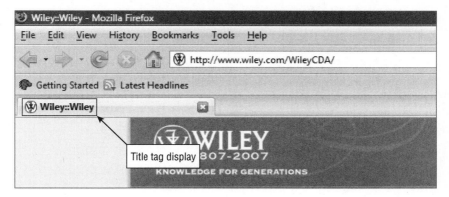

High-level headings (H1s) are also important when a crawler examines your web site. Your keywords should appear in your H1 headings and in the HTML tags you use to create those headings. An H1 tag might look like this:

```
<h1>High-Level Heading</h1>
```

FIGURE 4-3

The Google Chrome browser shows the title tag in the current tab. Note there is no reverse bar in Chrome.

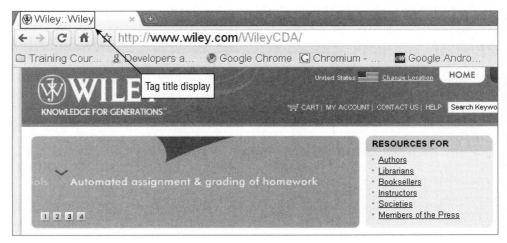

Anchor tags, also called *anchor text*, are used to create links to other pages. An anchor tag can point users to another web page, a file on the Web, or even an image or sound file. You're probably most familiar with the anchor tags used to create links to other web sites. Here's what an anchor tag might look like:

```
<a href="http://www.targetwebsite.com/">Text for link</a>
```

Figure 4-4 illustrates how that link might appear to users as they navigate a web page.

FIGURE 4-4

The anchor tag is used to create links to other pages, files, or images on the Web.

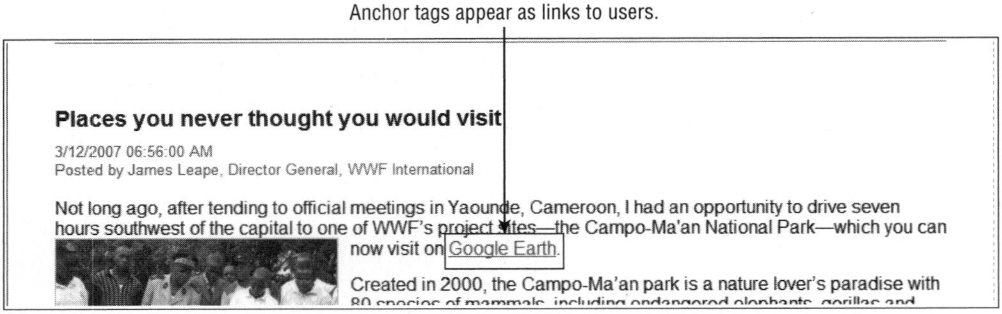

Anchor tags appear as links to users.

Places you never thought you would visit

3/12/2007 06:56:00 AM
Posted by James Leape, Director General, WWF International

Not long ago, after tending to official meetings in Yaounde, Cameroon, I had an opportunity to drive seven hours southwest of the capital to one of WWF's project sites—the Campo-Ma'an National Park—which you can now visit on Google Earth.

Created in 2000, the Campo-Ma'an park is a nature lover's paradise with 80 species of mammals, including endangered elephants, gorillas and

A *link tag* is combined with the anchor tag. That link can be text-based, and that text is where search engine optimization comes into play. How many times have you seen a web site that includes text with underlined words, all of which are related to the topic covered on the site? Those links are tagged for optimization. When a search engine crawler examines your web pages, it will look for links like the one shown in the figure.

What's important about anchor text is that it enables you to get double mileage from your keywords. When a search engine crawler reads the anchor text on your site, it sees the links that are embedded in the text. Those links tell the crawler what your site is all about, so if you're using your keywords in your anchor text (and you should be), then you're going to be hitting both the keyword ranking and the anchor text ranking for the keywords that you've selected.

Of course, there are always exceptions. In fact, everything in SEO has exceptions, and with anchor text the exception is that you can overoptimize your site, which might cause search engines to reduce your ranking or even block you from the search results altogether. Overoptimization occurs when all the anchor text on your web site is exactly the same as your keywords, but there is no variation or use of related terminology in the anchor text.

The other half of anchor text is the links that are actually embedded in the keywords and phrases used on the web page. Those links are equally as important as the text to which they are anchored. The crawler will follow the links as part of crawling your site. If they lead to related web sites, your ranking will be higher than if the links lead to completely unrelated web sites.

These links can also lead to other pages within your own web site, as you may have seen anchor text in blog entries do. The blog writer uses anchor text, containing keywords, to link back to previous posts or articles elsewhere on the site.

One other place that you may find anchor text is in your site map. Naming your pages using keywords when possible helps improve your site rankings. Then to have those page names (which are keywords) on your *site map* is another way to boost your rankings, and thus your traffic. A site map (which is covered in more detail later in this chapter) is a representation of your site with each page listed as a name linked to that page.

Anchor text seems completely unrelated to keywords, but in fact it's very closely related. When used properly in combination with your keywords, your anchor text can help you achieve a much higher search engine ranking.

Avoiding the Minefield of Google Bombs

Sometimes web site owners intentionally include only a word or a phrase in all their anchor text with the specific intent of making the page linked from rank high in Google search results. It's usually an obscure word or phrase and enables them to say they rank number one for whatever topic that site covers. It also has malicious undertones. This is called *Google bombing* or sometimes *link bombing*. (Link bombing became a viable term because it works with other search engines too.)

Google bombs are typically used in political attacks. For example, the first Google bomb created caused the phrase "more evil than Satan himself" to return Microsoft as the number one search result. Another incident, in which a specific slur directed at George Bush returned the store for George Bush merchandise, was seen during the 2004 presidential election.

Originally, Google ignored the problem, stating that Google bombs weren't a high priority and that it didn't want to compromise the integrity of the search engine, but eventually Google relented and changed the algorithm. Google bombs can still be used today — both for political purposes and for advancement of personal web sites — but it requires the enlistment of a community of bloggers and web site owners who are willing to use whatever obscure phrase is chosen and link it to the specified web site.

Links

To be of value, the links on your web pages must be related to the content of the page, and they must be active links to real web sites. *Broken links* can lower your search engine ranking. Links have always been an important factor in how web sites rank on the Web, but the abuse of linking that we see so often today started just a few years ago, about the time that Google became the big name in search.

When links became a ranking criterion, many black-hat SEOs began building *link farms*, which are sites that are nothing more than pages full of links designed to gain high search engine rankings.

It didn't take long for search engine administrators to figure out this sneaky optimization trick, so they changed the criteria by which links are ranked. Now link farms are fairly ineffective, but links on your web site are still important. Links show an interactivity with the community (other sites on the Web), which points to the legitimacy of your web site. Links aren't the only, or even the highest, ranking criteria, but they are important all the same.

CROSS-REF You'll find a complete explanation of links, linking, and how links affect your SEO in Chapter 15.

Popularity

One other consideration, even before you build your site, is the site's popularity. Many search engines include a criterion for the number of times users click on web sites that are returned in search results. The more often the site is selected from the search results, the higher in the ranking it climbs.

For you, that means you should begin building the popularity of your site even before it goes live. Begin building buzz about the site through advertisements, info-torials, and even newsletters or other e-mail announcements. Then redouble those efforts as soon as the site goes live to the public. *Social media* — services such as Facebook, Twitter, and MySpace — are another way to build buzz about a site, but there's a fine art to working within the community structure of social media. You can find more about the intricacies of using social media in SEO in Chapter 20.

Sometimes, SEO can seem like a conundrum. You optimize your web site for search engines in order to build popularity, but your ranking in the search engine can be determined by how popular your site is. There is no magic formula to help you solve the riddle of which comes first, popularity or SEO, so both have to happen together. The one certainty is that it requires time and consistent effort to draw visitors to your site.

Other criteria to consider

In addition to those four main elements you should plan to include on your site, there are a few others. For example, the *body text* on your web site will be examined by the crawler that indexes your site. Body text should contain enough keywords to gain the attention of the crawler, but not so many that it seems like the site is being stuffed with such words.

Alternative tags for pictures and links are also important. These are the tags that might appear as a brief description of a picture or graphic on a web site that fails to display properly. The alternative tags — called *alt tags* — display a text description of the graphic or picture, so that even if the actual image doesn't appear, there's some explanation of what should be there. Alt tags are a good place to include additional keywords.

Most users will never see your alt tags. They appear to screen readers that persons with sight disabilities may use, and they appear when a graphic image won't load on a page. Sometimes this is a problem with the visitor's Internet service; other times visitors intentionally turn off images to enable web pages to load faster.

Yet even if the majority of your visitors don't see these tags, crawlers do — and the alt tag provides you with an additional place to use keywords that are important for establishing the subject of your web site, as well as for boosting your site's recognition for those keywords.

Understanding Web Site Optimization

Web site optimization is all about creating a site that is discoverable by search engines and search directories. It sounds simple enough, but there are many aspects of site optimization to consider, and not all of them are about the keywords, links, or HTML tagging of your site.

Does hosting matter?

This question comes up frequently when a company or individual is designing a web site. Does it matter who hosts your site? The answer is no, but that's not to say that domain hosting is unimportant. Elements of the hosting have a major impact on how your site ranks in search results.

One of the biggest issues that you'll face with domain hosting is the location of your hosting company. If you're in the United States and you purchase a domain that is hosted on a server in England, your search engine rankings will suffer. Geographically, search engine crawlers will read your site as being contradictory to your location. Because many search engines serve up results with some element of geographical location included, this contradiction could be enough to affect your ranking.

The length of time for which you register your domain name could also affect your search engine ranking. Many hackers use *throw-away domains*, domain names that are registered for no more than a year, because they usually don't even get to use the domain for a full year before they are shut down. In fact, the typical malicious web site is online for less than four months, and usually for no more than a couple of weeks to a month. For this reason, some search engines have implemented ranking criteria that give priority to domains registered for longer periods. A longer registration also shows a commitment to maintaining the web site.

Domain-naming tips

The question of what to name a web site is always a big one. When selecting a name, most people think in terms of their business name, personal name, or a word or phrase that has meaning for them. What they often don't consider is how that name will work for the site's SEO. Does the name have anything at all to do with the site, or is it completely unrelated?

Have you ever wondered why a company might be willing to pay millions of dollars for a domain name? The domain name business.com was purchased for $7.5 million in 1999 and was recently thought to be valued at more than $300 million. Casino.com went for $5.5 million and worldwideweb.com sold for $3.5 million. What's so important about a name?

Choosing the right site name

Where SEO is concerned, the name of your web site is as important as many of the other SEO elements that you need to consider. Try this test. Use your favorite search engine to search for a topic, perhaps "asphalt-paving business." When your search results are returned, look at the top five results. Most of the time, a web site containing those words will be returned in those top five results, and it will often be in the number one slot.

In other words, if your company name is ABC Company but your business is selling nutmeg graters, consider purchasing the domain name NutmegGraters.com, instead of ABC Company.com. ABC Company may not get you in the top of search rankings, but the very specific nature of your product probably will; and both the content of your site and your domain name will attract crawlers in the way you want. Using a domain name containing a keyword from your content usually improves your site ranking.

A few more things that you should keep in mind when you're determining your domain name include the following:

- Keep the name as short as possible. Too many characters in a name mean increased potential for misspellings. It also means that your site address will be much harder for users to remember unless it's something really startling.

- Avoid dashes, underscores, and other meaningless characters. If the domain name that you want is taken, don't just add a random number or piece of punctuation to the name in order to "get close." Close doesn't count here. Instead, try to find another word that's relevant and possibly included in the list of keywords you'll be using. For example, instead of purchasing www.yourwebsite2.com, try something like www.yoursitesubject.com.

- Opt for a .com name whenever possible. There are a lot of domain extensions to choose from, such as info, biz, us, tv, names, and jobs, but if the .com version of your chosen domain name is available, that's always the best choice. Users tend to think in terms of .com, and any other extension will be harder for them to remember. Com names also tend to receive higher rankings in search engines than web sites using other extensions, so if your competition has www.yoursite.com and you choose to use www.yoursite.biz, chances are good that the competition will rank higher in search results than you.

  Try this: Choose a random term and then use your favorite search engines to search for that term. Looking only at the top one or two pages of search results, how many of those sites have an extension other than .com? If you do see extensions other than .com, they're likely to be .org, .net, .gov, or .edu — and you probably won't see many of those. That's how prevalent .com is, and it illustrates why you should try to use it whenever possible.

Considering URL structures

One more thing to think about as you're choosing your domain name is how URLs will be structured as you begin to put your site together. Some URLs are very long and seem completely random. For example, take a look at any given product page URL for Amazon.com. If you copy and paste that URL into a document, it could be two or three lines long, and it won't mean a thing to *you* after the Amazon.com part.

Ever notice how Amazon.com product pages rarely (if ever) seem to turn up in search rankings? That's because the pages are dynamic, and a URL that exists on Amazon today may not exist there tomorrow. *Dynamic URLs* change. Often. And for a variety of reasons. Sometimes dynamic URLs are used on product pages, but they can also be used when content is drawn from a database on a visitor-by-visitor basis or when visitor tracking information is included in the URL.

Typically, search crawlers can't effectively crawl sites that have dynamic URLs because the crawler can't trigger the dynamic URL the way a user does. One way to deal with dynamic URLs is to use a program that rewrites them.

URL rewriting is a common practice in SEO, especially since Google stated that it can't effectively crawl dynamic URLs. Unfortunately, even URL rewriting comes with a set of drawbacks. For example, because even a rewritten dynamic URL tends to be very long, they often wrap — or become two lines — in error messages or when used in blog posts or forums. The result is sometimes an incomplete URL that can't be followed.

URL rewriting also introduces the possibility for errors, especially if the rewriting is done manually in the coding for a web page.

A better option is to use *static URLs*. Static URLs remain the same all the time. You can see static URLs all over the Web. Even blog posts have a temporary dynamic URL, but then once the post goes into archives, the URL becomes static and doesn't change again. It helps to more effectively rank web pages that change temporarily and then become permanent.

Another advantage of static URLs is that, when used, these URLs can contain keywords that are meaningful not only to search crawlers, but also to the people who visit your web site. Static URLs are easier to read. They usually contain mostly words, with few numbers, and they never include randomly generated identifiers.

As you're putting your site together, consider how it's going to grow and how you'll be naming the pages that you add to it. Part of that consideration is entirely site design and will be determined by the programming language that you use to create your site; but much of it involves forethought about how such matters will be handled. Discuss with your web site designer how you would like to have the URL structure handled. The designer will know how to ensure that your URLs are as usable as the rest of your site.

Again, it's important to realize that domain naming is only one facet of SEO strategy. It won't make or break your SEO, but it can have some effect. Therefore, take the time to think about the name you plan to register for your site and then how you plan to structure your URLs as your site grows.

If you can use a name that not only reaches your audience, but also lands you a little higher in search results and makes it easier to create useful URL structures, then by all means purchase it; but if no name really seems to work in the SEO strategy for your site, don't get discouraged. You can make up for any domain-naming issues by implementing solid keyword strategies, tagging strategies, and other elements of SEO. Do try to keep your URL structure simple, though, even when your domain name might not be your first choice.

Understanding usability

Usability. It means different things to different web site designers. It's also been at the top of every user's requirements list since the Web became part of daily life. When users click through to your web site from a search results page, they want the site to work for them. That means they want to be able to find what they're looking for, to navigate from place to place, and to be able to load pages quickly, without any difficulties.

Web site users are impatient. They don't like to wait for pages to load, they don't want to deal with *Flash* graphics or *JavaScript,* and they don't want to be lost. These are all elements of usability — how the user navigates through and uses your web site. And yes, usability has an impact on SEO, especially from the perspective of your site links and loading times.

When a search engine crawler comes to your site, it crawls through the site looking at keywords, links, contextual clues, meta and HTML tags, and a whole host of other elements. The crawler moves from page to page, indexing what it finds for inclusion in search results; but if that crawler reaches the first page and can't get past the fancy Flash you've created, or if it gets into the site and finds links that don't work or that lead to unexpected locations, it will recognize this and make note of it in the indexed site data. That can damage your search engine rankings.

Navigation knowledge

When you consider web site navigation, there are two types: *internal navigation* and *external navigation*. Internal navigation involves the links that move users from one page to another on your site. External navigation refers to links that take users away from your page. In order for your navigation to be SEO-friendly, you have to use both types of navigation carefully.

Look at a number of different high-ranking web sites. How is the navigation of those sites designed? In most cases, you'll find that the top sites have a left-hand navigation bar that's often text based, and some have a button-based navigation bar across the top of the page. Few have only buttons down the left side, and all of them have text links somewhere in the landing page.

The reason why the navigation structure for many sites looks the same is because this plan works. Having a text-based navigation bar on the left works for SEO because it enables you to use anchor tags with the keywords you're using for the site. It also enables crawlers to move from one page to another with ease.

Buttons are harder for crawlers to navigate, and depending on the code in which those buttons are designed, they might be completely invisible to the crawler. That's why many companies that put button-based links at the top of the page also include a text-based navigation bar on the left. The crawler can still move from page to page, but the user is happy with the design of the site.

The other elements that appear on nearly every page are text-based links within the content of the page. Again, those links are usually created with anchor tags that include the keywords the site is using to build site ranking. This is an effective way to gain site ranking. The crawler comes into the site, examines the linking system, examines the content of the page, compares these items, and finds that the links are relevant to the content, which is relevant to the keywords. That's how your ranking is determined. Every element works together.

Take the time to design a navigational structure that's not only comfortable for your users, but also crawler-friendly. If it can't always be perfect for the crawlers, make sure it's perfect for users. Again, SEO is influenced by many different factors, but return visits from users are the ultimate goal. This may mean that you have to test your site structure and navigation with a user group and change it a few times before you find a method that works both for returning users and for the crawlers that help to bring you new users. Do those tests. That's the only way you'll learn what works.

Usability considerations

It's not always possible to please both your site users and the crawlers that determine your page ranking. It is possible, however, to work around problems. Of course, the needs of users come first because once you get them to your site you want them to come back. On the Internet, it's extremely easy for users to surf away from your site and never look back — and returning visits can make or break your site. The catch is that in order to build returning visitors, you have to build new visitors, which is the purpose of SEO. That means you need search engines to take notice of your site.

When it seems that users' preferences are contrary to crawlers' preferences, there is a solution: a *site map*. There are two types of which you should be aware. A basic site map is an overview of the navigational structure of your web site. It's usually text based, and it's nothing more than an overview that includes links to all the pages on your web site. Crawlers love site maps. You should, too.

A site map enables you to outline the navigational structure of your web site, down to the second or third level of depth, using text-based links that should include anchors and keywords. An example of a site map for the Work.com web site is shown in Figure 4-5.

When a site map exists on your web page, a search engine crawler can locate the map and then crawl all the pages that are linked from it. All those pages are then included in the search engine index and will appear on search engine results pages. Where they appear on those SERPs is determined by how well the SEO is done for each individual page.

A second type of site map, the *XML site map*, is different from what you think of as a site map in both form and function. An XML site map is a file that lists all the URLs for a web site. This file is usually not seen by site visitors, only by the crawlers that index your site. Chapter 18 offers more specifics on XML site maps.

A site map enables you to include links to all of your pages, two to three levels deep, that include keywords and anchor tags.

Components of an SEO-Friendly Page

Building an SEO-friendly web site doesn't happen by accident. It requires an understanding of what elements search engines examine and how those elements affect your ranking. It also requires including as many of those elements as possible on your site. It does little good to have all the right meta tags in place if you have no content and no links on your page.

It's easy to get caught up in the details of SEO and forget the simplest web-design principles — principles that play a large part in your search engine rankings. Having all the right keywords in the right places in your tags and titles won't do you much good if the content on your page is nonexistent or completely unreachable by a search engine crawler.

Understanding entry and exit pages

The entry and exit pages are the first and last pages of your web site that a user sees. It's important to understand that an entry page isn't necessarily the home page on your web site. It can be any other page where a user lands, either by clicking through search engine results, by clicking a link from another web site or a piece of marketing material, or by bookmarking or typing directly into the address bar of a browser.

Entry pages are important in SEO because they are the first page users see — the electronic equivalent of a first impression. The typical web site is actually several small, connected sites. Your company web site might contain hubs, or central points, for several different topics. For example, if your site represents a pet store, then you'll have hubs within it for dogs, cats, birds, fish, and maybe exotic animals. Each hub will have a main page — which will likely be your entry page for that section — and several additional pages leading from that central page to other pages containing relevant content, products, or information about specific topics.

Understanding which of your pages are likely entry pages helps you to optimize those pages for search engine crawlers. Using the pet-store example, if your home page and all the hub pages are properly Search Engine Optimized, you potentially could be ranked at or near the top of five different sets of search results. When you add additional entry pages deeper in your web site structure (that is, a dog-training section to the hub for dogs), you've increased the number of times you can potentially end up at the top of search engine rankings.

Because entry pages are important in the structure of your web site, you want to monitor those pages using a web site analytics program to ensure they are working the way you expect them to work. A good analytics program, such as Google Analytics, will show you your top entry and exit pages.

Exit pages are those from which users leave your site, either by clicking through an exiting link, selecting a bookmark, or typing a different web address into their browser address bar. Exit pages have two purposes. The first is to drive users from their entry pages to a desired exit page. This is called the *path* that users travel through your site. A typical path might look something like this:

> SERP ➤ Home ➤ Women's Clothing ➤ Product Pages ➤ Shopping Cart ➤
> Checkout ➤ Receipt

In this example, Home is the entry page and Receipt is the exit page. By looking at this navigational path, you can tell how users travel through your page and where they fall off the page; but there's an added benefit to understanding the navigational path of your users. When you know how users travel through your site, you can leave what's called a *bread-crumb trail* for them. That's a navigational indicator on the web site that enables them to quickly see where they are on your site, as shown in Figure 4-6. This is the navigation path shown on the Wal-Mart web site. You can quickly see where in the navigational structure of the site you're located.

The bread-crumb trail not only helps users return to a previous page in the navigational path; it also makes it easier for a web crawler to fully examine your site. Because crawlers follow every link on your page, this is an internal link structure that leads crawlers to individual pages that you want included in search engine results.

FIGURE 4-6

The navigational path can be shown on each web page in the path to help users quickly see where they are located on the site.

Navigation path

Choosing an Analytics Program

An important element in any SEO plan is analytics — the method by which you monitor the effectiveness of your web site. Analytics are the metrics that show you how pages, links, keywords, and other elements of your web site are performing. If your web host hasn't provided you with an analytics program, find one. Not having an analytics program is like walking around in the dark, hoping you won't bump into a wall.

Many web site owners shy away from analytics packages because they believe them to be complicated and expensive. However, they don't always have to be. You can find a good analytics program that's not only easy to use, but also inexpensive or even free; but use caution about making ease and low cost the deciding factors when selecting an analytics program.

The program will give you the power to see and control how your web site performs against your goals and expectations. You want it to show you everything you need to know, so here are some considerations when you're evaluating analytics programs:

continued

continued

■ What reports are included in the tools you're examining, and how will you use those reports?

■ How do you gather the information used to create the metrics you need?

■ How often are your reports updated?

■ How much training is necessary to understand your application and the reports provided?

■ Do you get software installation or is the product provided strictly as a web-based service?

■ What is the *total cost of ownership*?

■ What types of support are available?

■ What is the typical contract length?

Many analytics programs are available. Google Analytics, AW Stats, JayFlowers, ClickTracks, and dozens of others all offer something different at a different price tag. If *free* is what you can afford, don't assume you'll get a terrible package. Google Analytics is one of the free packages available, and it's an excellent program, based on what used to be the Urchin Analytics package (which was quite costly). Other programs cost anywhere from $30 to $300 a month, depending on the capabilities you're purchasing.

Cost is not the most important factor, however. Ultimately, your main consideration should be how the analytics package can help you improve your business.

Using powerful titles

Page titles are one of the most important elements of site optimization. When a crawler examines your site, the first elements it looks at are the page titles; and when your site is ranked in search results, page titles are again one of the top elements considered. Therefore, when you create your web site, you need great page titles.

Consider several key factors when coming up with your page titles:

■ Unless you're Microsoft, don't use your company name in the page title. A better choice is to use a descriptive keyword or phrase that tells users exactly what's on the page. This helps to ensure that your search engine rankings are accurate.

■ Try to limit page titles to less than 50 characters, including spaces. Some search engines index only up to 50 characters; others might index as many as 150. Regardless, maintaining shorter page titles forces you to be precise in the titles that you choose and ensures that your page title will never be cut off in the search results.

NOTE The World Wide Web Consortium (W3C) has determined that the outside length of a page title should be no more than 64 characters. Search engines vary in regard to the size of title that's indexed. Using 64 characters or less is an accepted practice that still leaves your page titles cut off in search engines that index only up to 40 or 50 characters. For this reason, staying at or below the 40-character length is a smarter strategy within your SEO efforts.

- Don't repeat keywords in your title tags. Repetition can occasionally come across as spam when a crawler is examining your site, so avoid that in your title if possible, and never duplicate words just to gain a crawler's attention. It could well get your site excluded from search engine listings.

- Consider adding special characters at the beginning and end of your title to improve noticeability. Parentheses (()), arrows (<<>>), asterisks (****), and special symbols such as ££££ can help draw a user's attention to your page title. These special characters and symbols don't usually add to or detract from your SEO efforts, but they do serve to call attention to your site title.

- Include a call to action in your title. There's an adage that goes something like, "You'll never sell a thing if you don't ask for the sale." That's true on the Web too. If you want your users to do something, you have to ask them.

All of your page titles should be indicated with the title tag when you code your web site. The title tag isn't difficult to use. Here's an example of such a tag:

```
<title>A Descriptive Web Site Title</title>
```

If your page titles aren't tagged properly, you may as well not be using them, so take the time to ensure that your page titles are short, descriptive, and tagged into your web site code. By using title tags, you increase the chances that your web site will be ranked high within search engine results.

Creating great content

Web site content is another element of an SEO-friendly site that you should spend plenty of time contemplating and completing. Fortunately, there are ways to create web site content that will make search crawlers love you.

Great content starts with the right keywords and phrases. Select no more than three keywords or phrases to include in the content on any one of your web pages. Why only three? Wouldn't more keywords and phrases ensure that search engines take notice of your site?

Actually, when you use too many keywords in your content, you face two problems. First, the effectiveness of your keywords will be reduced by the number of different ones you're using. Choose two or three for each page of your site and stick with those.

Second, you may be delisted or ignored because a search engine sees your SEO efforts as *keyword stuffing*. It's a serious problem, and search engine crawlers will exclude your site or pages from indexes if they contain too many keywords.

After you have the two or three keywords or phrases that you plan to focus on, you need to actually use those keywords in the page content. Many people assume that the more frequently you use the words, the higher your search engine ranking will be. Again, that's not necessarily true. Just as using too many different keywords can cause a crawler to exclude you from a search engine index, overusing the same word will also cause crawlers to consider that as keyword stuffing. Again, you run the risk of having your site excluded from search indexes.

The term used to describe the number of times a keyword is used on a page is *keyword density*. For most search engines, allowed keyword density is relatively low. Google is very strict about ranking sites that have a keyword density of 5 to 7 percent; much lower or much higher and your ranking is seriously affected or completely lost. Yahoo!, MSN, and other search engines allow keyword densities of about 5 percent. Going over that mark could cause your site to be excluded from search results.

Keyword density is an important factor in your web site design, and is covered in more depth in Chapter 5; but there are other content concerns, too. Did you know that the freshness and focus of your content also affects how high your web site ranks? One reason why many companies began using *blogs* on their web sites was because blogs are updated frequently and they're highly focused on a specific topic. This gives search engines new, relevant content to crawl.

Consider implementing a content strategy that includes regularly adding more focused content or expanding your content offerings. It doesn't have to be a blog, but news links on the front page of the site, regularly changing articles, or some other type of changing content will help gain the attention of a search engine crawler. Don't just set these elements up and leave them, however. You also have to ensure regular updates and keep the links included in the content active. Broken links are another crawler pet peeve. Unfortunately, with *dynamic content,* links will occasionally break. Make sure you're checking this element of your content on a regular basis and set up some kind of user-feedback loop so broken links can be reported to your *webmaster*.

Finally, when you're creating your web site content, consider interactive forums. If you're adding articles to your site, give users a forum in which they can respond to the article, or a comments section. This leads to more frequent updates of your content, which search crawlers love. In short, forums provide users with an ongoing, interactive relationship with your web site, and give an extra boost to your search engine ranking.

Maximizing graphics

Images or graphics on your web site are essential. They're also basically ignored by search engines, so what's the point of putting them on your site? There's a good reason that has nothing to do with SEO. Without images, your page is just boring text. You're not going to be happy with using plain text instead of that cool, new logo you had designed for your company, and neither are your users. They want to see pictures.

If images are a must on a web site, then there should be a way to use those images to increase your web site traffic or to at least improve your site ranking. And there is.

One technique that will help your SEO make use of graphics on your site is to tag those graphics with *alt tags* inside the *img tags*. The alt tags are the HTML tags used to display alternative text when a graphic is present. An alt tag should be a short, descriptive phrase about the image, which includes the keywords used on that page when possible.

The img tags are the tags used to code the images that appear on your web site. Here's an example of what an img tag, with an included alt tag, should look like:

```
<img src="pic1.jpg" alt="alternative text"/>
```

Here's how that tag breaks down: `<img src="pic1.jpg"` is your image tag; `alt="alternative text"/>` is your alternative text tag. The alternative text tag is where your keywords should be included if at all possible.

You want to tag your images as part of your SEO strategy for two reasons. First, crawlers cannot index images for a search engine (with an exception, which is covered shortly). The crawler "sees" the image and moves on to the text on the page. Therefore, something needs to take the place of that image, so the crawler can index it. That's what the alternative text does. If this text includes your keywords, and the image is near text that also includes the keywords, then you add credibility to your site in the logic of the crawler.

The second reason you want to tag your images as part of your SEO strategy is to take advantage of image-based search engines, such as Google Images. These image-based search engines are relatively new, but they shouldn't be undervalued. Just as a search engine can find and index your site for users searching the Web, image-based search engines find and index your images. Then, when users perform a search for a specific keyword or phrase, your image is also ranked, along with the text on the pages.

Image searches are gaining popularity, so crawlers like the one Google uses for its Google Images search engine will gain momentum, and image searches will add to the amount of web site traffic that your SEO strategies help to build. Conversely, while not discounting the value of images, don't overuse them on your web pages either. As with any element of a web page, too much of a good thing is not good.

Problem Pages and Work-Arounds

No matter how much time and consideration you put into your SEO strategy, some elements of your web site will require special consideration. Certain sites — such as portals — need a different approach than a standard web site might require. How you deal with these issues will have an impact on the effectiveness of your SEO efforts.

Painful portals

The use of portals — web sites that are designed to funnel users to other web sites and content — as a search engine placement tool is a hotly debated topic. Many experts will start throwing around the word "spam" when the subject of SEO and portals comes up; and there have been serious problems with portals that are nothing more than search engine spam. In the past, portals have certainly been used as an easy link-building tool offering nothing more than regurgitated information. Sometimes the information is vaguely reworded, but it's the still the same information.

Search engine operators have long been aware of this tactic and have made every effort to hinder its usefulness by looking for duplicate content, interlinking strategies, and other similar indicators. Using these techniques, search engines have managed to reduce the usefulness of portal web sites as SEO spam mechanisms.

However, because search engine operators need to be cautious about portals that are nothing more than SEO spam, if your site is a portal, then optimizing it will be a little harder. As with all web site design, the best objective for your site, even for a portal, is to help your visitors achieve a desired result, whether that's purchasing a product, signing up for a newsletter, or finding desired information. If you make using your site easy and relevant, your site visitors will stay on your site longer, view more pages, and return to your site in the future. Portals help you reach these goals by acting as excellent tools for consolidating information into smaller, more manageable sources of information that users find easier to use and digest.

Too often, people optimizing web sites focus on the spiders and forget about the visitors. The sites you are developing have to appeal to the visitors and provide them with the information they're looking for, or all you will have at the end of the day are hosting bills and low conversion rates. Portal web sites enable you to create a series of information resources that provide full information on any given topic, while structuring a network of information covering a much larger scope.

Though the visitor is of significant importance when building a web site, the site itself is of primary significance, too. There's no point in creating a beautiful web site if no one's going to see it, and portals are a fantastic tool for increasing your online visibility and search engine exposure, for a wide variety of reasons.

Perhaps the most significant of these reasons is the increase in keywords that you can use in portal promotion. Rather than have one web site with which to target a broad range of keywords, portals enable you to have many web sites, each of which can have its own set of keywords. For example, instead of trying to put "deer hunting" and "saltwater fishing" on the same page, you can create a hunting portal that enables you to have separate sites for deer hunting, saltwater fishing, and any other type of hunting activity you'd like to include.

On one page it's much easier to target the two key phrases "deer season" and "Mississippi hunting license" than it is to target two key phrases like "deer season" and "marlin fishing." Targeting incompatible keywords or phrases — that is, keywords or phrases that aren't related to a larger topic — makes it harder to have both readable, relevant content and reach the keywords that you need to use.

There are other advantages to creating web portals as well. Having a portal enables you to have multiple home pages, which gives you the opportunity to create sites that consistently appear in a top ranking. You also have more sites to include in your other SEO strategies and more places to include keywords. However, there is a fine line between a useful portal and one that causes search engines to turn away without listing your portal on SERPs.

WARNING Don't link all your sites to all the others within your portal using some link-farm footer at the bottom of every page. You may not even want to link all of them to the others on a site map or links page. Instead, interlink them in an intelligent way. When you want to lead visitors to another site in the portal, or when you want those users to be able to choose which site is most useful to them, you can create intelligent links that have value for the site user. This value translates into better rankings for your web site.

As with most issues in web design, keep it user-friendly and attractive. If you have any concerns that the actions you're taking with your site or the design methods that you're using could lead to negative results for the SEO of your site, don't use them. If you have a feeling that a strategy won't work, it probably won't, and you're wasting your time if you use a design you're not comfortable with.

Fussy frames

Some web site designs require the use of *frames*. Frames are sections of a web site, with each section constituting an entity separate from the other portions of the page. Because the frames on a site represent separate URLs, they often create display issues for users whose browsers don't support frames, and for search crawlers that encounter the frames and can't index sites where the frame is the navigational structure.

You have a couple of options when frames are essential to the design of your web site. The first is to include an alternative to the framed site. This requires the use of the noframes tag. This tag directs the user's browser to display the site without the framed navigational system. Users may see a stripped-down version of your site, but at least they can still see it. When a search crawler encounters a site made with frames, the noframes tag enables it to index the alternative site. It's important to realize, however, that when you use the noframes tag, you need to load the code for an entire web page between the *opening tag* and *closing tag*.

WARNING When you're creating a noframes tag for a framed site, the content of the noframes tags should be exactly identical to the frame set. If it's not, a search crawler could consider it spam, and then your site would be penalized or even delisted.

Another issue with frames is that search engines often display an internal page on your site in response to a search query, but if this internal page does not contain a link to your home page or some form of navigation menu, users are stuck on that page and cannot navigate through your site. That means the search crawler is also stuck in that same spot. As a result, the crawler might not index your site.

The solution, of course, is to place on the page a link that leads to your home page. In this link, include the attribute TARGET = "_top". This prevents your site from becoming nested within your own frames, which locks users on the page they landed on from the search results. It also makes it possible for crawlers to efficiently crawl your site without getting stuck.

That link back to your home page will probably look something like this:

```
<a href="index.html" TARGET = "_top">Return to Home Page</a>
```

Frames are difficult, but not impossible, to get around when you're putting SEO strategies into place. It's a good idea to avoid them, but they won't keep you completely out of search engine rankings. You just have to use a different approach to reach those high rankings you desire.

Cranky cookies

Cookies are one of those irritating facts of life on the Internet. Users want web sites tailored to them, and cookies are one way companies have found to do that. When users enter a site and customize some feature of it, a small piece of code — the cookie — is placed on the user's hard drive. Then, when the user returns to the site in the future, that cookie can be accessed and the user's preferences executed.

When cookies work properly, they're an excellent tool for web designers. When they don't work as they should, problems arise. The main issue with cookies is that some browsers allow users to set how cookies will be delivered to them; and some *source code* prompts the user to be asked before a cookie is accepted. When this happens, the search engine crawler is effectively stopped in its tracks, and it doesn't pick back up where it stopped once the cookies are delivered. In addition, any navigation that requires cookies prevents a crawler from indexing the pages.

To overcome this issue, you must code cookies to ensure that the source code is not designed to query the user before the cookie is delivered.

Programming Languages and SEO

One aspect of web site design you might not think of when planning your SEO strategy is the programming language used to develop the site. Programming languages all behave a little differently. For example, HTML and PHP use completely different protocols to accomplish the visuals you see when you open a web page. (When most people think of web site programming, they think in terms of HTML.) In reality, many other languages are also used for coding web pages — and those languages may require differing SEO strategies.

JavaScript

JavaScript is a programming language that enables web designers to create dynamic content. However, it's not necessarily SEO-friendly. In fact, JavaScript often completely halts a crawler from indexing a web site, and when that happens the result is lower search engine rankings or complete exclusion from ranking.

To overcome this, many web designers *externalize* any JavaScript that's included on the web site. Externalizing the JavaScript means that it is actually run from an external location, such as a file on your web server. To externalize your JavaScript:

1. Copy the code, beginning at the starting tags, and paste it into a Notepad file.

2. Save the Notepad file as `filename.js`.

3. Upload the file to your web server.

4. Create a reference on your web page to the external JavaScript code. The reference should be placed where the JavaScript will appear, and might look like this: `<script language="JavaScript" type="text/javascript" src="filename.js"></script>`

This is just one of the solutions you can use to prevent JavaScript from becoming a problem for your SEO efforts. There are many others, and depending on your needs you should explore some of them.

> **NOTE** Sometimes people use JavaScript as a means to hide content or links from a search engine. However, search crawlers can read JavaScript, and most can even follow the links that are in JavaScript, so if you try to hide content or links behind JavaScript, you run the risk of having your site labeled as search engine spam. There's more information about search engine spam in Chapter 17.

Flash

Flash is another of those technologies that some users absolutely hate. That's because Flash, though very cool, is resource intensive. It causes pages to load slower, and users are often stuck on an opening Flash page and can't move forward until the Flash has finished executing. When you're in a hurry, which is almost always, it's a frustrating situation to deal with.

Flash is also a nightmare when it comes to SEO. A Flash page can stop a web crawler in its tracks, and once it is stopped, the crawler won't resume indexing the site. Instead, it will simply move on to the next web site on its list.

The easiest way to avoid Flash problems is to simply not use it. If, despite Flash's difficulties with search rankings, your organization needs to use it, then you can code the Flash in HTML and an option can be added to test for the ability to see Flash before it is executed. Note, however, that there's some debate about whether or not this is an acceptable SEO practice, so before you implement this type of strategy in an effort to improve your SEO effectiveness, take the time to research the method.

Dynamic ASP

Most of the sites you'll encounter on the Web are *static web pages*. These sites don't change beyond any regular updates by a webmaster. Conversely, *dynamic web pages* are web pages that are created on the fly according to preferences that users specify in a form or menu. These sites can be created using a variety of different programming technologies, including *dynamic ASP*. The problem with these sites is that they don't technically exist until the user creates them. Because a web crawler can't make the selections that build these pages, most dynamic web pages aren't indexed in search engines.

There are ways around this, however. Dynamic URLs can be converted to static URLs with the right coding. It's also possible to use *paid inclusion services* to index dynamic pages down to a predefined number of levels (or number of selections, if you're considering the site from the user's perspective).

Dynamic ASP, like many of the other languages used to create web sites, carries with it a unique set of characteristics. But that doesn't mean SEO is impossible for those pages. It does mean that the approach used for the SEO of static pages needs to be modified. It's an easy enough task, and a quick search of the Internet will almost always provide the programming code you need to achieve SEO.

PHP

Search engine crawlers being what they are — preprogrammed applications — there's a limit to what they can index. PHP is another programming language that falls outside the boundaries of normal web site coding. Search engine crawlers see PHP as another obstacle if it is not properly executed.

Properly executed means that PHP needs to be used with search engines in mind. For example, PHP naturally stops or slows search engine crawlers, but with some attention and a solid understanding of PHP and SEO, it's possible to code pages that work.

One thing that works well with PHP is designing the code to look like HTML. It requires an experienced *code jockey*, but it can be done. And once the code has been disguised, the PHP site can be crawled and indexed so that it is returned in search results.

Other Design Concerns

You're likely to encounter numerous problems with SEO when designing your web site. Some are easy to overcome, others can be quite difficult. And still others aren't problems you have to overcome per se, but issues you need to be aware of or you risk being ignored by search engine crawlers.

Among the tactics that might seem okay to some, but actually aren't, are the so-called *black-hat* SEO techniques. These are practices that are implemented with a single goal in mind: increasing search engine rankings, no matter how inappropriate they might be. Some companies deliberately use such techniques when creating web sites, even if the results that are returned have absolutely nothing to do with the search terms users entered.

Domain cloaking

On the surface, *domain cloaking* sounds like a great idea. The concept is to show users a pretty web site that meets their needs, while at the same time showing search engines a highly optimized page that probably would be almost useless to users. In other words, it's a slimy trick to gain search engine ranking while providing users with a nice site to look at.

It starts with *content cloaking*, which is accomplished by creating web site code that can detect and differentiate a crawler from a site user. When the crawler enters the site, it is redirected to another web site that has been optimized for high search engine results. The problem with trying to gain higher search results this way is that many search engines can now spot it. As soon as they find that a web page uses such a cloaking method, the page is delisted from the search index and not included in the results.

Many unscrupulous SEO administrators will use this tactic on throw-away sites. They know the site won't be around for long anyway (usually because of some illegal activity), so they use domain cloaking to garner as much web site traffic as possible before the site is taken down or delisted.

Duplicating content

When you're putting together a web site, the content for that site often presents one of the greatest challenges, especially if it is a site that includes hundreds of pages. Many people opt to purchase bits of content, or even *scrape* content from other web sites to help populate their own. These shortcuts can cause real issues with search engines.

Suppose your web site is about some form of marketing. It's very easy to surf around the Web and find hundreds (or even thousands) of web sites from which you can pull free, permission-granted content to include on your web site. The problem is that every other person or company creating a web site could be doing the same thing. The result? A single article on a topic appears on hundreds of web sites — and users don't find anything new when they search for that topic and every site has the same article.

To help combat this type of content generation, some search engines now include as part of their search algorithm a method to measure the *freshness* of site content. If a crawler examines your site and finds that much of your content is also on hundreds of other web sites, you run the risk of either ranking low or being delisted from the search engine's indexing database.

Some search engines now look for four types of duplicate content:

- **Highly distributed articles:** These are the free articles that seem to appear on every single web site about a given topic. This content has usually been provided by a marketing-savvy entrepreneur as a way to gain attention for his or her project or passion. But no matter how valuable the information, if it appears on hundreds of sites, it will be deemed duplicate and reduce your chances of being listed high in the search result rankings.

- **Product descriptions for e-commerce stores:** The product descriptions included on nearly all web pages are not included in search engine results. Product descriptions can be very small, and depending on how many products you're offering, there could be thousands of them. Crawlers are designed to skip over most product descriptions. Otherwise, a crawler might never be able to work completely through your site.

■ **Duplicate web pages:** It's pointless for a user to click through a search result only to find that your web pages have been shared with everyone else. These duplicate pages gum up the works and reduce the level at which your pages end up in the search results.

■ **Content that has been scraped from numerous other sites:** *Content scraping* is the practice of pulling content from other web sites and repackaging it so that it looks like your own content. Although scraped content may look different from the original, it is still duplicate content, and many search engines will leave you completely out of the search index, and hence the search results.

Hidden pages

One last SEO issue concerns the damage to your SEO strategy that *hidden pages* can inflict. These are pages in your web site that are visible only to a search crawler. Hidden pages can also lead to issues such as hidden keywords and hidden links. Because keywords and links help to boost your search rankings, many people try to capitalize on this by hiding them within the body of a web page, sometimes in a font color that perfectly matches the site background.

There's no way to beat the detection of hidden pages. If you have a web site and it contains hidden pages, it's just a matter of time before the crawler figures out that the content is part of a hidden SEO strategy; and once that's determined by the crawler, your site ranking will drop drastically.

404 error pages

One problem that visitors may encounter is broken links that don't lead to their intended target. Instead, these links take the user to a worthless page that usually contains a message such as *"error 404."* Not very descriptive, is it? When users encounter an error that they don't understand, it simply adds to the frustration of being blocked from going where you want to go.

Error pages happen: links break, pages become outdated, and — especially if you're linking to a search engine results page — people type incorrect URLs into their browsers all the time. It's what you do about these issues that will determine whether your user heads off to another site or surfs back to your site in an effort to locate what they were looking for.

No one wants their site visitors to encounter an error page, but sometimes you can't help it. For those times when it does happen, you want the page to be as useful as possible to your visitors. Adding elements that tell the visitor more about what happened and what their options are is the best way to accomplish that. That "error 404 page unavailable" message doesn't give them anything to work from.

Instead, you can use your error page to provide a list of links that are similar to what the user was trying to reach in the first place. Or you can offer a search box that enables users to search for information similar to what was on the page that they couldn't reach. The worst thing you can do is nothing.

Give your visitors options that are designed to keep them on your web site. And one more thing: Don't overwhelm them. An error page should look like an error page, even if it's more useful than the simple "this page doesn't exist" error; but it should also be simple. However, don't make your error pages look like the rest of the site. You might assume that providing users with your site's usual look and feel and navigational structure is the best way to ensure that they don't leave, but that's not the case. When you don't distinguish an error page from the rest of your site, two things can happen.

First, users get confused. The error page looks like the rest of your site, so it's not immediately recognized as an error. Second, the navigational or link structure that you include on the page might not work properly, which translates to even more frustration for the visitor.

When designing error pages, your best option is to keep it simple and make it useful. Do that and you will likely ensure that your visitors stay on your site. At the same time, you're providing useful information that can be loaded with keywords and other SEO elements. The result is the best of both worlds: managing search engines while impressing your visitors with the usefulness of your site.

Validating Your HTML

HTML code is a pretty straightforward programming language. However, like any language, a document written in HTML can contain a lot of meaningless garbage that doesn't seem to interfere with the message but leaves the document less than pristine. In fact, if your web site designer leaves a snippet of trash in your HTML code because it didn't overtly affect the site and the designer didn't want to take time cleaning it up, it could spell disaster for your SEO.

With HTML there's a lot behind the scenes that site visitors don't see. There are the tags and elements that must be there for users, of course, and then there are the tags and elements that aren't ever visible, so whether they are there or not doesn't seem to matter — but of course it does.

When you recognize that a search engine crawler looks at text, and that HTML is a type of text, then your HTML begins to take on new meaning. If your site contains something that shouldn't be there, visitors may not see it but search crawlers will, and it could affect the quality score of your site.

Because HTML can be manipulated on the back end, a set of guidelines and best practices has been developed by the World Wide Web Consortium (W3C). These guidelines and best practices were created to help web designers use HTML in the most efficient and effective manner. Unfortunately, the designers don't always pay attention, and sometimes the HTML of a site can be littered with unneeded elements that affect your search engine rankings.

The best thing to do is validate your HTML, or check to ensure that it complies with W3C standards. You could do that manually, by going through every single line of code in your web site, but that would take a very long time when you consider that some web sites contain millions of lines of code.

Instead, you can use a tool such as the free HTML Validator (`http://validator.w3.org/`) that the W3C makes available to examine (or validate) your HTML to ensure that it adheres to the W3C guidelines. To use this tool, just enter the URL of your web site, and the validator will run a diagnostic on the site and return the results to you. You can then use that information to ensure that your site is free of the clutter that turns crawlers off.

After Your Site Is Built

Building the right site to help maximize your SEO efforts is a difficult task; and when you're finished, the work doesn't end. As mentioned earlier, SEO is an ongoing strategy, not a technology that you can implement and forget. You need to spend time reviewing your practices, examining results, and making adjustments where necessary. If this ongoing maintenance is ignored, then your SEO efforts up to this point will quickly become time that would have been better spent standing on the street with a sign around your neck advertising your web site. That might be more effective than outdated SEO.

Beware of content thieves

Maintenance of your SEO strategies is also essential to helping you find problems that might be completely unrelated to SEO. For example, SEO strategies can help you locate content thieves. One such strategy is tagging your web site. Some people (including black-hat SEOs) take snippets of content from your site to use on their own. If you tag your content cleverly, you can use some very distinctive tags, which will help you quickly locate content that has been stolen.

Another way in which SEO helps you to locate stolen content is through tracking. Presumably, if you're executing SEO strategies, then you're also monitoring your site metrics with a program such as Google Analytics. Watching the metrics used by one of those analytics programs can help you locate content thieves. For example, if you look at your incoming links on one of these programs, you might find that people are coming to your site from a completely unexpected location. If that's the case, you can follow the link back to that site to find out why. A site using stolen content is easy to find using this method. Many services are available that will help you track your web site content. Those services are covered in more depth in Chapter 12.

Tagging works well for finding content thieves, and you can also use domain cloaking to thwart automatic content scrapers. Recall that this is a process by which your web site appears to be located somewhere other than where it actually is. This is accomplished using an HTML frameset that redirects traffic from one URL to another. For example, if your web site address is `www.you.somewhere.com`, you can use domain cloaking to have your site appear to be `www.yourbusiness.com`.

As you learned earlier in this chapter, a problem with using domain cloaking is that it can confuse a search engine crawler, because the same content appears to be on two pages, although it's only one page that redirects. Another problem is that some search engine crawlers can't read the frameset that's used to redirect the user, which means your site may end up not being ranked at all. Domain cloaking is a tactic that should be used only in special cases — namely, where content is truly unique and could possibly affect your SEO rankings (or that of someone who might steal it) in a dramatic way.

Dealing with updates and site changes

One last problem you may encounter after you've initially set up your SEO strategies is the updates and changes that your site will undergo. Web site owners often think that once the SEO is in place, it's always in place and they don't have to think about it again. That attitude can lead to a very unpleasant surprise.

When your site changes, especially when there are content updates or changes to the site structure, links can be broken, tags may be changed, and any number of other small details may be overlooked. When this happens, the result can be a reduced ranking for your site. Site crawlers look at everything, from your tags to your links, and based on what they see, your ranking could fluctuate from day to day. If what the crawler sees indicates that your site has changed in a negative way, the site's ranking will be negatively affected.

As you know, many factors affect the way your site is ranked in a search engine. You've seen an overview of a lot of them in this chapter, and you'll see them all again in more depth in future chapters. Realize that SEO is not a simple undertaking. It is a complex, time-consuming strategy for improving your business. Without attention to all of the details, you could be wasting your time. Plan to invest the time needed to ensure that your search engine optimization efforts aren't wasted.

Chapter 5

Keywords and Your Web Site

Keywords. That's a term you hear associated with search engine optimization all the time. In fact, it's very rare that you hear anything about SEO in which keywords aren't involved some way; so what's so special about keywords?

Simply put, keywords are those words used to catalog, index, and find your web site; but of course, it's not nearly as simple as it sounds. There is a fine science to finding and using the right keywords on your web site to improve your site's ranking. In fact, an entire industry has been built around keywords and their usage. Consultants spend countless hours finding and applying the right keywords for their customers, and those who design web sites with SEO in mind also agonize over choosing just the right ones.

Using popular — and effective — keywords on your web site will help to ensure that it is visible in the search engine results, rather than be buried under thousands of other web site results. There are keyword research tools that can help you find the exact keywords to use for your site and therefore for your search engine optimization. Understanding the use of keywords — where to find them, which ones to use, and the best ways to use them — enables you to have a highly visible and successful web site.

The Importance of Keywords

On the most basic level, keywords capture the essence of your web site. Keywords are the words or phrases a potential visitor to your site enters into a search engine to find web sites related to a specific subject, and the keywords that you choose will be used throughout your optimization process. As a small-business owner, you will want your web site to be readily visible when those search engine results come back. Using the correct keywords in your web site content can mean the difference between being listed as one of the first 20 sites returned from search engine results (which is optimum) or being buried under other web sites several pages into the results (which means hundreds of results are returned *before* your site). Studies show that searchers rarely venture past the second page of search results when looking for something online.

Consider for a moment the telephone book's Yellow Pages. Suppose you're looking for a restaurant. The first thing you're going to do is find the heading *restaurant*, which would be your keyword. Unfortunately, that's pretty broad, and even in a smaller city, there might be a page or more of restaurants to look through. If you're in a large city, there might be hundreds of pages.

If you are so inclined, you can narrow your search to Chinese restaurants, which will greatly reduce the number of entries that you have to search through. Basically, that's how keywords work in search engines and search engine optimization. It's also a good example of how people search: They begin with the broadest concept and then gradually narrow their search criteria, based on what they learn in each step of the process.

Recall from the discussion of Long Tail search in Chapter 2 that what leads visitors to your site can be either the broad search term or the more narrow (and very specific) term. Based on that concept, choosing the appropriate keywords for your web site will improve your search engine rankings and lead more search engine users to your site.

How do you know which keywords to use? Where do you find them? How do you use them? Knowing the answers to these questions will save you a great deal of time when creating a web site. Where you rank in search engine results is determined by what keywords are used and how they are positioned on your web site. It's critical to choose appropriate keywords, include variations of those keywords, avoid common (or *stop*) words, and know where and how many times to place them throughout your web site.

Used correctly, keywords should enable you to be placed in the first page or two of the most popular search engines, and in some cases even as the number one result. This tremendously increases the traffic to your web site. Keep in mind that the majority of Internet users find new web sites by using a search engine. High search engine rankings can be as effective as, if not more effective than, paid ads in marketing your business.

The business you receive from search engine rankings will also be more targeted to your services than it would be with a blanket ad. By using the right combination of keywords, your customer base will consist of people who set out to find exactly what your site has to offer, and those customers will be more likely to visit you repeatedly in the future.

To decide which keywords should be used on your web site, you can start by asking yourself the most simple, but relevant, question: "Who needs the services that I offer?" It's an elementary question, but one that will be most important in searching for the correct keywords and having the best search engine optimization.

For example, if you were marketing specialty soaps, you would want to use words such as soap (which really is too broad a term), specialty soap, bath products, luxury bath products, or other such words that come to mind when you think of your product. It's also important to remember to use words that real people use when talking about your products. For example, using the term "cleaning supplies" as a keyword wouldn't result in a good ranking because people thinking of personal cleanliness don't search for "cleaning supplies." They search for "soap" or something even more specific, like "chamomile soap." Your customers are usually your best source of information about the search terms they use to find your products or web site.

One way to figure out what terms people use is to ask them. Most customers don't mind answering a brief questionnaire, especially when some incentive is involved. Many companies have luck eliciting feedback by offering entry into a drawing for a prize or even a discount coupon to people who participate in surveys. Some people will offer opinions just because you ask. If you have a blog or forum on your web site, that's a good place to pose a question about the terms people use when they think of your site or products.

In addition to the terms that you think of and that your customers tell you they use, people also look for web sites using variations of words and phrases — including misspellings. An example might be "chamomile." Some people may incorrectly spell it "chammomile" or "camomile," so including those spellings in your keywords can increase your chance of reaching those searchers. In addition, remember to use capitalized and plural keywords. The more specific the words and the greater the number of variations, the better the chances that your web site is targeted. Be careful to avoid words such as "a," "an," "the," "and," "or," and "but." These are called *stop words*, and they're so common they are of no use as keywords.

NOTE Just to illustrate how important misspellings actually are, here's a little-known fact: Google is actually a misspelling of the word that Google founder Larry Page intended to use. He meant to use the word "googol," which is a mathematical term that refers to a 1 followed by 100 zeros, but he spelled the term wrong and now we have Google, a name that is so popular and widely known that the dictionary now includes it as a verb (as in "to google" something).

Understanding Heuristics

In order to maintain a web site with the best search engine optimization possible, you have to be familiar with *heuristics*. This is simply a term for recognizing a pattern and being able to solve a problem or come to a conclusion quickly and efficiently by consulting what you already know about that particular pattern. In other words, using heuristics is a way to solve a problem, although it's not always the most accurate way.

Patterns, proximity, and stemming

Heuristics are important in search engine optimization because they allow for variations in the way that users search for a particular keyword or phrase. Because a combination of factors must come together to create a ranking for your web site, heuristics make it possible for some, but not all, of those factors to be present.

> **TIP** **The Greeks had a word for it.** The root of the adjective "heuristic" comes from their term for "invent" or "discover." *Heuristics* has come to mean a way of education or computer programming that proceeds by experiment or observation, rather than theory, and sometimes employs *rules of thumb* to find solutions or answers. We all act "heuristically" every day.

For example: Let's say you run a travel-planning web site. If a web user is searching for "spring-time vacations," a search engine crawler will visit many sites, with varying keywords, keyword placement, and keyword density. In effect, it will give each a score, calculated on a baseline for relevance. It may find one site with the phrase, "some writers get their best ideas in springtime or while on vacation." But it won't score that site high, because it doesn't meet baseline criteria very well. The keywords are separated and the context is wrong. In addition, links from that site are unlikely to support the idea of planning a springtime vacation. The search engine likes your travel-planning web site better, because it has a lot to say about "springtime vacations."

The crawler doesn't stop with your site, however, and it doesn't look just at the words in your links, although it helps if those say "springtime" and "vacation," not something vague like "trips." The crawler will actually go to your links to see if they're truly helpful for the user who wants something about "springtime vacations." If your links are irrelevant to that, the crawler may decide you're running a link farm, designed to catch its attention without really delivering. Conversely, if a high percentage of your links are actually related to springtime vacationing — travel information, garden shows, trips to tulip festivals — then the crawler may score you high and put your site high on the list it compiles for the user. That user, after all, is the crawler's customer — and you hope also yours.

The crawler has operated *heuristically*, making its best judgments at each stage of the process by examining the patterns and proximity of words used on a web page.

Keywords apply to heuristics because they provide the pattern by which a problem (that is, the search) is solved. Why do you need to know all of this? Because understanding the pattern by which your site is ranked will help you understand just how important it is to properly choose and place keywords that will improve your search engine ranking.

Think of it (as in the preceding Tip) as a rule of thumb. Heuristics provides a working guideline by which a search term is ranked. Certain words or phrases used in certain patterns can be indicative of a specific topic.

To take the concept of patterns and proximity one step further, there is another element in the way words can be used together called *stemming*. Essentially, stemming is the growth of one related word from another, using prefixes and suffixes.

In other words, all the forms of a root word can be considered stemmed words. For example, if you've chosen "book flight" for your travel web site, then the stemmed keywords for that phrase might be as follows:

- Booking flights
- Books flights
- Pre-book flights
- Re-book flights
- Re-booking flights
- Pre-booking flights
- Re-booked flights

Suddenly, one word becomes many, which means you have many more opportunities to use that base word.

A lot of discussion about SEO has gone into the debate about how effective it is to use stemming in your web site content. The general consensus seems to be that stemming is a good method for boosting the number of times you can use a keyword on any given page.

Here's the rub: You still should be cautious of overusing any keyword or set of keywords. Some search engines have started to recognize only the root word of a keyword. For example, if you use the terms "pre-book flights," "book flights," and "re-book flights" in the same article on a page, the search crawler might recognize all forms of "book" as the same word. In other words, it's possible the crawler could view your combined use of these terms as more than is considered ethical by the standards of keyword density. So what's a person to do?

Use the words but be mindful of the 7 to 10 percent keyword density already discussed. The idea of stemming becomes very useful when you find you're having trouble using your desired keyword or phrase often enough on a web page without making the tone of the page completely foreign. If you're using several forms of a word, however, you can do that to meet your goals for keyword use and still create content that flows naturally.

It all goes back to creating pages for your user. Don't use a keyword on your page just because a search engine might like it. Landing in a search engine's favor should only be a goal as long as it leads you toward creating a useful and informative site for visitors. If those visitors find your content hard to read because you're showing the maximum allowable number of keywords even though they don't make any sense on your web page, you'll turn your visitors away, and then what's the point of your efforts?

Remember too that rankings are achieved through a complex combination of factors, not all of which are completely predictable. These guidelines are just that — but they can help you set a standard for how you plan to use keywords.

Heuristics and site usability

Heuristics applies to more than just the keywords that you use on your site. Heuristics also applies to web site usability, and a set of heuristic guidelines for site usability was first established by Jakob Nielsen in 1990. At the time, he developed a list of 10 items that when included in web site design would make a site more usable for individuals. In 1994, Nielsen updated that list of heuristics so that it now includes the following items:

- **Visibility of system status:** This principle says that the user should always know what's going on through feedback from the system that's provided in a timely manner.

- **Match between the system and the real world:** According to this, the system should speak the user's language. This means that keywords, phrases, and concepts should be used in a natural language that is familiar to the user and not be just technical or marketing buzzwords.

- **User control and freedom:** This principle says that users often mistakenly make choices they don't really want. For that reason, it's essential to offer the capability to undo or redo an action. A good example of this is having back and forward buttons in a web browser.

- **Consistency and standards:** Each time users click a button or see a word, they should not have to wonder what that action or word means. Consistency and standards apply to both languages and actions, and should be predictable across the Internet.

- **Error prevention:** Users are frustrated by errors, so you should design your site with the prevention of errors in mind. However, if you recognize a place where users *might* encounter an error, then using a confirmation system is recommended.

- **Recognition rather than recall:** Don't make users remember things from one screen or dialog to another. Instead, create your pages with clearly visible instructions, actions, and objects. If you must create an element that requires additional instructions, make those instructions easy to access, and clearly mark them as instructions.

- **Flexibility and efficiency of use:** This principle applies to both novice users and experienced users of your site. According to this rule, your site should apply to both groups of users by providing customizable actions.

- **Aesthetic and minimalist design:** Remember the adage KISS (keep it simple, stupid)? Well, your users may not be stupid, but they still want you to keep your site as simple as possible. If your products, services, or information are complicated to locate, you'll lose site visitors very quickly. They'll go to a site where it's easy to find what they're looking for.

- **Help users recognize, diagnose, and recover from errors:** Users want error messages that help them navigate through and correct an error as quickly as possible. Make sure that error messages aren't cryptic, and provide clear, easy-to-follow instructions.

- **Help and documentation:** It's always best *not* to have to refer users to help and documentation files, but sometimes it can't be avoided. If that's the case for your site, be sure your help and documentation files are easy to navigate and written in a clear, understandable language.

Of course, most of these heuristics apply more specifically to web site design and less specifically to keywords and SEO. Still, because SEO really should be part of overall site usability, these are important principles to keep in mind when you're designing your web site and implementing your keyword strategies. As mentioned previously, don't design your web site for SEO; build it for users, with SEO as an added strategy for gaining exposure. Always keep the user in mind because if users won't come to your site, or won't stay on your site once they're there, there's no point to all the SEO efforts you're making.

The Ever-Elusive Algorithm

One element of search marketing that has many people scratching their head in confusion is the algorithms that actually determine what the rank of a page should be. These algorithms are proprietary in nature, so few people outside the search engine companies have seen them in their entirety. In fact, there is some debate about whether any single person in a search engine company completely understands the entire algorithm used by the search engine. They're just that complicated.

Even if you were to see the algorithm, you'd have to be a math genius to understand it. That's what makes figuring out the whole concept of optimizing for search engines so difficult. Search engines are very complicated programs, even to the most brilliant mathematical minds.

To put it as plainly as possible, the algorithm that a search engine uses establishes a baseline to which all web pages are compared. The baseline varies from search engine to search engine. For example, more than 200 factors are used to establish a baseline in the Google algorithm; and though some people have figured out some of the primary parts of the algorithm, there's just no way to know all of the parts, especially when you consider that Google makes about half-a-dozen changes to that algorithm each week to reflect changes in the way people actually perform searches. Some of those changes are major, others are minor — but they all make the algorithm a dynamic force to be reckoned with.

Knowing that, as you create your web site (or update it for SEO), you can keep a few design principles in mind — the most important of which is to design your web site for people, not search engines. Going back to the example of building a site about springtime vacations, you would want to include information and links to help users do just that: plan their springtime vacations.

When a crawler examines your site and it contains links to airfare sites, festival sites, garden shows, and other related sites, the crawler can follow these links, using the algorithm to determine whether they are related, and your site will rank higher than if all the links lead to completely unrelated sites (which tells the crawler you've set up that bogus link farm previously discussed, causing it to either rank your site very low or not at all.)

The magic number for how many links must be related and how many can be unrelated is just that: a magic number. Presumably, however, if you design a web page about springtime vacations

continued

continued

and it's legitimate, all the links from that page (or to the page) will be related in some way. The exception might be advertisements, which are clearly marked as such.

Even your ads should tie into your web-page content (and, it therefore stands to reason, to your keywords). Because a lot of advertising is keyword driven these days, ads for saddles on a page about booking a hotel room would likely present a red flag that tells a search engine crawler something is wrong. Ads should match your site, or at least be appealing to your audience. If they're unrelated, your audience won't be interested. Moreover, featuring only links for advertisements won't gain you much ground with a search crawler. Crawlers like links that lead to related information on other web sites, not just related products.

The same is true of keywords. Some search engines prefer that you use a higher keyword density than others. For all search engines, content is important, but the factors that determine whether or not the content helps or hurts your ranking differ from one search engine to another. And then there are meta tags, which are also weighted differently by search engines.

This mysterious baseline that we're talking about varies from search engine to search engine. Some search engines look more closely at links than others do, some look at keywords and context, some look at meta data, but most combine more than one of those elements in some unknown ratio that is completely proprietary.

That means if you design your web site for search engines, then you'll always be playing a vicious game of cat and mouse; but if you design your web site for people, and make the site as useful as possible for visitors, then you'll probably remain in all of the search engines' good graces.

What's more, if you're really paying attention to your customers' behavior when they're on your site, you won't always be a step behind the search engine. Eventually, you'll be in step and maybe even a little ahead, because a search engine has only one purpose: to provide relevant information to searchers in the manner they want to access it.

Natural Language vs. Boolean Searches

The preceding information about heuristics leads to this conclusion: Search crawlers and search engines employ some level of heuristics in ranking web pages and returning results. Crawlers look at patterns to determine what a page is about, and search engines look for patterns in search queries to compare to the patterns recognized by crawlers and then return results.

The complex aspect of this theory is that we have a living, growing, and constantly changing language, which means that the patterns of usage for that language are also constantly changing. To keep up with that, search engines also have to be living, growing, and constantly changing. That's why heuristics is such an important concept in understanding how to target your web site for search engines.

The easiest way to understand it is to compare past search behavior with present search behavior and look at how search engines have evolved.

In the beginning there was Boolean

The way people search today is nothing like how they searched when search engines first came into being. Remember Archie, Gopher, Jughead, and Veronica from Chapter 1? Those early indexing and search programs were rather limited, and to find anything in the index you had to be highly specific. In fact, when it was just Archie and Gopher, you had to know the exact location of the document or file you sought.

It wasn't until Jughead and Veronica showed up that you could actually search for something; and back then, search was rudimentary at best. When search did finally become a possibility, there were some stringent guidelines about how a file could be found. The *natural language search* that is so common today would have turned up nothing in those early days of search.

Instead, users had to specify they were searching for "this but not that" or "exactly this phrase." Enter *Boolean logic* — exactly the method needed to find the right file or document in the index of your choice. Boolean logic is based on an algebraic system of logic introduced by George Boole in the mid-nineteenth century.

Essentially, Boolean logic is a way of breaking data down into sets until a very small data set remains that meets the requirements set forth in the original query. For example, in terms of search, there might be 1,000 pages on the Web dedicated to pools. Furthermore, there might be 1,000 pages dedicated to saltwater. If you're searching for the term "saltwater pools," a search might return all 2,000 of those pages. Pretty overwhelming.

When you combine the two terms, however, to find only the pages that have both "salt-water" and "pools" on them, only a fraction of the original 2,000 pages would apply, as Figure 5-1 shows.

To take the example one step further, you can reduce the data set even more by adding a qualifier, such as "not chlorine." When you add that qualifier, another chunk of data is eliminated, leaving fewer selections that meet your query of "pools, saltwater, but not chlorine," as Figure 5-2 illustrates.

This example represents three of the *operators* that are used in Boolean searches: *and, or,* and *not*. Because Boolean logic is based on an algebraic system of logic, each of those operators can be represented with a symbol:

- **And:** +
- **Not:** −
- **Or:** The default, which returns all the pages with either words, regardless of their proximity. It is represented by a blank space between words.

A Venn diagram is often used to display the Boolean overlap of data sets.

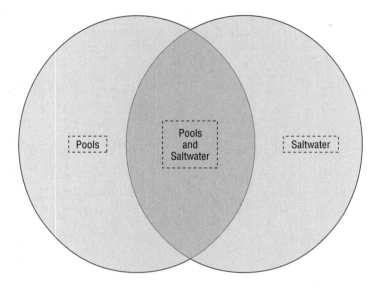

Looking at the example, to search for "pools" and "saltwater," the following combinations show what results would be returned:

- **Pools saltwater:** Would return all pages with the term "pools" or "saltwater" on them
- **Pools+saltwater:** Would return all pages with both of these terms on them
- **Pools+saltwater-chlorine:** Would return all pages with both "pools" and "saltwater," unless those pages also had the term "chlorine" on them

You can see how Boolean logic reduces the amount of data that could apply to a query by dividing it into sets. One additional operator, the *near* operator, reduces the size of those sets even further. It's represented by placing parentheses around the word or phrase that you want to find. This tells the search engine to look only for pages that contain the words within in the parentheses if those words are near each other.

In the swimming pool example, placing parentheses around the term "saltwater pools" will eliminate all results except for those that have these two words near each other. Visually, it might look something like the graphic in Figure 5-3.

You began with 2,000 possible pages, but by applying data sets using Boolean logic operators, you narrowed your choices down to a small handful. Now you're more likely to find what you're looking for, and to find it quickly.

FIGURE 5-2

Adding a qualifier to your query further reduces the appropriate data set.

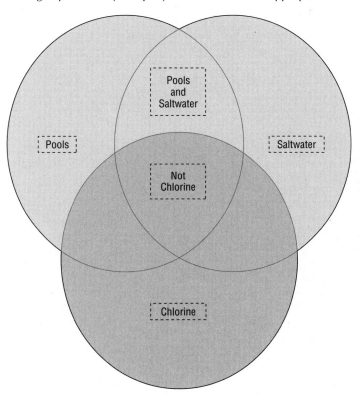

In the early days of Internet searching, Boolean logic helped users locate the files and documents they sought. From a heuristics point of view, Boolean logic provided the perfect problem-solving capabilities for search. But even technologies mature over time ...

Search language matures, naturally

Boolean logic provided a perfect foundation for search language. In fact, many people today still use Boolean operators when searching for something very specific on the Internet; but many more do not.

Over time, the number of files and documents on the Web has grown to monstrous proportions, as has the number of people searching for those files and documents. It's only natural that the way people search for data changes as well.

FIGURE 5-3

Adding the *near* operator eliminates all but a few of the possibly relevant pages in search results.

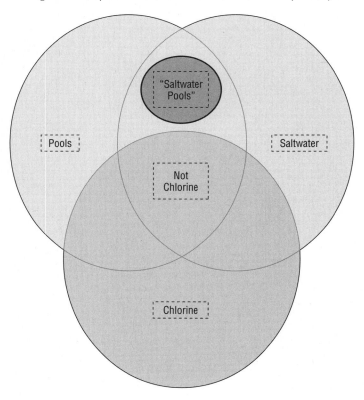

Today, most people simply construct search queries as they would speak. For example, if you were looking for information about homemade candles in Kentucky, that's probably the search string you would use: "homemade candles in Kentucky."

No plus signs, minus signs, or parentheses — just the complete thought that crossed your mind. You might even add another word or even several to the query (e.g., "history of homemade candles in Kentucky," or "where to buy homemade candles in Kentucky").

Search engines today are much better equipped to handle these natural language searches because, ironically, they apply some elements of Boolean logic on the processing side of the query. Search engine designers have paid attention to the evolution of how people search for information and have adapted search engines to work with that evolution.

Searchers can enter a question, a phrase, or even a string of related words without any operators at all, and the search engine will usually apply the correct Boolean operators to the search by using data that has been collected into databases. The operators are applied to search queries according to the construction of the search query, which is used to set up the correct data sets. For an obvious example, common words such as "of," "to," and "in" are ignored because they appear far too frequently in the English language to be useful.

NOTE The same basic rules apply to languages other than English. All languages include a set of common words that are used to qualify and modify more important words. These are the words that a search engine ignores.

Today, using mostly the *and* and *near* operators, search engines examine a search query and deduce that it could be relevant to specific topics based on the proximity and relationship of words in the query. This is accomplished by ranking the importance of word proximity and the patterns of relationship. For example, if you search for "home made candles in Kentucky," the top search results will show the web sites containing the most occurrences of those words together.

In this case, the number one result at the time of this writing for a Google search (shown in Figure 5-4) is a web site called *Scent of Kentucky,* and their headline is "Candles, home made by *Scent of Kentucky*."

FIGURE 5-4

A natural language search has relatively accurate results in today's search engines.

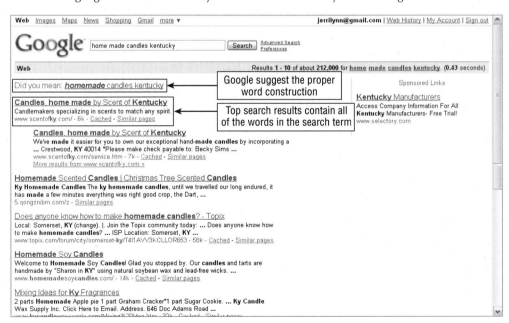

As shown in the results, the actual spelling of "homemade" is a single word, not two. In fact, Google suggests re-searching the results with the proper spelling. However, for brevity, and to illustrate the importance of paying attention to all of the details related to your keywords, I've left the example constructed improperly.

Users can still apply Boolean operators to search queries today if they want to, and doing so will narrow the results that are returned; but it is no longer necessary, given the power of today's search engines. They have improved almost to the point where they seem to know what you're thinking, so why bother?

It's that very thought process that makes keywords so vitally important to your web site. Potential visitors will put forth the least amount of effort necessary to find the solutions they seek. Search engine designers understand that and work hard to create search engines that are intuitive enough to return accurate results, despite a lack of Boolean operators. Your keyword selections need to be equally intuitive if your SEO efforts are to be successful.

Picking the Right Keywords

Keywords are really the cornerstone of any SEO program. Your keywords play a large part in determining where in search rankings you'll land, and they also mean the difference between a user finding your page or not. Selecting the right keywords for your site means the difference between being a nobody on the Web and being the first site that users click when they perform a search. Therefore, when you're picking keywords, you want to be sure that you've selected the right ones. How do you know what's right and what's not? You'll be looking at two types of keywords: brand keywords and generic keywords.

Brand keywords are keywords associated with your brand. It seems pretty obvious that these keywords are important; however, many people don't think they need to pay attention to these keywords because they're already tied to the site. Not true. If you don't use the keywords contained in your business name, business description, and specific category of business, you're missing out. If you don't own them, who will? And if someone else owns them, how will they use those keywords to direct traffic away from your site?

Generic keywords are all the other keywords that are not directly associated with your company brand. For example, if your web site, TeenFashions.com, sells teen clothing, then keywords such as clothing, tank tops, cargo pants, and bathing suits might be generic keywords that you could use on your site.

Before going too much farther in this description of keywords and how to choose the right ones, you should know that keywords fall into two other categories: keywords you pay a fee to use (called *pay-per-click*), and naturally occurring keywords that just seem to work for you without the need to pay someone to ensure they appear in search results (called *organic keywords*).

When you think about purchasing keywords, these fall into the pay-per-click category. When you stumble upon a keyword that works, that falls into the organic category. As you begin considering the keywords that you'll use on your site, the best place to start brainstorming is with keywords that apply to your business. Every business has its own set of buzzwords that people think of when they think about that business or the products or services related to the business. Start your brainstorming session with words and phrases that are broad in scope, even if they may not bring great search results. Then narrow your selections to more specific words and phrases, which will bring highly targeted traffic. Table 5-1 shows how broad keywords compare to specific key phrases.

TABLE 5-1

Broad Keywords vs. Specific Key Phrases

Broad Keywords and Phrases	Specific Key Phrases
Knives	Hunting knives
Indian knives	American Indian knives
Damascus knives	Vintage Damascus knives

Recall from Chapter 2 the information on Long Tail search. The keywords that appear in the left column of Table 5-1 are those at the broad head of search. These are some of the most competitive keywords available, and they typically require a paid keyword campaign to even come close to the top ranking. But that doesn't mean you should discard them from your keyword options.

The amount of potential traffic that can be generated by these broad keywords is huge if you can rank high enough. Just keep in mind that it will probably take a lot of time and a large budget to land on the first page of results, not to mention in the number one spot.

Conversely, the keywords in the right column are Long Tail keywords. They're more specific and will probably draw smaller amounts of traffic to your site. The traffic that Long Tail keywords draw, however, tends to be *qualified traffic*, meaning those visitors are more likely to reach a conversion goal you've established for your web site.

For example, people searching for "vintage Damascus knives" already know what they're looking for. If your web site features those knives and information about them, and it's properly loaded with the right keywords, then you're more likely to land in the top search results; and when those searchers see you in the top results and click through to your site, they're more likely to make a purchase, sign up for a newsletter or mailing list, or help you reach whatever other goal you might have for that page.

Another advantage to Long Tail keywords is that it's easier to achieve organic SEO with them. Specific key phrases tend to be in lower demand than broader, more popular terms, so a little work and attention to detail should help you rank well for these terms. Ultimately, it may result in less traffic than a broader term, but the traffic it does drive to your site should be much better targeted, which may work out better for you in the long run.

In short, as you consider the keywords that you want to use in optimizing your web site, think in terms of both broad words and deep phrases. They have different requirements and payoffs, but both will prove useful in your SEO efforts.

Chapter 8 contains more details about choosing the right keywords and key phrases. The principle for choosing keywords is the same, whether the words you're using are in PPC programs or occur organically, so all of the elements of keyword selection for both categories are covered there.

NOTE   When you're considering the words that you'll use for keywords, also consider phrases of two to three words. Because key phrases can be much more specific than single words, it's easier to rank high with a key phrase than with a keyword. Key phrases are used in the same ways as keywords, they're just longer.

What's the Right Keyword Density?

Keyword density is hard to quantify. It's a measurement of the number of times that your keywords appear on the page versus the number of words on a page — a ratio, in other words. For example, if you have a single web page that has 1,000 words of text and your keyword appears on that page 10 times (assuming a single keyword, not a keyword phrase), then your keyword density is 1 percent.

What's the right keyword density? That's a question that no one has been able to answer definitively. Some experts say that your keyword density should be around 5 to 7 percent; others suggest that it should be higher or lower. No one seems to agree on exactly where it should be.

Because there's no hard-and-fast rule, or even a good rule of thumb, to dictate keyword density, site owners are flying on their own. What *is* certain is that using a keyword or a set of keywords or phrases often begins to look like *keyword stuffing* to a search engine, which will negatively impact the ranking of your site.

Not enough keyword density and your site ranking suffers. Too much keyword density and your site ranking suffers. Fortunately, you can at least find out what keyword density your competitors are using by looking at the source code for their pages.

TIP   Looking at your competitors' source code is also a good way to find out *which* keywords they're using. The listed keywords should appear in the first few lines of code (as indicated in Figures 5-6 and 5-8).

To view the source code of a page if you're using Internet Explorer, follow these steps:

1. Open Internet Explorer and navigate to the page for which you would like to view the source code.

2. Click View in the standard toolbar. (In Internet Explorer 7.0, select Page.) The View (or Page) menu appears, as shown in Figure 5-5.

3. Select View Source. A separate window will open displaying the source code from the web page you're viewing, as shown in Figure 5-6.

If you're using the Firefox browser, the menus are slightly different and the source code looks a little different. These are the steps for Firefox:

1. Open Firefox and navigate to the page for which you would like to view the source code.

2. Click View in the standard toolbar. The View menu appears, as shown in Figure 5-7.

FIGURE 5-5

Use the Page menu in Internet Explorer 7.0 to view the source code for the displayed web site.

FIGURE 5-6

The source code for the displayed web page appears in a separate window.

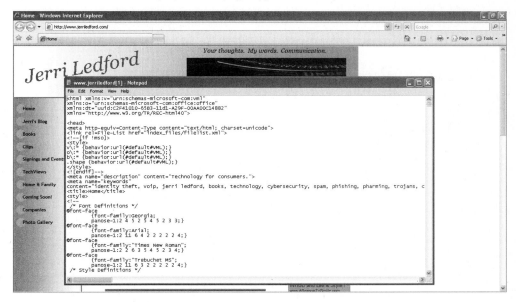

FIGURE 5-7

The Firefox View menu is located in a different place and labeled differently than in Internet Explorer.

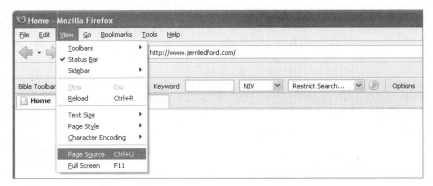

3. Select Page Source to open a separate window that displays the source code for the web page, as shown in Figure 5-8. Alternatively, you can use the keyboard combination Ctrl+U to open the source code window.

FIGURE 5-8

Although the source code is the same, different browsers display it differently.

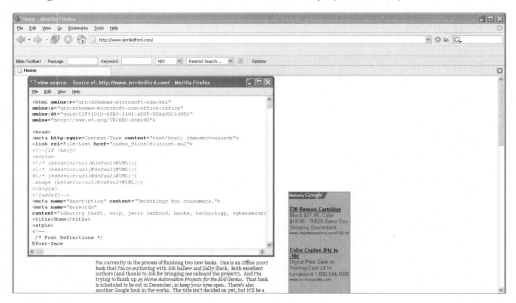

The source code looks a little different in Internet Explorer than it does in Firefox, but the basic information is all there. That said, it's not very easy to get through this information. All of the page text is jumbled in with the page encoding. It may take some time to decipher, but ultimately, this is the best way to find out not only what keywords the competition is using, but also how they're using them, and how often the keywords appear on their pages.

Taking Advantage of Organic Keywords

We've already covered brief information about organic keywords. As you may remember, organic keywords are those that appear naturally on your web site, and they contribute to the search engine ranking of the page. By taking advantage of those organic keywords, you can improve your site rankings without spending additional budget dollars. The problem is that gaining organic ranking alone can take four to six months or longer. To help speed the time it takes to achieve good rankings, many organizations (or individuals) use organic keywords in addition to some type of PPC (pay-per-click) or *pay-for-inclusion* service.

To take advantage of organic keywords, you first need to know what those keywords are. One way to find out is to us a web site application that collects visitor data, such as the one that Google provides, Google Analytics. Some of these services track the keywords that push users to your site. When viewing the reports associated with keywords, you can quickly see how your PPC keywords draw traffic, and what keywords in which you're not investing still draw traffic.

Another way to discover organic keywords is to consider the words that would be associated with your web site, product, or business name. For example, a writer might include various keywords about the area in which she specializes, but one keyword she won't necessarily want to purchase is the word "writer," which would be naturally occurring on the site.

The word won't necessarily garner high traffic for you, but when that word is combined with more specific keywords, perhaps keywords that you acquire through a PPC service, the organic words can help to push traffic to your site. Going back to the writer example, if the writer specializes in writing about AJAX, then the word "writer" might be an organic keyword, and "AJAX" might be a keyword that the writer bids for in a PPC service.

That way, when potential visitors use a search engine to search for "AJAX writer," the writer's site has a better chance of being listed higher in the results rankings. Of course, by using more specific terms related to AJAX in addition to writer, the chances are pretty good that the organic keyword combined with the PPC keywords will improve search rankings. Therefore, when you consider organic keywords, think of words that you might not be willing to spend your budget on but that could help improve your search rankings, either alone or when combined with keywords in which you are willing to invest.

Where organic keywords are concerned, more specific is better. In fact, if you have a series of specific phrases that relate well to your site but to few other sites, those are good phrases to focus your organic efforts on. Those words should not only rank well in terms of Long Tail search, but also bring more qualified visitors to your site and serve as a solid foundation for any future PPC campaigns that you may begin.

Avoid Keyword Stuffing

Recall from earlier in the chapter that keyword stuffing is the practice of loading your web pages with keywords in an effort to artificially improve your ranking in search engine results. Depending on the page that you're trying to stuff, this could mean using a specific keyword or key phrase a dozen times or hundreds of times.

Temporarily, this might improve your page ranking; but if it does, the improvement won't last, because when the search engine crawler examines your site, it will find the multiple keyword uses.

Search engine crawlers use an algorithm to determine whether the *keyword density* — the number of times that a keyword or phrase is used on your site — is reasonable. If it's not, then the crawler will discover very quickly that your site can't support the number of times you've used that keyword or key phrase. The result will be a lower quality score for your site, and the site will be either dropped deeper into search rankings or removed completely from search results (which is what happens in most cases).

There are no search engine guidelines that state, "It's appropriate to use keywords on your web site *X* number of times," because then everyone would use their keywords similarly and they would hold no value in search rankings at all. As it is, many web site owners try to skew search rankings with complicated (and not always ethical) keyword strategies. Therefore, it's up to you to determine how many times you should include keywords in your tags, titles, text, links, headings, and content, and to hope that whatever you decide is the right solution.

Keyword stuffing, purposely or not, occurs in several ways on web pages. The first is when the content writer or web designer includes a block of text on the web page (usually at the bottom, but it can be anywhere) that is nothing more than a repetition of the chosen keyword, as shown here:

AKC Breeding AKC Breeding AKC Breeding

AKC Breeding AKC Breeding AKC Breeding

AKC Breeding AKC Breeding AKC Breeding

AKC Breeding AKC Breeding AKC Breeding

Sometimes this repetitive block of text is shown in the same font as the other text on the page, but it's not at all unusual for a block of text like this to be the same color as the page background so that it is invisible to visitors, but perfectly readable by search engine crawlers. When it's invisible to visitors, it's called *invisible keyword stuffing*.

You also run the risk of accidently falling victim to keyword stuffing on your page. This can happen when you place too many keywords into tags, text, and other elements of your web page. As a general rule, keep the keyword density of your page at 7 to 10 percent of the total words on your web page. For example, if your page has 300 words of text, then no more than 21 to 30 of those words should be keywords. In addition, those 21 to 30 words should be distributed between the text and the back-end meta tags.

As mentioned earlier, 7 to 10 percent keyword density isn't a rule, but a guideline that you should try to stay close to. Some search engines will allow a little higher keyword density before flagging your site as a spam site, whereas others might allow less than 10 percent. It's a game that you'll have to play for a while in order to learn what works and what doesn't.

One way to ensure that you're not overdoing it with your keywords is to use several different keywords or phrases that are unique to that page. These keywords should come from the keyword groups that you learned about at the beginning of this chapter. If a keyword is not essential in helping site visitors understand a product, service, or concept, don't use it simply as a tactic to increase your rankings. Don't be tempted. The result of that temptation could be the exact opposite of what you're trying to achieve.

Keywords are still one of the least expensive methods of advertising your web site. They are also a moving target, not a simple select-and-forget-it solution. You'll have to put plenty of ongoing effort and experimentation into learning what works and what doesn't with your PPC ads and keyword placement. If you keep your efforts consistent and regular, though, you'll eventually find the right combination — one that not only provides the increased traffic and conversions you're looking for, but also does it within the confines of your budget.

More About Keyword Optimization

There is much more to learn about keywords and pay-per-click programs. In Chapter 6, you'll learn more about how to conduct keyword research, what pay-per-click programs are, and how to select the right keywords for your web site. Always keep in mind that keywords are just tools to help you improve your search rankings. When designing your site, the site should be designed to inform, enlighten, or persuade your site visitor to reach a goal conversion.

That's what SEO is truly all about. Keywords may be a major component of your SEO strategies, but the ultimate goal of SEO is bringing in more visitors who reach more goal conversions. Without those conversions, all the site visitors in the world won't mean anything more than that people dropped by.

Chapter 6

Pay-per-Click and SEO

P ay-per-click (PPC) is one of those terms that you hear associated with keywords so often you might think they were the conjoined twins of SEO. They're not, really. Keywords and PPC do go hand in hand, but it is possible to have keywords without PPC. It's not always advisable, however.

Hundreds of PPC services are available, but they are not all created equal. Some pay-per-click services work with actual search rankings, whereas others are more about text advertisements. Then there are the category-specific PPC programs, such as those for keywords, products, and services.

The main goal of a pay-per-click program is to drive traffic to your site, but ideally you want more out of PPC results than just visits. What's most important is traffic that reaches some conversion goal that you've set for your web site. To achieve these goal conversions, you may have to experiment with different techniques, keywords, and even PPC services.

Pay-per-click programs have numerous advantages over traditional search engine optimization:

- **No changes to a current site design are required.** You don't have to change any code or add any other elements to your site. All you have to do is bid on and pay for the keywords you'd like to target.

- **PPC implementation is quick and easy.** After signing up for a PPC program, it might take only a few minutes to start getting targeted traffic to your web site. With SEO campaigns that are strictly organic and don't include pay-per-click, it could take months for you to build the traffic levels that PPC can build in hours (assuming your PPC campaign is well targeted).

IN THIS CHAPTER

How PPC affects SEO

Before you PPC

How pay-per-click works

Pay-per-click categories

Keyword competitive research

Choosing effective keywords

Writing ad descriptions

Monitoring and analyzing results

■ PPC implementation doesn't require any specialized knowledge. Your pay-per-click campaigns will be much better targeted, however, if you understand keywords and how they work.

As with any SEO strategy, PPC has its limitations. Bidding for keywords can be fierce, with each competitor bidding higher and higher to reach and maintain the top search results position. Many organizations even have a dedicated person or team that's responsible for monitoring the company's position in search results and amending bids accordingly.

Monitoring your position is crucial to maintaining good placement, however, because you do have to fight for your ranking, and PPC programs can become prohibitively expensive. The competitiveness of the keywords or phrases and the aggressiveness of the competition determine how much you'll ultimately end up spending to rank well.

NOTE One issue with PPC programs is that many search engines recognize PPC ads as just that — paid advertisements. Therefore, although your ranking with the search engine for which you're purchasing placement might be good, that doesn't mean your ranking in other search engines will be good. Sometimes it's necessary to run multiple PPC campaigns if you want to rank high in multiple search engines.

Understanding How PPC Affects SEO

There's a lot of debate about how an organization should use organic keyword marketing versus PPC marketing. There seem to be two (and possibly three) distinct opinions about what should and shouldn't be done in regard to these different types of marketing.

The first position is that pay-per-click programs can hurt organic keyword programs. According to supporters of this position, PPC programs damage organic rankings because the act of paying for a listing automatically reduces the rank of your organic keyword efforts. Those who subscribe to this theory believe that there is no place for PPC programs.

Another position in this argument is that PPC has no effect at all on SEO. It's a tough concept to swallow, because one would naturally assume that any organization *paying* for a specific rank in search returns would automatically push organic keyword returns into a lower slot (which supports the first theory). Those who follow this theory believe that there is no need to invest in PPC because you can achieve the same results with organic keywords, though it takes much longer for those results to become apparent.

The most widely held belief, however, is that a combination of PPC and organic keywords is the best approach. This theory would seem to have a lot of validity. According to some researchers, pay-per-click programs tend to be much more effective when an organization also has organic keywords that rank in the same area as the PPC ranks. For example, if you've bid on a keyword that's consistently placed number two or three in search engine returns and you have organic keywords that fall in the next few slots, you're likely to enjoy better conversion numbers than either organic keywords or PPC programs can deliver on their own.

It's important to note here that all search engines make a distinction between PPC and organic SEO. PPC doesn't help your organic rankings. Only those activities such as tagging your web site properly, using keyword placement properly, and including great content on your site will help you on the organic side. PPC is a *search marketing strategy*.

> **NOTE** Throughout this book, you'll like see the terms *SEO* and *search marketing* used interchangeably. Very strictly speaking, search marketing and SEO are quite different activities. Search marketing — sometimes called *search engine marketing (SEM)* — includes any activity that improves your search engine rankings, paid or organic. SEO, however, usually refers strictly to the free, organic methods used to improve search rankings. Very often, the two terms *are* used interchangeably by people using SEO and search engine marketing techniques. SEO and SEM experts, however, always clearly differentiate the activities.

Before You PPC

Before you even begin to use a PPC program, you should consider some basics. A very important point to keep in mind is that just because you're paying for placement or advertising space associated with your keywords, you're not necessarily going to get the best results with all the keywords or phrases that you choose. With PPC services, you must test, test, and test some more. Begin small, with a minimum number of keywords, to see how the search engine you've selected performs in terms of the amount of traffic it delivers and how well that traffic converts into paying customers.

An essential part of your testing is having a method in place that enables you to track your return on investment. For example, if your goal is to bring new subscribers to your newsletter, you'll want to track conversions, perhaps by directing the visitors funneled to your site by your PPC link to a subscription page set up just for them. You can then monitor how many clicks actually result in a goal conversion (in this case, a new subscription). This helps you to quickly track your return on investment and to determine how much you're paying for each new subscriber.

Before investing in a PPC service, you may want to review a few different services to determine which is the best one for you. When doing your preliminary research, take the time to ask the following questions:

- How many searches are conducted each month through the search engine for which you're considering a PPC program?
- Does the search engine have major partners or affiliates that could contribute to the volume of traffic you're likely to receive through the PPC program?
- How many searches are generated each month by those partners and affiliates?

- What exactly are the terms of service for search partners or affiliates?

- How does the search engine or PPC program prevent fraudulent activity?

- How difficult is it to file a report about fraudulent activity and how quickly is the issue addressed (and by whom)?

- What recourse do you have if fraudulent activity is discovered?

- Do you have control over where your listing *does* appear? For example, can you choose not to have your listing appear in search results for other countries where your site is not relevant? Can you choose to have your listing withheld from affiliate searches?

When you're looking at different PPC programs, look for those that have strict guidelines about how sites appear in listings, how partners and affiliates calculate visits, and how fraud is handled. These are important issues, because in each case you could be stuck paying for clicks that didn't actually happen. Be sure to monitor any service that you decide to use to ensure that your PPC advertisements are working properly and seem to be targeted well.

It often takes a lot of testing, monitoring, and redirection to find a PPC program that works well for you. Don't be discouraged or surprised if you find that you must try several different programs or many different keywords before you find the right combination. Through a system of trial and error and diligent effort, you'll find that PPC programs can help build your site traffic and goal conversions faster than you could with organic SEO alone.

How Pay-per-Click Works

Pay-per-click marketing is an advertising method that enables you to buy search engine placement by bidding on keywords or phrases. There are two different types of PPC marketing.

In the first type, you pay a fee for an actual SERP ranking, and in some cases you also pay a per-click fee, meaning the more you pay, the higher in the returned results your page will rank.

The second type is more along true advertising lines. This type of PPC marketing involves bidding on keywords or phrases that appear in, or are associated with, text advertisements. Google is probably the most notable provider of this service. Google's AdWords service, shown in Figure 6-1, is an excellent example of how PPC advertisements work.

Determining visitor value

The first thing that you need to do when you begin considering PPC strategies is to determine how much each web site visitor is worth to you. It's important to know this number, because otherwise you could find yourself paying far too much for keyword advertising that doesn't bring the traffic or conversions that you expect. For example, if it costs you $25 to gain a conversion (or sale) but the value of that conversion is only $15, then you're losing a lot of money.

FIGURE 6-1

PPC advertisements are those that you see at the top and on the sides of search pages.

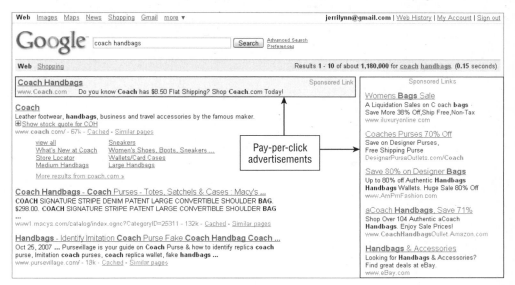

To determine the value of each web site visitor, you need some historical data about the number of visitors to your site in a given amount of time (e.g., a month) and the actual sales numbers (or profit) for that same time period. This is where it's good to have some kind of web metrics program to keep track of your site statistics. If you divide the profit by the number of visitors for the same time frame, the result should tell you (approximately) what each visitor is worth.

For example, suppose that during December, your site cleared $2,500. (In this admittedly simplified example, we're ignoring various other factors you would have to figure into an actual profit and loss statement.) Suppose also that during the same month, 15,000 visitors came to your site. Note that this number is for all the visitors to your site, not just the ones who made a purchase. You divide your $2,500 profit by *all* the visitors, purchasers or not, because this gives you an accurate average value of every visitor to your site. Not every visitor will make a purchase, but you have to go through a number of nonpurchasing visitors to get to those who will purchase.

Back to the formula for the value of a visitor: Divide the site profit for December ($2,500) by the number of visitors (15,000) and the value of your visitors is approximately $.17 per visitor. This value is approximate because during any given month (or whatever time frame you choose) the number of visitors and the amount of profit will vary. The way you slice the time can change your average visitor value by a few cents to a few dollars, depending on your site traffic. (Again, the example is based on the value of all visitors, not just conversions, which might be a more valid real-life way of calculating the value of individual visitors; but this example is simply to demonstrate the principle.)

The number you get for visitor value is a sort of break-even point. It means you can spend up to $.17 per visitor on keywords or other promotions without losing money; but if you're spending more than that *without increasing sales and profits*, you're going in the hole. It's not good business to spend everything you make (or more) to draw visitors to the site, but note the preceding italicized words.

If a $.25 keyword can raise your sales and profits dramatically, then it may be worth buying that word. In this oversimplified example, you need to decide how much you can realistically spend on keywords or other promotions. Maybe you feel a particular keyword is powerful enough that you can spend $.12 per click for it, and raise your sales and visitor value substantially. You have to decide what profit margin you want and what promotions are likely to provide it.

As you can see, there are a number of variables. Real life is dynamic and eludes static examples. Whatever you decide, you shouldn't spend everything you make on PPC programs. There are far too many other things that you need to invest in.

Popular keyword phrases can often run much more than $.12 per click. In fact, some of the most popular keywords can run as much as $50 (yes, fifty dollars) per click. To stretch your PPC budget, you can choose less popular terms that are much less expensive but that provide good results for the investment that you do make.

Putting pay-per-click to work

Now that you have your average visitor value, you can begin to look at the different keywords on which you might bid. Before you do, however, you need to look at a few more things. One of the main mistakes made with PPC programs is that users don't take the time to clarify what it is they hope to gain from using a PPC service. It's not enough for your PPC program to have a goal of increasing your ROI (return on investment). You need something more quantifiable than just the desire to increase profit. How *much* would you like to increase your profit? How many visitors will it take to reach the desired increase?

Let's say that right now each visit to your site is worth $.50, using our simplified example, and your average monthly profit is $5,000. That means that your site receives 10,000 visits per month. Now you need to decide how much you'd like to increase your profit. For this example, let's say that you want to increase it to $7,500. To do that, if each visitor is worth $.50, you would need to increase the number of visits to your site to 15,000 per month. Therefore, the goal for your PPC program should be *to increase profit $2,500 by driving an additional 5,000 visits per month*. Now you have a concrete, quantifiable measurement by which you can track your PPC campaigns.

Once you know what you want to spend, and what your goals are, you can begin to look at the different types of PPC programs that might work for you. Although keywords are the main PPC element associated with PPC marketing, there are other types of PPC programs to consider as well.

Pay-per-Click Categories

Pay-per-click programs are not all created equal. When you think of PPC programs, you probably think of keyword marketing — bidding on a keyword to determine where your site will be placed in search results; and that's an accurate description of PPC marketing programs as they apply to keywords. However, there are two other types of PPC programs — and you may find that targeting a different category of PPC marketing is more effective than simply targeting keyword PPC programs.

Keyword pay-per-click programs

Keyword PPC programs are the most common type of PPC program. They are also the type this book focuses on most often. By now you know that keyword PPC programs are about bidding on keywords associated with your site. The amount that you're willing to bid determines the placement of your site in search engine results.

In keyword PPC, the keywords used can be any word or phrase that might apply to your site. However, remember that some of the most common keywords have the highest competition for top spot, so it's not always advisable to assume that the broadest term is the best one. If you're in a specialized type of business, a broader term might be more effective; but as a rule of thumb, the more narrowly focused your keywords are, the better the results you are likely to have with them (and PPC costs much less if you're not using a word that requires a $50-per-click bid).

NOTE Did you know that Google and Yahoo! have $100 caps on their keyword bids? Imagine paying $100 per click for a keyword. Those are the kinds of keywords that will likely cost you far more money than they will generate for you. It's best if you stick with keywords and phrases that are more targeted and less expensive.

The major search engines are usually the ones that come to mind when you think of keyword PPC programs, and that's fairly accurate. Search PPC marketing programs like those offered by vendors such as Google, Yahoo! Search Marketing, and MSN are some of the most well-known PPC programs.

Product pay-per-click programs

You can think of product pay-per-click programs as online-comparison shopping engines or price-comparison engines. A product PPC program focuses specifically on products, so you bid on placement for your product advertisements.

The requirements for using a product PPC program are a little different from keyword PPC programs, however. With a product PPC, you must provide a *feed* — think of it as a regularly updated price list for your products — to the search engine. Then, when users search for a product, your links are given prominence, depending on the amount you have bid for placement. However, users can freely display those product listings returned by the search engine in the order of price from lowest to highest if that is their preference. This means that your product may get good placement initially, but if it's not the lowest-priced product in that category, it's not guaranteed that your placement results will stay in front of potential visitors.

Some of these product PPC programs include Shopping.com, NexTag, PriceGrabber, and Shopzilla.

NOTE   Although product PPC programs are popular for controlling the placement of your product listings, some services, such as Google Base, enable you to list your products in their search engines without cost. These product PPC programs still require a product feed, however, to keep product listings current.

Implementing a product feed for your products isn't terribly difficult, although, depending on the number of products you have, it can be time-consuming. Most of the different product PPC programs have different requirements for the product attributes that must be included in the product feed. For example, the basic information included for all products is an item title, the direct link for the item, and a brief description of the item.

Some of the additional attributes that you may need to include in your product PPC listings include the following:

- Title
- Description
- Link
- Image link
- Product type
- UPC
- Price
- MPN (manufacturer's part number)
- ISBN
- ID

Some product PPC programs require XML-formatted feeds; however, most will allow *text-delimited Excel files* (simple CSV files). This means you can create your product lists in an Excel spreadsheet and then save that spreadsheet as text delimited by selecting File ➤ Save As and ensuring that the file type selected is text delimited.

Service pay-per-click programs

When users search for a service of any type, such as travel reservations, they are likely to use search engines related specifically to that type of service. For example, a user searching for the best price for hotel reservations in Orlando, Florida, might go to TripAdvisor.com. Advertisers — in this case, hotel chains — can choose to pay for their rank in the search results using a service PPC program.

Service PPC programs are similar to product PPC programs, with the only difference being the type of product or service that is offered. Product PPC programs are more focused on e-commerce products, whereas service PPC programs are focused on businesses that have a specific service to offer.

Service PPC programs also require an RSS feed, and even some of the same attribute listings as product PPC programs. Some of the service PPC programs you might be familiar with are SideStep.com and TripAdvisor.com. In addition, many product PPC programs have expanded to include services. One such vendor is NexTag.

TIP In addition to the three categories of PPC programs discussed in this text, there is an additional one. Pay-per-call is a type of keyword advertising in which search results include a phone number. Each time a call is connected through that phone number, the company that owns the number is charged for the advertising, just as if it were paying for a traditional pay-per-click service.

PPC Is *Not* Paid Inclusion!

One distinction that is important to understand is the difference between PPC and *paid-inclusion (PI) services*. Many people believe that PPC and PI services are the same type of marketing, but there can be some subtle differences. For starters, paid-inclusion services are used by some search engines to enable web site owners to pay a one-year subscription fee to ensure that their site is indexed with that search engine at all times. This fee doesn't guarantee any specific rank in search engine results; it only guarantees that the site is indexed by the search engine.

Yahoo! is one company that uses paid inclusion to populate its search index. Not all the listings in Yahoo! are paid listings, however. Yahoo! combines both normally spidered sites and paid sites. Many other search engines have staunchly avoided using paid-inclusion services — Ask.com and Google are two of the most notable — because most users feel that paid inclusion can skew the search results. In fact, search engines that allow only paid-inclusion listings are not likely to survive very long, because people won't use them.

There is a bit of a gray area between paid inclusion and PPC. That area begins at about the point where both services are paid for. Detractors of these types of programs claim that paying for a listing — any listing — is likely to make search returns invalid because it is believed that search engines give higher ranking to paid-inclusion services, just as they do to PPC advertisements.

Keyword Competitive Research

Keyword research is the core of any SEO campaign and it is vitally important when developing PPC programs. You should choose carefully the keywords that you believe will be most effective, because the keywords selected during the research phase will be included in your web site copy, as well as your PPC programs, and many other types of campaigns. For starters, you should select valid keywords from a variety of sources, including the following:

■ **Your own knowledge of the product or service that you're marketing:** From your own knowledge, you should be able to choose at least one word that characterizes the product or service. If you're unable to select that word, spend some time getting to know your products and services better.

■ **Your customers:** Your customers will be able to tell you what keywords they think of or use when searching for your product or service. Customers can be your best source for valid and relevant keywords, because you're trying to reach people just like them.

■ **Competitors' web sites.** Check your competitors' web sites for additional keywords that you may not have considered during your initial brainstorming session. Obviously, if your competitors are using these keywords, there will be some competition for them, but better to have the competition than to be left outside the arena while the games are taking place.

CROSS-REF   Remember checking out competitors' web sites back in Chapter 5? The same method of viewing the source code for those sites is the method that you would use here to check for keywords on your competitors' sites. If you need a reminder, flip back now to review the section on keyword density.

Keyword suggestion tools

One tool that you should use when developing your keyword list is a *keyword suggestion tool*. Keyword suggestion tools are just that: tools that provide a list of suggested keywords based on a base word that you enter into the search tool. Some of the words returned may not have occurred to you when you were brainstorming keywords and soliciting feedback from your customers about the words they would use. In addition, keyword suggestion tools provide some of the information that you'll need to determine how much competition there is for the keywords and phrases you're considering using.

In the past, measuring the competition for your search terms was done by performing a search for each keyword or phrase using one search engine at a time. When the SERPs were returned, you could see how many times that keyword or phrase turned up. It was a tedious and ineffective method of keyword research. Today, keyword suggestion tools speed the competitive research process.

Here's how it works: You first input your proposed keywords into a keyword suggestion tool, which examines a database containing millions of instances of keyword usage. Using these tools, you can quickly learn how many users are conducting daily searches for that term, how many of those searches resulted in an actual visit, and what related search terms were used.

Many keyword suggestion tools are available on the Web. Some of the top tools, which you may already be familiar with, include the following:

- **SEO Book Keyword Suggestion Tool:** The SEO Book Keyword Suggestion tool, shown in Figure 6-2, shows you how many searches have been conducted over a given month in various search engines for a keyword or phrase related to the search term you enter into the tool. You can find the SEO Book Keyword Suggestion Tool at `http://tools.seobook.com/keyword-tools/seobook/index.php`.

- **Wordtracker:** Wordtracker enables you to search for terms in the database of terms collected. This program tells you how often a keyword or phrase was searched for. In addition, the list of keywords and phrases returned may include words or phrases that you haven't considered using.

  You may also find keywords on this list that have low competition rates but high relevancy. For example, Figure 6-3 shows some of the results for a Wordtracker search for the term "beach." A free version of Wordtracker is available at `http://freekeywords.wordtracker.com/`.

- **Trellian Keyword Discovery Tool:** The Trellian tool is a subscription tool (about $70 per month) that enables users to ascertain the market share value for a given search term, see how many users search for it daily, identify common spellings and misspellings, and discover which terms are affected by seasonal trends. Figure 6-4 shows the some of the results that are returned with a Trellian search for "Sydney Hotel." As shown in the figure, each keyword or phrase returned includes information about the number of searches for the word, and Trellian can analyze each word or phrase further.

- **Google AdWords Keyword Tool:** Google's Keyword Tool provides suggestions for additional words that you may not have considered. The results shown in Figure 6-5 (using the term "business technology writer") include some graphs related to the number of times the words are searched for and to the competition that you might face if you select a particular word. However, there are no actual numbers, so your decisions about competition will include a high degree of guesswork.

  What you might find unique about the Google Keyword Tool is its capability to examine your web page or even your entire web site and make suggestions for keywords and phrases that might be useful in marketing your site. The results of such a search, as illustrated in Figure 6-6, may include terms that you haven't considered.

Ongoing keyword testing

One thing that you should remember as you're using any of these keyword suggestion tools is that you're checking not only how competitive a keyword is, but also whether it's popular; and you're keeping your eyes open for those unexpected keywords that are not highly competitive but are completely relevant to your site.

FIGURE 6-2

SEO Book's Keyword Suggestion Tool is a simple-to-use tool to help you find keywords related to your topic word.

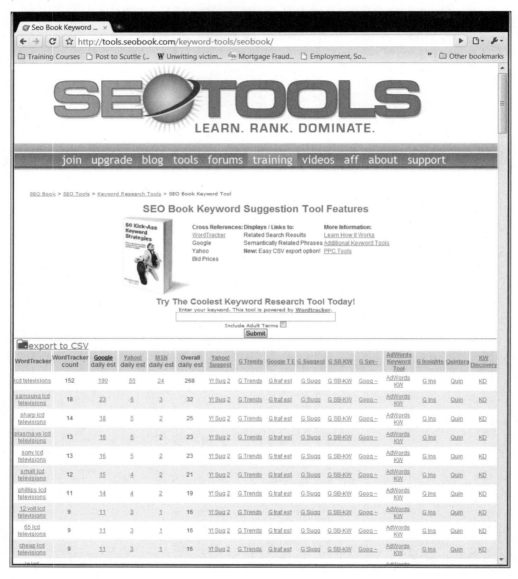

FIGURE 6-3

Wordtracker shows not only related words, but also where those words rank in searches.

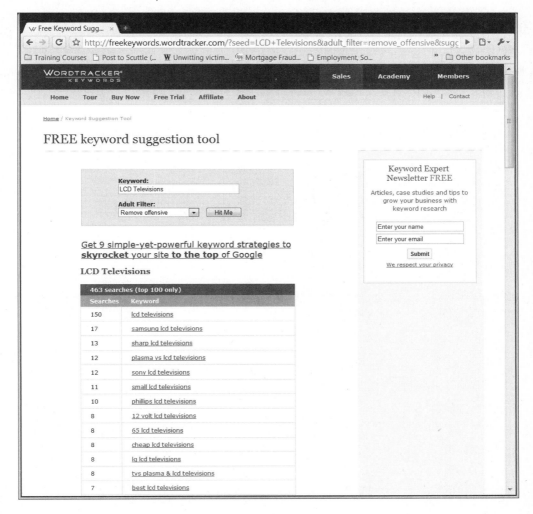

FIGURE 6-4

Trellian provides slightly different information about each keyword or phrase, and is a subscription service.

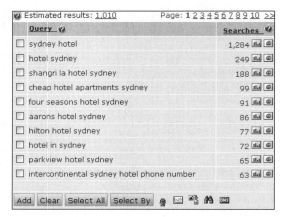

While you're testing potential new terms, it's also a good idea to test any keywords that your site is already using to see which ones are effective and which are not. The keywords that are effective — meaning those that result in visitors and goal conversions — are the keywords to hang on to. Any that aren't performing well should be replaced with new keywords.

This means your keyword research is an ongoing chore. Because your site is likely to change over time, your keywords will also change. Therefore, it's necessary for you to conduct regular keyword research to determine which keywords or phrases are working and which are not, as well as to add new keywords to your list.

In doing your keyword research, here are some basic guidelines you can follow to ensure that you're conducting the most thorough research while being highly efficient:

- Search from the point of view of your potential customers.
- Select as many relevant keywords or phrases as possible.
- Monitor your keywords to see which attract your target audience. Keep those that perform and replace those that do not.
- Select keywords and phrases that aren't the most competitive but aren't the least competitive either. These medium competitive words should yield good results without eating a ridiculous amount of your budget.

FIGURE 6-5

Google's Keyword Tool offers no concrete numbers, just graphical representations for popularity and competition.

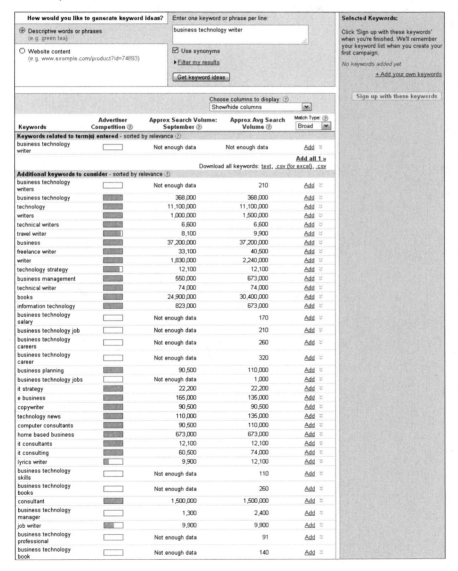

Keywords	Advertiser Competition	Approx Search Volume: September	Approx Avg Search Volume	Add
Keywords related to term(s) entered - sorted by relevance				
business technology writer		Not enough data	Not enough data	Add
				Add all 1 »
		Download all keywords: text, .csv (for excel), .csv		
Additional keywords to consider - sorted by relevance				
business technology writers		Not enough data	210	Add
business technology		368,000	368,000	Add
technology		11,100,000	11,100,000	Add
writers		1,000,000	1,500,000	Add
technical writers		6,600	6,600	Add
travel writer		8,100	9,900	Add
business		37,200,000	37,200,000	Add
freelance writer		33,100	40,500	Add
writer		1,830,000	2,240,000	Add
technology strategy		12,100	12,100	Add
business management		550,000	673,000	Add
technical writer		74,000	74,000	Add
books		24,900,000	30,400,000	Add
information technology		823,000	673,000	Add
business technology salary		Not enough data	170	Add
business technology job		Not enough data	210	Add
business technology careers		Not enough data	260	Add
business technology career		Not enough data	320	Add
business planning		90,500	110,000	Add
business technology jobs		Not enough data	1,000	Add
it strategy		22,200	22,200	Add
e business		165,000	135,000	Add
copywriter		90,500	90,500	Add
technology news		110,000	135,000	Add
computer consultants		90,500	110,000	Add
home based business		673,000	673,000	Add
it consultants		12,100	12,100	Add
it consulting		60,500	74,000	Add
lyrics writer		9,900	12,100	Add
business technology skills		Not enough data	110	Add
business technology books		Not enough data	260	Add
consultant		1,500,000	1,500,000	Add
business technology manager		1,300	2,400	Add
job writer		9,900	9,900	Add
business technology professional		Not enough data	91	Add
business technology book		Not enough data	140	Add

115

FIGURE 6-6

Google's Keyword Tool can also examine your site and make keyword suggestions for you.

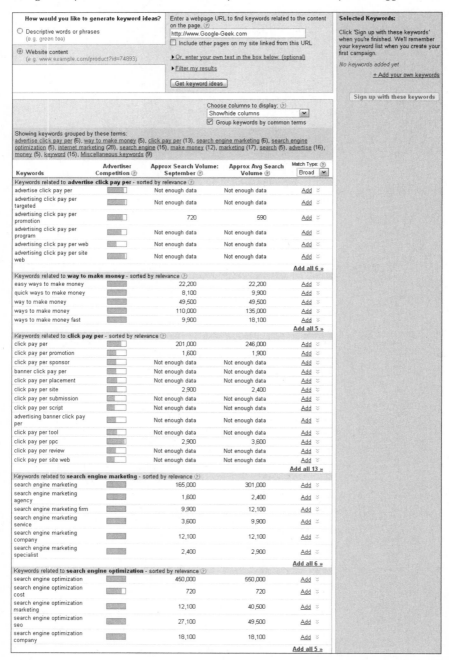

Choosing Effective Keywords

When you're using keyword marketing to optimize your site, you can run into a lot of frustrating situations. Despite your best efforts, it's possible that the keywords you select are just not generating the traffic that you need. Conversely, sometimes keywords that work well in the beginning will stop working. You can tell when this happens because the numbers associated with your keywords (assuming you're using a metrics program to track them) drop without warning or explanation.

Many things can cause your keywords to stop being as effective as they were in the past; and often it won't be the result of anything you did or didn't do. That's why it's essential to regularly develop concepts, test, the concepts and implement new keywords for your PPC programs and for your web site.

Creating your first keyword list

The initial idea of keyword research can be daunting. Just thinking about trying to come up with the perfect combination of words to drive customers to your site, improve your conversion rate, and make yourself visible to search engines can give you a serious tension headache. Even using some of the techniques discussed in this chapter to find the right keywords and perfect your methods of research takes time. It's not something that you can just jump into today and be successful at before the sun sets. You will be far more successful if you start slowly and build your way to greater success.

You already know that you must first create a list of potential keywords, and that brainstorming and asking customers are two ways to build that list. You can also include all the keywords that are suggested by keyword suggestion tools, and you might even consider pulling out a thesaurus to find additional words and phrases that you haven't considered. Come up with enough words to cover all the services your site offers and avoid broad or generic terms that are so all encompassing they apply to any site that's even remotely related to yours. These words are incredibly difficult to rank high with and won't drive quality traffic to your site. Instead, focus on words that are relevant but not overly used, and always keep your eyes open for those words that are very specific but highly targeted to your site.

When you are creating your first keyword list, include all the words that you can come up with. This part of selecting your keywords and phrases is actually easy. Just include everything and don't worry about the quality of what you're including until later. However, because it is so easy to create this first list, many people assume that PPC marketing is easy. This first step may be, but it does get much harder as you research and qualify words and phrases and then work those words and phrases into PPC marketing programs.

Because keywords and phrases will need constant revision, you should always be creating that *first* keyword list. Keep a running list of words that apply to your site. Each time something is changed on the site, or something changes in the field that you're in, you have to go through all these steps again. If you are not constantly testing, analyzing, adding to, and removing keywords and phrases as appropriate, you'll find that PPC programs that worked well in the beginning lose effectiveness over time.

Understand that your competition will be constantly monitoring and revising *their* keyword and PPC strategies; and if you're not regularly taking advantage of all your keyword resources, you might as well hand over your customer list to your competition, because they're going to end up with all your customers anyway.

Keywords are what draw potential customers to your web site. These potential customers are either visitors who are ready to buy now or browsers whom you can motivate into making a purchase or reaching a goal conversion that you've established. Therefore, when you're building your initial keyword list, keep in mind that you're using a little educated guessing to reach highly qualified site visitors. Later, you can rely on specific keyword-related tools and analysis to replace your educated guesses with more concrete keywords and phrases that will help you reach your goals.

Forbidden search terms and poison words

When you're creating your keyword lists, remember that some search terms will result not in higher quality visitors, but instead in either a low ranking or even complete removal from search listings. These aren't just ineffective keywords and phrases. These are what are called *forbidden search terms* or *poison words*. These words are known to decrease your pages' rankings if a search engine finds them in your site's title, description, or even in the URL. These words can either kill or lower your pages in rankings.

Here's the challenge with the forbidden or poison terms: There's no central, consistent, or standard list of terms to which you can turn for guidance on the words you should not use. For example, vulgar words are usually considered to be forbidden or poison, but do a search for one of these words and you'll be returned a fair number of results. However, using these words in your site tagging as a means to rank high in a search will result in your site being buried or even omitted from search results.

Although there are no official lists of words that search engines use for filtering inappropriate keywords, you can figure out some guidelines for yourself. Two types of words have the potential to create issues for your site if you use them as keywords within the site or for PPC marketing purposes:

- Vulgar words
- Politically incorrect words (which are especially dangerous in countries such as China and North Korea where censorship is prominent)

Despite the apparent simplicity of the preceding guidelines for types of words to avoid, it's really not that simple. Many words are excluded or flagged by a search engine because they are associated with search engine spam. When a search engine suspects that a word or term is being used strictly to rank highly, even when it is included on a page full of unrelated content or links, search engines will flag that word or phrase and consider closely its relationship to other words and links on a page before making a ranking determination. The problem with that, however, is that as soon as search engines crack down on a word or phrase, another one pops up to take its place.

Don't confuse *poison words* with *keyword poison*. Keyword poison is actually the overuse of keywords on your site. When you're including keywords on your site, you should use them only as often as necessary and not one time more than that. If you throw your keywords into the site randomly, you're poisoning the search term ranks and run the risk of having your site knocked farther down in the ranking or even having it delisted completely as spam.

Finally, forbidden search terms and poison words are different from *stop words*. Stop words are those words that are so common on the Web that they are usually ignored by search engines and are completely useless in your PPC programs and other keyword marketing efforts. Here's a brief list of some of the most common stop words, though dozens more might be included:

- A
- An
- The
- But
- E-mail
- When
- Where
- How
- Free
- If
- And
- While
- Or

To illustrate how stop words are ignored in a search query, consider the search term "the sunny beach." As shown in Figure 6-7, when this search term is used on Google, the word "the" is ignored (as indicated by its solid black coloring and lack of linking). Only the words "sunny beach" are included in the search (as indicated by the darker lettering of the words and the fact that they are links).

Forecasting search volumes

After you have decided on your initial keyword list — and even after you've narrowed the list down some — you need to begin looking at the budget that you have for use with a PPC program. One way to determine how much mileage you'll get for the budget dollars that are allocated to your PPC program is to forecast search volumes. Forecasting enables you to control your marketing expenditures by predicting the performance of your keyword choices and desired positions. Simply put, for every amount invested, a company can predict a corresponding amount in sales.

FIGURE 6-7

Common words, called stop words, are ignored when searches are performed.

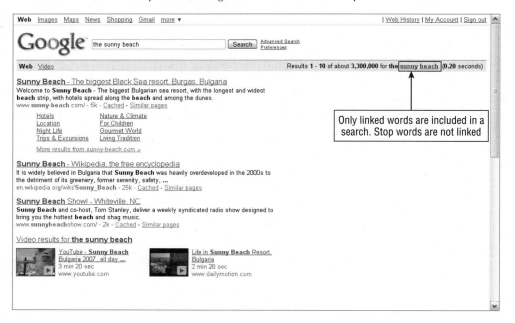

Before you get too deeply into forecasting search volumes, however, you should try to determine what rank will work best for you. A number one rank is not always the best strategy for everyone. You will probably need to balance the volume of your keyword costs (clicks) with the *cost per acquisition (CPA)*. For example, if it costs you $2 per click to reach a number one slot in search results and your budget is $100 per month, then you can only afford about 50 clicks per month (volume). These 50 clicks per month don't equate to a great volume; therefore, you might consider a slightly lower ranking in the SERPs that will generate more volume within the budget that you have to spend.

Conversely, there is an exponential decrease in the number of clicks that you'll receive as you decrease your ranking position. In general, there is about a 20 percent difference between the first and second ranking slots on a SERP. Each ranking slot below that increases the difference, so some experts estimate that being ranked first on a SERP might produce at least 10 times the traffic generated by a site ranked tenth.

Comparing this information with your budget, you can decide whether it's cost effective to stay in a lower position, or whether bidding for a higher spot would net greater click potential. Here's the bigger question, however: Ranking higher will result in much more traffic, but does the additional traffic result in more goal conversions? If not, then spending the extra money to reach the top ranking slot is probably a waste of money.

Using the same example, if you're paying $2 per click for a top ranking that generates 50 clicks per month, but only 1 percent of those visitors make a purchase from your site, you don't have a good conversion rate. But if you were to change your keywords a bit to make them more specific and then reduce your cost per click to $1 for a slightly lower rank (let's say a number three ranking slot) that generates 100 clicks per month, and those 100 clicks also resulted in a 1 percent conversion, you're still reaching more conversion goals, and therefore making more money with the lower rank than you would be with the higher rank.

How exactly do you forecast search volumes and the cost associated with those volumes? It's best to start by researching a keyword list that includes 100 to 300 keywords and phrases. Use a varied keyword list that includes both broad and specific terms; and during your research, use both personal investigation and keyword selection tools to determine the click volume and the cost per click for each of those terms. Using this information, you can then estimate search volumes and the cost of those search volumes, but additionally you can estimate other performance metrics that will help you to determine both the cost and the value of the keywords that you've selected. Those additional metrics include the following:

- Projected impressions
- Estimated click-through rate (CTR)
- Estimated clicks per month
- Average cost per click (CPC)
- Estimated budget requirements

Using this information, you can increase the effectiveness of the budget that you invest in your PPC program. For instance, keywords with lower CPC rates typically have less competition than more expensive ones. If you can select some of these keywords that are more efficient for creating goal conversions, then you've invested less in your PPC program for better results.

As you're estimating your search volumes and the budget that you'll invest in your PPC program, understand that all these projections are based on historical data. This means that you should collect data about your keywords and use it to improve your PPC program effectiveness over time. Additionally, many other factors — seasonal changes, sales, competition, and even landing pages — can affect your actual performance results. This is yet another reason you should continuously monitor and revise your keywords and phrases and your PPC marketing efforts.

Forecasting search volumes and budget considerations is just the first step toward creating a PPC program that both meets your needs and fits within your budget. In addition to initial forecasting, you also need to conduct ongoing *keyword testing*.

Keyword testing is the process by which you examine keywords and how many searches they're included in, as well as the competition for those keywords. Once you've completed that research, you begin to implement your keywords on your site very slowly, monitoring the results of your site traffic and goal conversions after each new word or set of words is added.

It's a time-consuming activity, but keyword testing has the potential to improve your PPC program results if you take the time do it properly. Through careful testing, you can learn what your most effective keywords are; and then you can use those keywords to improve your position and impressions.

One way to start the testing process is by understanding exactly what you are testing for. Are you testing to see how effective your most recent ad copy is? How do landing pages hold up in attracting and keeping site visitors? If those landing pages are experiencing a lot of *bounces*, you may need to work with them to create more stickiness. Other questions you may want to answer to ensure you understand what you're testing for include the following: Are visitors reaching goal conversions? Does ad placement really make a difference?

As you're considering keyword testing, you may decide that you just don't have time to efficiently forecast your PPC traffic. However, not taking the time to do the testing can result in wasted budget dollars. Adding keywords doesn't mean that they, or a PPC program, will be effective. It's necessary to conduct the proper testing to ensure that your PPC program is as efficient and effective as possible.

Finalizing your keyword list

A lot of effort has gone into creating, researching, and narrowing your keyword list so far. Now it's time to finalize that list and begin putting your keywords and your PPC programs to work for you.

Of course, "finalizing" your keyword list doesn't really mean that it's completely final. As you've learned already, a keyword list (as it applies to PPC programs) is an ongoing element in your PPC program. You should be continuously changing and updating your keyword list — and this can be a very time-consuming process.

The Long Tail of Search

The Long Tail of search (covered in Chapter 2) is a concept described by Chris Anderson, an editor at *Wired* magazine. It refers to the less-competitive keywords — usually three- to five-word phrases — that site visitors use to find web sites. The idea of less-competitive keywords and phrases relates to the more specific terms that you can use to describe the products, services,

continued

continued

or information available on your site. The basic idea of the Long Tail of search is that you begin any search with a very broad term. For example, if you're searching for Italian dinner recipes, that term is too broad to return a manageable number of useful results.

Using the Long Tail theory, more precise and less common keywords and phrases are usually the most effective. These are located at the end of a long tail of possible words. Normally, a product site lands visitors by two types of keywords and phrases:

- General keywords and phrases
- Long Tail keywords and phrases, such as specific product names

The magnificence of the Long Tail of search is that you don't know how effective it is until you have optimized your site and have some content on your site to attract it. Sure, there will be some Long Tail queries in your logs, but only a fraction of what could be there.

To capture the Long Tail of search, you need to create a rich foundation of content. The tricky part is knowing what content to create. If your focus is on providing value to your customers, it will be easier for you. You need to create content that's not only relevant to your product or service, but also related to your product or service, even if the relationship is remote. You do this because you need to target not only people who know about you and your product, or who know just what they need — that's pretty simple — but also people who have the same problems as your target audience and who are looking for a solution.

However, there are a few things that you can do to ensure that your final keyword list is the most effective and up-to-date list available to you:

- Remove all unrelated search terms from your list. An unrelated term is one that doesn't apply to your site in any way. You may have words or phrases on your list for which you have no web site content at all. You have two options here: Either create new content specifically for those words, or just discard the words in favor of better-targeted and more efficient PPC marketing.

- Remove words for which the competition is too high. Unless you have an unlimited budget for your PPC program, you should eliminate keywords for which the competition is fierce. You won't gain a number one slot by eliminating broad terms, but you may find that your job in optimizing your site becomes much easier.

- Remove any keywords that your potential audience is likely to overlook or not use at all. You can usually tell what types of keywords your potential visitor will use when searching for your site, service, or product. This also means you should remove any words that are industry buzzwords but that someone outside of the industry might not consider using.

After you've narrowed your words to the most relevant keywords and phrases with an acceptable amount of competition, it's time to start putting those keywords to work. Placing the keywords in the right place and using them properly will go a long way toward making your PPC program successful. You'll learn all about that in Chapter 7.

Writing Ad Descriptions

Keywords and PPC programs are just the beginning of your PPC campaign. Once you have the keywords that you plan to use, you have to begin putting them to work, and creating PPC ads is one way to do that. Creating a PPC ad isn't usually too difficult. Each search engine or PPC company does it differently, but most offer tutorials that walk you quickly through the ad process.

There's a difference, however, between creating an ad and creating a great ad. Anyone can create an ad; but if you really want to get the most from your PPC program, you need to create great ad descriptions that quickly arouse the interest of potential visitors and entice them to visit your site. That's not always an easy task, and it can be downright difficult.

With a typical search engine description, the object is to entice as much traffic to a site as possible in the hope of converting that traffic into customers. PPC requires a little a different approach. You don't want to pay for unlikely prospects, so the description used in your PPC ads should be designed to eliminate casual surfers who are just window shopping, while attracting those who want nothing more than to buy your products, hire your services, or sign up for your newsletter. For this reason, your PPC ad description should describe exactly what your business offers. At the same time, proven marketing copy techniques should be employed to ensure that the description is enticing enough to attract ideal prospects.

Relevancy is the name of the game when it comes to copywriting for paid listings, not only for your potential customers, but increasingly to meet the stringent requirements of the search engines themselves. Including your keyword in the title and description of your listing can increase your click-through rate, and relevant listings are rewarded not only with more clicks from consumers, but also with a higher position on SERPs.

Writing ad copy for search engine listings is not only about knowing the right formula for creating a good ad. Following good copywriting guidelines gets you past tough search engine editors and in front of potential consumers. With that in mind, here are some suggestions for writing great ad copy:

- **Use your keywords:** Including your keywords in your advertisements can increase the efficiency of those ads. Additionally, if you're using the keywords that you've selected, then your ads are likely to appear in conjunction with related topics, making it easier for you to entice traffic.

- **Qualify your traffic:** Creating an advertisement that people will click on is not enough. You must create an ad for the *right* people to click on. Not all traffic is equal. Even people who search with the same phrase might have different needs. Your ad should appeal to your target audience while signaling to others that your business would not be a good fit for their differing needs.

■ **Include a feature and benefit in your ad description:** Include at least one of each for the product or services that you're advertising with the PPC program. Generally, you'll have very little space in which to include a description, so choose the words that you plan to use very carefully.

■ **Use a call to action:** Too often, advertisements are created without including a call to action; but studies show that including a call to action will increase your conversion rates, whereas ads that do not contain a call to action tend to perform less efficiently and effectively than those that include it.

■ **Stand out:** Many PPC advertisers in the same business as yours will have very similar PPC advertisements. If you can create ads that stand out from these other, often more generic ads, you have a much better chance of achieving an effective PPC program. It is well worth your time to spend some planning hours creating an ad that helps you stand out from the crowd.

Monitoring and Analyzing Results

It's been mentioned several times in this chapter, but it bears repeating again: You're not finished with your PPC campaign after you have it set up. PPC is not a one-shot program you can set up and then walk away from and expect to work properly. Crucial to the success of any PPC campaign is that it be monitored regularly, because positions can and do change every day. Apart from position monitoring, it is also important to track and analyze the effectiveness of individual keyword phrases on a monthly basis. Viewing click-through rates and studying visitor habits can provide valuable insight into their motivations and habits, and help you further refine your PPC program.

These monitoring and analyzing activities must be ongoing. It's not enough to say, "I'll check on this PPC program next month." Monitoring and analyzing PPC results should become part of your daily routine. In some cases, your rank in a search engine can change very rapidly. If you're focused on your PPC program, however, you'll likely find far more success (or at least the potential for success) if you regularly monitor and analyze the program's results.

Chapter 7

Maximizing Pay-per-Click Strategies

Pay-per-click can be a useful tool in SEO, but to be truly useful you must use keywords correctly on your web site. If you don't, you can spend a ton of money on PPC advertisements that perform in a mediocre way at best. Including the right keywords in the right places is essential for the best possible performance of your keyword ads, as well as for your SEO.

How do you know where to put your keywords? In some places, keywords work themselves in naturally. Text is a good example of that. If you're true to the concept and subject of your site, a certain number of automatic keyword placements within the text will happen; but there are other places, on the back side of a web page that visitors never see, where keywords are essential.

Using them correctly in those places can mean the difference between a site that performs well in search engine rankings and one that doesn't. It can also make a huge difference in the success of PPC advertisements. It all comes down to the keywords, so you must know how to use them well.

IN THIS CHAPTER

Understanding keyword placement

Alt and other tags and attributes

URLs and filenames

Writing keyword advertisement text

Creating great landing pages

Understanding and using A/B testing

Avoiding keyword stuffing

Understanding Keyword Placement

Having the right keywords is far more than just ownership. Once you have them, you have to use them properly in order to gain any value from them at all. For example, you might know the hottest keyword on the Internet, but if you don't use that keyword on your web site properly, it won't do you much good at all.

Once you've developed the perfect list of keywords, what are you supposed to do with them? In previous chapters, you've heard a little about the tags, text, and links where you can use your keywords, but it's not as simple as just throwing a keyword in here and there. You must know where and how to place them on your site properly so that search engines will interpret them properly and take notice of your web site.

Alt Attributes and Other Tags

You've probably heard the term *alt tags* at least once or twice. It's been mentioned more than once in this book — especially in Chapter 4 where a basic description of how these tags are used was discussed. Of course, hearing the term and understanding how it works are two different things, so let's dig a little deeper into the information you might need about alt tags.

The first thing you should understand about alt tags is that they're not really *tags* at all. Rather, the proper name for these items is *alt attributes*. The term *attributes* is used because these are (more accurately) different attributes that enhance the tags you use on your web site. Alt, which stands for alternative, is a specific type of attribute that refers specifically to the alternative text you may see in place of graphics.

Most people who are not professional web designers use the terms *tags* and *attributes* interchangeably. That's why you often see alt attributes referred to as alt tags.

Alt attributes aren't a major SEO element. In fact, these attributes are designed more for screen readers than anything else. They're used to replace images, tables, or other elements of a web page that don't translate well when read by a screen reader. If used properly, however, you can take advantage of alt attributes to add keywords to your web pages. Just remember that you're designing this particular element of your page specifically for visitors, not search engines.

To make them as useful as possible, alt attributes should *briefly* describe the image or element they are replacing. How briefly is the source of much debate. Some experts say only 5 to 10 words, others say as many as 125 characters (which can equal more than 10 words if they're not too long).

Ideally, you should keep your alt attributes to between 50 and 125 characters, using only the words that are necessary to describe what visitors with images turned off or visitors who are using screen readers can't see. Your alt attributes are not the place to tell your story; rather, they are a place to let your reader know what was there and how it applies to the story. Choose your words wisely, and make them powerful. And if you can include keywords in the process, great; if not, it's not the end of the world and probably won't have a negative impact on your search engine rankings.

An example of an alt tag might be the description of a picture of the Mona Lisa on your web site. Your alt tag, then, should look like this:

```
Alt="Mona Lisa"
```

The alt tag usually falls at the end of the image tag. An image tag might look something like this:

```
<img width="100"
height="100"
src="monalisa.jpg"
alt="Mona Lisa">
```

The image code breaks down as follows:

`<img width="100"`: The width (in pixels) of the image

`Height="100"`: The height (in pixels) of the image

`Src="monalisa.jpg"`: The source of the image file

`Alt="Mona Lisa">`: The alternative text that's displayed when the image is not

One more note about alt tags: To be really effective, these tags should be used for every single image on your web site. That could become an arduous task if your site hasn't been properly coded to start with (and depending on the number of images that you have on your site). However, the addition of these tags should be advantageous to your SEO efforts as long as you don't overstep the unspoken boundaries of alt tags.

Alt tags in graphic links

Until this point, you've heard that alternative text for graphics (or graphic links) should always be included in your web pages. Now is when you find out the exceptions to that rule. Alternative text, in the form of alt tags, is very useful in circumstances where visitors to your site are using text-only browsers, when those visitors have graphic capabilities turned off on their browsers, or when they use screen readers to read your web pages to them. That's what makes alt tags so important.

However, if your web site features a lot of repetitive images, it might be redundant for you to use the same alt tag repeatedly. Furthermore, when you're using graphics (such as pictures and clip art) as links, visitors will quickly tire of seeing `alt="hyperlink"`. Unless the graphics used on your page and in your links contain information that is vitally important to your web site, you can usually use one instance of a descriptive alt tag, and then for each repetitive picture use an empty alt tag: `alt=""`.

If you're using alternative tags for graphic links, then you can differentiate each one by using the web site address that you're linking to in the alt tag. However, don't use web addresses that string on for three or four lines. Instead, use a basic web address (`www.basicaddress.com`). For example, Figure 7-1 shows what graphic links look like without alt text, and what both graphic links and graphics look like with alt text.

You should avoid using overly long alt tags, no matter what type of graphic you're using them with. A good rule is that your alt tag should be no more than one line long; and if you can create effective, shorter tags, that's much better.

FIGURE 7-1

Alt text helps visitors who don't have or don't allow graphics displays, and those with screen readers.

Graphic files without alt text   All text for both a graphic and a link

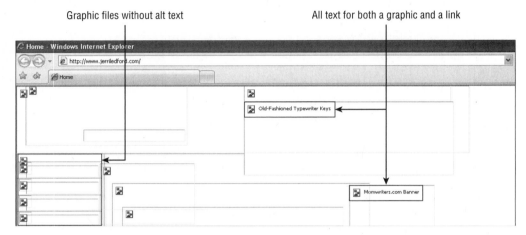

If an image on your site is strictly text — for example, a company logo that is stylized text — one way to handle it would be to create stylized text using a style sheet to suggest some particular properties through typeface, size, or color. For example, using the CSS rule strong, the code for your text might look like this:

```
{ background: #ffc none; color: #060; font-weight: normal;
font-family: "Comic Sans MS", Western, fantasy; }
```

The problem with creating stylized text in place of a text-only graphic is that sometimes it just doesn't work as well. The company logo that was mentioned earlier *might* be acceptable in a text-only format, but only if the logo was designed that way to start with. If the logo has any graphic element in it at all, even though it is text, changing the display to a nongraphic style would cause you to lose the brand recognition that comes with the logo.

Another problem that you may run into when creating alt tags is bulleted lists that contain decorative (graphic) bullets. One way to handle alt text for bullet images is to write the tag using an asterisk or a dash to indicate each new bullet point, like this

```
alt="*"
```

or

```
alt="-"
```

Your other alternative is to use an alt tag that actually describes the graphic used for the bullet point:

```
Alt="black musical note"
```

Alt tags, whether you're using them in graphical links or just in place of graphics, are one way for people who can't see your images to understand your site. Many times, graphics play a large part in how your site displays; but if you're using them simply to repeat keywords on your web page, without providing information that replaces the graphic, avoiding them is the best option.

Aside from alt attributes, several different tags and attributes are used when placing keywords into the coding of your web site. This chapter covers five of them, but there are far more attributes on a typical web page. For example, although it's not covered in this chapter, bgcolor is an attribute that's often used on a web page to specify the background color of the page.

Title tags

Title tags are perhaps the most important SEO tags for any web site, and if you can place your keywords in the beginning of the title tag, that greatly improves the effectiveness of those tags. The maximum number of characters allowed by most search engines for title length varies. For example, Google allows up to 66 characters (including spaces) for title tags, whereas Yahoo! allows up to 120. If your title tags exceed those limits, they'll be truncated to fit into the maximum space allowed.

To ensure that you're getting the most value for the character limitations of title tags, the World Wide Web Consortium (W3C) recommends that web site designers keep their titles 64 characters or less in length. You can do that, or you can monkey around with them to develop titles that work with both Google and Yahoo! (and any other search engine).

The way to do that is to create a title that's as understandable at 66 characters as it is at 120 characters. That often takes a lot of consideration for the best phrasing, but it can be done. It's up to you whether you want to put time into that effort. Well-written, 66-character titles can be just as effective as longer titles.

Search engine spiders use these title tags as the main source for determining the web-page topic. Spiders or crawlers examine the title, and the words used in it are then translated into the topic of the page. That's one reason it's always best to use your keywords in your page title, and to use them as close to the beginning of the title as possible. The text included in the title tag is also the text that will appear in SERPs as the linked title on which users will click to access your page.

For example, suppose you have an informational web site that provides guidelines for choosing retirement funds. If the most important keywords for your web site are "retirement funding" and "retirement income," then a page title (which is the text used in the title tag) along the lines of "Retirement Funding Options to Increase Income" is highly relevant to the topic of the site. As spiders crawl your site, because the title tag is the first element encountered, the spider will read it and then examine your site, as well as the keywords used in other places on your site (which you'll learn about shortly), to determine how relevant the title is to the content of the site.

That's why it's vitally important to target the most critical keywords in the title tag. You may use 20 keywords on your web page, but two or three of those keywords (or even just a single phase) are the most important keywords you've selected. These are the keywords that should be used in your title tag.

Another important practice to remember when using title tags in your web site design is to create a unique title for every page in the site. Make the title as descriptive as possible — and, again, use the most important or effective keywords you've selected for the page, because the words you use in your title tag will appear in the reverse title bar, or the tab title, of your web browser, as shown in Figure 7-2.

FIGURE 7-2

The text within the title tag appears in the reverse title bar, or the tab title, of your web browser.

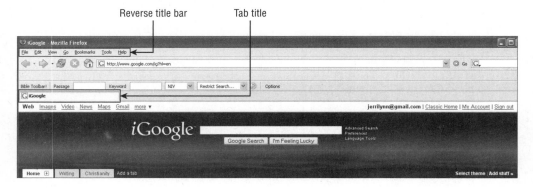

Now that you know why you should use a title tag, the next questions to answer are what exactly does a title tag look like, and where do you use it?

The best way to learn where you should place your title tag is to look at the source code for other web sites. As Figure 7-3 shows, the title tag is located within the head tag, along with the meta description tag and the meta keyword tag.

FIGURE 7-3

The title tag is located within the head tag, along with the meta description and meta keyword tags.

Opening head tag   Title tag

This illustration is taken from the actual source code for a real web site. However, it's difficult to see exactly how the title tag comes between the opening and closing head tags, so here's a view that's a little more simplistic:

```
<HEAD>
<TITLE> Home </TITLE>
<META name="description" content="Technology for consumers.">
<META name="keywords" content="identity theft, voip,
jerri ledford, books, technology, cybersecurity, spam, phishing,
pharming, trojans, computer virus, malware, cyberstalking,
cyberharrassment, security">
</HEAD>
```

If you take this code apart line by line, here's what you have:

<HEAD>: This is the opening head tag.

`<TITLE> Home </TITLE>`: This is the title tag, including both the opening code and the closing code.

`<META name="description" content="Technology for consumers.">`: This is the meta description tag, where you place a brief description of your site, keywords included.

`<META name="keywords" content="identity theft, voip, jerri ledford, books, technology, cybersecurity, spam, phishing, pharming, trojans, computer virus, malware, cyberstalking, cyberharrassment, security">`: This tag is where you list the keywords that you're using to describe your site. These could be either organic or purchased keywords.

`</HEAD>`: This is the closing head tag. It indicates that the information in the header of the page has ended.

The head tags and title tags shown here are considered *container tags*. Container tags act as a bucket into which certain information can be dumped. For the head tag, it *contains* the header information; for the title tag, it *contains* the title information. It's important that the title tag appear somewhere within the *opening tag* and *closing tag* of the header. If the title tag is located in other places in your web site coding, it won't render properly, and you'll be left with a web site that doesn't behave the way that you expect it to.

When creating your title tags, remember that the best title tags are those that contain targeted keywords, that help develop the brand for the site, and that are both concise and attention grabbing. Usually, the text included between the opening and closing title tags also translates into the linked text that is displayed in search engine rankings. In other words, the title tag provides the first (and sometimes only) impression of your web page. It can either draw in visitors or cause searchers to choose a different search result altogether.

Meta description tags

Meta description tags are also important for every page on your web site. The text beneath the linked title in search results (shown in Figure 7-4) comes directly from the information included in the meta description tag.

There's a lot of debate regarding the value of the meta description tag. Most believe that search engines don't give these tags any special weight beyond relevance — the meta description tag must include information that's relevant to your web site.

The catch with meta description tags is that they work differently for different search engines. For example, Google gives very little weight to meta descriptions. Instead, the Google search engine looks at the text on a page. In addition, on the SERPs, Google doesn't always display the meta description text either. What does show is the content surrounding the instance of the keyword on your site. Google calls this a *snippet*.

The Yahoo! search engine, however, does put weight on meta description text, and it uses that text directly under the web site link on SERPs.

FIGURE 7-4

In some search engine results, the text displayed below the title comes from the meta description tag.

Meta description text

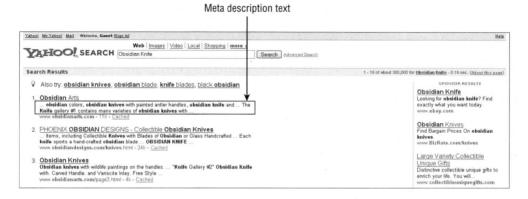

What does this all mean to you? First, it means that your meta description tag isn't the most important piece of coding on your web page. Second, it also means that you don't want to skip over the meta description tag, because some search engines actually do use it, and that bit of text could be what leads visitors to your web site when they find your site in search engine rankings.

In summary, you should include the meta description tag on each page of your web site using the following guidelines:

- Different search engines allow different description text lengths. A good rule of thumb is to keep your descriptions to around 25 to 30 words, or about 150 characters. That's about enough space for one to two descriptive sentences; anything more than that will likely be cut off in the search results display anyway.

- Every page in your web site should include its own unique meta description tag. Even if a search engine isn't using the text to rank your site, it may still display that text to searchers; and it's always better to have it, in the event that the searcher sees it, rather than the searcher being presented with nothing more than the title of your page or completely irrelevant text that does nothing to pique the searcher's interest.

- Meta description tags should include keywords with high levels of importance or effectiveness. Use only your most important keywords in your description tags. Even if the search engine doesn't count these words for ranking purposes (and keep in mind that some might), having the most relevant keywords means that searchers can determine exactly what the page is about, which helps them decide to swing over to your site to find what they're looking for.

- Meta description text should not be the same as the text included in the title tag. Nor should it be the same as the first paragraph of text on a page or the teaser for the page (if you use one). Meta description text should be unique, powerful text similar to what is used in advertisements.

Like the title tag, the meta description tag belongs inside the <Head> </Head> section of your web pages. Ordinarily, web site designers include the meta description tag after the title tag and before the meta keywords tag, but that's not a practice set in stone. As long as the meta description tag appears between the opening and closing head tags, it will be read by crawlers as it should be.

When creating your meta description tag, this is what it should look like:

```
<META name="description" content="Your description goes here.">
```

For example, the meta description tag that I might use for my personal web site would look like this:

```
<META name="description" content="Technology for consumers.">
```

It's important to note that not everyone agrees on the value of the meta description tag. However, it takes very little time to include this tag (or any of the tags included in this section of the book) in your web site coding; therefore, including it should be a given. As with many different strategies in SEO, these tags are not a sure thing, and they do not represent an absolute solution to ensuring that your site ranks well. Nonetheless, they are one more element that could affect your ranking, so including them should be automatic.

Anchor text

Anchor text is probably one of the most important elements of keyword use. Anchor text is text found on a given web site that appears to be a hyperlink. Figure 7-5 illustrates how anchor text appears on a page.

Chances are good that you see anchor text every day. In fact, anchor text has become such a major inclusion on web pages that companies often use it without any thought as to how it could affect their search engine rankings.

Anchor text has already been covered in Chapter 4, but how you use it is crucial because it is one of the most important search engine ranking factors. When a search engine looks at your web page, it automatically follows all the links that you have on the page. If those links (or even a large portion of those links) are text-based links, that's even better, because then the search engine sees not just the link to another page, but also your keywords. It's not enough just to make all your links text based, however. There's a fine art to taking advantage of the power of anchor text.

The first thing you should understand is that there are two kinds of anchor texts: yours and everyone else's. I'm not being facetious here. It really is important that you consider not only how you link with other people, but also how they will link back to you. For example, if you do a Google search for the term "click," you'll find that the Adobe web site is at or near the very top of the list. This isn't because Adobe loaded down their web site with the keyword "click."

FIGURE 7-5

Anchor text is the linked text on a web page. It plays a large part in determining your search engine ranking.

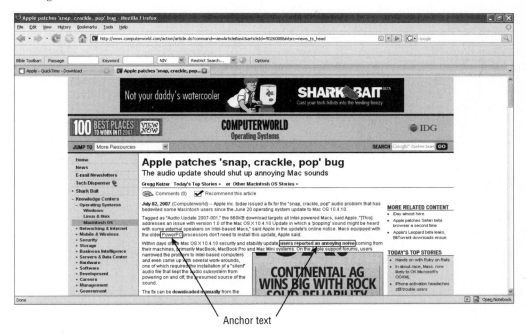

Anchor text

What has actually happened is that many people link to the Adobe PDF reader using the word "click" in their anchor text. This isn't hard to believe, because most web sites that offer downloadable PDF files usually include a text link to "Click here to download" or something similar.

As you can see, it's not just your own anchor text that matters. How your site is included in others' anchor text is also important. We'll come back to how other people link to you. For now, consider how you use anchor text in your web site. As we've already established, anchor text is the linked text on your web site. This text can be linked either to other pages within your own web site or it can be linked to other web sites that are relevant to the content of your site. That's the real key to why anchor text can be so powerful — the relevance of the link and the words used to create the link.

When a search engine crawls your site, it's looking at several different factors:

■ The topic of the site as indicated by the words used in the text

■ The links leading away from the site

■ The links leading into the site

Of course, these aren't the only factors that matter, but they're among the top-ranking factors, because how these elements are handled determines how user-friendly (and authentic) your site is. Therefore, if your site caters to gourmet cooks, then the information on your site might include articles about gourmet techniques, gourmet recipes, and links to web sites where site visitors can purchase gourmet ingredients or tools.

When the crawler examines your site, it's going to see that the topic of the site is gourmet cooking (which will be determined by the keywords you use in the site text). Then it's going to follow all the links on your site. If those links happen to be text-based links that use your keywords, and they lead to web sites that are relevant to the topic of your site, you're going to score well with the search engine crawler. The result is that you'll appear higher in SERPs than you would if you didn't have relevant keywords in your text and links.

You should use care when creating anchor text links, however. If you use the wrong words, then you won't get nearly the mileage that you need from the links. One mistake some web site owners make is to create web pages with the anchor text "click here." That phrase is not only completely overused and largely ignored by web crawlers, but it's also in no way related to the content of the site. When a crawler examines the anchor text, it doesn't see relevant keywords, even if the links lead to web sites that are related to the content of the site. Think of your anchor text as a chance to showcase the relationships you have with related companies.

What works best is to use as many of the keywords as you can from the list of relevant keywords that you developed during the planning process. Going back to our gourmet cooking example, if you use an anchor text link that reads "Gourmet Ingredients" and links to a web site that sells gourmet foods, a search engine sees both your key phrase (Gourmet Ingredients) and a link that leads to a web site that sells gourmet ingredients. Therefore, for the effort of creating that small piece of anchor text, you not only have a valid reason to use your keywords and phrases, but you also have a link that leads to a relevant web site.

If you were adding the anchor text for Gourmet Ingredients to your web page, you must add a piece of HTML like the following in each spot where you want the anchor text to appear:

```
<a href="http://www.gourmetingredientslink.com">GourmetIngredients</a>
```

Then, on your web site, the user sees what is shown in Figure 7-6.

One more strategy for anchor text that you should consider is varying the anchor text. When you repeat the same anchor text multiple times on a given web page, it begins to lose its effectiveness, and in fact it can cause a search engine crawler to rank your site lower in the SERPs. It's much more effective to use multiple keywords and phrases as anchor text on a web page. This enables you to vary the anchor text but maintain a consistency in the keywords and phrases you use.

The other type of anchor text is that which others use to link back to your site. This anchor text is often overlooked as an SEO strategy, but it's one of the most effective types of optimization that you can use. Here's an example: One savvy marketer on the Internet decided to see how quickly he could make his site rank high in the Google SERPs. He used anchor text links on his page, and then solicited *reciprocal links* based on highly targeted keywords and phrases that were relevant to his site. The result? Within four days, the web site had shot to the number four position in the Google SERPs.

FIGURE 7-6

Anchor text may also be called text links.

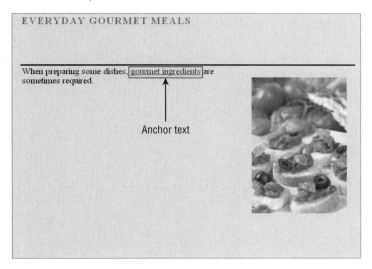

There are two elements to consider in this anecdote. The first is that the web site owner sought reciprocal links. These are links to your page from another web site, in return for your site linking to them. The reciprocal links are most effective when they come from sites that are relevant to your web site; but most often, you'll have to seek the links out. Furthermore, in order to take advantage of all the value of reciprocal links, you also need to ensure that your site is linked to in a certain way. Instead of having another site just link to your main page, it's most effective to provide a potential linking site with the code that includes the anchor text you want to use.

The second element of the anecdote to which you should pay special attention is that the links used by the webmaster were highly targeted keywords. In order to learn which keywords will be most effective for your site, you should refer to your keyword research. The keywords that are searched for most often but are as narrowly related to your site as possible are the keywords that you should consider using in your anchor text. The whole point of anchor text is to optimize your site to gain higher search engine rankings, which in turn brings visitors to your site.

How often should you use anchor text on a web page? That's one of those magic numbers that no one really knows for sure. Different people will tell you different things. Some say no more than two or three times, others say no fewer than 10 or 12 times. A good rule of thumb is to use anchor text as many times as you can justify its use. Don't load your content with anchor text just to have the links, but if you have a relevant link that can be included, don't skip it just because you've used anchor text five other times on the page.

Determining what anchor text is essential and what isn't is a personal decision. However, if you're using a good analytics program that tracks the links on your web pages, you should be able to determine which anchor text links are most effective and how using them on a page affects your normal traffic flow. Anchor text is a good way to improve your search engine ranking, but as you've seen many times before in this book, your web pages should be designed with the user in mind.

One more note about anchor text before moving on. One of the most effective ways to use anchor text is in *dynamic content*. Dynamic content is content that changes regularly. Most often, that means blogs. Anchor text is well suited to blogs that change daily or weekly. This is fresh content (which is also a plus for improving your search engine rankings). It gives you an opportunity to change your anchor text regularly. Search engine crawlers get bored, too, and if you can provide them with dynamic content that contains relevant anchor text, those crawlers will look on you with favor.

WARNING One anchor text tactic to avoid is *Google bombing* (or *link bombing*). Google bombing refers to the methods used by black-hat SEOs to artificially inflate their web site ranking by connecting an unrelated keyword to a specific web site. For Google bombing to work, more than one web site designer must be willing to participate in a link exchange that will then grow exponentially because of the "apparent" popularity of the site.

Header tag content

Another attribute that should be included in web site design is the *header tag*. These header tags are a bit different from the head tags discussed earlier in this chapter that indicate the heading of your pages. Instead, these are the attributes that set up the different levels of headings and subheadings on your web site. There can be as many as six different levels of headings, though most web sites typically use four at most.

The debate about the value of header tags in SEO is a long-standing one. Some feel that header tags have zero value for impressing search engines regarding the importance of text on a page, whereas others feel that header tags are absolute necessities if you plan to put emphasis on certain keywords in the headings and subheadings of your web site.

The truth probably falls somewhere between the two points of view. Looking at header tags from a strictly design point of view, you should absolutely include them in your site.

Headers indicate to users the topic of a page and what the segments of body text are about. They also give readers an idea of what they should be taking away from the content they're reading. For example, if you have a web site that contains an article outlining all the medical reasons why readers should purchase a new mattress, then your level-one header would likely be the title of the article. The level-two headers indicate the main subheadings within the article, and the level-three headers indicate the sub-subheadings. It might look something like this:

Losing Sleep Over Poor Sleep Habits?

Your Mattress Could Keep You Awake

Too Firm?

Too Soft?

Choosing the Right Mattress

That heading hierarchy reads like this:

H1: (Page Topic) Losing Sleep Over Poor Sleep Habits?

H2: (Main Topic) Your Mattress Could Keep You Awake

H3: (Sub Topic) Too Firm?

H3: (Sub Topic) Too Soft?

H2: (Main Topic) Choosing the Right Mattress

Headings on a web page behave the same way that headings on a page behave. They denote important information and enable users to quickly skim the page to find the information they're seeking. On the Internet, that's vitally important, because site visitors don't always read all the text on a page.

More important, header tags on a web page give you an opportunity to use your most important keywords in a contextually appropriate manner. Specifically, search engine crawlers take into consideration the text within a header tag and how it fits with the body text around it (which is discussed in the next section). Again, looking at the different levels of headings, first-level headings should contain the most important keywords on your web page, assuming they can be used naturally within the heading.

It's important to make that distinction — keywords should work in your headings. If they don't, avoid using them. It's okay to include headings that contain no keywords at all. What's most important is that the headers help readers to easily read the content in which the headings are included.

If you're using your most important keywords in level-one headings, then lower-level headings (levels two through six) should contain decreasingly important keywords.

Don't fall for the erroneous assumption that because level-one headings contain your most important keywords, you should use them all over your web pages. It doesn't work that way. Most SEOs and web-design experts will tell you that you shouldn't use a level-one heading on your web page more than once. Using it more could cause a search engine crawler to decide that you're spamming the search engine, which will result in lowered rankings and might even cause your web site to be delisted from search results entirely.

It also doesn't follow that because level-one headings are important you should make them long, rambling monstrosities. A good rule of thumb is to keep your headings, no matter what level they are, between five and ten words in length. You don't want them too short, because then they're useless for scanning, but too long has the same effect. As with so many things SEO, use only the number of words that you absolutely need to get your point across and not a single word more.

The heading tags are similar in format to other tags that you've examined to this point:

```
<H1>Header 1</H1>
<H2>Header 2</H2>
<H3>Header 3</H3>
<H4>Header 4</H4>
<H5>Header 5</H5>
<H6>Header 6</H6>
```

Header tags should be included immediately before the body-text tags of your site, and the text of the header goes in between the opening and closing tags. These are automatically sized headings, though you can change the size of the headings using *cascading style sheets (CSS)*. Cascading style sheets are a language that enables you to create your web site using a specific style. For example, in some programs you can create a web site using a preset theme. This theme usually contains all the CSS information needed to ensure that the design of the site — from text to layout — is consistent across all pages of the site.

If you're manually coding your web site (writing the HTML yourself, instead of using pre-designed sites from an application such as Microsoft FrontPage or Adobe Dreamweaver), you would use CSS to ensure that your site is consistent from page to page. The nice aspect of CSS is that you can change your header sizes to suit your needs.

Unfortunately, some less-than-honest SEOs have determined that CSS can be used to artificially implant header tags into a web site in a way that doesn't actually change the size of the text included in the header tag. However, using this method to fool search crawlers into seeing more headings than are actually on a page could backfire, leaving you much lower in the rankings than you would prefer to be.

Body text

Body text is the text that is visible to readers of your site but not included in a header. When you look at the pages of this book, for example, the text that's between headings is the body text. It's the same for web pages.

Although you've already used keywords in several places on your web site, body text is another place where you'll want to include your keywords when possible. There is no hard-and-fast rule about the number of times that your keywords should appear on a page, but a good rule of thumb is to use them about once every paragraph or two, with the condition that they make sense in the content of the site.

What many people who are optimizing their sites don't realize is that all the strategies for SEO can be overdone, including the use of keywords in the body text of your site. You should use these words regularly in your text, but don't use them out of context or just as a ploy to improve your search engine standings. If the keywords don't work in the normal flow of the text on the page, don't include them. Nonsense will gain you no points at all with search engine crawlers.

Body text should be placed into your web site using the body-text tags: `<body>`Insert Body Text`</body>`. These are not the only body-text tags that you'll use, however. In addition to the tags that indicate where your body text begins and ends, there are also tags that indicate special formatting in text. Those tags are as follows:

```
<b>Bold</b>
<i>Italics</i>
<strong>Strongly Emphasized</strong>
<em>Emphasis</em>
<li>New Line in List</li>
```

Each of these tags indicates special formatting for the word or phrase within the opening and closing tags, and the special emphasis makes a search engine crawler take notice of those words. Therefore, try to use keywords within those tags if possible. However, the same rule that applies to body text applies to these formatting options: Only use keywords where appropriate, and avoid stuffing keywords into your site simply to improve your search engine rankings. If you use those tactics, they will likely fail.

Making your web site's body text visible (or readable) to search engine crawlers isn't all that complicated. Even so, many site designers still struggle with the issue, because certain text styles cannot be indexed by search engines. These styles are often used on web sites in an effort to improve the appearance of the site. Some of the text visibility issues that site designers contend with include the following:

- Text embedded in JavaScript applications or Macromedia Flash files
- Text contained in image files (including those with the extensions .jpg, .gif, .png, and .bmp).
- Text that is accessible only on a submission form or another portion of the page that requires some action or interaction with the user

If search engine crawlers can't see your web site text, they can't index that content for visitors to find. Therefore, having *seeable* content is essential to ranking well and getting properly indexed. In some cases, you must use a graphic, a special type of formatting such as JavaScript or Flash, or even forms that contain text. If you must use these unreadable forms of text, try to optimize your site by using keywords in headings, title tags, URLs, and alt tags on the page. Just remember that you shouldn't go overboard with embedding keywords into headings or other tags.

WARNING Never try to hide text on your site in an attempt to fool search engine crawlers into thinking your site is something it's not. If you try to include text on your site that's the same color as the background, or if you use other types of CSS tricks, you run the risk of being detected by search engine crawlers — and even if those crawlers don't detect your trickery, it's just a matter of time before some competitor or even one of your users discovers your dishonesty and reports your actions.

Writing well for search engines is both an art and a science, and is covered in more depth in Chapter 13.

URLs and Filenames

The URL (Universal Resource Locator) is the literal address of your web site on the Internet. It's the address that site visitors type into their browser's address bar to reach you, or in some cases it's the link those users click to find you.

Ideally, your URL should be as descriptive as possible without being long and hard to remember. As you've already learned, a URL such as `www.atopkeyword.com` is much more effective than a URL such as `www.partofyourcompanynameonline.com`.

But there is more to a URL than just the base name. For example, your site's structure probably has several levels of pages and files. Therefore, the base URL will include a path to additional pages and folders. Unfortunately, if you have a site that has hundreds of pages or dynamic content, you could end up with a URL that looks like this:
`http://www.yoursite.com/o/ASIN/B00023K9TC/ref=s9_asin_title_1-1966_p/ 102-8946296-2020168?pf_rd_m=ATVPDKIKX0DER&pf_rd_s=center-1&pf_rd_r= 1A562KV3VPEPKDF3Z65D&pf_rd_t=101&pf_rd_p=291577501&pf_rd_i=507846.`

There are a couple of problems with the preceding URL. First, there's no way visitors can remember all of it. Second, you've lost valuable keyword real estate because the URL is an undecipherable collection of letters and numbers.

A better option with your URLs is to try to keep it as short and descriptive as possible. Suppose that the preceding long URL was one that leads users to a handmade, red, scallop-shell necklace that you have for sale. Rather than create a long URL that has no meaning at all, you could create a URL for the page featuring the necklace that reads something like this:
`http://www.yoursite.com/products/necklace/shells/id=507846_red_scallop`

That short URL is much more memorable than the longer one. Individuals might still have difficulty remembering all of it, but it's more likely they will remember that than one that's full of random letters and numbers. This illustrates the two key bits of advice you should take away from this discussion: URLs should be descriptive without being overly long, and they should give visitors a good idea of what to expect on the page. Using this method of creating URLs for the pages in your web site, you create the potential for including keywords in your URL, which not only helps as crawlers look at your site, but also when your URL is posted as a link on other web sites or mailing lists.

Note that you should keep URLs limited to as few *dynamic parameters* as possible (like the product ID in the example URL). A dynamic parameter is the part of the URL that provides data to a database so the proper records can be retrieved. The product ID or category ID are good examples of dynamic parameters. Another good example might be the pages of a blog. Each page will usually contain one post, or posts for a week or a month. Those pages are most often created using dynamic parameters in the URL to indicate that the information stored in a database is what should be retrieved when a user visits the site.

The URL that you select for your web site and those that you create for your web pages are important pieces of text. Those URLs can be crawled by search engine crawlers, and they should be easy for visitors to use, to remember, and to understand. These tips, like many of the others covered in the book up to this point, are all small parts of SEO. It's when all the small parts come together that your SEO efforts make great strides.

Chapter 8

Increasing Keyword Success

It would seem that picking out the right keywords and then employing them in keyword advertisements would be an easy enough task, but don't let the simplicity of the concept fool you. There is much to learn about how to use your keywords effectively to draw traffic to your web site.

One of the biggest mistakes web site owners or designers make is to assume that once the site is properly tagged and *seeded* with keywords, their work is finished. It's not. There's more to do. You can't just throw your keywords into your site's meta tags and content and then purchase a few PPC advertisements and expect to rise to the top of search engine rankings. There's a fine science to writing PPC ads and managing your keywords.

Even if you nail all the aspects of keyword placement and pay-per-click advertising, when site visitors click onto your site, what's going to greet them? Your *landing page* is as important as the text that you place on your site or the ads that lead visitors to your page; and sometimes even just creating the right advertisement text, based on the right keywords, requires some comparison testing.

Keyword marketing and *keyword advertising* are not simple processes. They're also not processes that you can do once and forget about. To be truly effective, you should be working with your keywords on an ongoing basis. Only through regular, consistent attention can you increase your keyword success and maximize the return on your keyword investment.

NOTE Notice the use of both the terms *keyword marketing* and *keyword advertising*. These are not the same activities. Keyword marketing deals primarily with unpaid marketing activities, whereas keyword advertising is generally understood to mean paid keyword activities.

Return on investment (ROI) is a term that you'll hear frequently associated with keyword advertising (and most other types of advertising and technology, too, but we're not interested in those right now). There is more detailed information in Chapter 10 about PPC ROI, but the important point to understand here is that PPC advertising is becoming increasingly expensive. It's also important that you be able to justify your keyword investments with solid returns such as sales or *goal conversions*.

However, keyword advertising is by no means as expensive as more traditional methods of advertising have been. If you have a small advertising budget and think that PPC advertising is going to be the best way to maximize it, you could be correct — if you keep up with the maintenance and ongoing efforts that are required for keyword advertising, and combine those efforts with effective keyword marketing techniques.

Once you've made the decision to go with a PPC program, the real work begins. As you learned in Chapter 6, PPC really does have a place in SEO, when it's executed properly. Chapter 7 and this chapter show you how comprehensive PPC can be. Now it's time to see how involved a PPC advertising campaign really is; not so much in the setup and execution of that campaign (that information is coming in Chapters 9 and 10), but in the goals and maintenance of the campaign.

Pay-per-click strategies can be very complex, and due to the nature of keywords and how search engines evaluate keywords, that complexity is constantly changing. That means you should be consistently evaluating your keyword strategies and focusing (or refocusing) on the elements that play a large part in determining that success: advertisement text, anchor text, landing pages, and A/B testing.

What's Better: Traffic or Conversions?

The idea of traffic or conversions is a hotly debated topic among SEO managers. Ultimately, the point of SEO (and PPC) is both. You need to draw people to your web site, but you also need those people — visitors — to convert to customers. Then you need them to come back and do it all over again in the future. That's how you measure the success of your efforts.

Setting goals

To be successful, however, you have to start with a plan — usually in the form of goals that outline what you hope to accomplish with your SEO and PPC efforts. For example, your goal for SEO might be to use search engines to draw visitors to your site *who reach a conversion*. Your goal for your PPC campaign might also be to draw people to your site who reach a conversion.

Note the twofold goal here. First, you need to draw people to your site — that's the *traffic*. Second, you need them to do something specific on your site — that's the *conversion*. Ranking well in search engines or otherwise drawing a lot of traffic to your site is useless if you can't get those visitors to convert to customers.

How do you get visitors to convert to customers? It starts with a good goal. Believe it or not, coming up with the right goal is harder than it sounds, because goals are only valuable if they reflect the ultimate mission of your company or organization. For example, if you're a news organization that happens to sell books or magazine subscriptions on the side, your main goal will probably be to get visitors to sign up for a newsletter or mailing list. If your site is designed to sell products or services, then your goal is likely to be the completion of a sale. Goals are as varied as the different types of web sites on the Internet:

- Filling out a form
- Subscribing to a mailing list
- Registering with your site
- Visiting a physical location
- Simply reading content
- Commenting and participating in forums
- Subscribing to a news feed
- Buying a product or service

Achieving conversions

A conversion is the completion of whatever goal you have set for a web site or a page on a web site. For example, if your goal is to have your site visitors subscribe to your mailing list, then the representation of the conversion might be a page that appears to visitors after they've subscribed that says, "Thank you for subscribing to our newsletter. Your first issue will arrive in your inbox soon."

The way that you'll track the success of your goals is by comparing the number of people who start the process that leads to the goal to the number of actual conversions that you have. Whether you're using SEO techniques or PPC to reach that conversion page, the number of conversions you reach will determine the success of your efforts.

Many SEOs are focused on the search engine rankings, because ranking high means a lot of traffic; but a lot of traffic doesn't automatically translate to a lot of conversions. A high search engine ranking means only that more people see your web site in search results, so you're more likely to have a lot of visitors. It is your site, however, that determines whether those visitors will convert into customers. Traffic without conversions is worthless, though the measurements may seem impressive.

So which do you shoot for? The answer is both. Actually, goals, traffic, and conversions are not separate measurements at all. They're all connected. You must have a goal in order to know what segment of potential visitors to target. You must have traffic to reach a conversion. And you must have conversions to have return visitors (and to evaluate your efforts). With that in mind, before you begin writing the text for your advertisements, and even before you choose the keywords that you'll use in your SEO and PPC efforts, you have to know what you want to accomplish. That provides the road map indicating how you move forward.

Clear goals help you to easily define what conversions must take place in order to meet those goals. Then (and only then) can you look at how to use SEO and PPC strategies to accomplish conversions.

CROSS-REF Goal conversions are more than just a fancy metric that you can use to impress the powers that be. They're actually connected to values that help you project the worth of specific customer actions and track the success or failure of your PPC and SEO efforts. There's more about goal conversion values in the "Keyword Budgeting" section of Chapter 10.

Pay-per-Click Advertisement Text

The text of your PPC advertisement will be the single most important element in determining the success or failure of your PPC campaign, and by extension the SEO of your site. Are PPC advertising and SEO two *different* and *separate* activities? Yes, and no.

Yes, PPC and SEO are completely different activities. PPC is all about using paid keyword advertisements to draw visitors to your site. SEO is about optimizing your site for search engines so you'll rank well and draw more visitors to it.

And no, PPC and SEO are not separate activities. SEO purists balk at the idea of combining the two strategies, because in a purist's mind, SEO should be effective without any paid efforts. The truth, however, is that a combination of PPC and SEO is not only beneficial, but also essential when trying to increase the traffic on your site and the revenues that the site generates. PPC is a strategy that includes placing advertisements on other web sites that lead back to yours. In the bigger pictures, however, PPC is a way to improve off-site SEO elements, especially if the keywords you're using in your PPC campaign are the same keywords you're using in your SEO efforts (and they should be).

In fact, because both are tied to the same keywords, your success or failure in one area will ultimately be a direct reflection of your success or failure in the other. You have to think of these strategies as being interconnected.

A successful PPC campaign leads targeted, qualified visitors to your site through direct links from (you hope) related sites. A successfully researched and implemented SEO strategy defines and optimizes your site for keywords related to the site topic that help visitors to find you by using search engines.

The combination of the two, then, ensures that your site is drawing *qualified visitors* and that it meets whatever needs the visitors have that lead them to you. Interconnected. Yes, you could have one without the other, but the results wouldn't be as successful.

Once you understand the relationship between PPC and SEO, you can begin to consider what it takes to make PPC ads successful. It all starts with the right advertisement text. And before you can even begin to write your keyword advertisement text, you should have a finalized list — or even multiple finalized lists — of keywords selected.

If you've used a keyword-research worksheet (like the ones included in Appendix D), you can easily use the list created with that worksheet to group your keywords according to the *intent* with which visitors use them.

Category words and product words

Keywords fall into two basic categories: *category words* and *product words*. Category words are broad (think Broad Head) and are usually used when a visitor is in the early stages of the buying process. A visitor is probably more interested in researching an idea or product than in purchasing at this stage.

Product words are more specific (think Long Tail), and these are the words that people search for when they're ready to make a purchase. For example, if your keywords include "dayspring," "spa," "aromatherapy," "lavender soap," "relaxing herbal wrap," and "mud bath," your category words and product words might be organized like those shown in Table 8-1. It's important to keep your keywords grouped together, in particular because they are associated with the different pages of your web site. It's these words that you'll be working with as you create your keyword advertisement text. According to research done by major search engine companies, using keywords in your advertisement text can increase your advertisement click-through rates by as much as 50 percent. Keywords are important to your advertisement text, and the right keywords for the advertisement are vitally important.

TABLE 8-1

Related Keyword Groups

Category Words	Product Words
Aromatherapy	Dayspring Spa
Spa	Lavender soap
Mud bath	Relaxing herbal wrap

Another thing to consider before you begin to write your keyword advertisement text is what you hope to accomplish with the text. Do you want visitors to buy something? Do you want them to call your office for more information? Do you want them to sign up for a newsletter or some other service? It's important to know what you want users to do when they see the advertisement, because you'll use some form of this goal in a *call to action* in the advertisement.

It helps if you write down several clear, different sentences that express the goal conversions you want visitors to reach. You don't have to worry about writing the sentences in short form right now. Just brainstorm and get the ideas down on paper. You can whittle away unnecessary words as you move forward with writing the text.

One last thing to consider before you begin writing your PPC ad text is the immediate benefits of your product or service. These, too, will be used in ad text, so take the time to write down several benefits that you might draw from as you're creating your ad text.

Writing the ad

Once the preliminaries are done, you can begin to write your text. This job starts with knowing your audience. Very often, when writers are creating ad text, they fail to take into consideration the audience they're trying to reach. You need to not only identify your potential audience, but also understand how to reach them. Language is in a constant state of flux, and each generation of people communicates differently, so different tones and styles of writing will be needed to reach them.

A good example is the difference between the teenage generation and the senior generation. For example, if you're trying to reach teens with your video editing software, you'll want to write your advertisement in a language that catches their eye and is understood. If your advertisement includes the call to action, "Show the world you're an emo!" those teenage users will immediately understand that it means, "Show the world you're part of the emotional crowd." Senior visitors would be unlikely to get that unless they happen to have grandchildren who have explained that the term *emo* in teen-speak refers to people who openly share their emotions (incidentally, *emo* can also be a subdesignation for groups such as goths, punks, and metal heads).

Conversely, if you were trying to reach the seniors, your slogan might be something like, "Share your precious memories." This acknowledges the experiences of a senior and says, "We can help you share your recollections with anyone you want." To a teen, it says *boring!*

When you know your audience, you can write ad text that is specifically targeted to the most qualified potential visitors for your site. Sometimes, you'll want to reach more than one group of people. In this case, you'll want to write different ads for each group. Don't try to reach everyone with a single ad. You won't. Instead, you'll come closer to reaching no one at all.

Each PPC program has its own unique guidelines for ad text, so take the time to learn the requirements for the PPC program that you've selected. In addition, the only PPC programs that rank advertisements solely on the amount that the ad's owner bids on placement are with secondary search engines such as Marchex and Kanoodle. Most PPC programs from major search engines use an algorithm that combines the amount paid for each click with the relevance of that ad and how compelling the position of the ad is to the user.

Ad position is everything. For example, Google ranks ads in different places either at the top or side of a page (see Figure 8-1). The best placement, obviously, is at the top of the page. It's expensive to land that spot, though, so if that's really where you want to be, plan to shell out some big bucks. Side-of-the-page advertisements are less expensive, but also still ranked by relevance. How relevant and compelling your ad is, combined with the amount you're willing to pay per click, will determine where in that placement scheme your ad will land.

FIGURE 8-1

Keyword advertisement rankings are determined by relevance and advertising budget.

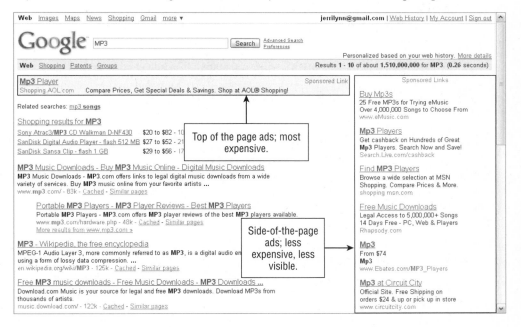

In summary, if your ad text is well written and performs well, then you could potentially pay less for the ranking you want, or pay the same and achieve a better ranking than you expected.

Note the following ad-text requirements that will typically apply to nearly all PPC programs:

- **Include keywords in your ad text:** As you've already seen, ads that contain keywords can perform up to 50 percent better than ads that don't include them.

- **Make your offer:** Tell potential visitors exactly what you offer and why they want it. Just be careful not to exaggerate claims about the benefits of your products and/or services. Keep your claims accurate and compelling.

- **Call visitors to action:** Numerous studies have proven that using a call to action actually does work. Include a call to action in your ad text to motivate potential visitors to click through the ad to your web site to accomplish whatever it is you want them to do. One word of caution, however: Many PPC programs will not allow, or strongly recommend against, using the phrase "Click Here Now." It's a seriously overused phrase that conveys neither creativity nor motivation.

- **Include keywords:** Keywords should be used in both the ad title and the body of the ad text if possible. Keywords are what make PPC ads relevant and compelling — and when your ads are relevant and compelling, you get far more exposure for a smaller cost per click.

- **Create a sense of urgency:** It's one of the oldest sales tricks in the book, but it still works surprisingly well. You can create a sense of urgency in your potential visitors by using phrases such as "limited availability" or "offer expires soon." Have you ever been told by a salesperson that you're looking at the last or one of the last items available, whether it's a car, a television, or something else? Did you feel a sense of urgency to make the purchase more quickly than you would have if you knew that many more of that item were left? That's the purpose of creating urgency — it drives the user to take action, which is the goal of your advertisement.

- **Draw clicks, not views:** Write your advertisement with the intention of enticing users to click on it. Although you have been cautioned against using the phrase "Click Here Now," that *should* be the goal of your advertisement. The purpose in PPC advertisement is to draw potential visitors to your site. With that in mind, you should design your PPC ads to draw clicks, not simply *impressions*. It's not enough for users to see your advertisement. You won't build any brand recognition that way, and users won't see it now and return to your site later. They'll view it, forget it, and move on. Be sure that your ads are designed to collect clicks, not eyeballs.

- **Write your ad long and then cut it:** Writing your ad long is a copywriting trick that helps to distill the ad to only the most relevant and enticing text. Begin by writing your ad in full sentences, using each of the preceding elements, and then cut those sentences down to only the strongest words that will entice potential visitors to click on them. Look at the ads that already appear in the PPC program that you've selected. This will indicate how long your ad should be and what works for others. You can then build on that to create ads that work for you.

- **Use strong, motivating words:** Because you'll have a very limited amount of space in which to write your ad, be sure that you're using the most powerful words that you can conjure up. For example, instead of using the word "skilled," use the word "professional." Instead of "markdown," use "discount." Strong, carefully chosen words convey more meaning and emphasis, and they do it in less space than other words or phrases.

■ **Experiment tirelessly and endlessly:** If your PPC ad is perfect right out of the gate, it will truly be an anomaly. What's more likely to happen is that you write a PPC ad, it performs okay, and then you try something a little different. That's how it should be with PPC ads. It takes continuous monitoring and testing to find the right combinations of words, punctuation, keywords, and placement to hit the sweet spot in PPC advertising. And even once you do, you'll likely find yourself having to readjust the ad frequently because of changes in your products or services. Set aside at least an hour or two to put into your PPC ad campaign. Only through experimentation and testing can you achieve PPC success.

PPC advertising has plenty of appeal. It's quick, it's effective, and it's nowhere near as expensive as other types of advertising. But as you've learned here, don't assume that PPC advertising is all sunshine and light. It requires work and commitment to find the methods and combinations that work for you. Once you've done that, you have to make the click worth the visitor's time. To do that, you need to create great *landing pages*.

Understanding Landing Pages

Landing pages are those pages that potential site visitors reach when they click your PPC (or other) advertisement. These pages are usually not connected to your web site in any way. They are not linked through the site map or through the body of your web site; and to ensure that they're fully disconnected from all other methods of discovery, landing pages should not be spidered (which is accomplished using Robots.txt, but that's covered in Chapter 18).

It sounds like a disaster in the making, right? In fact, these landing pages are designed for two purposes. First, a landing page is designed specifically to funnel visitors to a goal conversion when they click your advertisement. Second, landing pages are designed as a way for you to keep track of how well your PPC ads draw not just qualified traffic, but conversion traffic.

If the goal of SEO is to draw to your web site more qualified traffic that converts more often, then landing pages are your means to monitor whether or not that's happening. A landing page also gives you an opportunity to create a relationship with a new site visitor who has clicked your link for one specific purpose. After you meet that person's needs, you can funnel the user into the remainder of your site to see what else you have to offer.

There is some debate as to the value of landing pages that don't link to any other source on the web site. Some experts think that once you've pulled visitors to the landing page, then the more you engage them, the more likely they are to return to your site and eventually reach a goal conversion. That may be true.

Using that assumption, there would seem to only be one kind of landing page: the landing page associated with a PPC campaign. However, there is a second type of landing page that mirrors the other pages on your web site, including all the same navigation links and the same feel as the rest of the site. Essentially, however, these pages require the same efforts during creation and testing that landing pages for PPC ads require.

The landing page shown in Figure 8-2 actually does have live links, but they do not allow visitors to interact further with the site. All the links on that page lead to the conversion goal that OptiLink has created for the site.

FIGURE 8-2

The landing page for an OptiLink ad funnels visitors toward the singular goal of purchasing the product.

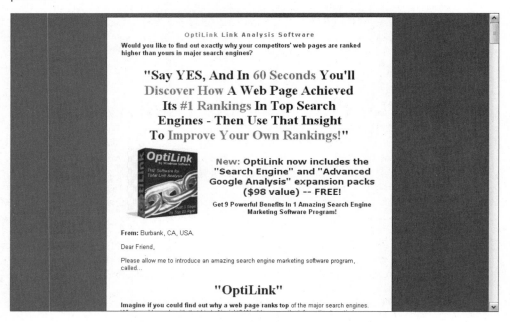

A page that looks more like the rest of your web site might look like the one shown in Figure 8-3. The FTD landing page looks just like the rest of the site and includes links that enable users to interact with other pages of the site. However, notice that the URL for the landing page

```
http://www.ftd.com/5970/?campaign_id=google_yellow+rose&KW_ID=p36936100
```

is different from the URL that appears when the user clicks to another page in the site:

```
http://www.ftd.com/5970/catalog/category.epl?index_id=occasion_birthday
```

FIGURE 8-3

The FTD PPC landing page looks like the rest of the web site and enables visitors to interact as they would with any page.

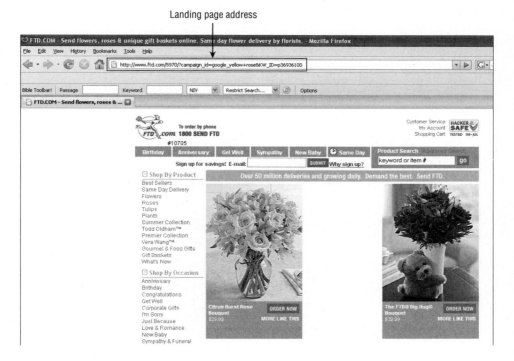

This is your indication that the page is actually the landing page for a PPC ad. It would appear, then, that FTD has another way of tracking conversions from that page, rather than from other pages on the site.

One more tidbit about landing pages before going through the list of elements that should be included in such pages. It's usually a wise idea to create several different landing pages and test them to determine what type of page works best for your PPC ads. It's even possible you'll learn that your PPC landing page should be a dynamic one that changes with each visitor who clicks through the link in the PPC ad. This is a determination that you can make only through testing.

Remember earlier in this chapter when you separated your keywords by intent? Now is when that exercise will come in handy. The intent of the visitor who comes to your site through your PPC ads (or through any other method of SEO that you use) will determine how your landing page should work. Users looking for information will make *reference landings*, meaning they aren't in the right frame of mind to purchase anything yet; they are still working through the sales process.

Visitors nearing the end of the buying process already know what they are looking for and will make *transactional landings* on your page. That means they've come to your site from a specific keyword, chosen because they know what they want. All that remains is the final decision to buy. If your site offers the right product or service at the right price, you should see a large number of conversions from these visitors.

When you're creating your landing pages, you want them to be an extension of the PPC ad for which they are designed. For example, if you're advertising Navajo turquoise jewelry, your landing page must be targeted to the correct market. It will only confuse and frustrate visitors if they are expecting Navajo turquoise jewelry for people but only find turquoise jewelry for (or on) dolls.

To further extend the concept of understanding your audience, your landing page should also provide what is promised. If your ad promises Navajo turquoise jewelry and your visitors are directed to something else, then they're not going to stick around to learn about what you offer. Finally, just as you would use a call to action with your PPC advertisement, you want to use such a call on your landing page. The purpose of the landing page is to create conversions, and you have to ask for the sale (or other interaction) to receive it.

Keep in mind that your call to action might actually be for the user to sign up for a newsletter or to participate in a survey. Whatever that call to action is, present it to your visitor on the landing page.

Here are some additional tips to help you design landing pages that convert visitors who click through your PPC ads:

- **Create specific landing pages for each PPC ad:** Individual landing pages enable you to tailor the pages to specific audiences, which can increase the chances of conversion.

- **Quickly orient visitors to the purpose of the landing page by using direct and concise headlines:** When users click through an ad to your landing page, they must immediately see that the page will help them reach whatever goal they have in mind. If they don't see this, then they will quickly click back to their search results.

- **Don't overcrowd your landing pages:** Too much information, too many graphics, or too many multimedia elements can make it difficult for users to load your landing page. Even if they do load it, they are likely to become sidetracked or overwhelmed. Keep your landing page, and indeed all your pages, clean and include plenty of white space.

- **Include everything that visitors need to complete a conversion:** That means users should be able to sign up for your newsletter, make a purchase, or fill out a form, from the landing page. If users have to click much deeper into your site, you may lose them.

- **Test, test, test:** You'll hear that mantra over and over again with many different SEO strategies. For landing pages, you may have to test several versions before you find one that works for the ad you're currently running. Remember too that when you change the ad, the landing page needs to change with it. It's an ongoing process that's never quite finished.

Understanding and Using A/B Testing

You've heard it so many times by now that you're probably sick of it, but testing is your best friend during any SEO efforts, and specifically with your PPC efforts. The most common and the most easy-to-use form of testing is *A/B testing*. In its simplest form, A/B testing is testing one ad version against another.

For a PPC advertisement effort, that means testing two or more ads at the same time. This section provides some guidelines when testing different ads.

First, understand what you hope to achieve with the testing. Are you trying to increase traffic? Are you trying to increase conversions? Or do you want to increase or change some other element of your PPC performance? Ask yourself these questions and then use the answers that you come up with as a guideline for making changes to test.

When you know what you're trying to accomplish, you must start your testing with an ad that serves as your baseline. In order for this to happen, you have to first create at least one PPC ad and then allow it to perform long enough to have a good baseline of data against which you can compare future ad designs.

Once you have your baseline established, you can begin comparing that ad against new ads that you've created to test different elements of the PPC ad. Some of the elements you can test include the following:

- Headline
- Keywords
- Call to action
- Ad text
- Different landing pages

The key to successful A/B testing is to change only *one* element in the test ads at a time. Moreover, once that element has been changed, you have to give the ads time to develop performance data so that you can tell which of the ads is performing better. If you change more than one element at a time, then you'll find yourself in the untenable position of having to decide which ad changes affected the traffic and conversion rates. Stick to one change at a time in order to make it easier to track which changes cause what results.

When you're A/B testing your PPC ads, you should have both a *control ad*, the one you used to create your baseline, and a *test ad*. If you don't have a control ad, then you don't have anything to compare your results against. You must run both the control ad and the test ad at the same time in order for your testing results to be accurate and meaningful.

Using A/B testing, you can learn what works and what doesn't in your PPC advertisements. It's not the most sophisticated testing method that you can use, but it's the easiest and it's highly accurate. Testing your ads will help you tweak and fine-tune them until they are as successful as possible.

Tying It All Together

Keyword success, PPC success, and even the success of your SEO efforts as a whole, are derived from a carefully balanced blending of creating the right goals, choosing the right keywords, writing effective ad copy, and designing landing pages with the intent of potential visitors in mind. Simply creating a site and throwing up some PPC ads based on a few randomly selected keywords won't bring the results that you're looking for.

Neither will building crafted PPC ads based on the wrong keywords, or carefully chosen keywords that don't reflect the goals that you have for your site. You probably see where this is headed, don't you?

To be truly successful, all these elements must work in concert with one another, much like the various instruments of an orchestra. Yes, you can have a single instrument without an orchestra, but the effect of one is not nearly as moving as the result of the entire group. In other words, if you haven't done it yet, take the time now to define just exactly what it is you want to accomplish with your web site.

Only after that goal is cemented can you begin to find the right keywords, create PPC ads that are effective, and develop landing pages that funnel visitors to the conversions you're reaching for. Be prepared to put a lot of work into the process, and plan to test extensively until you find the winning combination. Through those efforts, you'll achieve the success that's so important in SEO — with your keywords and your PPC ads.

Chapter 9

Understanding and Using Campaign Targeting

Mass marketing techniques that were used in the twentieth century, like many other techniques from that era, are pretty much outdated. Reaching potential customers using television and newspaper ads still works, but it's not always the most efficient way to advertise.

Traditional methods of advertising target a large group of people. Generally, that means large numbers of the people who see an ad won't be interested in it at all. As a result of that blanket type of advertising, companies spend a (relatively) large amount of money to reach a small segment of the population.

One way that advertisers have found to improve the success rates of their advertisements is through *contextual targeting*. Contextual targeting is basically the practice of placing ads in a specific medium based on the elements surrounding the ad.

Here's an example: Open up any women's magazine (or men's, or even children's) and look at the advertisements. Frequently, at least one of the articles in the women's magazine is about weight loss. Alongside the text of the article in the pages, and at the end, you might find advertisements for online dieting services, diet pills, or even gym memberships.

These advertisements are placed in context based on the content of articles, with the assumption that someone reading an article on weight loss might be interested in dieting services, diet pills, or gym memberships. This is *contextual advertising* — the act of placing ads in the context of the surrounding content.

Contextual advertising provides a big step toward reaching specific groups of people, but it's not nearly enough. With today's technology, a much more targeted advertising method should be possible, one that works within the confines of the medium that potential customers are using. In many cases, that medium is now the Internet. Of all the places where advertisers can reach highly qualified potential customers, the Internet is the best — as long as the targeting methods are appropriate for the audience.

In addition to contextual targeting, another method of reaching a narrower, but more qualified, group of potential customers is *demographic targeting*. For example, if you are trying to sell a music-sharing service, your main target age group might be the 18- to 25-year-old crowd; but if you are advertising a drug used to treat sickle cell anemia, you would target your advertising to 22- to 35-year-old African Americans.

What Is Behavioral Targeting?

As effective as demographic targeting can be, however, it's still not the best way to reach highly qualified leads on the Internet. What works much better is *behavioral targeting*. Behavioral targeting is a relative newcomer to advertising targeting. It's the practice of serving ads to users based on their search behaviors and web-surfing habits. Behavioral targeting can be used on both media sites (such as MSN or Computerworld) and destination sites (such as Amazon.com). The difference is how you track visitors to each type of site. For media sites, you track visitors' behavior across the pages that they visit. Specifically, the keywords of the pages are monitored to determine what topics interest the visitor.

For destination sites, tracking is a little different. Instead of general pages, the products that visitors look at, purchase, and have purchased in the past are taken into consideration before an ad is served. When you access Amazon.com, for example, the recommendations that Amazon suggests to you after your first visit are just one example of behavioral targeting. Your past (and present) behavior determines what Amazon.com serves you as ads and even to some degree as content.

Benefits of Behavioral Targeting

Behavioral targeting is so effective because search marketing has expanded so much. In the past, search marketing was only about search. Today, search marketing can target demographics, *dayparting* (addressed in Chapter 10), and behavior; and because today's audiences are more fragmented than ever, the more specific marketing efforts can be, the more effective they'll be.

Behavioral marketing has many other benefits, too. For example, although behavioral targeting results in fewer impressions, it also results in a higher conversion rate, because the ad is more targeted than a contextual ad might be. Additional benefits of behavioral targeting include the following:

- **More click-throughs:** Click-throughs reflect the visits by potential customers or site visitors when they click *through* your PPC (or other) ad and land on your site.

- **More conversions:** As you've learned already, behavioral targeting tends to reach fewer people, but it results in more goal conversions. Because your goal conversions should be designed to result in either a sale or the collection of data to help you reach a sale, the conversion rate for ads placed using behavioral targeting is much higher.

- **Improved return on investment (ROI):** Return on investment is the metric that seems to drive everything these days. Behavioral targeting helps to improve the ROI of your PPC and other advertising programs because ads placed using behavioral targeting are focus on the type of audience that is most likely to make a purchase, provide data, or sign up for a newsletter or other service.

Taking Advantage of Behavioral Targeting

Another element that makes behavioral targeting more attractive is the growing ability of companies to capture and record behavior. This is accomplished through the use of *cookies*, which are small pieces of code that make it possible for companies to track how people behave on a web site or even across a network of sites without capturing any specific personal information about those people.

The concept is simple: A company places a cookie on a user's hard drive, and then using that cookie tracks what the user searches for online and then where the user travels within those search results. Suppose, for example, that you're contemplating buying a hybrid car. If you are like most car buyers, the first thing that you're likely to do is research hybrid cars on the Internet. If a search company (or some other organization) is tracking your search movements, they'll learn that you're researching hybrid cars.

At this point in the purchasing process, you're not ready to commit to buying a car, so an advertiser may hold its ads back, not wanting to pay for exposure that results in no conversions. However, the company that placed the cookie on your hard drive can continue to monitor your searches and movements on the Web. Then, when you begin to search for the phrase "buying a hybrid car" or something similar, the search company can alert the advertiser, who will then place an ad in front of you. This ensures that you're in the right frame of mind to see the ad, which means that you're more likely to *click through* the ad and reach a conversion goal than other surfers might be.

Advertising research indicates that an ad must be placed in front of a visitor about three times before that visitor even registers the ad. Using behavioral targeting, you can create those three impressions at just the right time, so that when visitors reach the buying phase, your ad is there, offering them exactly what they seek.

Meeting the customer halfway

The truly useful element of behavioral targeting is not that you're tracking users' behaviors, but that you're meeting these potential customers in the place where they are most likely to make a purchase, sign up for your newsletter, fill out a form for more information, or accomplish whatever conversion goal you've established.

This *search profiling* — tracking users' pre- and post-search behavior — also has the added benefit of enabling you to target your ads much more effectively in the buying process. It's the part of behavioral targeting that seems to draw the most attention — but it provides more than just pre-purchase (or pre-conversion) advertisements. You can also use search profiling as part of behavioral targeting to develop appropriate *post-search ads*.

Post-search ads appear on the landing pages that you or others have created. These ads are highly targeted to the people who are most likely to click through a PPC ad to reach the landing page. Once there, the ads offer additional related products and services. These post-search ads are popular because they tend to get more traffic than other types of advertising, leading to more goal conversions than other types of advertising.

When behavioral targeting is used, several methods are used to evaluate behavior, including the following:

- **Expected behavior:** Expected behavior is just that — what you would expect users to do on a given type of site. For example, if you operate a site that requires users to log in to use the site, even if it's a free site, you expect users (who are also qualified sales leads) to fill out the form necessary to sign up for your web site service. This behavior can sometimes enable you to see patterns that you would not otherwise see in the behavior of your customers or potential customers.

- **Repetitive behavior:** This is the same type of behavior from potential customers over and over again. This could include anything from users accessing your pages in a certain order to users repeatedly jumping to your site on a specific page or at a specific time. This repetitive behavior makes it much more possible for you to define patterns of behavior that lead to purchasing decisions or to other decisions that lead to the targeted goal conversion.

- **Sequential behavior:** This occurs when users sign on to your site and then visit pages or perform actions in a sequential manner. Monitoring sequential behavior helps you to discover established routines that lead to goal conversions. When you know what users are likely to do, because their habits are consistent, you're more likely to stay one step ahead of your competition.

In addition to these broad categories of behavior evaluation, there are many categories of behavior that are much more specific. Here's a short list of some of the categories that can be monitored using behavioral targeting:

- Mobile users
- Internet power users (those who are always online)
- Gamers
- Auto buyers
- Home buyers
- Personal investors
- Credit card shoppers
- New/expecting moms
- Hotel seekers
- Vacationers
- Luxury car researchers
- Sports car researchers
- SUV researchers
- Pickup truck researchers
- Passenger car researchers
- Movie watchers

Using these categories of behavior monitoring, it's much easier to target your ads to just the right people at the right time. Let's say you've discovered that many people buy from your site after first clicking through some of the articles there. If you see this in the sequential behavior of several users, you can begin to infer that if you place additional relevant content (that's not too sales intensive) on your site, then at a certain point in the process users will be more likely to click through your advertisements.

It's all in the timing

The problem with behavioral targeting is that the companies that conduct professional behavioral targeting activities can't monitor all the different behaviors. The preceding list includes some of the behaviors that the MSN search engine monitors. However, other search engines might monitor some of these behaviors and not others; and those other search engines might monitor some behavior that is not included in that list.

It's possible to create a system by which you monitor a specific behavior that's important to you. Maybe you're selling a product such as plasma screen televisions, and maybe the behaviors that you want to monitor are the research phase of the buying cycle and the buying phase of the buying cycle. You can monitor both behaviors if you have a clear understanding of what you're looking for. All it takes is the creation of a cookie or set of cookies that will monitor those behaviors.

The key here is determining the searches or page views that are going to lead to the conversion that you are trying to accomplish — in this case, selling a plasma screen television. There is no hard science to tell you what behaviors will definitely lead to a sale; however, there are some indications as to what point searchers must reach before they are willing to buy.

For this example, let's assume that the ideal time to place your ad in front of them is when they have returned to the Internet for a second time to research plasma screen televisions. At this point, you can place your ad in front of these searchers, and the ad is more likely to result in a goal conversion. To track these movements, you would need cookies to track the specific behavior that you've determined leads to goal conversion, as well as the pages that the potential customers are viewing. You may even want to include a cookie that helps you exclude site visitors who have already reached the goal conversion that you've established.

Additionally, your web site will need the capability to read these cookies and then serve up the right content to the user, based on the contents of those cookies. It's a complicated process, but with the right web designer, it's a very doable one — and it really shouldn't be all that expensive.

Additional Behavioral Targeting Tips

Behavioral targeting may sound like the solution to all your advertising worries, but it does have a few drawbacks. By its nature, it reduces the number of potential customers who will see your advertisement. This could mean that you'll miss some segments of the market (such as those who don't yet know that they are interested in what you're offering but would be if you presented an ad to them).

For this reason, behavioral targeting shouldn't be the only method you use to target your potential customers. Yes, it's a method that will make your PPC campaigns more effective, and that alone may be all that you need to be convinced that behavioral targeting is right for you, but it may not be in all cases.

Take the time to research the behavioral-targeting capabilities of whatever vendor you choose, but don't put all of your hope in it. For most people it works great, but not as a stand-alone targeting method. To be truly effective, you should use programs that leverage contextual targeting, demographic targeting, and something you'll learn about shortly: *placement targeting*.

Multiple users require multiple placement methods

You may also want to use other targeting methods because some households have one computer with multiple users. This can cause the wrong person to be served with the wrong ad. In a typical family, for example, you have two parents or adults and maybe a teenager who are all using the same computer. Mom spends some time online looking at recipes and e-commerce sites to make the job of taking care of her family easier. Dad spends a lot of time looking at sports scores. The teenager spends a lot of time downloading music and playing games.

When Dad goes to the computer to look up scores, he may find an ad for cookware, because Mom was the last person to use the computer. Or Mom may be served an ad about a new gaming system. The behavioral targeting is working properly, but because there are multiple users on the same computer, any given user may end up seeing the wrong ad.

To some extent, the different profiles enabled by the Windows operating system can mitigate this problem. Cookies are stored according to user profile, but that assumes that each member of a family or each different computer user actually has (and uses) his or her own profile. It's not a foolproof system; and because it's not, you should consider the possibility that this could skew your behavioral targeting effectiveness.

Behavioral targeting and privacy concerns

One more problem, and perhaps the most bothersome issue about behavioral targeting, is the privacy issue. In today's market, nearly everyone is concerned about privacy. With the drastic rise in the number of identity thefts, people are guarding their personal information more closely than in the past, and many people object to having their online activities monitored, even for a benign purpose such as attempting to provide the best possible advertisements.

NOTE To some people, behavioral targeting sounds a bit like adware or spyware, both of which are methods of collecting information from users without their permission. Moreover, adware is used with the express intent of pushing unwanted advertisements out to users. Behavioral targeting is designed to better target your advertisements; however, users are aware that their movements are being tracked, and they agree to that tracking. Behavioral targeting also enables more than just pushing relevant advertisements. It also enables an organization to learn how it can serve users better according to their activities while they are on the organization's web site.

Legislation can also make it more difficult to monitor people's behaviors closely without their consent. To ensure that potential customers are not offended before the relationship even begins, many companies are including opt-in (or out) methods to enable users to decide for themselves whether they want to be targeted.

Study after study has found that your potential customers may be willing to let you track their movements — with a couple of conditions. The first is that they know you're tracking them.

This requires providing some kind of privacy notice that enables potential users to decide not to allow you to track their movements. In the case of those who have no interest in being monitored, you'll have to find some other way to serve them the right advertisements at the right time.

The second condition is that your potential customers want to see some kind of value from allowing you to access their personal information. This value could be that you provide them with higher-quality information, better-quality services, or lower prices (among other things). Whatever the value to your potential customers, the higher it is the more likely your potential customers will be to participate in your efforts, and to let you use information about their movements on the Internet to serve them targeted advertisements.

One of the most fortunate aspects of behavioral targeting is that you don't need personal information for the targeting to be effective. Because all the tracking done with behavioral targeting is monitored by cookies, the only information that's collected is movement behavior. What you are doing is persuading potential customers to participate in the collection of their web movements by offering them value for doing so.

Then There Is Placement Targeting

Behavioral targeting is one way to serve the right ads to your customers at the right time, but there's another way to target your ads: *placement targeting*. Placement targeting is targeting your keyword advertisements to a specific web site or even to a certain location on a web site because that's where you believe you'll get the best response to those ads.

Don't confuse placement targeting with contextual targeting. Contextual targeting is placing an ad within the context of a given page. That's what happens when keyword ads that are relevant to a given web page are shown based on the keywords for that web page. Contextual targeting refers to ad relevance.

Placement targeting, however, refers to location relevance. Where on a given web site will an ad perform the best? Where will it reach the right site visitors at the right time? Placement targeting is a bit of an art, and it usually takes continual testing to figure out what spots on a page work best for which ads.

Within the context of keyword advertising, placement targeting is best used with Long Tail keywords on niche web sites, because placement-targeted ads are usually charged according to *cost-per-thousand impressions (CPM)* — for every 1,000 times an ad is shown, you are charged according to the amount that you've bid for that ad. There are some keyword advertising programs (such as Google's AdWords) that allow placement-targeted ads based on CPC (cost-per-click) or *cost-per-action (CPA)*, but not all services allow that.

Making Placement Ads Work for You

Generally, placement-targeted ads have a bad rep. These ads don't always perform as well as other keyword ads, but when they do perform well, they usually result in more conversions, because they are targeted to visitors who are farther along in the buying process.

The trick is to find the way in which placement-targeted ads work best for your products and services. That requires testing and monitoring. Anytime that you choose to use placement-targeted ads, you should plan to spend some time monitoring those ads closely. In addition, be prepared to cancel ads that don't generate conversions. Replace them with new ads, and then monitor those.

As you can see, placement ads require a lot of attention. A few guidelines can help, but like all other types of keyword ads, there are no guarantees:

- **When possible, choose placement ads above the fold:** Most of the keyword advertising services that allow placement ads also allow you to choose where on the page you want the ad to appear. Above the fold is key. You'll pay more for it, but ads shown below the fold will have fewer actual impressions — even though people click on the page, they may not scroll down to see your ad.

- **Use both text and graphic placement ads:** Placement ads are most often thought of as being graphic ads, but they can also be text ads (contextual ads). If you have the option, use both and monitor which work best. As with everything else in keyword advertising, there is no definitive answer regarding which works best. For some, graphic ads will be best, for others it will be text.

- **When using graphic ads, make sure they're not too small:** What is too small varies from ad to ad, but in most cases, anything under 600 pixels is too small. Still, don't just take my word for it. Try different sizes to find out which ones work best for you.

- **Choose exact locations over specific web sites when possible:** Obviously, the more control you have over a placement ad, the better your chance are of having placement ads that work. When you have the option to choose a specific location on a web site, rather than just a specific web site, take it. You won't always have that option, but it's helpful when you do.

Just remember that where your ad appears determines what you'll pay for it. Is it worth it for your ad to be at the top of the page when it costs you $5 per thousand impressions and you only receive one conversion a month from that ad? I don't know, but you should. It could be that an ad on the side of the page will be just as valuable and cost less. You have to figure out what a conversion is worth to you and then decide what type of ads you should pursue based on that figure.

CROSS-REF You can find more information about determining visitor value and the cost of conversions in Chapter 6.

Placement ads are just another option for placing your keyword advertisements where they might be seen by the most interested visitors. Alone, placement ads probably won't be the ads that bring the majority of traffic to your web site, but when combined with other types of ads — behavior-targeted ads, contextual ads, and so on — they can be a viable part of your SEO strategy.

Chapter 10

Managing Keyword and Pay-per-Click Campaigns

Keywords and PPC campaigns, like any type of advertising campaign, need to be monitored carefully to ensure that they are as effective as possible. Of course, you'll also want to be sure that you're spending only as much of your advertising budget as you need; but determining those factors requires monitoring activities, spending, and conversions, and managing the strategies that you use to improve those factors.

The one factor that will influence your PPC campaigns the most is money. Be it in the form of your PPC budget, the amount of money that you need to save, or determining your ROI, you'll be constantly justifying your pay-per-click advertising with financial values. Tracking those values isn't difficult, but it can be time-consuming.

Moreover, the competition for keywords and PPC advertisements can be fierce. If you're not constantly tweaking your PPC campaigns to make them as effective as possible, then you'll be throwing your budget away like empty candy wrappers.

Keyword Budgeting

Part of the allure of PPC advertising is that it appears to be a low-cost alternative to other types of advertising. The initial attraction is that it seems you can reach more people using less of your advertising budget. The reality could be much different, however.

PPC programs are designed to create competition between bidders. You find the perfect keyword, and then you get caught up in a bidding war. Before you know it, you've upped your maximum bid per click. In addition, to accommodate this, you've upped your daily maximum budget. It doesn't take long for this addiction to lead to one of two possibilities: Either your entire advertising budget is completely consumed by your PPC campaign, or, worse, your PPC costs skyrocket to the point that your advertising budget is gone and then some. Either way, you'll never be able to justify what you've invested into pay-per-click advertising because it's just too much.

When the PPC campaign takes over the budget, eventually the campaign will fail. It's impossible to realize any return on investment when the bids on a keyword skyrocket. As a result, because there is no ROI, your company is likely to cut your PPC campaign completely from its advertising budget; or, if you're an individual, you could end up deep in debt chasing the best keywords.

That's why it's essential to start with the budget when designing your PPC campaign. Only with a carefully considered and strategically planned budget can your PPC campaign be both effective and profitable.

The value of a conversion

Before you can begin to determine your PPC budget, you must first determine what a goal conversion is worth to you. Determining the value of a conversion can be a bit tricky. Note, too, that the value of a conversion is different from the *cost per conversion*. The value of a conversion is how much you stand to profit when one of your PPC ads leads to a conversion.

If you have an e-commerce business, then it should be easy for you to determine the value of a conversion: It's equal to the average profit per order. For example, if your average profit per order is $5, then you can assume that the value of a goal conversion associated with your PPC campaign is $5.

If you're not running an e-commerce business, determining the value of a conversion might be a little more difficult. For example, if you're operating a content site, then your targeted goal conversion might be a newsletter sign-up. What's the value of that newsletter sign-up to you? It varies from company to company, but if your newsletter draws advertisers, your advertising income might be what your conversion value is based on.

For example, if your monthly newsletter has 10,000 subscribers and your advertising income is $10,000 a month, then a subscriber is worth $1. Therefore, a good value to assign to your goal conversion (which in this case is for a site visitor to sign up for your newsletter) is $1.

Another way to assign a conversion value to a nonmonetary goal is to use a system of points. Of course, the number is still going to be somewhat arbitrary, but what you're really after here is a way to measure goals and compare the effectiveness of your marketing efforts.

Using the newsletter example we started with above, look at how the points system works.

First, assign points to your goals:

- Open the e-mail newsletter — 1 point
- Click a "read more" link that leads to your web site — 5 points
- Click an advertiser's ad within the newsletter — 10 points
- Create an account on your e-commerce site — 50 points

Note that the points on these goals increase with the value of the goal. You may not have an exact monetary value, and it may even be worth more to you for your readers to click an ad than to create an account. The point value is something you should determine based on the importance of your goal, but you should have an idea of how valuable each activity is, even if you can't assign an exact dollar amount to it.

Now you can track different (and completely hypothetical) newsletter marketing campaigns to see how they measure up. For this example, let's assume that your newsletter goes out to 15,000 subscribers:

- **Campaign 1** results in 14,500 subscribers who actually open the newsletter, 1,500 who click through a "read more" link, 1,275 who click an ad in the newsletter, and 320 who create new accounts.
- **Campaign 2** results in 14,000 subscribers who open the newsletter, 750 who click through a "read more" link, 998 who click an ad in the newsletter, and 675 who create new accounts.

Looking at these numbers (forgetting for a moment that there are points assigned to each of these actions), it looks as though campaign 1 was the more successful of the two. But when you assign a point value to the goals included, it changes the picture a bit:

- **Campaign 1** = 14,500 + 7,500 + 12,750 + 16,000 = 50,750
- **Campaign 2** = 14,000 + 3,750 + 9,980 + 33,750 = 61,480

After you tally up the points, you begin to see the real value of conversions and how mixing up the right marketing magic can make all the difference. Sure, the points are arbitrary, but they give you a clear picture of the value of a conversion and how your keyword and SEO efforts affect that conversion.

Budgeting based on conversions

With your conversion value determined, you can begin to determine your PPC budget, and it starts with determining how much you want to spend on PPC overall. This amount (whether it's $50 or $50,000) is your firm limit. Very often, PPC costs can increase over time, so it's important to pay particular attention to the maximum you set.

To budget for your different keywords, you need a few additional metrics for each keyword:

- Average conversion rate
- Goals for number of conversions desired
- Cost per keyword

To find the average number of conversions, you need to multiply the number of clicks per day by the percentage of conversions associated with that keyword. To determine your daily budget for a keyword, multiply the average value of a conversion by the average number of conversions in a given day. To find the monthly budget, multiply the daily budget by the number of days in the month. The whole equation should look something like the following (the numbers used here are for example purposes and have no corresponding metrics):

- **Average Number of Conversions** = 15 (clicks per day) × .08 (% conversion rate) = 1.2 (conversions per day)
- **Daily Keyword Budget** = $5 (average conversion value) × 1.2 (conversions per day) = $6 (daily budget)
- **Monthly Keyword Budget** = $6 (daily budget) × 30 (days in the month) = $180 (monthly budget)

One more thing about these equations: The budget illustrated would be your absolute maximum budget, because spending that amount would equate to spending all the profits that you're making with your PPC campaign. Obviously, you won't want to do that. Breaking even is not the point of PPC advertising, making a profit is. Therefore, it would be more realistic to expect to spend about $3 to $5 a day on that one keyword. That would make your keyword budget in a 30-day month $90 to $150 each month.

A Different Kind of Auction

As we talk about auctions and bidding on keywords, you may be thinking of that end table you bought at the Auction Barn a few years ago. That's not quite the same thing. Although you *say* you're bidding on the keyword, what you're actually bidding on is the placement of an advertisement containing the keyword — and there are numerous placements, numerous times per day, and probably millions of searches in which the ad could theoretically be displayed.

For example, let's say your maximum bid is $1 on a keyword of your choice. This means that every time your advertisement is shown, you can be charged up to $1. If someone else comes along and bids higher than you, that person's ad will be shown in a more optimal place than yours.

continued

continued

Because it's possible that you're being charged $1 every time your ad is shown, your advertising budget could be inflated to a sizable bill within 24 hours if your ad were shown every time the keyword you're bidding on was shown. Therefore, to keep the advertising budget manageable, you can put a cap on your budget for each keyword.

If your budget for that keyword were $25 a month, and the word stayed at the $1 level (it can drop below that at any time, depending on what your competition's highest bid is), your ad could be shown 25 times a month; but the price of words (or the ads in which they appear) is dynamic, going up and down as other ad owners increase or decrease their bids. If the price drops below $1, this increases the number of times your ad can be shown, and any amount over that $1 bid decreases the number of times it will be shown.

We'll get into this in a little more detail as we discuss bid management and such practices as bid jamming.

That's for a single keyword, however. If you're bidding on 20 keywords, and you choose to pay the same amount for all those keywords, then your overall monthly PPC spend would be $1,800 to $3,000 per month. Most small and medium-size business can't afford to sink that much money into a PPC program, so you have to find a way to reduce that amount. That's usually accomplished by beginning with a few of the keywords that you've defined and then replacing the ones that don't work with others from the list that you've defined.

It's important to remember, however, that PPC shouldn't be the only element within your SEO budget. In fact, PPC should equate to only 20 or 30 percent of your total SEO budget. Other SEO efforts should also be ongoing, so that over time your organic keywords and other SEO efforts become as effective as your PPC and other paid marketing campaigns.

Understanding Bid Management

According to some experts, online marketers will spend more than $20.9 billion on PPC campaigns by the year 2013. This means that PPC campaigns are going to become more competitive and more expensive in the very near future. To help you compete, you'll need to monitor and manage your keywords very closely. *Bid management* is the method by which you control the amount spent on keywords. There are two methods for bid management: *manual bid management* and *automated bid management*.

Manual bid management

Manual bid management is bid management that you conduct on your own. To manually manage your PPC bids, you must keep up with what your competition is doing, track your conversions, test and monitor the performance of existing and new keywords, watch your PPC campaigns for fraud, and make changes to all campaigns when necessary. And if you happen to be running PPC campaigns with more than one PPC provider, you must do all that for every group of PPC ads you're running. It's a very time-consuming process.

That fact alone is enough to make some people opt to use automated bid-management software or services; but even with automated bid management, there are a few strategies that you'll need to manage on your own:

- **Don't obsess over the number-one slot:** It's contradictory to what you would assume, but you don't really need to be number one. Nor can you afford to be number one in most cases. The number-one slots are usually snatched up by large companies that are using PPC to boost their sales, and they often have seemingly unlimited budgets to spend on their PPC efforts. That means if you're fighting for the number-one slot, you're likely to spend so much on that spot that your PPC campaign will be pointless.

  Another reason to avoid the number-one slot is that most people don't trust the first ad or search result on which they click. Many people will click through several ads before they make a purchase, provide information that generates a lead, sign up for a newsletter, or-whatever else it might be that you're hoping to entice them to do. Having your ad or search result a little further down than number one — say, number three or four — will result in great savings and probably be just as effective, if not more so, than if you were paying for the number-one slot.

- **Select keywords for the stages in the buying process that you're targeting:** This goes back to separating your keywords by intent (which was covered in Chapter 5). Manual bid management is often about choosing the right keywords. If you can define various steps in the purchase process, then you can target each step in a different way, investing less in the research stage and more in the final purchasing stage. If you're not selling products, then there may still be stages in which you can invest, and determining which of those stages is most valuable to you will help you decide how to best spend your PPC budget.

- **Delete duplicate words from your keyword lists:** Many organizations have several different keyword lists for different departments or different stages, and often a keyword will apply to several of those lists; but you shouldn't include a keyword on more than one list for your organization. If you do, you'll be bidding against yourself for placement.

- **Monitor your keywords and PPC campaigns every day:** Even if you're using a bid-management application or software, hands-on management is still required. You'll need to monitor and make decisions for the application or software. Usually an hour or two a day is enough.

Manual bid management isn't nearly as effective or manageable as having an automated bid-management solution, unless you only have a few keywords to monitor. If you're like most companies, though, you have dozens or even hundreds of keywords to stay on top of, and handling all those keywords and PPC campaigns manually could be so time-consuming that it's all you would ever do.

Automated bid management

Automated bid management can take one of three forms: as part of a solution provided by your analytics or PPC program provider, as desktop software, or as a hosted service. Many analytics providers (such as Google Analytics) and PPC program providers include some form of keyword-management reports and capabilities with their products, such as the Google Analytics report shown in Figure 10-1. These reports are great for basic keyword and PPC campaign management, but they often lack the functionality that desktop software and hosted services provide. However, if you're only managing a handful of keywords, then the capabilities provided by your analytics provider should be all you need.

FIGURE 10-1

Google Analytics provides reports that illustrate keyword values.

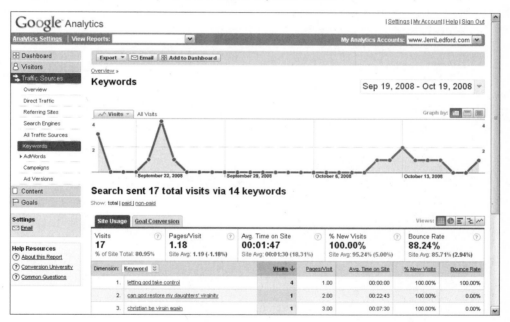

If you're managing more than a handful of keywords, then you'll need something much more powerful to help you stay on top of your keywords and PPC campaigns. One option is desktop software, which is software that you install on your computer. You maintain the software, and it helps you to manage your PPC campaigns and keyword bids. Most desktop software is sufficient for your needs, but because it requires that you maintain the resources to operate the software, manage the software updates and upgrades, and in general manage and monitor it, you may decide that a *hosted bid-management application* is a better choice.

Hosted bid-management applications, like the one shown in Figure 10-2, are those provided by third-party vendors. The vendor manages the software, the resources required to maintain the software, and all the maintenance for both software and resources. An added benefit of using a hosted application is that often the application is much richer and more robust than one you could manage and maintain on your own.

FIGURE 10-2

SearchIgnite offers a hosted bid management application to keep you on track.

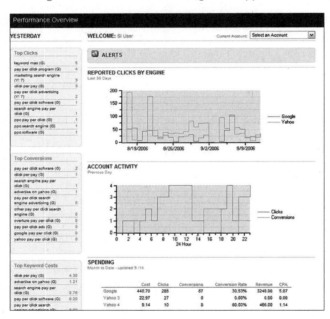

Dozens of companies offer bid-management services, including WebSideStoryBid, SearchIgnite, PPCPro, KeywordROI, and BidRank, to name only a few. Each vendor offers some similar and some different features for the applications that they provide, and the cost of hosted bid-management software can be from $125 per month to more than $1,200 per month. The cost depends on the number of keywords you're tracking and the different features that are available. Some management-application providers will also allow you to create custom management applications that fall into the same cost range.

When you're considering an automated bid-management product, you should look for several features. The most basic of these include the following:

■ **A single interface for multiple PPC campaigns:** You will most likely be running PPC campaigns from several different providers, so you need a solution that enables you to manage all of those campaigns, regardless of provider, from a single control panel.

■ **Conversion tracking:** This includes conversion rates and cost per sale for each keyword that you're tracking.

■ **Global change capabilities:** When you make a change to your PPC campaign, whether it's changing a word, changing your strategy, or changing your bids, you may need to have those changes reflected in multiple places. Good bid management software is capable of making global changes — you make the change one time, and all the campaigns you specify are updated automatically.

■ **Keyword monitoring capabilities:** Bid-management software should enable you to see where your keywords are performing at any given time.

■ **Automatic bid-management capabilities:** One trick that some companies use to keep the competition at bay is called *bid jamming*. Because keyword bids, unlike those in a traditional auction, are dynamic and can go both up and down, the auction isn't over when you've paid a lot and won your word. You'd like to rebid it at a lower price. That's where the keyword jammer, by offering only a penny less than your inflated bid, tries to keep you at that level and drain your SEO budget. (Of course, you can play the same game by letting the jammer have the word and then becoming a bid jammer yourself.) Automatic bid management can keep you from going crazy by ensuring that you're bidding at the most efficient level all the time.

■ **Fraud monitoring and documentation:** *Click fraud* can be very costly. A good bid-management software application will monitor your PPC campaigns for signs of click fraud.

■ **Reporting capabilities:** Nearly every bid-management application includes the capability to generate and share reports. What those reports contain varies from vendor to vendor. Be sure to check the types of reports that are available with the solution you are considering.

Costly Click Fraud

One of the most onerous problems with PPC campaigns is click fraud. Click fraud happens when a person, group of people, or automated script clicks on PPC advertisements. Because the concept of PPC is that advertisers pay each time someone clicks on their ads, this drives the cost of ads higher and higher without resulting in any conversions.

Click fraud happens for many reasons, the most common being that a competitor is trying to drive competition out of the market. By arranging for a competitor's ads to be clicked on repeatedly without any intention of making a purchase or completing whatever goal conversion the competitor

continued

continued

has established, the overall cost of the advertisement can be inflated, while the average conversions and the value per visit are deflated.

Some advertisers also believe that PPC providers commit (or encourage) click fraud because they benefit from the additional clicks. In fact, there have been several court cases that resulted in settlements when PPC providers such as Google and Yahoo! were sued for contributing to or allowing click fraud.

One of the most frustrating aspects of click fraud is that unless all the clicks come from the same IP address, it's hard to prove that click fraud is actually happening. Some criminals have even created programs, called *clickbots*, that can create clicks from what appear to be different IP addresses. In other cases, people are paid to read and click advertisements. In some cases, there are indicators of click fraud: an inflated number of clicks without conversions, clicks that all occur from the same computer or even the same city, and a large number of clicks within a short period of time, especially if the pattern of clicks is unusual.

If you suspect that you're being targeted by click fraud, immediately contact the fraud department of your PPC provider. If you don't receive satisfactory results from reporting the activity, then you should consider pursuing legal action. Click fraud can cost your company thousands, even tens of thousands, of dollars. Worse, click fraud can destroy your PPC advertising campaign. Monitor your stats closely for any signs that you may be falling victim to click fraud.

In addition to the basic features that you should look for in bid-management software, you may want to consider some additional features. These are not essential features, but they offer additional value and make monitoring your PPC campaigns and keyword bids a much easier process:

- **Rank management:** Most bid-management software is based solely on the bidding guidelines you define. However, some software can adjust your bids automatically according to the rank of a given keyword. This can be helpful if what matters to you is the rank that your ad reaches, rather than the cost of the click.

- **Balancing strategies:** These are capabilities within bid-management software that maintain a steady conversion rate by adjusting bids according to the number of conversions. This also helps to ensure that your ROI remains steady, rather than fluctuating according to the cost of your bids.

- **Gap management:** In PPC bidding there's a phenomenon called a *gap* that appears between bids. For example, the cost per click, according to ranking, might look like this: $.56, $.53, $.49, $.28, $.27, $.26. The large drop from $.49 to $.28 is called a gap. These gaps are caused when large companies bid the same amount for each of their keywords, regardless of the average bid or the bid necessary to reach a specific rank.

  When you're looking at a gap in bidding, it's often possible to fill the gap and still reach a great ranking. Using the preceding example, if you were to bid $.30, you could jump to the fourth position; but to make it to the third position you would need to increase your cost per click a full 21 cents. For the difference between the number four and the number three spot, the additional expenditure doesn't make sense.

Some bid-management software offers gap management and will alert you when there is a gap you can take advantage of. And taking advantage of these gaps can result in lower PPC costs with the same or better results.

- **Keyword-suggestion tools:** Keyword-suggestion tools aren't necessarily part of the bidding process, but they can still be useful and should be considered when you're looking at bid-management software. Keyword suggestion tools can provide additional resources or options for your PPC keywords, which can result in finding lower-cost keywords that perform as well as those that cost considerably more.

Bid management is a time-consuming process, but you can take advantage of bid-management applications and software to reduce the amount of time you spend managing your PPC campaigns and to increase the effectiveness of those campaigns.

Tracking Keywords and Conversions

One of the keys to a successful PPC campaign is tracking the performance of those campaigns — both the performance of the keywords and the number of conversions that result from a campaign — and adjusting your campaign according to those tracking results. This tracking helps you achieve the best possible performance level for the least cost. In short, conversion tracking is the most important part of any PPC campaign.

Conversion tracking can be accomplished in one of several ways:

- **Tracking tools integrated with your PPC program:** Some PPC providers (most notably Yahoo! Search Marketing and Google AdWords) provide tracking tools built into their PPC control panels. Figure 10-3 shows some of the reports that are available with Google AdWords, but AdWords is also paired with Google Analytics, so reports can be much more detailed. These tools enable you to track traffic, conversions, and possibly even value per visit.

- **Third-party tracking tools:** These tools tend to be more powerful than those offered by PPC providers. The most important area of increased functionality is the capability to track PPC campaigns across companies. Because most web site owners have PPC campaigns running from more than one PPC provider, having the capability to manage and control all those campaigns from a single location can be very valuable.

- **In-house tracking tools:** Because some companies are unable to find tracking tools that provide the information they need, they create their own tracking tools in-house. If you have the capability to create in-house tracking tools, you can have tools that provide only the specific information you need.

- **Tracking using a spreadsheet:** Before there were PPC campaigns and the tracking tools that go along with them, web site owners would track their online advertising using a spreadsheet, developed to include all of the different categories that needed to be tracked. Today, there are still some web site owners who prefer to track their PPC campaigns (and their other online advertising campaigns) using the "old-fashioned" spreadsheet. It's one of the least expensive ways to track your PPC campaigns, but it's also one of the most time-consuming. Should you decide that a tracking spreadsheet is the way to go, consider including columns for the following:

- Keywords
- Headlines
- Ad Copy
- Click-Through Ratio (CTR)
- Keyword Cost
- Sales Indicators (to show which keywords resulted in sales)
- Information Requests Harvested
- Information Requests Resulting in Sales

FIGURE 10-3

Google AdWords offers a variety of reports to help you track the effectiveness of your keywords.

Campaign	Ad Group	Keyword	Keyword Matching	Keyword Status	Keyword Min CPC	Current Maximum CPC	Keyword Destination URL	Impressions	Clicks	CTR	Avg CPC	Cost	Avg Position
Starter Campaign	Starter Ad Group	Total - content targeting	Content					14,588	19	0.13%	$0.58	$11.08	5.6
Starter Campaign	Starter Ad Group	how to protect yourself from identity theft	Broad	Active	$0.05	$0.94	default URL	12	1	8.33%	$0.91	$0.91	13.2
Starter Campaign	Starter Ad Group	how to report identity theft	Broad	Active	$0.20	$0.35	default URL	37	1	2.70%	$0.30	$0.30	6.2
Starter Campaign	Starter Ad Group	how to stop identity theft	Broad	Active	$0.04	$0.70	default URL	6	0	0.00%	$0.00	$0.00	8.8
Starter Campaign	Starter Ad Group	identity theft	Broad	Active	$0.20	$0.81	default URL	197	0	0.00%	$0.00	$0.00	55.6
Starter Campaign	Starter Ad Group	identity theft precautions	Broad	Active	$0.05	$0.63	default URL	24	2	8.33%	$0.24	$0.48	5.1
Starter Campaign	Starter Ad Group	report identity theft	Broad	Active	$0.10	$0.77	default URL	53	0	0.00%	$0.00	$0.00	14.2

Report Generated: Aug 14, 2006 7:08:22 AM   Show report detail
Export Report   Create Another Report Like This   Aug 1, 2006 - Aug 13, 2006
View: Summary

Impressions	Clicks	CTR	Avg CPC	Cost	Avg Position
14,945	23	0.15%	$0.56	$12.77	6.31

Regardless of which method you decide to use to track your PPC campaigns, you need a way to differentiate one keyword ad from another. Some PPC providers require that this be done by inserting a snippet of tracking code on your web site. This code then catalyzes the tracking process so that when someone clicks through your PPC ad, you can track whether the click-through results in a conversion.

Following is an example of what the tracking code for your PPC campaign might look like if you're running a Google AdWords campaign. This specific code is intended as an example only. (If you try to use this code to track your web site, you'll find that it won't work because it was designed only as an example by the Google AdWords team.)

```
<!-- Google Code for Purchase Conversion Page -->
<script language="JavaScript" type="text/javascript">
<!--
var google_conversion_id = 1234567890;
var google_conversion_language = "en_US";
var google_conversion_format = "1";
var google_conversion_color = "666666";
if (1) {
var google_conversion_value = 1;
}
var google_conversion_label = "Purchase";
//-->
</script>
<script language="JavaScript" src="http://www.googleadservices.com/
    pagead/conversion.js">
</script>
<noscript>
<img height=1 width=1 border=0
src="http://www.googleadservices.com/pagead/conversion/1234567890/
?value=1&label=Purchase&script=0">
</noscript>
```

The code is placed in the HTML of your web site, according to directions provided by the PPC provider.

Another way to track your PPC campaigns is by URL. Using this method, each PPC ad is given a separate URL, which is used only by that keyword. Then, when a visitor clicks through a PPC ad and is taken to your web site, you will know which ad is working best according to the amount of traffic on the specific site.

This method does require that you have a way to track your web site traffic, but you should be doing that anyway. If you're not tracking it, how will you know what kind of traffic your web site gets?

Before you get too far into tracking your keywords and conversions, it helps to have a plan that clarifies what you want to gain from your PPC campaign. The first things that you'll need to know are the long- and short-term goals for your PPC campaign. You need to track both long- and short-term goals because without both you could find yourself throwing money into a PPC campaign that doesn't provide the results you need.

Far too often, web site owners find that they have instituted a PPC campaign that does really well in the beginning but then over time becomes more costly and less effective. If you're monitoring and handling all the elements of SEO for your site properly, then it won't be worrisome to discover that the effectiveness of your PPC campaign drops after a while — as long as the overall traffic to your site and the number of conversions on your site continue to rise.

This means that your organic SEO efforts are working. When this happens, it's time to consider other keywords for your PPC campaign. Instead of pouring more money into improving your ranking, which will decrease the return on investment from your PPC campaign, you might change the campaign by using different keywords.

WARNING As you're monitoring your PPC campaigns, make sure that your organic SEO efforts don't suffer because of your PPC efforts. Organic keywords are your true ticket to a high ROI. The more search engines rank you for free, the more effective you can make your investment in PPC. However, if you're not careful about the keywords that you use in PPC, the ads that you write for PPC, and the frequency with which you change your PPC campaigns, then you could end up cannibalizing your organic rankings — and when PPC replaces your organic rankings, you have to spend more money for lower results.

As you're tracking your PPC campaign, you should also have a set of *key performance indicators (KPIs)* that you compare your results against. KPIs are metrics that you develop based on the long- and short-term goals you have in place for your PPC campaigns. These indicators are of value for deciding when it's time to change some element of your PPC campaign.

Reducing Pay-per-Click Costs

The only phrase associated with PPC campaigns that you're likely to hear more often than *conversion rate* is *reducing costs*. Every penny invested in advertising and marketing needs to be well spent, and PPC campaigns are no exception. Budgets must be monitored and maintained, and that means finding a way to reduce the costs associated with your PPC campaigns.

During the early years of PPC advertising, you could pretty much figure a bid for a keyword or phrase and then assume that you didn't need to monitor it too closely; but that was before PPC advertising became one of the most effective advertising methods used on the Internet. Today, the competition for PPC keywords and phrases is very high, which means you're likely to spend a lot more money to achieve the same rank than you needed to in the past.

If you're not careful about your budgeting habits in the context of a PPC campaign, you could spend tons of money without getting better results. Management strategies, however, will help you reduce the cost of your PPC campaigns, while maintaining or even improving your click-through and conversion rates.

Managing PPC campaigns

When you consider management of your PPC campaign in the context of reducing the budget, there's a lot you can do to reduce your costs without decreasing the effectiveness of your campaign. Your first step should be to replace any poorly performing ads. Monitoring your ads should already be a key part of your PPC campaign, so determining those that aren't performing well should be easy.

Another way to reduce your PPC costs is to reduce the amount of your bid per keyword. As noted earlier, it's not necessary to strive for the top advertising slot. Reducing your keyword bid by a few cents per click can make a huge difference in the cost of the campaign. Many experts believe that the top rankings aren't always the best performing. The only way to know for sure is to test, and continuously.

Just remember that reducing your bid shouldn't necessarily mean reducing your budget. Instead, use your existing budget more effectively. If you cut your budget too much, you'll lower the number of times that your keyword ad is shown each day, which in turn lowers your conversion rate.

In addition to reducing the amount you're bidding on keywords, you should also examine the keywords you've selected to determine whether you can remove any that are too general in nature or are in high demand. *General* and *high demand* can be the same, but there can also be a subtle difference. General keywords are good for branding purposes (and branding purposes only), so they are automatically high demand and high cost. Competition for them is keen. However, less-general keywords (also called *Long Tail keywords*) can also be high demand. For example, if you're in the tissue business, "tissue" is a coveted branding keyword and will cost you a lot. "Facial tissue" is less general, but it's still going to be in high demand and thus expensive. Unless it's essential that your brand be associated with one of these high-demand keywords, it's better to avoid them. That way, you won't be paying a lot for keywords that won't increase your number of qualified clicks all that much.

The more popular a keyword is, the more you'll pay for it — and with many high-demand keywords, the resulting traffic may not be as well targeted as it could be. This means a reduced number of conversions, resulting in a lower ROI. It's far better to choose keywords and phrases that are not in as much demand but are more targeted. You'll pay less for these keywords and will likely end up with much more qualified traffic from them, which translates into more conversions and a better ROI.

Match types can also help you control your PPC budget. A match type is the condition under which you prefer that your PPC ad is shown. For example, if you've selected a keyword or phrase — let's say "SEO consultant" — for your PPC advertisement, you can specify if you would like to have that ad shown only under certain conditions.

When you set up your PPC campaign, most PPC providers offer the option to choose a match type, though it might not be immediately obvious. By default, your match type will be the broadest match possible (because that means more money for the search engine), but there are several general match types that you could use:

- **Broad match:** A broad match occurs when your ad is shown to the broadest possible segment of searchers. What that means is that anytime someone searches for "SEO consultant" your ad will be shown, regardless of whether those two words appear together or other words are included with them.

- **Phrase match:** A phrase match occurs when your ad is shown for searches that contain the key phrase you've selected, in the correct word order, but also including other words. Therefore, instead of showing your ad only for searches containing "SEO consultant," your ad might also be shown for searches such as "free SEO consultant," or "SEO web-design consultant."

- **Exact match:** An exact match takes place when your PPC ad is shown only for searches that contain the exact words that you've selected, in the exact order in which you've selected them, with no other words included in the phrase. In other words, if you choose an exact match for "SEO consultant," then the only time the ad will be shown is when a user searches for "SEO consultant."

Match types offer an excellent method for reducing the cost of your ads while increasing the effectiveness of the ads. You should use caution when narrowing your match types too much, however, because you could miss possible clicks from people who aren't exactly sure what they're looking for.

One more method for decreasing your PPC budget is to modify your PPC strategy. This actually should be an ongoing strategy for any PPC campaign, even if you're not trying to reduce your budget. Monitor and review your amount of PPC spending versus the number of conversions you achieve. Then use this information to make changes to your keywords and ad copy to increase the effectiveness of your PPC campaigns.

Negative keywords

Negative keywords are words that cause a PPC ad *not* to be shown. These are words that can be associated with the topic that you're targeting, but not with the specific product or service that you're advertising. For example, if your web site sells traditional Christian music, it's unlikely that you will want your ad to show for people who are looking for rock, pop, blues, or rap music. You can flag those words as negative keywords to reduce the number of times that your PPC ad is shown.

Some PPC providers actually have a *negative keyword tool* that makes it easy for you to add negative keywords to your PPC campaigns. If your PPC provider doesn't have such a tool, then you can add negative keywords to your keyword lists by placing a negative (-) sign in front of them. Using the music example, then, your negative keyword list might look something like this:

-rock

-pop

−blues

−rap

Negative keywords should result in better-qualified traffic from your PPC ads, but some people are concerned that negative keywords can have an adverse effect on their PPC campaigns because they reduce traffic from the ads. If your main purpose for having a PPC campaign is to gain exposure for your web site, then negative keywords could have an adverse effect. If, however, the purpose of your keyword advertisements is to increase the amount of qualified traffic and conversions, then negative keywords are a great strategy to help reduce the cost of your PPC campaign while improving the quality of your clicks.

Finding negative keywords adds another dimension to creating your keyword lists. You must be careful when using negative keywords in keyword groups. You want to choose negative keywords that won't affect other PPC ads within the keyword groups that you're using.

The most obvious place to begin looking for negative keywords is within your keyword list. If you're brainstorming keywords, you're likely to come up with some that don't apply to your products or services but that *could* trigger your ad to be shown. You can also use a keyword-suggestion tool to suggest the different keywords and phrases associated with your products or services. Negative keywords usually appear all over the lists that are suggested by these tools.

It's possible to go overboard with negative keywords. You don't want to include so many negative keywords that your ads are never shown. Just use them when the keywords that could trigger your ad truly are unrelated to your products and services.

Dayparting

One of the most effective methods for reducing the cost of your PPC campaign is to target your campaign to the most effective times of the day or days of the week. Called *dayparting*, this strategy requires that you monitor your PPC campaigns to determine which days and hours of the day your campaigns perform the best.

Not all PPC companies offer dayparting capabilities, but many do, and some even enable you to set up automatic bid adjustments according to your dayparting schedules. This helps to reduce the cost of your ads while showing them during the most effective times of the day or days of the week.

There are other reasons you might want to use dayparting aside from the savings. Some companies use dayparting to improve the demographics to which their ads are shown. Different demographic groups use the Internet at different times of the day. For example, if you're targeting teens, you might find that they are most active online between the hours of 3:00 P.M. and 10:00 P.M. Once you know that, you can schedule your ads to be shown more often during those times, and the result should be that more teens see those ads.

The best way to determine the most active times for your ads is to look first at the metric for average time on your site. The average time it takes visitors to click through your ad indicates their level of interest. For example, if you find that people who click through your ads between 8:00 A.M. and 5:00 P.M. spend twice as much time on your site than those who click through at other times, then you can assume that those who visit your site during the daytime hours are more interested in what you have to offer. As a general rule, those who are more interested will contribute more goal conversions.

After you have determined during what hours your site visitors spend the most time, you can look at the number of visitors who access the site during that time and the number who result in goal conversions. These numbers should give you a pretty clear idea of what your dayparting schedule should look like. An example of a dayparting schedule is shown in Table 10-1.

Looking at the schedule, it's easy to see the pattern in the average number of seconds that visitors spend on your site. Between 9:00 A.M. and 11:00 A.M., visitors spend slightly more time than they do during the lunch hours. However, users spend the most time on the site (by seconds) between 2:00 P.M. and 6:00 P.M. These are the hours in which you should invest the most.

In addition, you can see that the company is closed all day on Sunday and before 9:00 A.M. during the week, and is short staffed all day on Saturday. These are times when you would want to keep your ad exposure low or nonexistent.

NOTE Dayparting also has an additional benefit that many people don't think about. It can help you reduce the instances of click fraud that you may face. Because your ad is shown only at specific times, it is less available for your competition or other malicious souls to use it to drive up your PPC advertising costs.

TABLE 10-1

Typical Dayparting Schedule

Hours	Monday	Tuesday	Wednesday	Thursday	Friday	Saturday	Sunday
8–9	Closed	Closed	Closed	Closed	Closed	Closed	Closed
9–10	32.7	33.5	31.6	33.4	33.3	Short Staff	Closed
10–11	31.1	38.2	35.6	39.2	36.9	Short Staff	Closed
11–12	21.0	21.6	20.5	18.5	22.0	Short Staff	Closed
12–1	18.6	17.2	19.4	18.4	16.5	Short Staff	Closed
1–2	18.3	18.1	18.9	19.1	17.7	Short Staff	Closed
2–3	45.9	39.2	41.7	49.9	43.6	Short Staff	Closed
3–4	56.7	57.9	51.0	60.3	51.1	Short Staff	Closed
4–5	59.9	56.7	55.3	59.7	60.4	Short Staff	Closed
5–6	60.4	61.7	55.8	59.0	59.3	Short Staff	Closed
6–7	18.7	23.5	19.1	18.0	17.9	Short Staff	Closed

Dayparting also works for days of the week and is especially useful if your products or services are seasonal in nature. For example, if you find that your ads generate the most traffic on weekends, then you may decide that exposure during the week isn't as important as exposure on the weekend. In that case, you can keep your exposure during the week to a minimum and increase it dramatically over the weekend. This should result in lowering your budget; or, at the very least, your budget should stay the same while the effectiveness of your PPC campaign increases noticeably.

CROSS-REF Another strategy that can help you reduce your PPC costs is geo-targeting. You'll find more information about geo-targeting in Chapter 16.

Improving Click-Through Rates

Some of the efforts you make to reduce the cost of your PPC campaigns can also lead to improved click-through rates. It's essential that you work toward increasing these rates. Even though more clicks drive up the cost of your PPC campaign, they also lead to more sales or conversions.

Aside from the efforts that you've already seen (such as dayparting and better targeting), you can also improve your click-through rates by improving the ad copy in your PPC campaigns. Ad copy is covered in more depth in Chapter 13, but for now you should know that there are a few strategies for beefing up that copy:

- **Include special offers or incentives in ad text:** If you have coupons to offer, discounts available, or even free gifts with a purchase or other special offers and incentives, be sure those are included in your PPC ad text. People are drawn to specials, and advertising them should increase the number of visitors to your site.

- **Consider including prices in ads for products or services:** Many people shy away from advertising their prices, but those prices (especially if they're real bargains) can entice customers. If you have great prices, tell the world. Just make sure you check out the competition before you decide you have the best prices on the Internet!

More About Click Fraud

As noted earlier, click fraud is becoming an increasingly difficult problem with PPC advertising. Don't fall victim to the lure of participating in some click-fraud scheme to increase your click-through rates. The results will be disastrous.

continued

continued

Click fraud is a crime. Just as you should avoid being victimized, you should avoid taking part in falsely inflating the number of click-throughs on PPC ads either for personal gain or simply as a way to harm the competition.

Click fraud can be conducted in several ways. Competitors may click through your ads repeatedly to increase the number of click-throughs for which you are charged. Some advertisers have been billed for more than $100,000 in PPC costs because a competitor arranged to have their PPC ads clicked repeatedly.

In an effort to insulate themselves from criminal charges, and to create as much havoc as possible, some advertisers will employ *clickbots*, programs that search for and click on PPC links to drive up prices. These clickbots are usually automated and very often can't be traced back to their owners.

Click fraud is also conducted by a program called Paid-to-Read (PTR). Underhanded businesses hire readers to read and click through PPC ads. Again, this can be costly, but even more worrisome is the fact that PTR schemes are difficult to track because multiple people using valid IP addresses are clicking through the ads. It's much harder to track multiple individuals than to track a single individual at one location using a repetitive activity or clickbots to commit click fraud.

Click fraud is monitored by watching the sources of PPC traffic. If a large number of clicks come from the same IP address, it's obvious that fraud is being committed. Often, though, this isn't the way it happens. Criminals use IP-alternating software programs to click on ads. These clicks appear to come from legitimate site users.

Another indication of click fraud is when a number of ad clicks seem to occur within a short time frame (for example, 100 clicks over the course of 10 minutes). Monitoring traffic patterns is one way that anyone committing PPC may be caught.

In the past, anyone caught conducting click-fraud schemes would receive what equaled a slap on the wrist. Today, however, many search engines are being made to answer for click fraud and the associated costs that PPC users are having to pay because of it, so those search engines are cracking down. If you get caught conducting a click-fraud scheme, you could face stout fines and possibly even a criminal prosecution that could result in jail time.

Click fraud is a serious crime. Don't be victimized — and don't be tempted to victimize someone else.

- **Highlight a key feature of your product or service:** Key features can be used to draw additional clicks, and they should be better-qualified clicks than if you just include the name of a product or other more general information.

- **Create a sense of urgency:** People are motivated by time limits. If you have a limited-time offer, make sure your PPC ad makes it clear that there's a special going on, but only for a given amount of time. You can also create a deadline, which will motivate potential customers to click through your ad.

- **Use a call to action:** People often hesitate to take action on their own. Your PPC ads will be much more effective if you include a call to action that gives people a reason to click through your ad. Buyers need directions, and they want you to make as many decisions for them as possible, so if you can definitively tell customers they should take some action (such as *click here for more information*), they're more likely to click through your ad.

When you're creating PPC ads, you also want to use the most active language possible. The following two ads are for the same product, but the first is written in a weak style, using language that's not compelling enough. The second ad improves on those factors, making the ad more effective for your PPC campaigns:

- **Mediocre ad:** Learn about government grants. E-book provides details about grants available to you.

- **Better ad:** Free money from Uncle Sam! Learn how to land federal grants and free money!

The hook and the active language in the second ad make it much stronger (and therefore more effective) than the first ad, even though they both say almost the same thing.

Don't be afraid to play with your ad copy a little if you find that your PPC ads aren't performing as well as you would like them to. Changing the copy just a little can sometimes make a huge difference.

The ROI of PPC

Return on investment (ROI) is the final word on the success of many PPC campaigns. However, sometimes organizations look at ROI differently than they should. Most people associate ROI with strictly a monetary value. In truth, however, there's much more to it than just money.

If you're interested in learning just the monetary value of your PPC ROI, it's easy enough to figure. Some PPC companies or the tracking companies that you use will provide the metrics for you. However, if you need to figure it yourself, the equation is simple:

```
Profit = Sales — Ad Spend — Expenses
ROI = Profit/Ad Spend
```

That's all there is to figuring out your monetary ROI. With PPC campaigns that are properly managed, the ROI on your PPC campaigns should be impressive, but there is much more to PPC ROI than this.

Other aspects of ROI that should be considered are not money oriented, though they should always be coupled with monetary valuations. For example, if the goal of your PPC campaign is to gather information about your customers, then one of your ROI measurements should be how successful your PPC campaign is at gathering that information.

Another ROI measurement could be brand loyalty or even satisfaction. Your additional ROI measurements should be based on your PPC campaign and the goals of that campaign, but don't base your whole campaign only on the monetary ROI, even if it turns out that monetarily your PPC campaign is very successful. Monitoring all your ROI measurements will help you keep your PPC campaign on track.

Chapter 11

Keyword Tools and Services

With so many keyword and PPC tools and services, it's hard to know which one to choose. You'll find, though, that only a few companies are major players in this space. The top three are Google AdWords, Yahoo! Search Marketing, and Microsoft adCenter. Others exist, of course, but these three are the best known.

They also represent both directories and search engines, which gives you a good idea of how the different types of PPC services work. The basics from the advertising end are about the same. It's the setup and some of the more advanced features that are different.

When you're looking for a PPC program, remember that you'll probably use more than one, and some companies use several to reach both broader and narrower markets. Which company you choose and whether you choose to work with more than one company should be determined by your needs. When you're considering PPC agencies, here are some qualifications to keep in mind:

IN THIS CHAPTER

Google AdWords

Yahoo! Search Marketing

Microsoft adCenter

- ■ **Length of service:** How long has this company been around? If you're considering a new agency, use caution. New companies aren't necessarily stable and you might get your campaign started only to have the company gobbled up by another — or it could just fall off the face of the Internet.

- ■ **Industry participation:** The PPC industry has been around a while, but like anything associated with the Internet, it changes often. Find out how invested your target company is in the industry. Industry investment usually means long-term plans and goals within an industry. It also means that the company is more likely to stay in good standing with customers.

- **Features and feature combinations:** Your company requirements might differ from other companies. Look at the different features and feature combinations that are offered by your target PPC provider. Some of the services that should be available include bid management, education, reporting, link submission, copywriting, and even some elements of research. Determine what features you must have and then find the vendor that can provide them.

- **Number of campaigns:** Some PPC providers restrict the number of PPC campaigns you can run at any one time. Others have restrictions on the types of campaigns you can run (that is, global versus local). Be sure to ask about limitations in this area; otherwise, you'll find out later that it's an important issue to address up front.

- **Average spend:** Can your prospective PPC company give you an estimate of the average spend for companies that use its services? This average helps you to quickly determine if your budget is sufficient.

- **Client referrals:** Client referrals are an often-overlooked aspect of PPC company research. What are other clients saying about the service? You can look for these comments online or ask the company specifically for referrals. However, if you ask the company to provide referrals, keep in mind that they will point you *only* in the direction of good referrals.

Should You Hire a PPC Management Firm?

Many companies use multiple PPC services and have dozens or even hundreds of pay-per-click campaigns running at any given time. Keeping up with all those ads and campaigns can be a real chore; and if it's not your core capability, it could take you away from activities that would be more profitable for your company.

To help keep up, some companies hire PPC management firms to take care of the daily tasks involved in running multiple PPC campaigns — keyword research, writing ad copy, tracking analytics, determining the return on investment for each campaign, and any of the other tasks that attend pay-per-click campaigns; but is hiring a PPC management firm the right choice for you?

Ultimately, that's a decision that you have to make after weighing the costs and benefits. The services provided by PPC management firms can cost you anywhere from about $1,000 per month for basic services to as much as a $200,000 flat fee for a complete campaign-management package over a specified amount of time. The question is whether it's worth it for you to pay this fee to free up your time so you can focus on other activities.

If the answer to that question is yes, then you should begin the search for the right firm. Not all firms are created equal. You want to find the firm that will provide for all your PPC needs at the lowest cost. Among the things that you should look for in a PPC management firm are the following:

- **Appropriate focus:** Some firms promise clicks and traffic when what you really need are leads and sales. Be sure the firm you're considering is focused on capturing the leads and sales that you need to make your PPC campaigns truly valuable.

continued

continued

- **Landing page creation, management, and tracking:** The landing page is your best tool for tracking the success (or failure) of any given PPC campaign. If a firm wants to direct all your traffic to your home page, you'll have a hard time figuring out what's working and what's not. Choose a firm that understands and will capitalize on the value of the landing page.

- **Conversion tracking:** Conversions are another measurement of success. The firm you are considering should have successful methods for tracking conversions.

- **Support:** A PPC management firm is not valuable to you if you can't reach them when you have questions. Make sure that you are assigned an experienced PPC manager whom you can reach when you call. At the very least, be sure you have a clause in the contract that specifies a return call within a short period of time (a few hours is usually reasonable).

These are just a few of the facets of PPC campaign management that you should look at. Take the time to create a list of questions to ask when interviewing prospective PPC management firms, and don't forget to check references. Have frank, pointed conversations with several current and previous customers, and always ask the question, "Would you work with this firm again?"

A PPC management firm might be just what you need to help reduce the burden of managing multiple PPC campaigns. Just make sure you know what you're getting into before you sign a contract with one of these firms.

Google AdWords

Google AdWords is the PPC company you've probably heard the most about. AdWords is one of the top search engine marketing programs, and Google is one of the biggest providers of search and many other services as well.

Being the biggest doesn't always mean being the best, though. When you're evaluating the PPC companies you might use, be sure to check not only the traffic rate, but also the conversion rate if possible. It's great if your ads receive a lot of impressions, but if those impressions don't turn to clicks, you'll find that your PPC campaign is not at all effective.

You may have heard the name *Google AdWords* so often that you assume there's nothing else — and certainly it's one of the most diverse PPC companies out there. It offers not only search engine marketing, but also marketing by radio and even a telephone service that potential customers can use to call you. Google also offers TV, newspaper, and embedded-video advertising. Even the radio and phone models of AdWords are charged on a bid-per-keyword basis. Additionally, AdWords is linked to Google's AdSense program, which is an advertisement publishing program whereby web site owners place ads on their web sites, and when users click through those ads and make purchases, the web site owner is paid a small amount. Many web site owners use this service to help offset the cost of having a site.

AdWords ads are shown when someone searches on Google, AOL Search, Ask.com, or Netscape. This gives Google AdWords one of the largest markets available for keyword advertisements. Of course, a larger market doesn't guarantee a higher-quality lead, so when using AdWords, it's essential that you pay attention to the details that help place your ads when they're most effective.

Signing up for Google AdWords is quick and easy. When you begin the registration process, you must choose between the basic and standard editions of AdWords. The basic edition is great if you've never used a PPC program before. It includes one set of keywords, basic reporting capabilities, and basic targeting. The standard edition includes multiple sets of keywords and more-advanced targeting and reporting, in addition to a few other tools.

If you begin with the basic starter edition, you can graduate to the standard edition when you're ready. When you do, your starter campaign will be moved to your standard AdWords account, so you don't lose any of your existing advertisements. Regardless of which option you choose, you'll step through the process of setting up your first AdWords PPC ad when you sign up for the account. After creating an account, however, the ad won't be active until you fund the account.

Funding just means that you provide Google with a credit card number that they can use to charge your monthly advertising costs. Once you fund the account, your ads will begin showing immediately, based on the budget that you created when you set up the account.

Google enables you to change your budget, or even your ads and keywords, without too much trouble. When you sign in to your AdWords account, you should see four tabs across the top of the page, as shown in Figure 11-1. These tabs lead to different segments of the AdWords web site that enable you to manage your ad campaigns and your AdWords account.

Campaign management

The Campaign Management tab is where you'll perform most of the tasks to manage your account. This tab contains an overview of the ads that you have running, as well as links to an account snapshot, tools for managing your accounts, conversion tracking tools, a web site optimizer, an ad creation marketplace, and an ad audio library.

The account snapshot, shown in Figure 11-2, shows a quick overview of your campaign performance, as well as any alerts that you might need to see.

The Tools link is where you're most likely to find the tools that you need to edit, change, or delete your ad campaign. When you click this link, you're taken to another page with links to applications such as the Keyword Tool, the Traffic Estimator, and the Ad Creation Marketplace, which is a fee-based service that makes it easy for you to hire someone to help you create your PPC ads.

The conversion tracking provided by Google AdWords will provide you with a basic understanding of how well your ads are converting customers. The actual conversion metrics are on the Campaign Summary page of the Campaign Management tab, but on this page you can find educational information about conversion tracking and *cross-channel tracking*. Cross-channel tracking is a method for tracking all your ads through all the media available on AdWords — PPC ads, radio ads, newspaper ads, and so on.

FIGURE 11-1

Use the navigation tabs in Google AdWords to manage your campaigns and your account.

The Website Optimizer link takes you to a page that shows you results from different campaigns that you might be testing. The first time you come to this page, you are prompted to go through a tutorial, create a plan for the testing that you'll be doing, and view a sample report. Once you've clicked through these elements, you can click the Get Started button to begin using the Website Optimizer. You'll be taken to a page like the one shown in Figure 11-3 that you can use to create a new experiment or testing session.

The Ad Creation Marketplace is a service that enables you to hire someone to create your PPC ads. Using the ad specialists they have available will help you ensure that you're generating the most effective copy possible.

The Ad Audio Library is one of the newest features of AdWords. This feature enables you to create audio ads for use with the audio capabilities that Google AdWords has recently put into place.

FIGURE 11-2

The account snapshot is a brief overview of your AdWords campaign.

FIGURE 11-3

Use the Website Optimizer to test different configurations for your PPC ads.

Open any of these links to be taken to a page that displays additional information, capabilities, and training materials about that feature.

Reports

The Reports tab is where you'll find all your reporting capabilities. Figure 11-4 shows the opening page of the tab, where you can see existing reports and the links to create new reports. The reports available here include the following:

- Statistical reports
- Financial reports
- Conversion reports

FIGURE 11-4

The Report Center provides an overview of your current reports and specifies which reports are set to run automatically.

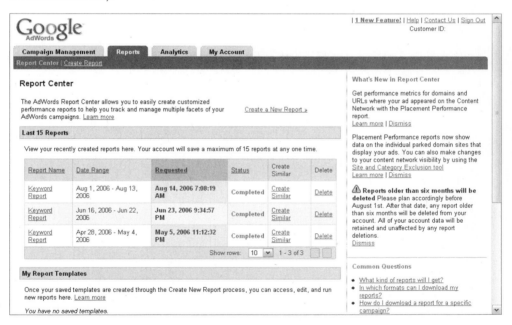

In addition to these reports, you can also create your own reports, building from a foundation of those available. These reports can provide information about many aspects of your campaign, including the following:

- Keyword performance
- Ad performance

- URL performance
- Ad group performance
- Campaign performance
- Account performance
- Search-query performance
- Placement performance

These reports can be customized based on specialized dates or date ranges, level of detail viewed, and several other options. Filters enable you to further customize the reports to return only the information you need.

Finally, you can download and print reports and even have reports run automatically on a specific day of the week or month and sent directly to your e-mail inbox. This ensures that the report is generated on the same day you need it, even if you're too busy to stop and think about it.

Analytics

Analytics reports measure different aspects of your PPC campaigns, such as keywords used to find your site, entry path, exit path, conversions, and even the amount of time spent on the site. Instead of just supplying the basic analytics with AdWords, Google takes it one step further and enables you to connect your AdWords campaigns with your metrics in Google Analytics. The result is a much clearer picture of how your campaigns are running in the context of how other SEO efforts are affecting your site.

If you don't have Google Analytics, it's easy to get and it is free. AdWords will walk you through the process of setting up your Analytics account and within a few days you should begin seeing metrics from your web site traffic. You will, of course, need to tag your PPC campaigns so that you can differentiate one from another in your Google Analytics reports, but the help files on the Google Analytics web site (www.google.com/analytics) can help you tag your campaigns in just a short while.

My Account

Keeping track of your invoices, billing information, account access, and account preferences can be a nightmare if all that information is located in different places, but with AdWords it is all on the My Account tab.

When you first open the tab, a billing summary is displayed, as shown in Figure 11-5. This summary shows basic information about your last couple of billing cycles. For more information or to change your billing methods, click the Billing Preferences link near the top of the page.

This tab also provides a link that enables you to manage who has access to your account. This is an especially handy feature when you would like to enable other people in your organization to access your AdWords account. Just be cautious about allowing others to access your account, because once you have added someone else, that person is capable of changing and deleting reports, and even deleting other users, including you. Be sure that you trust anyone you plan to add to your account.

FIGURE 11-5

Use the My Account tab to see a detailed billing summary of previous invoices.

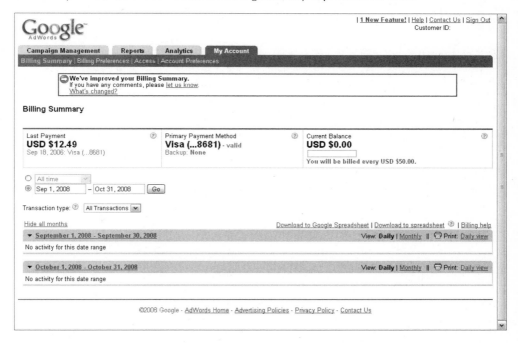

Print Ads

One last tab that might appear on the AdWords page is the Print Ads tab. A newer feature of AdWords, this page enables you to create your own print-newspaper ad, specify the newspapers in which you'd like it to appear, including which sections your ad should be shown in. Once you've selected these options and created your ad, you can bid for placement, just as you would bid for keyword placement.

Although the Print Ads feature of AdWords has little to do with your PPC campaigns, it is an interesting way to increase the effectiveness of your advertising without necessarily increasing your total advertising budget; and if the print ads are bringing traffic to your web site, you still need to maintain your SEO efforts, including PPC advertising.

Yahoo! Search Marketing

Another type of search engine is the directory search engine. Directories don't display search results based on keywords; instead, they display results by category and subcategory. Web sites are usually categorized by the site, not by pages on the site. This means that your overall listing in directory search results will depend largely on either paid placement or correctly categorizing your site as tightly as possible.

Yahoo! Search Marketing is a PPC program that's similar to AdWords, but there's one big difference: Yahoo! is a very commercial search engine, which means that many of the search results are paid-placement ads or are web sites that have been added by the web site owner. Editors usually review and approve submitted listings before these are shown in search results.

Yahoo! is also a portal that contains many different services, such as instant messaging, e-mail, maps, and much more (Google is structured in a similar manner). Being a portal means that Yahoo! has many loyal users who are likely to see your ads once you begin a PPC campaign with Yahoo! Search Marketing.

When you sign up with Yahoo! Search Marketing, you have two options for the type of account you'd like to have. These options are different from Google, because you can have a free PPC plan that you use, create, and maintain on your own, or you can choose to have a Yahoo! specialist help you create your campaign. If you decide to use a Yahoo! specialist, you pay a one-time $199 setup fee.

As with Google, there's no reason to pay when you first begin your PPC advertising with Yahoo! Search Marketing. You can start with the basic, free PPC service; and if you find that your ads don't perform well or that you need help managing your campaigns, you can always upgrade to the paid service. You even have the option of creating your first ad without providing billing information to activate the ad. As with Google, the ad won't begin showing in search results until you have activated it with billing information.

After you complete the sign-up process and log into your account, the setup is similar to AdWords. The tabs are a little different, but it all works basically the same. The tabs available in Yahoo! are the Dashboard tab, the Campaigns tab, the Reports tab, and the Administration tab. In addition, links on the pages will take you to other features and capabilities.

Dashboard

The Dashboard in Yahoo! Search Marketing is shown in Figure 11-6. It gives you a brief overview of some of the metrics related to your PPC campaigns. For example, one of the report snapshots that you'll see is for account performance. This is just a quick-and-dirty look at the number of clicks, the number of impressions, and the cost of your PPC campaign.

One feature that doesn't exist on the dashboard (it would be nice to have) is the capability to add or remove metrics based on your specific needs. Perhaps Yahoo! will include it in future versions of the program. For now, what you see is what you get — and it's enough to get you started.

FIGURE 11-6

The account dashboard provides an overview of some of the most important PPC metrics.

Campaigns

The Campaigns tab is where you'll manage and monitor your PPC campaigns. When you click the Campaigns tab, you're taken to a Campaigns Summary page. This page shows you all the campaigns you're running at any given time, the status of those campaigns, and basic metrics such as click-through rate, cost per click, and daily spending limit.

Each campaign that's listed is linked to a campaign detail page, such as the one shown in Figure 11-7. The information on this page is related strictly to that campaign, but you can dig deeper into the information by clicking one of the *ad groups* listed in the Ad Group column. When you click an ad group, you're taken to a page that lists the keywords you have chosen for that ad group, along with basic metrics such as maximum bid per click, average position, impressions, clicks, and more. There's also an Editorial column that enables you to see at a glance whether your keyword has been approved or disapproved.

NOTE Circumstances may prevent your keywords from being approved. For example, if you have duplicate keywords, then you'll receive notice of it as soon as you try to set up your campaign; or if you have keywords that are trademarked, then they may be disapproved for legal reasons. If a keyword that you want to use is not approved, try selecting a different but similar phrase.

FIGURE 11-7

The campaign detail page shows high-level data about your entire PPC campaign.

Each of the keywords in the list shown on the Ad Group page is actually a link to one more level of detail. When you click a keyword, you're taken to a keyword detail page. This page shows information such as your maximum bid for the keyword, a forecast for position or number of times the ad will be shown based on your budget, and a prediction for how much higher you will rank if you increase your daily bid. Editing features such as keyword replacement and changing your destination URL are also available.

Now let's go back to the top-level Campaigns page. When you're ready to create a new campaign, you can click the Create Campaign button to start a wizard that will walk you through the creation process. If you have not yet funded your account by providing billing information to Yahoo!, then this button will not appear and you can't create additional campaigns.

The Campaigns Summary page is one of three pages available on the Campaigns tab. The other two are the Editorial Status page, which details the editorial status of any new campaigns and keywords, and the Search page, which enables you to search your campaigns by keyword. This is a useful tool if you're running more than a handful of campaigns.

Reports

The third tab in the lineup is the Reports tab. From this tab, you can view the available reports that Yahoo! provides (shown in Figure 11-8), but you cannot create custom reports. The extent of the customization that you can achieve here is changing the date ranges to something other than the default.

Using the Reports tab, you can view reports at the summary level or access more detailed reports such as Ad Performance.

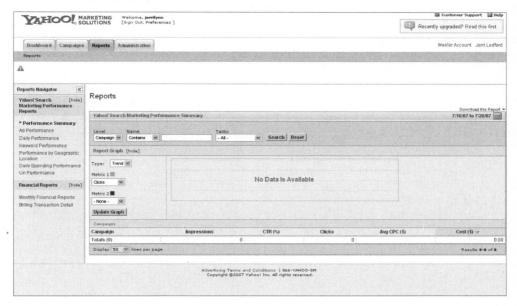

Even though you can't customize Yahoo!'s reports, a good selection of reports is available. The main report on the Reports tab is a summary. It's another of those at-a-glance reports that provides the most commonly accessed basic metrics. In addition to the summary report, eight other reports are available:

- Ad Performance
- Daily Performance
- Keyword Performance
- Performance by Geographical Location
- Daily Spend Performance
- URL Performance
- Monthly Financial Reports
- Billing Transaction Detail

Administration

The last tab, Administration, is where you'll handle all the housekeeping issues associated with your Yahoo! Search Marketing campaign. When this page opens, you're taken to an administrative summary that details information about several different aspects of your Yahoo! Search Marketing account. The information available to you includes the following:

- Account General Information
- Account Daily Spending Limits
- User Administration
- Billing and Payment Information
- Tactic Settings

User Administration is where you'll handle adding users from other accounts to your account, deleting users from your account, and creating new user accounts. You also have access to the Master Account User profile, which enables you to change passwords and assign the level of administration that master users and account users can have.

The Tactic Settings area has another set of useful capabilities. Tactic Settings are those that guide how your PPC ad is distributed. With Yahoo! Search Marketing, you have the option of allowing sponsored searches, different types of content matching, and excluded words. These settings help you to further target your PPC campaign in order to obtain the best results possible.

There are some differences in the capabilities of Google and Yahoo!, but those differences should be easy to get used to once you begin using either of the programs. Both are designed in a way that makes it easy to quickly orient yourself and begin using the programs. One advantage of Yahoo! over Google, however, is that Yahoo!'s help files are less circular and much easier to understand. A major difference between the two engines is that Yahoo requires a minimum bid of $.10 for each keyword, whereas Google's minimum bid on keywords can be as low as $.01.

Microsoft adCenter

Microsoft adCenter used to be known as MSN AdCenter. Microsoft has rebranded the advertising program to draw it closer to the Microsoft family of products, but it's essentially the same adCenter that has always ranked among the top PPC programs available.

PPC ads through Microsoft adCenter are distributed on the MSN web portal and on the Live Search network. Setting up your Microsoft adCenter account is a little different from setting up a Google or a Yahoo! account. Microsoft requires you to provide your billing information up front, even before you create your first ad. There is also a one-time setup fee of $5 that is charged to the credit card you provide for payment. This setup fee is charged immediately to your account.

Once you've provided billing information, you can begin to set up your first adCenter ad. When you sign into adCenter, you're taken to a general page that includes four tabs, which you can use to manage your adCenter ads. These tabs are Campaign, Accounts & Billing, Research, and Reports.

Campaign

The Campaign tab in adCenter is like its counterparts in both the Google and Yahoo! programs. When you click the Campaign tab, you're taken to an overview page (shown in Figure 11-9) where you can create or import PPC campaigns. To create a campaign, click the Create Campaign link to start the creation process.

You'll be asked to provide all the same information that you have to enter for both Yahoo! and Google campaigns, including a name for the campaign and the information necessary to target your customers. Once you've completed this step, you move on to creating your ad and developing your budget.

FIGURE 11-9

The Campaign overview page is where you begin creating your first campaign.

One thing you'll notice that's a little different in the adCenter campaign creation process is the capability to target even your first ad to specific times or days of the week. Other PPC providers may offer this service, but Microsoft's adCenter is the only one that enables you to set up a schedule when you create the first campaign. As you may remember from the discussion on dayparting in Chapter 9, this strategy can help you better target your ads to the time periods when your click-throughs and conversions are likely to be the highest.

The importing capability is also unique to adCenter. Using this capability, you can import PPC ads that you've created in Excel or another spreadsheet program. If the ads were not created in Excel, you should save the file as a .csv file for importing.

Accounts & Billing

The Accounts & Billing tab is where you'll find controls for your PPC accounts and billing information. When you click the Accounts & Billing tab, you're taken to an Account List page like the one shown in Figure 11-10. From this page you have access to three additional tabs: Company Information, Payment Methods, and Billing.

FIGURE 11-10

Use the Account List page to access company and billing information about your adCenter campaigns.

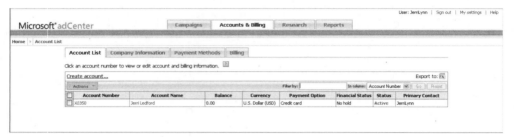

The tabs make it obvious that you can access different information about your accounts from this page, but there's a much easier way to access that information. Instead of clicking a tab to read specific information, you can simply click the account number to access all the basic information on one page. From there you can make whatever changes need to be made, including changing billing information and canceling campaigns.

Some of the tabs provide additional features. For example, on the Billing tab, you can pull up billing statements, which can't be accessed by clicking the account number on the Account List page.

Research

Maintaining a PPC campaign means continuously researching new keywords. The Research tab in adCenter gives you the option to generate new keyword lists based on a single keyword, a key phrase, or a web site. On the Keyword Research Tools tab, simply enter the keyword, phrase, or web site that you would like to use as a basis for your keywords and click Submit. A keyword list like the one shown in Figure 11-11 is generated.

If you find keywords on the list that you would like to add to your existing list, place a checkmark next to the box beside the keyword in the column on the left. It will be transferred to the column on the right. When you're finished, you can copy and import the desired keywords into your keyword list.

A useful feature of the keyword research tool provided by adCenter is the metrics that are provided with each keyword. Each keyword in the list generated by the research tool has two numbers next to it. The first is the number of searches for that word or phrase during the previous month. The second is the number of searches that have been done using those keywords in the current month. These numbers help you to quickly see how popular your selected keywords are.

FIGURE 11-11

Use the Research tab to generate new keywords to add to your PPC campaigns.

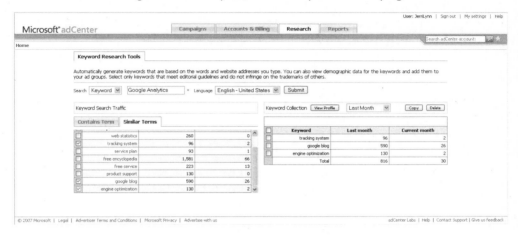

Reports

The final tab in the adCenter dashboard is the Reports tab. Like Yahoo! and Google, this tab contains reporting capabilities to help you monitor and maintain your PPC ads. When you click the Reports tab, you're taken to the Create New Report page, where you can do just that. Once you've created a first report, it will appear on the Recent Reports tab with any other reports that you may have run in the past. You can choose to leave the report there or delete it if you no longer need it.

Also within the Reports tab is the Report Templates tab. This is where you'll find any templates that you've created for reports. Storing a template here makes the process of generating more specialized reports much faster. You don't need to create a new report type each time you need to generate it. Simply save the report as a template; and then the next time you want to run a report, select the template during the report creation process.

Overall, Microsoft adCenter is a little different from either Yahoo! or Google, but the same basic concepts and capabilities apply. One big difference among the three PPC programs, however, is traffic. According to studies done by industry analysts, Google tends to have very high traffic but it's one of the least expensive PPC programs. It would seem that Google, then, would be the logical choice for a PPC campaign. However, it's possible that under the right circumstances, Microsoft's adCenter might have a much better conversion rate. It's one of the most expensive PPC programs you'll find, but the audience is smaller, so the traffic is better targeted and the conversion rate can be much better for some ads.

Yahoo! has the highest traffic of any of the three, but the conversions at Yahoo! are not as high as at either Google or adCenter. Some experts believe that it all comes out in the wash.

For example, because Google has high traffic, medium conversions, and low cost, it can be as effective as adCenter with its higher costs, lower traffic, and higher conversions.

It makes it difficult to decide where you should invest your PPC budget, which is why many organizations opt to use more than one PPC campaign provider. Using multiple PPC vendors means better coverage with your PPC ad, which can lead to better conversions.

Chapter 12

Tagging Your Web Site

Y

ou may remember from Chapters 4 and 7 that we covered some of the HTML tags most commonly used in SEO. These include title tags, heading tags, body tags, meta tags, and the alt tag. No web site should be without those tags in the HTML that makes up the site. However, those tags aren't the only ones that you should understand.

There are several others you might find useful. In fact, a basic understanding of HTML is nearly essential for achieving the best SEO possible for your web site. Sure, you can build a web site using some kind of web-design software such as Expression Web or Adobe Dreamweaver, but those programs won't necessarily ensure that all the essential HTML tags are included in your site, or if they are included that they are accurate and useful. It's far better if you know at least enough HTML to understand where your HTML tags are placed and how to put them there without trashing the design of the site.

Another important aspect to tagging your web site is using the right strategies to ensure that the tags are as effective as possible. For example, some HTML tags are strictly for formatting (such as the `<bold>` tag), but formatting a word with `<bold>` doesn't tell the search engine that the word is important. Using a more appropriate HTML tag (such as `<strong>`) works much better.

These are all elements of site tagging that you should know, so if you haven't already taken steps to ensure that your site is tagged properly, do it now. Search engine crawlers don't read web sites or web pages. They read the text on those pages, and HTML is a form of text. With the right HTML tags, you can tell a search engine far more about your site than the content alone will tell it.

IN THIS CHAPTER

Why site tagging is important

How site tagging works

Additional HTML tags

Advanced tag structure

Using redirect pages

Why Site Tagging Is Important

You might be thinking that if site tagging is addressed three times in this book, then it must be very important to SEO — and you would be correct. Even beyond the keywords and the PPC campaigns, site tagging is one of the most effective ways to ensure that your web site shows up on search engine results pages.

The HTML tags that you include on your web site tell search engine crawlers much more about your site than your content alone will tell them. Don't misunderstand. Content is an essential element for web site design, but it's a more customer-facing portion of the design, whereas HTML is a crawler-facing portion — and before customers will see your content, crawlers must see your HTML.

Your SEO ranking will depend in large part on the tagging that controls your page behind the scenes. Customers never see it, but without it they never see you.

How Site Tagging Works

Site tagging, as you already know, is about putting the right HTML commands in the right place. The challenge is understanding what types of tags to use and what to include in those tags. The basic tags — title, heading, body, and meta tags — should be included in every page that you want a search engine to find.

In order to make these tags readable to the search engine crawlers, however, they need to be formatted properly. For example, with *container tags*, you should have both an opening and a closing tag. The opening tag is usually bracketed with two brackets (<tag>), also known as the *greater than* and *less than* symbols. They have no mathematical significance in HTML, but that doesn't mean they are insignificant! The closing tag is also bracketed, but it includes a forward slash before the tag to indicate that the container is being closed (</tag>). Notice that the tag name is repeated in both the opening and closing tags. This just tells the crawler or web browser where a specific type of formatting or attribute should begin and end. Therefore, for example, when you use the Bold tag, only the words between the opening and closing tags will be formatted with a boldface font, instead of the entire page being bold.

Another element of web site design that you should know about and use is called *cascading style sheets (CSS)*. It's not a tagging method, but rather a formatting method. You should use CSS so that formatting tags are effective strictly in formatting, while the other tags actually do the work needed to get your site listed naturally by a search crawler.

Think of cascading style sheets as boxes, one stacked on top of another. Each box contains something different, with the most important elements being in the top box and decreasing to the least important element in the bottom box. With cascading style sheets, you can set one attribute or format to override another under the right circumstances.

A complete discussion of creating cascading style sheets is beyond the scope of this book. There's enough to learn about CSS to fill at least two additional books, and in fact dozens have been written about it.

When you're using an attribute from a CSS, however, it's easy enough to incorporate it into your web page. The following is a snippet of HTML that uses a cascading style sheet to define the heading colors for a web page:

```
<HTML>
   <TITLE>Your Web Page Title</TITLE>
   <STYLE>
     H1, H2 { color: purple }
   </STYLE>
   <BODY>
     <H1>First Heading</H1>
     <P>Enter any text that you would
         like to have appear here.
     <UL>
       <LI>List item one.
       <LI>List item two.
       <LI>List item three.
     </UL>
     <H2>First subheading</H2>
     <P>Another paragraph of text can go
         here. Add whatever you like.
   </BODY>
</HTML>
```

Looking at this bit of code more closely, you can see the following tags:

<HTML>: This tag indicates that HTML is the language used to create this web page (were this part of an entire web page).

<TITLE>Your Web Page Title</TITLE>: This indicates the title of the page.

<STYLE>: This is the beginning of a CSS indicator for the style of the web page. In this case, the style applies only to the headings.

H1, H2 { color: purple }: This is the indicator that heading styles one and two should be purple.

</STYLE>: This is the closing CSS indicator.

<BODY>: This indicates the beginning of the body text.

<H1>First Heading</H1>: This is the first header. In the live view of this page on the web, this heading would be purple.

<P>Enter any text that you would like to have appear here.: This is your first paragraph of text.

213

<UL>: This is the opening tag for an unordered list.

<LI>List item one: This is the first item in your list.

<LI>List item two: This is the next item in your list.

<LI>List item three: This the last item in your list.

</UL>: This indicates the closing tag for the unordered list.

<H2>First subheading</H2>: This is the first subheading. In the live view of this page on the Web, this heading would be purple.

<P>Another paragraph of text can go here. Add whatever you like.: Again, another paragraph of text.

</BODY>: This is the closing body tag. It indicates that the body text of the web page is complete.

</HTML>: This is the closing HTML tag, which indicates the end of the web page.

Figure 12-1 shows how this little snippet of HTML code looks when it is uploaded to the Web and displayed on a site visitor's web browser.

FIGURE 12-1

CSS, or Cascading Style Sheets, is used within HTML to define the style of a document on the web.

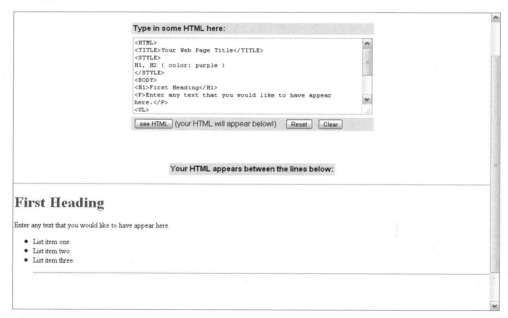

It's not difficult to use CSS for the stylistic aspects of your web site. It does take a little time to get used to using it, but once you do it's easy. Moreover, when you're using CSS to control the style of your site, you don't need to use HTML tags, which means those tags will be much more efficient.

Additional HTML Tags

You've already been introduced to the most important HTML tags for SEO, but there are literally dozens of such tags that you could use on your site. Some of them are more important than others. That doesn't mean they will be the deciding factor in your search engine ranking. It does mean that if you can include them, they'll help. This section describes some of these other useful tags.

Nofollow

One of the first tags you should consider using, as long as you can use it appropriately, is the *nofollow tag*. This tag, which is represented by <rel="nofollow">, is an attribute that tells a search engine crawler not to follow a certain link on your web site. For example, if you want to include an example of a bad site (such as a hacker's site or an SEO spam site) you may want visitors to see it, but not search crawlers. That link could reduce your search engine ranking because it's a known bad site, and when you include the link to it without blocking search crawlers, the crawlers assume that you're endorsing the site.

To save face and still have a link to your example, you can use the <nofollow> tag in the URL. The coded URL without the tag looks like this:

```
<a href="http://www.examplesite.com/">Bad Site</a>
```

When you add the tag it looks something like this:

```
<a href="http://www.examplesite.com" rel="nofollow">Bad Site</a>
```

Your URL with the <nofollow> tag could also look like the following because it doesn't matter where in the link tag you put the <nofollow> attribute:

```
<a rel="nofollow" href="http://www.examplesite.com">Bad Site</a>
```

Again, the <nofollow> tag isn't essential in your SEO efforts, but it could help prevent your site ranking from being lowered, and maybe even increase its ranking a little. At any rate, anything that keeps your ranking from falling is a good measure to take.

Strong and emphasis

When you're formatting the text on your web site, how do you format the bold and italic words? Do you use the `<b>bold</b>` and `<i>italics</i>` tags? If you do, you should consider using the CSS formatting discussed earlier. When you format a word with `<bold>`, the actual site visitor can see and understand why the word is bold. A search engine crawler, or a screen reader, cannot. All the crawler or screen reader sees is the `<bold>` tag. There's no *emotion* associated with it.

A much better use of your HTML is to use the `<strong>strong</strong>` and `<em>emphasis</em>` tags. The `<strong>` tag translates into bold formatting, and the `<emphasis>` tag translates into italics formatting, as shown in Figure 12-2. The difference is that when search engine crawlers or screen readers encounter these tags, they know to pay attention to the word or words that are included in the container.

FIGURE 12-2

Using the correct formatting on your web site gives strong or emphasized words more weight with search crawlers.

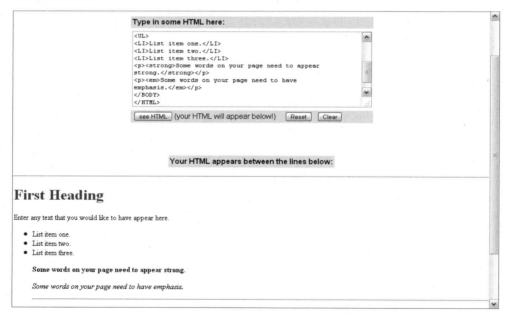

Those words within the container will also be given more weight, so if you simply boldface or italicize your keywords, they will look just like any other words on the page when the crawler or screen reader comes through. Conversely, using the `<strong>` and `<emphasis>` tags around your keywords tells those bots to notice that these words have importance and are more than simply additional words in the text of a page.

Noframes

Another useful tag, which we touched on briefly in Chapter 3, is the `<noframes>` tag. This tag is supposed to make your framed web site appear to search engine crawlers as if it has no frames. Crawlers can't read multiple frames on a page, so if you're using frames it's going to be much harder to get your site ranked in the search engine results.

The `<noframes>` tag will help, but it's not entirely foolproof. Even using the tag, you can still run into problems with browsers and crawlers. Some crawlers won't crawl a site even if it has `<noframes>` tags, so try to avoid using frames if that's possible. If you do have to use frames, be sure to include the `<noframes>` tag. Table 12-1 shows the difference between the HTML construction of a normal page, a frame page, and a frame page with the `<noframes>` tag.

As you can see in Table 12-1, the `<noframes>` tag appears after the `<frameset>` tags, but it's still read by the crawler; and in most cases, the `<frameset>` tags are ignored. As a result, your page, without the frames, is what is indexed by the crawler.

TABLE 12-1

Normal, Frames, `<noframes>` Comparison

Normal Page	Frame Page	Frame Page with `<noframes>` Tag
`<HTML>`	`<HTML>`	`<HTML>`
`<Head>`	`<Head>`	`<Head>`
`<Title>Page Title </Title>`	`<Title>Page Title </Title>`	`<Title>Page Title </Title>`
`</Head>`	`</Head>`	`</Head>`
`<Body>`	`<Frameset>`	`<Frameset>`
Body Text goes here	Frame Code goes here	`<Frameset cols="25%,*">`
`</Body>`	`</Frameset>`	`<Frame SRC="nav.html">`
`</HTML>`	`</HTML>`	`<Frame SRC="display.html">`
		`</Frameset>`
		`<Noframes>`
		`Alternative HTML goes here`
		`</noframes>`
		`</HTML>`

WARNING *Deprecated tags* are ones that are no longer useful. They have either been replaced by better tags or are not used enough now to be considered good form. An example of a deprecated tag (as of HTML 4.0) is `<center>Center a Block of Text</center>`. Because the use of CSS is becoming so widespread, some tags are being replaced by the style sheet. Be careful not to use deprecated tags in your web site design. Using them could cause your search engine ranking to drop because they make the site appear to be poorly maintained.

Table summary tag

Remember the discussion of alt tags in Chapter 7? Those are the tags that are used to present alternative text when images are essential to understanding the content of your page. Well, just as you need alt tags for your graphics, you also need *table summary tags* for your tables.

The table summary provides web crawlers and screen readers with alternative text for the table. For web crawlers, this means that instead of seeing a graphic, the crawler sees your description, which can include keywords if they are appropriate.

To use a table summary tag it should be inserted in your table code before the table caption tag. It should look something like this:

```
<TABLE border="1"
        summary="This table provides information about average 12
                year old girls: average height, weight, and
                percentage with brown eyes.">
<CAPTION><EM>Characteristics of Average Girls</EM></CAPTION>
<TR><TH rowspan="2"><TH colspan="2">Average
    <TH rowspan="2">Brown<BR>eyes
<TR><TH>height<TH>weight
<TR><TH>Females<TD>1.7<TD>0.002<TD>43%
</TABLE>
```

As you can see in Figure 12-3, you (or your visitors) won't be able to see the table summary text in the table in the lower-left corner. That's just fine. It's not meant for you to see. It's meant for search crawlers, and it gives you another opportunity to include a well-written sentence or two that provides relevant keywords or key phrases. Well-chosen words in this tag help both search crawlers and visitors using screen readers to fully understand the data used in the table.

Acronym/abbreviation tags

Another tag that you should consider using on your web pages is the <acronym> or <abbr> (abbreviation) tag. These tags simply tell a web crawler or text reader that an acronym or abbreviation is being used and what the full text for that acronym or abbreviation is.

The advantage to having your abbreviations and acronyms included in HTML tags is that if those words happen to be keywords for your page, the full text can be read by the crawler, rather than just the letters in the abbreviation or acronym.

When you're using acronym tags in your HTML, this is how they should look:

```
<acronym title="Search Engine Optimization">SEO</acronym>
```

The abbreviation tags should look like this:

```
<abbr title="United States of America">USA</abbr>
```

FIGURE 12-3

Site visitors won't see a summary in the table shown here, but crawlers and screen readers will.

On a web page (as with table summaries), you won't see anything more than the actual abbreviation. However, crawlers and screen readers will read the tag and interpret the abbreviation correctly. Without this little attribute, abbreviations can seem like nonsensical, unrelated words stuck in the center of text and can potentially cause search crawlers to flag your site as having elements of spam.

These two tags, although named differently, do exactly the same thing. Thus, many web designers have begun to use the abbreviation tag, rather than the acronym tag. Regardless of which tag you choose to use, it at least offers an additional way for you to include your keywords on your page if they happen to have an associated abbreviation or acronym.

Virtual includes

A *virtual include* is a tag that enables you to use repetitive information on your site without having to code it multiple times. For example, if you have a navigation bar on the left side of your first page that will appear exactly the same way on every other page, you can use a virtual include to repeat that navigation bar without needing to code the bar repeatedly throughout your site.

Tagging: Social Bookmarking

Tagging used to refer just to the tags that you placed in your web site's HTML to indicate certain types of formatting or commands. Tagging today often refers to something entirely different. When you hear the terms *tagged* or *tagging* in conversation today, they could very well refer to a phenomenon called *social bookmarking*.

Social bookmarking is a way for Internet users to store, share, classify, and search Internet bookmarks. There is some debate about how important social bookmarking is in SEO, but the consensus seems to be leaning toward the idea that social bookmarking, along with many other social media optimization (SMO) strategies, is quickly becoming a serious consideration for SEO. SMO is covered in more detail in Chapter 20, but let's take a quick look at social bookmarking here.

Social bookmarking is provided by services such as del.icio.us, Digg, Technorati, Scuttle, and Furl.net, which are taking the Internet by storm. They're often referred to as Web 2.0 services, because they involve a high level of social interaction, which is the fastest growing element of the Internet today.

In social bookmarking, people create their own topics and lists for places on the Internet that they like or dislike. They can then give the places they choose a category (or tag) and a rank. After they have ranked a site, they have the option to send that ranking to anyone who has subscribed to their RSS feed.

The implications this can have on SEO are dramatic. For example, suppose that one person visits your site during a web search and finds that it's easy to use and contains all the information this person was looking for. This user could very well tag various pages on your site that he or she found to be particularly helpful. The tag is then distributed to all of the people who are subscribed to that user's RSS feed. It's word-of-mouth marketing — called *viral marketing* in the industry — at its best.

Suppose one person tells 25 others, 20 of whom then visit your site. Maybe 15 of those people (60 percent) tell another 25 people each. The list keeps growing and growing, exponentially. It's much like those dreaded chain letters everyone dislikes so much, but here the participation is voluntary and the results are better — the only long-term implication of social bookmarking is improved traffic for your web site.

In other words, not only should you pay attention to social bookmarking, you should take advantage of it. That is, make your site worthy of bookmarking. Bookmarks appear to web crawlers as links to your page, and that makes them very valuable SEO tools. For some search engines, the more bookmarks that lead back to your site, the more votes you have on their popularity scale.

Begin by visiting some of the social bookmarking sites on the Internet. Learn how they work and then set up your own account. Next, create your own list of links, which includes your web site(s), of course, as well as any other web sites that users might find relevant or useful. It's important for you

continued

continued

to be genuinely involved in the community, and not just out to promote your own site. Otherwise, community members will quickly recognize your motives and the effects could be devastating.

On the web site side, be sure to include the code snippets provided by social bookmarking organizations that enable users to tag your site easily. Then, maintain it all. Don't just forget about your account completely. If you do, eventually it will disappear, along with all the advantages of having one. Instead, continue using social bookmarking. Over time, the rewards will be increased traffic to your web site.

Virtual includes can be used with ASP and PHP applications, but we'll only look at the straight HTML version here. If you want more information about writing includes for another application, try using Google to find that information. You can find many good, and free, tutorials on the Internet.

If you want something a little more comprehensive, check out *Professional Search Engine Optimization with ASP.NET* by Christian Dane and Jaimie Sirovich (Wiley, 2007). That's just one book of many in the Wrox Series that provides additional SEO information for specific programming languages.

One more thing you should know about virtual includes is that they only work with servers that allow *server side includes (SSI)*. This means that users coming from a server that does not allow SSI will not be able to see your virtual includes. That will leave large holes in your site for them; and in the case of navigation bars, it could make it difficult for them to navigate around your site.

Despite this possibility that your page may not render correctly, you may still decide to use virtual includes. If you do use them, here's how a navigation bar and a copyright notice might look on your page:

NOTE Server side includes are actually much more involved than this bit makes them appear. For example, you have to change the .html extension to .shtml in order for a server side include to work properly. If you think SSI can help you overcome a problem on your web site, then take some time to learn the intricate details of how they're written and how they work. Google is a great place to start.

```
<HTML>
<head>
Page Heading
</head>
<body>
<!--#include virtual="navbar.inc"-->
 The text of your web page goes here.
Remember that you want the text to be no
less than 250 words.
```

```
<!--#include virtual="copyright notice.inc"-->
</body>
</HTML>
```

Virtual includes can also be used to serve up variable elements on your web site, such as a visitor counter, changing error messages, or even a date that updates each time a visitor enters your site. The key is that this information is variable and changes frequently (or can be changed frequently), so including a single virtual include should reduce the amount of work you have to do in coding your web site to deal with this dynamic information.

If you do decide that virtual includes are the right choice for your site, don't overuse them. Virtual includes make a server work harder to provide information to site visitors, so make sure your server isn't overextended. If it is, the server will crash, bringing your site and everything else down with it.

This is less of a problem today than it has been in the past, but I still suggest ensuring that your server can handle the load. The last thing you want to have happen is for a spider to crawl your site and discover technical difficulties caused by an outdated server. Please the spider. Make sure your server is well suited for the demands you place on it.

Using Redirect Pages

One more item you should be aware of is the effect of redirect pages on your search engine rankings. The type of redirect that you use can affect how your site is treated by a search engine. One type of redirect page is permanent, the other is temporary. Each one has serious implications for your site ranking.

Three types of redirect pages are most commonly used in designing web pages:

- **301 redirect:** The 301 redirect is a permanent redirect page. The page appears to users as they are redirected from one web site to another or from one web page to another. The original page that is no longer available is removed within a few weeks when 301 redirects are used.

- **302 redirect:** The 302 redirect is a temporary redirect page. This page displays to users as they are redirected from one web site to another. The original page is temporarily unavailable, so when the 302 redirect is removed, the user goes back to the original site instead of the site used for redirection.

- **404 error pages:** A 404 error page redirects users to a page that displays an error message, usually one that says something like, "This page is no longer available; please check the URL and try again or use the refresh button on your browser."

It's important to understand that a search engine crawler reads a redirect according to the number that it is assigned. For example, although 301 and 302 redirects do the same thing, the codes are different: One tells the search engine crawler that the page no longer exists, and the other indicates that the page is only temporarily not being used.

Each redirect number should be used under different circumstances. For example, a 301 redirect should be used when you migrate all your web pages from one URL to another. A 302 redirect should be used when you have a temporary web site that you would rather have users see. For example, if you have a different look for your site during a holiday, you may choose to use the 302 redirect.

The 404 redirect is an error indicator. This is used when the web site that a user is trying to access errors out for some reason; either it no longer exists and there is no 301 redirect or there is an error in the coding for the site or the way the user typed the site address into the address bar.

Issues arise with redirect numbers when web site owners try to use the wrong code for the wrong reasons. Here's another example: Suppose you move your web site from one URL to another and you want to redirect your traffic to the new site. Using the 301 redirect is the correct choice in this case, because it tells the search engines that your site has moved and that the search equity built at the previous URL should be moved to the new URL.

With a 302 redirect, the search engines will never update their indexes to reflect the change in destination URL because you have indicated that the move is temporary.

Some savvy web site designers have decided that creating custom redirect pages is a good way to improve the SEO on their site, but unfortunately this doesn't always work the way it should. What happens is that the custom redirect page doesn't provide the proper redirect number to the search engine crawler, so it reads the site differently than a redirect page. This could affect your search engine rankings negatively, because the page appears to be unrelated to the other pages in your web site.

The best way to handle redirect pages for SEO purposes is to use the redirect pages in the manner in which they are meant to be used. Using them in any other way is risky in terms of your search engine results rankings.

Of course, it isn't just that simple. Once you've determined what redirect page type to use, then you actually have to include the code on the web page. Using a redirect written in HTML probably seems like the right answer, as I've pushed HTML to this point. In this case, however, HTML is probably your worst option.

In the past, HTML redirects were heavily abused to push web site visitors from legitimate web pages to spam pages. It was extremely frustrating for users to attempt to access one page only to be redirected to another. Search crawlers eventually began penalizing web sites that used HTML redirects, so even if your redirect is legitimate, it hurts your ranking.

A better way to include a redirect on your web page is through the .htaccess file. It's simple to do and effective. For example, if you're using a 301 redirect to move visitors from an old web page to a new one, then all you would need to do is add a snippet of code to your `.htaccess` file. The code might look like this:

```
Redirect 301 /oldpage/old.html http://www.yoursite.com/newpage.html
```

Note that there is no `http://www` before the old page from which you're redirecting. It's not necessary. All you need here is the path from the top level of the web site to the new page. However, it is necessary for the page that you're redirecting to. Also pay close attention to the spaces in this line of code, as they *must* appear in the right places or the code won't work properly.

What's This .htaccess Thing?

When you're working on the code side of your web site, you'll run across all kinds of elements that might affect the SEO and search ranking of your site. One of those things is `.htaccess`. It's a simple text file that you can include in the code of your web site to give directions to search crawlers.

The `.htaccess` file can be useful for a lot of different actions on your web site. Here's the short list:

- Password-protecting folders
- Creating custom error pages
- Changing file extensions
- Banning users according to IP address
- Preventing a site from inclusion in directory listings
- Using an alternative index file

The `.htaccess` file can be used for plenty of other directions to search crawlers, too, and it's easy enough to put together. All you have to do is create a plain text file with the desired commands. For example, you can include the code for the 301 redirect in the file.

Once you've created the file, save it as `.htaccess`, making sure that *nothing* is included before the `.htaccess` extension. Then, upload the file to your server using an FTP client. It's that simple.

After you've created and uploaded your `.htaccess` file, when a crawler comes along it reads the file and then better understands the structure of your site.

There are other ways to create your redirect files, too. You can use JavaScript, though it's generally not recommended for the same reason that HTML redirects are discouraged. You can also create redirects using any of these methods:

- Mod_Rewrite: This is a URL rewriting module. It's useful for ensuring that all the URLs used to access your site are uniform. To redirect users, all you have to do is create a URL rewrite file; then when users try to access the old URL it is automatically rewritten and they are directed to the new page.

- IIS: Internet Information Services. This requires that you create a redirect folder in the Information Services Manager.
- ColdFusion
- PHP
- ASP
- ASP.NET
- CGI Perl
- Ruby
- Ruby on Rails

For the last seven options on this list, a small snippet of code is required to create the redirect. That code and where it should be placed is specific to the language being used. Your programmer or web site designer should know how this is accomplished. If you're designing/coding your own web page, then a quick Google search should turn up very specific instructions about how to accomplish the redirect.

All the quirky little elements of site tagging and coding can have an effect on your web site ranking, although probably very few of these issues will completely determine your ranking. Remember that web crawlers examine hundreds of elements when determining your rank, but each piece of the puzzle should fit together to create a complete picture. You certainly don't want to have any pieces missing if there's any way to keep them all together.

Chapter 13

The Content Piece
of the Puzzle

"Content is king!" You've probably heard that phrase so many times it just sounds like nonsense. It shouldn't, though, because content truly is one of the most important aspects of your web site, from the perspective of both design and SEO.

Studies show that the number one reason people visit a web site is in search of information. Even the buying process isn't often accomplished in one visit. Instead, it sometimes takes visitors four or five visits to decide to make a purchase on your site — but it's your content that brings them back to your site those four or five times until they make the purchasing decision.

The loyalty factor is what content is all about. On the Internet, it's easy for users to click to a site only to find it's not what they are looking for and then to click away. Therefore, if you can target your site properly and serve up the right content to your site visitors at the right time, you can create a site that draws users back repeatedly. It's in that sense that content is king.

When content contributes dramatically to your customer loyalty, it's like royalty — something to be respected, babied, and even accorded some awe, because if your content is terrible, you won't get any return traffic on your site. Period. You might manage to still succeed with so-so content, but it won't be at all easy. You need and want the best.

IN THIS CHAPTER

How web site content affects SEO

Elements of competitive content

Using duplicate content

Avoiding search engine spam

Considerations for multilingual web sites

Content management systems

Understanding and using viral content

How Web Site Content Affects SEO

The crux of web site content is that it must be fresh and original in order to be most effective. If it's not, then the content can do more harm than good. As you've already seen, content is the one element that keeps customers coming back to your site. When customers return often, your site ranking improves, because that traffic registers the site with search crawlers as a valid and in-demand one.

When your content is lousy, though, your site is headed in the opposite direction. If you have content on your site that's stale or unappealing to site visitors, then the search engine crawler can register this, and your ranking is sure to drop lower and lower. You could possibly be delisted altogether.

How do you know whether your content is lousy or not? It's mostly a game of finding the right combination of content types and consistent updates; but before you can even get to the point of determining the right type of content, you need to create a content strategy.

Your content strategy is the plan by which you'll infuse your site with the right type of content at the right time. It starts with determining how to reach your target audience. By now, your target audience should be engraved on your forehead, but how you reach that audience is something entirely different. As mentioned in other chapters, if your audience is teenagers, the language and method with which you'll reach them will be different than if your audience is senior adults or stay-at-home moms, or even full-time professionals.

Once you have figured out which words and phrases your target audience are likely to use to find your web site, those will be some of the keywords you'll use in your content. Additional keywords may be discovered using some of the methods that have been covered in previous chapters.

Next, determine which users will benefit from visiting your site. Visitors click through a link looking for something. If you don't provide some benefit, then the users will click away nearly as fast as they found you. When determining what value you have to offer, don't think in terms of *your* desire to bring users to your site; think in terms of what those users are seeking. What do *they* want?

As you're considering what users want, keep in mind that there are various stages in the buying process (or any other process, for that matter). Visitors will come to your site looking for different information at each stage in the process.

For example, think about how you make a purchase. The first step is usually discovering that there's a product you didn't know about that you might want or need. Consider the iPhone, for example. You may already have a cell phone, but then you talk to some friends or colleagues who have the iPhone and maybe read a few articles or blog posts about it. You get just enough information to whet your appetite, but you already have a phone, so you're not rushing out to buy this new one. You just want to know what the buzz is all about.

You then file that information away, but you keep seeing and hearing about this phone that does nearly everything, so you take the time to learn more about it. At this stage, you're looking for deeper information. You might look at reviews, news, articles, blog posts — just about anything that provides more details. What features does the phone have? How have customers rated it? How expensive is it? Ideally, each piece of content that you read will provide progressively more information.

However, you're still not convinced you should buy it. All the information you've read needs to stew a little longer. After it's had time to ferment, though, you begin to think that maybe you can't live without an iPhone. After all, you can use it to access the Web, as a navigation system, and to access music and other applications that will help you be more productive or efficient.

Now you're considering buying, but (and isn't there always a but?) you need to justify the cost. At a price of $200 to $400 for a new phone when you already have one that works perfectly fine, you're battling with yourself about spending unnecessary money. At this point, now the information you're looking for serves two purposes: first, justifying the purchase, and second, finding the best value for your money, because if you're going to spend it (and you know you are), you want to know you're getting the best possible deal.

NOTE Value is more important to consumers than price in most cases, especially on a product such as an iPhone, which is consistently priced across all merchants. Added value in this case might mean an extended service plan, accessories, or even free shipping and a great return policy/process.

The final step in the buying process is making the actual purchase. Even for this step, you, as the business owner, have content opportunities that continue to build loyalty so customers will return to your site after the purchase.

Each step in this buying process requires a different level of content. Table 13-1 provides a breakdown of what content site visitors might expect to find at each stage.

Along with determining users' reasons for coming to your site, you should also be considering what might compel them to *return* to your site. Do you have regular sales of related products? Does your site offer some form of *dynamic content,* such as a blog or news page, that would draw them back? What other types of media (e.g., using videos or podcasting to present training materials) might you include on your site, and of what value would that be to your visitors?

Only when you've figured out what you can give your site visitors should you determine what you want from them. If you want them to sign up for a newsletter or make a purchase, include a call to action on your site and provide the tools they will need to complete the task that you want them to complete. *Every page on your web site should have a purpose.* You have to determine, on every page, what it is you want from visitors.

TABLE 13-1

Buying Process Content Opportunities

Stage	Defining Characteristics	Content
1	Curiosity	Answers to basic questions such as what it is and what's so much better about whatever has caught the visitor's attention. Companies often leverage this stage with prerelease hype and buzz created in blogs and news stories.
2	Deeper curiosity	You know the basics; what you're looking for here is some convincing: reviews, in-depth articles about benefits and uses, and comparisons of features — anything that provides additional, useful information is appropriate at this stage.
3	Justification and value	At this stage, you want it, you just need to be able to feel good about getting it. Any content that defines value — examples of how the product can be used to improve productivity or quality of life, particularly stories and reviews from real people — constitutes good content for this stage.
4	Purchasing and owning	Purchasing depends largely on loyalty and value. You build those in stages 1 through 3, but you want to keep up the momentum in this stage, so newsletters, e-courses, or other training content, and articles that explain features or accessories, can help keep customers returning to your site.

One more consideration as you're planning your content strategy: What do you do that's different from your competition? You should already have a good idea of what your competition is doing, and how it seems to work for them. What can you do differently (but just as, or more, effectively)? What sets you apart from all of the other web sites that appear in search results when a user is looking for what you offer?

Next, you need to determine what type of content you plan to include on your site to meet all the needs that have been defined by the preceding questions. There are several different types of content, and each type has its own implications:

- **Licensed content:** Licensed content is what you might buy from a content broker. For example, if you're looking for a quick way to populate your site with articles, you might turn to a company such as FreeSticky (www.freesticky.com)that offers many different articles you can use. The problem with this type of content is that it's often repeated all over the Internet. You're not the only one who will need to populate your site, and others will likely use some of the same services you do. Being used often doesn't make the content less valuable, but it's not going to rank as well with search engines because of the duplication.

- **Original content:** There are several types of original content. There's the content you write and share with others free, which is a good way to get links back to your site. You can use the content for a limited amount of time exclusively on your own site and then allow others to use it for nothing more than a link back to your site. This incoming link adds credibility to your site.

  Another type of original content is that which is distributed freely by visitors to your site. This original content can take the form of comments on your site or forum message boards. This type of original content is an excellent addition to your SEO efforts because it tends to be focused on a specific subject.

  Some original content is exclusive to your site. This is content that you create, and the only place it appears is on your web site. This is the most valuable type of content for your site, and it's the type search engine crawlers like the best. Think of it as giving the crawler some variety in its diet. It gets tired of the same thing day in and day out. The more original and exclusive content you can provide for a crawler, the better you'll rank in search results. It also doesn't hurt if that content has an appropriate number of keywords in it.

- **Dynamic content:** Dynamic content can be licensed or original. Blogs are the perfect example of dynamic content.

Once you have all these elements decided upon, you can begin to create your content. It sounds easy enough, but there's more to it than meets the eye. Not only does your copy need to be compelling to people, it also needs to be focused to help increase search engine rankings.

Elements of Competitive Content

When you begin to create your web site content, your audience is your customer or potential customer. Every word written for your web site should be written for the customer. Consider what type of information you have that would be of value to the customer, and those are the topics that you should be addressing.

Once you've determined what is most interesting to your target audience, it's time to get down to the task of actually writing the content. You can either write the content yourself or hire someone to write it for you. In addition, of course, there are the services that provide content to you, as noted earlier in this chapter. Assuming you're writing your own copy, you should be aware that some elements of web site content are more effective than others.

First, certain types of copy both draw more return visitors and please search engines. The most important of those types is content that updates and changes frequently. It's one of the reasons blogs have become such an overwhelming phenomenon. People like content that changes. We get caught up in the daily stories of people's lives, of business operations, and of useful information — and if your content changes daily, we're more likely to visit your web site.

Update your content as often as appropriate. It's always a bad idea to create content for content's sake. Try to add at least one page of new content each week. You *could* opt for a monthly schedule, but doing so would make it very difficult for people to remember you except for that one time per month when they're notified that your content has changed (assuming you have a notification system). Without any notification, they are unlikely to remember your site unless they have saved it as a favorite.

As a general rule, people today are so busy they can't keep things in their minds for more than a few hours. If you have a site that updates monthly and you tell customers or subscribers that you are having a sale next month, it's unlikely that many of them will remember. You lose the effectiveness of regularly updated content when you update only once a month or less.

When you're writing your content, there are some rules about how the content is best written for the Web. Words on a screen are viewed much differently from words on a page. Where possible, your customers should be able to interact with your words, so include links and other interactive features in your text.

Here are some additional guidelines to follow when creating your web site content:

- Make sure any content that you include on your site is contextually relevant. People and search engine crawlers will be looking at the relevance of content to your site and to any advertisements that led them to the site. Make sure everything you include is relevant in some way. It also helps if the content addresses a need the customer has.

- Use original content whenever possible. Original content is much more valuable than articles that have been distributed to you and all your competitors. Why should visitors come to your site if they can find the same information somewhere else?

- Ensure that all your content uses proper spelling and grammar. Nothing looks more unprofessional than web site content that seems as though the writer flunked English 101. It does happen, so if you're not an editor, find someone who is and ask that person to check your content before it is posted to your web site.

- Use mostly short sentences, with 10 words or less. If you must use a medium-length sentence, try to incorporate it with shorter sentences around it. Users don't have a lot of patience for long, rambling sentences in print publications, and even less patience for them on the Web (although you should vary a succession of short sentences with one a little longer — it keeps your writing from sounding like a kindergarten primer).

- Use short paragraphs with a lot of white space in between. In the print world, white space is your enemy. Too much white space means wasted space in print, but on the Internet, where real estate isn't quite as expensive, white space is essential to the flow of the content and readability. Reading on the screen is much more difficult for most people, so the extra white space helps them keep their place in the content. A good rule of thumb is to limit your paragraphs to no more than four or five short sentences.

- Use bulleted and numbered lists as often as possible without interrupting the flow of the article or the other content on your site. Such lists are easy to read. They provide the at-a-glance content that readers love and make it easy to find quickly the information they need.

- Break up your content with interesting titles, headings, and subheadings. Again, this is one of those elements of web site content that make it more at-a-glance in nature. The variety helps your readers quickly skim through to find the exact information they need. Titles, headings, and subheadings are much more important on the Web than they ever were in print.

- Use keywords where possible, but don't overdo it. You've heard this so many times by now that is should be second nature. Use keywords only where they make sense. Period.

- Use a call to action. Users will not take action if you don't invite them to, so invite them. When you need a form filled out, when you want them to join a mailing list, or when you want them to make a purchase, ask them. The adage "ask and ye shall receive" is just as valuable online as it is in offline.

Using Duplicate Content

Duplicate content is a hotly debated issue with regard to how it affects your web site ranking, and it's become an even bigger issue over time as spammers and other malicious Internet users have taken up the practice of *content scraping*, using the content from a web site on their own site with only minor changes to its appearance, not to the content itself.

Content scraping has become such a problem that search engines now look for duplicate copy, even when it is hidden behind a link like the Similar Pages link that Google uses for related content (see Figure 13-1). If they find it, your site may be lowered in the rankings or even delisted completely.

FIGURE 13-1

Google uses a Similar Pages link to group web sites with related content.

Google groups pages with similar content.

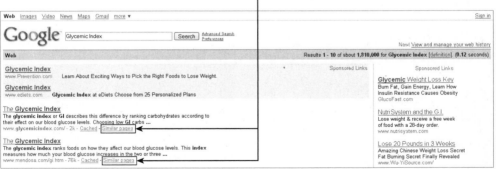

Still, the duplicate copy issue isn't as simple as it may seem. Some people think there's too much worry about it, whereas others insist the problem needs to be addressed — and both are right to some degree. Let me explain.

First, you need to understand that not all duplicate content is the same kind:

- **Reprints:** This is duplicate content published on multiple sites with the permission of the copyright holder. These are the articles that you or others create and then distribute to create links back to your site or to sites that are relevant to the content of yours. Reprints are not bad duplicate content, but they can get your site thrown into the realm of Similar Pages, which means they'll be buried behind other results.

- **Site mirroring:** This is the kind of duplication that can cause one or more of your sites to be delisted from a search engine. *Site mirroring* is keeping exact copies of your web site in two different places on the Internet. Web sites used to practice site mirroring all the time as a way to avoid downtime when one site crashed. These days, server capabilities are such that site mirroring isn't usually necessary, and search engines now exclude mirrored content because of the spamming implications it can have. Spammers have been known to mirror sites to create a *false Internet* for the purpose of stealing user names, passwords, account numbers, and other personal information.

- **Content scraping:** As mentioned earlier, content scraping is taking content from one site and reusing it on another site with nothing more than cosmetic changes. This is another tactic used by spammers, and it's also often a source of *copyright infringement*.

- **Same-site duplication:** If you duplicate content across your own web site, you could also be penalized for duplicate content. This becomes especially troublesome with blogs, because there is often a full blog post on the main page and then an archived blog post on another page of your site. This type of duplication can be managed by simply using a partial post, called a *snippet*, that links to the full post in a single place on your web site.

Of these types of duplicate content, two are especially harmful to your site: site mirroring and content scraping. If you're using site mirroring, you should consider using a different backup method for your web site. If you're using content scraping, you could be facing legal action for copyright infringement. Content scraping is a practice that's best avoided completely.

Stopping Copyright Infringement

Copyright infringement can happen to you, too. If you include original content on your site, it's very likely that someone will come along and copy that content without your permission for use on another site.

It's important for you to spend a little time each week checking for copyright infringement on your original articles. One way to do this is to pull a unique phrase from your article or other content and search for it on the Internet. If others are using your copy, it's likely that your unique phrase will pop up in the search results.

continued

continued

The problem with manually searching for unauthorized copies of your web site content is that it's very time-consuming, especially if you have hundreds of pages of content. Fortunately, you can find services and software applications that can help you quickly locate duplicate copies of your content.

One web-based service is provided by Copyscape (www.copyscape.com), shown below. You can use its free service to search the Web for content found at a specific URL. The results are usually accompanied by links to search other pages on your site.

Copyscape checks the Internet for copies of the content on your web pages.

One disappointment I noticed with the free version of Copyscape is that the pages returned in the search results were old pages. For example, some of the pages shown in the preceding figure for my web site no longer exist. It seems that in order to receive the most benefit from Copyscape, you need to pay for the premium version of the application.

Copyscape isn't expensive. Copyscape Premium is just $.05 per search, and Copysentry, an application that automatically monitors the Web for your content, is just $4.95 per month.

Another service you can use to monitor or search the Web for copyright infringement is CyberAlert (www.cyberalert.com). Several other services are also available if you decide you need such protection.

Even though reprints and same-site duplication are not entirely harmful, they are not helpful. You won't win any points with a search engine crawler if your site is full of content that's used elsewhere on the Web. Reprints, especially those that are repeated often on the Web, will eventually make a search engine crawler begin to take notice.

Once that happens, the crawler will try to find the original location of the reprint. It does this by looking at where the content appeared first. It also looks at which copy of an article the most links point to and what versions of the article are the results of content scraping. Through a process of elimination, the crawler narrows the field until a determination can be made. If it's still too difficult to tell where the content originated, the crawler will select from trusted domains.

After the crawler has determined which content is the original, all of the other reprints fall into order beneath it or are eliminated from the index.

If you must use content that's not original, or if you must have multiple copies of content on your web site, there is a way to keep those duplications from adversely affecting your search rankings. By using the `robots.txt` or `noindex` files, you can prevent duplicated pages from being indexed by the search engine.

The `noindex` tag should be placed in the page header for the page that you don't want to be indexed. It's also a good idea to enable the crawler that finds the tag to follow links that might be on the page. To do that, your code (which is a meta tag) should look like the following:

```
<meta name="robots" content="noindex,follow">
```

That tag of code tells the search engine *not* to index the page, but to follow the links on the page. This one small snippet of code can help you quickly solve the problem of search engines reading your duplicate content.

WARNING Don't make the mistake of using the `noindex` tag as a sneaky method of covering up duplicate content intentionally included to increase your search engine ranking. It will most likely backfire on you. The search engine crawler will eventually realize that your site doesn't rank well on all the criteria the engine uses to rank sites, and your search engine rankings will begin to fall.

The `robots.txt` tag can be used for a similar effect, but it won't be covered here. Look for information about `robots.txt` in Chapter 18.

Search Engine Spam

Search engine spam is one of the most difficult problems that search engine crawlers encounter. It can be a real problem for web site owners, too, because those who use search engine spam in an attempt to improve their site rankings make it even more difficult for legitimate web sites to achieve good rankings.

What exactly is search engine spam? Yahoo! defines it like this: "Pages created deliberately to trick the search engine into offering inappropriate, redundant, or poor-quality search results."

Other search engines have a similar definition for search engine spam. Ultimately, what your concern with search engine spam should be is to avoid it at all costs. There's a fine line between optimizing your web site and creating search engine spam — and you can cross that line unexpectedly. The problem is that search engines will penalize your site if they perceive any element of the site as being search engine spam. And in some cases, that penalty can be delisting your site from search rankings entirely.

There are more than a dozen types of search engine spam. Some types, such as content scraping, have already been covered. The following sections describe a few of the others, all of which you want to avoid.

Doorway pages

Doorway pages are often confused with landing pages, but they are not even close in their functions. Landing pages are designed to be rich in content, and visitors usually come to these pages through PPC ads. Doorway pages, conversely, are created specifically for search engines with the intent of increasing search engine results rankings.

Doorway pages usually use some form of redirection so that when visitors click through the link in the search engine results and land on the page, they are immediately taken to another page. This is accomplished with either a fast *meta refresh*, JavaScript, or *server-side redirection*. The meta refresh is a technique that is used less often now than in the past, because many search engines penalize web sites that use such a tactic.

NOTE Chapter 12 covers URL rewriting and page redirection. Using these techniques in the context of error pages and legitimately relocated pages is okay. It's only when using them as a dishonest method of drawing traffic to your site that you run the risk of affecting your search rankings.

In place of the meta refresh, some web sites have found clever ways to trick visitors into clicking a link that leads them forward to the web site they're being directed to. There are also some web sites that have designed *content-rich doorways*, which are doorway pages that have some element of content included as well as a basic navigational structure that's consistent with the rest of the web site. These pages, like other doorway pages, are still designed to draw high quantities of visitors, but do so using a type of false representation that results in dissatisfied users who move on to find what they were actually looking for. In other words, traffic numbers will be high, but conversions will generally be low.

Hidden and tiny text

If you plan to use hidden or tiny text on your page to draw search engine rankings, you should probably change your plans. The practice of using hidden and tiny text was used a lot in the past. Hidden text is accomplished by including keyword-rich text that is the same color as the background of your site. Because it blends in, it can't be seen by the visitors who come to your site, but it can be read by search engine crawlers.

Creating tiny text is also a fashionable, if dangerous, way to bump your search engine rankings. For example, some sites will create text that is -1,000 pixels (infinitesimally small) to load a page full of keywords.

The problem with using these black-hat techniques is that search engines have caught on to them, so they look for these tricks. When they find them, you'll be penalized or possibly even delisted. The offense is further compounded if you happen to use *keyword stuffing* in addition to hiding your text within your web site. Keyword stuffing is using a nonsensical stream of keywords, using keywords out of place on your site, or using strings of repeated keywords in your meta data. It can even be randomly including relevant keywords in various places blended with the background on your page. When you combine this method with hiding your text, it's just a matter of time before search engines refuse to include your site in their search rankings.

SEO oversubmission

Submitting your sites to search engines and directories is one tactic that some web site owners use to ensure that their sites are detected by search engines (and it is covered in more detail in Chapter 16); but most of the larger engines, while providing a way to submit a URL, actually suggest that the best way to be included in their index is to get a link to the URL.

Don't use automated submission services if you decide to submit your URL. Submit everything by hand, taking care to read the instructions completely.

Page jacking

Page jacking is a method of search engine spam that's similar in nature to scraping. The difference is that with page jacking, whole pages — and even whole web sites — are copied for the purpose of increasing search ranking and traffic for another site.

For example, a page-jacker might copy an entire site such as Microsoft and then *cloak* that site, hiding it behind his or her own page, but it still appears in search listings. Then, when unsuspecting users click through the listing for Microsoft, they're taken not to the Microsoft page, but to another page to which the page-jacker funnels them.

Not only is page jacking a good way to get your web site delisted from search engine results, it's also a crime that can result in a stiff fine and possibly jail time. That's because it's often associated with identity theft, identity fraud, and credit card or banking fraud. There are also trademark and copyright infringement issues associated with page jacking.

Bait and switch

Bait-and-switch cons are one of the oldest marketing cons that exist. It may have been tried on you at some point. Someone offers a product you want at a great price, but when you show up to purchase it, it's no longer available (if it ever was), and the salesperson tries to *switch* you to a more expensive product or one with less quality. This bait and switch still happens today, and it's now available in an online flavor.

Bait and switch in SEO is the practice of creating an optimized web page specifically for search engines with the intent of obtaining good rankings. When those rankings are obtained, the company replaces the optimized site with one that's less optimized and more normal. The result is nearly instant traffic when the site has been switched.

Bait and switch sounds good but most search engine crawlers revisit a site several times a month (and sometimes more often than that), and when the crawler revisits a bait-and-switch site, it sees that the content of the site has changed and adjusts search rankings accordingly. In other words, the person who sets up a bait and switch puts a lot of effort into a temporary optimization solution.

This is wasted effort. Why spend a lot of time creating optimization that will land you in top results only for a short while before your site is dropped altogether? Once your site is delisted, you have to go through the process of getting it included all over again. (It's even worse if your site is actually banned, as this means it will never be included in rankings again.) It makes much more sense to do your optimization the right way the first time. That way, when the crawler comes back through your site, it sees a consistent picture of it, and the ranking of the site will remain consistent and continue to climb. No unhappy surprises.

Cloaking

Cloaking is another sleight-of-hand SEO technique. For SEO purposes, cloaking a site is a method of delivering a page based on who is requesting the page. For example, if a web site is using cloaking, when a regular visitor comes to the site, that visitor will see one page. But when a search crawler comes to the site, it sees a much more relevant, better-optimized site.

Search engines frown on cloaking, and if you're caught using cloaking techniques, your site will be penalized or even delisted completely.

There is another reason why people use cloaking on their web sites. Instead of trying to trick search engines, some web site owners use cloaking to protect the source code of their web site. Because it's possible for anyone to choose Show Source or Display Source Code from a browser's tool menu, it's sometimes frustrating for organizations that want to keep their source code proprietary.

Instead of putting it out for the whole world to see, these companies use page cloaking, but this is not an advisable way to protect your code. Search engine crawlers don't like cloaked sites and your site will be penalized if you choose to use cloaking for any reason.

Hidden links

Hidden links are created using the same methods used to create hidden text. The difference between hidden links and hidden text is that with hidden links, the search crawler can follow the links to other sites or to other pages within the same site. Some sites use these hidden links because they want the SEO benefits of links, but they don't want to provide pathways off the page for site visitors. It's not worth it.

Because many search engines now pay close attention to the links that lead into and off a web site, hidden links have become more popular. However, they should not be used under any circumstances, because when your hidden links are discovered, and they will be, your site will be penalized by the search engine. And anything that reduces your site ranking or has the potential to affect the ranking in a negative way should be avoided.

Spamming a search engine for any reason is never a good idea, and you can be penalized even for inadvertently spamming, so take the time to learn what techniques could lead a search engine to believe that you're intentionally spamming it. Then, avoid those techniques no matter what might lead you to believe that spamming a search engine might be a good idea.

Considerations for Multilingual Sites

Creating SEO-optimized content for a multilingual web site presents a whole new challenge for SEO. Needing a multilingual site is a good problem to have, as it usually means that you have customers in multiple countries. However, it also means you have to double or triple your SEO efforts.

The good news is that optimizing your foreign-language web site is very much the same as optimizing your English one. You just do it in a different language. Here are some guidelines that should serve as reminders of what you should plan to do during the SEO process:

- **Translate keywords into the new language:** In some cases, you won't be able to translate your keywords into a matching word in another language. In that case, you'll need to choose new keywords.

- **Translate existing web content:** Again, translations can sometimes be squirrelly. Unless you're an expert in the language to which you're translating, hire someone to do it for you. A bad translation could cost you more in lost traffic than the services of a good translator.

- **Apply all the same SEO rules:** Everything you have learned for your English content is equally valid for your foreign content. Just because the language is different doesn't mean that the search engine or the search engine crawler is any different.

- **Include the proper links:** This applies both to and from your English site to your foreign-language site, but also includes the appropriate links to English on the foreign-language site.

- **Make language options clearly available:** If these options are not clearly marked, your foreign visitors could miss them, and then you'll lose visitors before they're fully engaged in your site.

SEO is really no different in any other language than it is in English. The biggest concern when translating your site to another language is the actual translation. The SEO efforts are essentially the same, but mangling the translation could cost you just as much as not having a foreign-language site at all.

Content Management Systems

Content is one of the most important elements of your web site because it can organically improve your search engine rankings. However, that only applies if the content is well written, interesting, and focused. If you have a web site that's hundreds of pages in size and those pages change regularly because of your content strategy, managing all that content can be a nightmare.

That's where a content management system (CMS) is very useful. A content management system is a tool used to create, update, publish, discover, and distribute content for your web site. This piece of software is usually very easy to use, and it quickly becomes one of the most useful tools you'll find for developing and maintaining your web site.

When should you use CMS?

Content management systems are hugely helpful for web sites that have hundreds of pages of content to manage. If your web site is smaller than that, should you use it? That depends on how you would answer the following questions:

- How much content do you actually have that *needs* to be managed?
- How much time do you have to manage it?
- How much of your budget do you want to invest in managing it?

For the last point, there is good news. Some content management systems are completely free. Drupal (http://drupal.org) is probably one of the best-known free systems. It's open source, which means that the software is both free and can be tweaked by you to meet your specific needs. It's through this collaborative development that open-source software applications are improved for everyone involved.

If you think you need a CMS that's a little more sophisticated (and expensive, as opposed to free), you can find those, too. The cost of the most basic CMS software starts at around $1,500 and increases to more than $7,000 for the initial license. More complex versions can cost as much as $500,000 for the initial licensing. Fees for additional licenses, extra features, or monthly maintenance fees may also apply.

Of course, price should not be the main reason you choose a content management system. Your CMS decisions should be based on your business needs, which obviously vary from one organization to another.

Choosing the right CMS

If you decide that a content management system is a tool you need for managing your web site content, you should take some time to investigate the different options available to you. Like any other software, not all CMS systems are created equal.

When you begin to look for the right CMS, the first thing you should do is consider your budget for the solution. Your budget will narrow your field some. Then you can begin considering different factors about each company that will help you narrow the field even more:

- **Company history:** Companies that are new to the market are risky, especially if they are drastically different from existing companies. The length of time that a company has been in business is a good indicator of its strength. This is not foolproof, but you can generally have more trust in companies that have been in business longer.

- **Workflow and collaboration features:** You know what you need to accomplish with a content management system. Whether it is plugging in content from vendors outside your company or allowing for collaboration within your organization, make sure that the services you are considering can meet all your needs both now and as your business grows. It's difficult to migrate from one content management system to another, so think long-term as you're making your decision.

- **Software integration:** Consider how the software will integrate with your organization. Do you need software that you install and manage from your own machines or will a web-based program serve your needs better? In addition, how will the system you choose work with the technology that you already have in place? If you have to invest in additional technology to support the CMS, the actual cost of the system will be higher than you originally anticipated.

- **Personalization options:** How much personalization do you need? Will multiple people need different capabilities? What about dealing with archived content? Personalization encompasses more than just defining how many users will use the CMS for different jobs. It also means looking deeper into all the situations in which a different element of CMS may be needed.

As with any technology, there are many other factors to consider, but the preceding questions will get you started. As you narrow the field, you can request references from organizations that currently use the CMS software you're considering. Keep in mind, though, that a vendor isn't going to supply a reference to an unhappy customer, so also check Internet forums and software reviews to round out your picture of the company that you're considering. A great resource for comparing CMS software is www.cmsmatrix.org.

How CMS affects SEO

One valid concern many web site designers have is how a content management system will affect their SEO efforts. In the past, CMS applications often published content with long, complex URLs or created multiple copies, which you now know is anathema to search engine crawlers. Today, however, CMS applications are much more SEO-friendly.

SEO has become a large part of owning any kind of web site. Even individuals now consider how they're going to get their sites to rank well in search engines, and small or even micro-businesses need an increasing amount of technological assistance, including SEO assistance. Therefore, CMS companies have listened when customers demanded a management system that plays well with search engines.

Today, most CMS applications are designed to improve your SEO, rather than to hinder it. Nonetheless, it's a factor that you should consider as you're looking for a solution. Ask very specific questions, such as "How does your software or application help with my SEO efforts?" and "What specific elements of your application or software will help to improve my SEO efforts?"

When looking at CMS applications, you should also consider the structure it uses to help you develop your content. Because a CMS is designed to maintain your content in an orderly manner, it can help to solidify your content strategy and your web site structure.

Understanding and Using Viral Content

If you've ever heard of *viral marketing*, you know that it involves marketing materials that are spread via social networking. For example, you may have an article that's largely a piece of marketing and that you post to a blog. The article is then tagged in a social network and begins to spread like a virus. Each time someone tags the article, more people see it. Then more people tag it and more people see it, and so on. It's a snowball effect applied to marketing.

Viral marketing of any other kind, however, begins with good content — *viral content*. The content that's spread virally by social networking doesn't have to be your only marketing; and in fact it will be much more effective if the content isn't overtly commercial at all. Users are much more interested in content that provides what they need at the time — real information — than in content that tries to sell them something.

That's where viral content comes in. Social networking and social media optimization are covered in depth in Chapter 18, but for now you should know that viral content should be written with the medium of distribution in mind. For example, if you plan to use blog tagging to distribute your content, then the proper format for that content should be a blog post, written short and to the point, but including useful information (that's more than just a link to another blogger's web site).

You can also include articles and news stories in viral content as long as you use the appropriate social networking systems to distribute them. If you've ever seen an article with a button at the bottom that says Digg This, you've seen the seed of viral content. Digg is a social networking site that visitors can use to share information of interest — and it's not the only one.

Dozens of *social bookmarking* applications have sprung up because Internet users find that social bookmarking is often a more reliable way to find the information they're looking for. It's the attitude that, "I must not be the only person in the world with this interest or problem, so what did others find useful?"

Social media — and by extension, viral content — really are the new search engine. You may as well learn how to leverage these technologies because they aren't going away.

The methods of SEO covered up to this point are mostly based on SEO that has worked in the past. As a dynamic entity, the Internet is changing all the time, and the most recent shift has been toward socially networked content systems. SEO for these types of content systems will require different strategies than the content systems of the past. It's something that you should start considering now. Taking advantage of these social networking systems sooner, rather than later, will help you at least keep up with the pack if not take the lead.

Chapter 14

Using Communities to Improve SEO

Perform a search on just about any search engine and somewhere in the results you're likely to find a community discussion of some kind. If the search you do is broad in nature, then the community will probably show up deeper in the results. If it's specific in nature, then it's very possible a community might be the first web page that comes up in the search. That's because communities often provide answers to very specific questions, or information about very specific concepts.

Communities have been around as long as the Web. In fact, the first web sites were actually communities that enabled people to share information globally. It was faster (and more effective) than faxing information around the world, and it enabled the rapid transmission of knowledge and experience with others.

Those early communities didn't necessarily share a lot of the aspects that communities these days do. There were none of the slick interfaces that you see today. You couldn't add avatars (those nifty little pictures that you see next to everyone's name in your favorite community). Moreover, the communities were used as a method of communication among very specific groups of people, such as engineers and scholars.

It didn't take long, however, for the community aspect of the Web to take off. We all want to add our two cents' worth. That's the entire essence of a community — and it's the reason why *Web 2.0* has become a concept that's both widely accepted and regularly leveraged to increase profits, build relationships with customers or vendors, and move organizations forward.

IN THIS CHAPTER

The value of communities

Leveraging communities for SEO

Choosing the right type of community

Proper care and feeding of communities

The basic concept of Web 2.0 is that the Web is socially driven, rather than technologically driven. It's true, really. Without people, the Web wouldn't exist — and without input from people, it would be nothing more than a digital catalog for products and services. With Web 2.0, however, the web has become the largest community in the world — or at least in the digital version of our world, which comprises thousands of smaller communities of like-minded individuals. Unlike the real world, however, people can belong to multiple communities. Moreover, one can even be a valued member of all of those communities, and that's an aspect of the Web that you don't want to miss out on when you're trying to get your web site noticed.

The Value of Communities

Communities as a means of SEO have only recently become popular. In the past, communities popped up as a by-product of content or because Internet users wanted a place to discuss their interests with other people who had the same interests. It wasn't until someone recognized that search engines actually listed community posts in search results that interest began to grow about how those posts could improve web site search engine rankings.

Even now, many SEOs look at web communities as more of a curiosity than another way to SEO your web site, but it's unlikely they'll maintain that view much longer. If you look at the underlying purpose of SEO — helping users find what they're looking for on your site — then communities, like other types of social media, are an essential part of creating a web site that people not only find useful, but also return to repeatedly.

CROSS-REF Social media present an entirely new debate about search engine optimization. You'll find out more about social media, the debates about how useful it is, and how you can use social media to improve web site traffic in Chapter 20.

Remember, too, that search engines rank web sites according to how useful they are to actual users; and communities provide a service to users that you probably can't provide without them, given the budget that you have. Communities provide a dialog, and most Internet users today demand that dialog. They also provide access to information that you might not think of providing to your web site visitors. Together, that means a richer experience that visitors value far more than content with which they cannot interact.

Community statistics

By nature, people need to interact with other people. One of the criticisms of the Internet is that it removes us from natural human interaction. Whereas people used to gather face to face to discuss, plan, and collaborate, the Internet has replaced those activities across an impersonal platform. You send e-mails instead of chatting by the water cooler. You transfer files instead of sitting in on planning sessions. A great deal of human interaction now takes place behind a monitor to the rhythm of keystrokes.

It's not at all surprising that people want more than that. No one denies that the Internet is a marvelous tool. It helps us find the information that we're looking for in a fraction of the time that it used to take. It is also a vehicle for sharing with others the information that we know.

Communities satisfy that need to share — to impress, to one up, or just to be passionate about a subject that's important to us. There are no age limits to that need. Studies show that 58 percent of *millennials* (that's the 18- to 25-year-old crowd) expect to create their own content online; and at least 25 percent of *matures* (that's the 61- to 75-year-old group) want to contribute as well. In fact, more than 40 percent of *all* consumers want to interact online through communities such as forums, reviews, comment functions, and media-sharing applications such as YouTube.

In other words, nearly half of all Internet users want to contribute to what you have to offer. They want to tell their side of the story. They want to share their experiences and opinions. In short, they want to be a part of a community.

A good example of how valuable being part of an online community can be might be the success of the Obama presidential campaign during the 2008 elections. Obama understood that to win the presidency, he would need to connect to and become part of the community. With the help of his campaign team, he did a great job of that connecting via campaign speeches, public appearances, and other traditional methods of campaigning for the presidency.

What Obama understood that the other candidates didn't, however, was that he could reach more people if he met them where they are — online. Even during his campaign he was addressing voters through YouTube and other community forums — and once he was elected he continued that trend with regular video updates. He has become a (very prominent) member of an online community of Internet users. Clearly, it worked well for him.

It can work well for you, too. Of course, Obama's case is somewhat exceptional. Already a well-known figure, he jumped into a popular, established community — YouTube and the political arena — and wasn't really expected to participate outside his own special realm. In your online world, you won't be as privileged. You'll have to meet certain expectations held by the visitors who come to your site.

User expectations

What exactly is it that users expect from your community? Quite a lot, actually. First, they expect to be able to participate. The whole reason communities have become a viable forum for improving your SEO is because people expect to join in. They expect to be able to create content, only they don't think of it as content. They think of it as sharing their knowledge and opinions with other people who are interested in what they have to share.

Second, community members also expect to have a reasonable amount of freedom to express their own thoughts and opinions. The fastest way to alienate visitors from your community is to create an inhospitable environment. You can do this by allowing others within the community to be harsh or rude. A certain amount of etiquette must be displayed within a community, and you'll learn more about that a little later in this chapter.

Third, your community visitors will expect *you* to participate. Maybe not you personally, especially if your organization is made up of more than a handful of people, but representatives of your organization will be expected to be visible within the community from time to time, and that doesn't mean only participating in your own community.

Participating means being active in communities other than your own, with the intent of helping the community as a whole. Self-serving participation will be sniffed out faster than a dog finds bacon; and once other members have decided that your motives are merely self-serving and not intended to help the larger community, you'll find resistance at every turn. You'll be ignored, and people will quit participating in the communities you've established, too.

In short, as a community member, you are expected to create discussions, join discussions, post helpful information, provide value, and in general be involved in other communities that are related to your interests, and perhaps even in some that are more personal to you.

Generally, web users are members of numerous communities. They participate on blogs, in forums, and in other ways for the web sites that are of interest to them — and that's an important distinction. Because an area is of interest to them, they are likely to be involved in multiple places that are loosely related (topically speaking) in an effort to gain more and have more impact. That's why you need to be involved in several other communities that are related to your own as well.

In the beginning, you may feel like a small fish in a big pond, but you will be seen. If you are contributing to the community in a useful way, eventually you will get attention. People will start to read what you're writing, they'll read all your posts or responses, and you'll gain their trust.

Ultimately, it's all about trust, which is the greatest expectation that community members have. They expect to be able to trust the other members of the community to participate in a valuable way. That's precisely why going into a community with nothing more than marketing in mind will get you shunned within that community.

People don't trust marketers and advertisers. They trust "regular" people. Some studies show that about 66 percent of Internet users *trust user-generated content* (that's your addition to a community) more than they trust any communications directly from a company. That alone is reason enough for you to seriously consider the value of creating and/or joining a community.

Leveraging Communities for SEO

If users expect to have a community in which they can participate and provide their own content, then it follows that you should be able to leverage that community for SEO purposes, right? Yes — and in fact many organizations do.

Most technology subjects are a great example of this. I was recently searching (through Google) to find out how to improve the battery life of my T-Mobile G1. Using the search term "improving G1 battery life," the search results page included a forum at cellphoneforums.net. There

I found a thread titled "Improving battery life on G1." Simple and to the point, and I found exactly what I was looking for in the first result.

Note two points here. First, the forum addressed something very specific: the battery life of the G1 cell phone. The search query that I used is a Long Tail query. "T-Mobile G1" or even just "G1" would be considered a broad query, because these are brand names and encompass all the different aspects of the phone. By narrowing the search query to the specific thing I was looking for — improving the battery life of the phone — I was able to avoid wading through thousands of irrelevant results.

Second, and this is something that we'll get into more detail about shortly, the title, or header, of the thread is nearly the same as the Long Tail query that I used to search for information. That's important, because titles and headers have more weight with search engines than simple text does. Sure, the text is important, because it's going to support the title, but search crawlers look at titles first.

The bigger picture here is that communities give you an opportunity to create optimization for Long Tail keywords without having to spend a lot of time doing it. A community forum, blog comments, and any other method that enables your visitors to contribute to the conversation will naturally bring Long Tail phrases into the picture, because it's those phrases that people tend to use when they're discussing a topic.

For you, that means being able to tap into the power of Long Tail search terms without having to spend time and money that are better spent focusing on your broad keywords (also called *core keywords*). Don't think you can create a community without some investment, though. You have to put some time and money into creating a great community, although there are ways to have others help you with some of that effort. First, though, a few more details on the benefits of creating communities on your web site.

Creating a dialog

Probably the biggest benefit of creating a community on your web site that enables your site visitors to create their own content is that in the process, you're also creating the opportunity to create a dialogue with your visitors that you might not otherwise be able to create.

In studies about the value of communities, organizations have been surprised at the dialogue communities create. Allowing visitors to have a voice on your site opens all kinds of doors to their input. In some cases, companies have found that user suggestions for improvement are right on target, adding a dimension to a product or service that hadn't been previously considered.

Users are also more willing to share their thoughts about your existing products or services in a community setting. Of course, you'll have a handful of people who are negative and have nothing useful to provide, but that's usually offset by the larger group of people who are positive about your offerings and are willing to share that opinion with other visitors. Their contributions often make the experience richer for new community members, which builds loyalty to your brand. It's also how buzz is started and propagated, and by now we all know that buzz is a very good tool for increasing your web site traffic.

Improving keyword effectiveness

Companies with communities also find that visitor input illuminates Long Tail marketing terms that weren't obvious before their input. This can be accomplished through comments, reviews, forums, and even something as simple as adding a tagging application that enables visitors to label your content according to their understanding of it.

Consider a tool like Scuttle, for example. A simple addition of the Scuttle tool, which is a tagging application, enables users to tag content on your web site with their own keywords. The keywords appear in a box (as shown in Figure 14-1), with larger keywords being prominent, highlighted keywords being popular, and the remaining keywords being suggestions that apply to the web page that's being tagged.

FIGURE 14-1

Tagging applications enable users to categorize your content using their own terms.

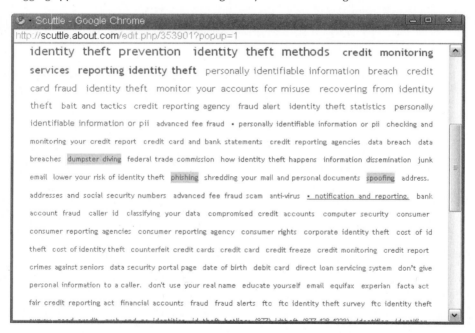

Other tagging applications even enable users to tag their own content so that other visitors can browse according to the tags, as shown in Figure 14-2. The same rules apply to these tags: Larger words are most popular; smaller words are used but are less popular. This particular tagging application doesn't include highlighting.

FIGURE 14-2

Some tagging applications enable users to tag their own content so that other users can browse by tag.

Allowing users to tag your content begins the SEO process without your input at all. You create content, the users classify it by keywords that make sense to them, and then other users come along and click on those keywords (because they also understand them) and find your article. This generates traffic for a very specific Long Tail phrase, which in turn increases your weight for that phrase with search engines.

For example, in Figure 14-2, you can see how visitors might browse by keyword tags. Let's take that a little farther, and click on the "Google Analytics" tag. For the particular web site that uses these tags, several pieces of content have been labeled with "Google Analytics." The first piece of content is an article entitled "Google Analytics Reports: Keywords."

Now let's see if we can find that same article using Google to search for "Google Analytics keywords reports." When I performed that search, the same article is in the number-one search results spot. Tagging helps visitors and crawlers to find the article based on the terms that readers think are important. Without the tagging, the article might appear as the first result for the phrase I used to search, but it would require additional input from the web site owner in the form of optimizing the site for that particular keyword.

Of course, the concept works with other types of community involvement as well. Forums are particularly useful for optimizing Long Tail search terms. Users search for very specific phrases, and sometimes even for questions. When you offer a forum that allows people to contribute using natural language, you stand a much better chance of turning up in the results for phrases that come naturally to your customers.

The same is true for reviews. Customer reviews are one of the most powerful tools you can employ if you own a product web site, because customers will review your products and services, and potential customers trust those reviews much more than they trust your marketing materials. Reviews also open the door for Long Tail keyword optimization in the same way that other community forums do.

Long Tail won't be the only keyword benefit that you see, however. Your core keywords will also benefit from customer input as well. Just as customers will use more (and different) Long Tail keywords, you'll also find that they use broad keywords more frequently, and completely in context, than you could use them in your own content efforts.

Ultimately, communities, when done well, can be a winning situation for the optimization of your web site. The key is that they should be done correctly. If you miss the mark with your community efforts, they may be just as ineffective as any other poorly done SEO strategy.

Choosing the Right Type of Community

If creating communities well (or creating good communities) is the order of business, where do you start? My advice is to determine the right kind of community for your web site. How do your visitors want to interact with you? What are they looking for? What kind of user-generated content do they want to provide?

The best course of action is to ask them. A simple survey of web site visitors should give you some good insights, but the short list below will help you to understand some of the options you have for providing the right space in which visitors can make themselves at home:

- **Comment-enabled blogs:** Everyone knows what a blog is, but if you have a blog on your site and you don't have comments enabled, you're missing out on an opportunity to provide your site visitors with their own forum for participation. Sure, comments create the possibility that you're going to have dissension and even outright nastiness, but the good comments will always far outweigh the ugly ones, and negative feedback can provide some of your most valuable information. Comment-enabled blogs are great for sites that are largely content based, and should usually be used in conjunction with other types of community forums that enable visitors a little more freedom of discussion.

- **User forums:** Message boards and discussion lists are two user forums that tend to generate a lot of traffic. Discussion lists — those that are strictly e-mail-based — aren't as effective for SEO as message boards, but they do give your site visitors a way to communicate with you and participate in a community. If message boards aren't an option for you, consider discussion lists — just don't expect a lot of SEO traction out of them unless you're archiving the messages online. Most sites are suited to message boards, though — especially technology sites or any site where visitors can benefit from additional instruction, tips, or how-tos.

- **Product reviews:** Online product reviews account for a huge percentage of product sales, especially among electronic gadgets and luxury-type items. People simply trust product reviews more than they trust marketing materials, and for a good reason: The people who buy and then review a product don't typically have any stake in rating it. They don't have to make grandiose claims because they don't care whether you purchase the product or not. Product reviews also work for service web sites, travel, and many other types of services available online. If you have a product or service offering, consider enabling public reviews on your site. If you want to get your customers talking, this is a great way to do it.

- **Content sharing:** Content sharing is less about *you* and more about your site visitors. Content sharing can be video, graphics, or even just simple text. It's most often lightly guided by suggestions from a moderator or manager, and gives community members a large space in which to contribute. Often, you'll see content sharing as a contest that encourages members to post their own videos (e.g., Google's 10^{100} project at www.project10tothe100.com), text, or images. The key thing to remember here is that users expect a little more freedom in a content-sharing community. You can still guide it, but give them plenty of room to stretch their creative muscles.

Remember, too, that you're not limited to just a single type of community. You can, and probably should, have more than one type of community available to your site visitors so they can participate in whatever way suits them best. You'll find that some visitors use only one way, while others might use all the participation tools you have available. Let them get involved. The benefits to you will be tremendous.

Proper Care and Feeding of Communities

Once you've decided how you want to get your web site visitors involved, it's time to start putting your community together. You've heard the adage "Build it and they will come"? Don't believe it. Simply forming a community and expecting your site visitors to do the rest of the work will leave you with a ghost town. If you want your community to grow and thrive, you have to do some work before the launch, during the launch, and after the site is up and running. In addition, it's more than just making sure that the right technology is there. You have to have a presence as well, both in your own community and within other communities in your industry.

Prelaunch preparations

Before you open the gates of your community, you need to make sure that it's a warm and welcoming place for your visitors to hang out. That means ensuring that not only is the right technology in place — technology in this sense is the structure of your community — but also that it's not a barren wasteland.

Many visitors won't want to be the first person to post in a given topic or subject; and of all the visitors to your community, only a small percentage (estimates are 20 to 40 percent) are likely to actually participate. The rest are visitors who simply lurk, watching conversations. Once in a great while, lurkers will add to the conversations that are going on — and sometimes, with a compelling reason, lurkers will even become regular participants.

It takes time for some visitors to be convinced that your community is the type of place where they want to have their voice heard. Of course, even a willingness to participate is worthless if your visitors can't figure out how to do it.

Tools

One of the first things you'll need to focus on when you begin building a community is the interface for it. A community interface should be not only usable for site visitors, but also useful for your site. What's the point in having a method for users to contribute if you can't show the world their contributions?

A good community tool, such as Jive Software's Clearspace Community, can offer both usability and usefulness. You should research several tools, but the one that you choose should make it intuitive for users to participate in the community you design. This includes making the tools for posting readily available and easy to access. It also means that the tools should be able to pull from your community any contributions that can be featured elsewhere on your web site.

For example, look at just about any web site that offers a user forum. The home page usually provides a widget or sidebar that features at least headlines from the posts in that forum. If you have a comment-enabled blog, then comments should be featured on your pages. You get the idea. Allow people to contribute and then make them stars by featuring their contributions.

Evaluate a few different software tools for community creation before you select one to ensure that it meets all your needs.

Building buzz

Before you ever open your community up to site visitors, you should begin building buzz around it. The more interest you can build before the launch, the easier it will be for you to get people to begin participating once the community has been opened to everyone.

One way to build buzz is for you, or a representative of your community, to actually begin participating in other related communities. Be sure that you include a signature line in all posts to other communities that points people to the community that will be opening soon. You have to be very careful about this, however, because the last thing you want to do is give the impression that you are only participating in a community as a way to promote your own.

Use proper etiquette when posting in other communities. Remember that the whole purpose of creating a community is to provide community members with something they need. You can begin this trend by providing insightful information in whatever other communities you participate in.

Another way to build buzz before the launch is to publish content across the Internet that announces — either subtly or blatantly — the opening of the community. Press releases are great for the blatant announcement. Articles, blog posts, and similar types of content are good for a more subtle approach whereby you provide information about your new community as an aside ("Oh, by the way, we're going to be opening our community to new members beginning ... ").

Beginning in beta

One more thing that you should do before you open your community to the population at large is to open the community in beta. Beta testing a community enables you to invite only select members to participate in that community. When choosing these members, try to select people who are relatively well known in your industry, who have something of value to offer others, and who are most likely to actually participate in the community.

It's also good to begin your beta testing with your community management team in place. This management team will be responsible for guiding the growth of the community. That includes initial, keyword-rich postings, as well as guidance for new users.

One more beta task is to get people talking. That's usually the hardest part of starting a community. You can use all kinds of tricks to get conversations started, but the best is to choose provocative subjects that are truly interesting to the people participating in your community and to reply to *every post* with words of encouragement and open-ended questions that help to encourage further dialogue.

Beta testing is your trial run for your community. It's where you'll work out the kinks and seed the community with interesting content, so that when you open it up to everyone and site visitors begin to appear, interesting threads are already in place. As mentioned earlier, most people prefer not to be the first person to start a conversation, so this helps to jump-start your community participation.

Once your community goes live

After beta testing your community for a while in order to begin building traffic among the people you've invited to participate and to begin jelling as a community, you can open it up for others to participate.

A good way to open your community for participation and to ensure that new members have someone they can turn to for questions or help with the community, is to create a contest or make it a game for existing community members to bring new members into the fold. The prize for bringing in the most new members might be something as simple as a $25 Amazon gift certificate, or even something directly related to your web site. What's important is that your existing community members (those who have been with you through the beta testing) are given an opportunity to be rewarded for their actions. People love rewards and will usually join in if the chances are good they might receive a reward.

One more thing needs to happen once your community goes live. You (or your representatives) need to continue to participate in other communities. If you quit participating in those communities where you built a presence before your own community went live, then you'll miss opportunities to contribute to your industry, as well as to bring new members into your own community. They may eventually find their own way there, but it can happen a lot faster if you're a visible member of the larger community.

Maintaining your community over time

After you get your community up and running — that is, after you have community members who are generating their own content and participating in discussions — you can't just disappear. You must maintain a presence in your own community in order for it to remain valuable to your community members. Once you quit participating in your own community, other people are likely to quit participating too, and everything that you've worked to create will slowly (or quickly) die.

In order for a community of any type to flourish, you must maintain some kind of presence, whether it's continued blogging, forum postings, or review comments. Reviews tend to be less difficult for you to maintain because people expect less response on a review, but without some kind of occasional appearance, people may begin to feel their efforts are wasted, even with a review-based community.

One way that community owners maintain a presence is to recruit community members into management positions. These can be volunteers, but they need to be tuned to your business goals and they need to appear to be part of your organization. Again, you don't need to pay them, and it may be best if you don't. It's not usually difficult to locate a champion among community followers. They just need to be focused on helping you achieve the goals that you've set out for your community.

Whether it's you or someone you've recruited to help you, the most difficult part of maintaining your community will be encouraging participation. People want to belong to a community. If they didn't, social medias wouldn't be nearly as popular as they are. It's just that sometimes people need a little guidance or encouragement.

You can encourage participation by paying particular attention to the people who are posting in your community. Praise them when appropriate and always be sure to follow up on every contribution that's made. If possible, make your follow-ups public.

People also like to be praised, and praise will take you a long way toward encouraging people to participate. So will questions. Everyone likes the opportunity to talk about things they feel passionate about. Ask an open-ended question, one that can't be answered with a simple yes or no, and put plenty of thought into the question so that they are insightful. If you're not truly interested, your community members will sense it and will go to sites where they believe the people involved are truly interested in what they have to say. If you don't know where to begin, look through previous postings to find threads that were dropped or never fully explored.

Communities provide an opportunity for you to create a relationship with your site visitors, and it's a relationship that can lead to excellent SEO opportunities for you. Take the time necessary to build a great community and you may find that the benefits are far greater than ever imagined, both from an SEO standpoint and from a customer relations point of view.

Chapter 15

Understanding the Role of Links and Linking

D uring the early days of the Internet, before it began to interest the general public, there were two ways to get around in it. You either had to have the URL of the page that you wanted to reach or someone had to send you a link to it. There were no search engines to help you find what you wanted.

Even though we have powerful search engines today to help us find information on the Web, linking from one page to another is still a powerful tool for helping users find your site. Links can also group together sites that are relevant, giving visitors additional options for the information they seek. Links, when used well on your site, also give you more leverage with search engines than a site without links might have.

How you populate your web site with links will determine how useful they are in improving your search engine rankings. This method is called a *link strategy*. There is a fine art to creating a linking strategy, however. It's not enough just to sprinkle a few links here and there within the pages of your site. There are different types of links that register differently with search engines, and it's even possible for your site to be completely delisted from search results if you handle your links improperly.

When you really begin to consider links and how they affect web sites, you realize that links provide the crucial connections that enable traffic to move around the Web. If you search for a specific term, when you click through the search engine results, you're taken to another web page. As you navigate through that web page, you may find a link that leads you to another site, and that process continues until you're tired of surfing and you close your browser. Even when the process starts differently — with you typing a URL directly into your web browser — it still ends the same way.

How Links Affect SEO

If keyword is the word you hear most often with SEO, then links, or linking, is the word you hear second-most often. Links are the foundation of topical communities, and as such they have as much, if not more, weight with search engine crawlers than keywords do.

A web page without links is like an uncharted island. It's sitting there, right in the middle of the ocean, but most people don't know it's there. The island could be littered with diamonds. The plants that grow there might heal every disease known to humans. None of that matters if no one knows the island is there. You can see where I'm going with this. The same is true with your web site. It doesn't matter how great the information, services, or products are if people can't find them. The site is as good as that undiscovered island.

The first purpose of links, then, is to connect your web site to others that are relevant to the information included on your site. In addition, links provide a method by which traffic to your site is increased, and isn't that the reason you're playing the SEO game? Your desire is to increase the traffic to your site, which in turn increases the number of products that you sell, the number of sales leads you collect, or the number of appointments that you set with highly qualified clients. In short, links lead to increased profit and growth. Of course you'd want to use them on your site.

Another reason links are so important is that links into your site from other web sites serve as votes for the value of your site. Usually, the more links that lead to your site, the more weight a search engine crawler will give the site, which in turn equates to a better search engine ranking, especially for search engines such as Google that use a quality ranking factor such as *PageRank*.

Understanding Google's PageRank

PageRank is a family of algorithms that assigns a numerical value to pages on the Web in an effort to determine the relevance or importance of those pages. PageRank, which was developed by Google founders Larry Page and Sergey Brin, is proprietary to Google, but other search engines use a ranking system to help determine the order of search engine results. (It's interesting to note that PageRank is named for Larry Page and doesn't refer to the rank of the page.)

The exact algorithms used by PageRank are not available to the general public. A version of the algorithms that you'll find here was filed with the patent for PageRank, but only Google knows every variable that's taken into account. It helps, however, if you understand how PageRank works, so the following example (from Wikipedia.org) should help clarify those calculations.

continued

continued

Simplified PageRank Algorithm

Assume a small universe of four web pages: A, B, C, and D. The initial approximation of PageRank would be evenly divided between these four documents. Hence, each document would begin with an estimated PageRank of 0.25.

If pages B, C, and D each link only to A, then they would each confer a 0.25 PageRank to A. All PageRank PR( ) in this simplistic system would thus gather to A because all links would be pointing to A.

$$PR(A) = PR(B) + PR(C) + PR(D).$$

Now suppose page B also has a link to page C, and page D has links to all three pages. The value of the link-votes is divided among all the outbound links on a page. Thus, page B gives a vote worth 0.125 to page A and a vote worth 0.125 to page C. Only one-third of D's PageRank is counted for A's PageRank (approximately 0.083).

$$PR(A) = \frac{PR(B)}{2} + \frac{PR(C)}{1} + \frac{PR(D)}{3}.$$

In other words, the PageRank conferred by an outbound link L( ) is equal to the document's own PageRank score divided by the normalized number of outbound links (it is assumed that links to specific URLs only count once per document).

$$PR(A) = \frac{PR(B)}{L(B)} + \frac{PR(C)}{L(C)} + \frac{PR(D)}{L(D)}.$$

In the general case, the PageRank value for any page u can be expressed as follows:

$$PR(u) = \sum_{v \in Bu} \frac{PR(v)}{L(v)}$$

That is, the PageRank value for a page u is dependent on the PageRank values for each page v out of the set Bu (this set contains all pages linking to page u), divided by the number of links from page v (this is Nv).

PageRank Algorithm Including Damping Factor

The PageRank theory holds that even an imaginary surfer who is randomly clicking on links will eventually stop clicking. The probability, at any step, that the person will continue is a damping

continued

continued

factor, d. Various studies have tested different damping factors, but it is generally assumed that the damping factor will be set around 0.85.

The damping factor is subtracted from 1 (and in some variations of the algorithm, the result is divided by the number of documents in the collection) and this term is then added to the product of the damping factor and the sum of the incoming PageRank scores.

That is,

$$PR(A) = 1 - d + d \left(\frac{PR(B)}{L(B)} + \frac{PR(C)}{L(C)} + \frac{PR(D)}{L(D)} + \cdots \right).$$

or (N = the number of documents in the collection)

$$PR(A) = \frac{1-d}{N} + d \left(\frac{PR(B)}{L(B)} + \frac{PR(C)}{L(C)} + \frac{PR(D)}{L(D)} + \cdots \right).$$

Therefore, any page's PageRank is derived in large part from the PageRanks of other pages. The damping factor adjusts the derived value downward. The second formula supports the original statement in Page and Brin's paper that "the sum of all PageRanks is one." Unfortunately, however, Page and Brin gave the first formula, which has led to some confusion.

Google recalculates PageRank scores each time it crawls the Web and rebuilds its index. As Google increases the number of documents in its collection, the initial approximation of PageRank decreases for all documents.

The formula uses a model of a random surfer who gets bored after several clicks and switches to a random page. The PageRank value of a page reflects the chance that the random surfer will land on that page by clicking on a link. It can be understood as a Markov chain in which the states are pages, and the transitions are all equally probable and are the links between pages.

If a page has no links to other pages, then it becomes a sink and therefore terminates the random surfing process. However, the solution is quite simple. If the random surfer arrives at a sink page, it picks another URL at random and continues surfing again.

When calculating PageRank, pages with no outbound links are assumed to link out to all other pages in the collection. Their PageRank scores are therefore divided evenly among all other pages. In other words, to be fair to pages that are not sinks, these random transitions are added to all nodes in the Web, with a residual probability of usually d = 0.85, estimated from the frequency that an average surfer uses his or her browser's bookmark feature.

Therefore, the equation is as follows:

$$PR(\rho\iota) = \frac{1-d}{N} + d \sum_{\rho j \in M(\rho\iota)} \frac{PR(\rho j)}{L(\rho j)}$$

continued

262

continued

where p1, p2, . . ., pN are the pages under consideration, M(pi) is the set of pages that link to pi, L(pj) is the number of outbound links on page pj, and N is the total number of pages.

The PageRank values are the entries of the dominant eigenvector of the modified adjacency matrix. This makes PageRank a particularly elegant metric: the eigenvector is

$$R = \begin{bmatrix} PR(p_1) \\ PR(p_2) \\ \vdots \\ PR(p_N) \end{bmatrix}$$

where R is the solution of the equation

$$R = \begin{bmatrix} (1-d)/N \\ (1-d)/N \\ \vdots \\ (1-d)/N \end{bmatrix} + d \begin{bmatrix} l(p_1, p_1) & l(p_1, p_2) & \cdots & l(p_1, p_N) \\ l(p_2, p_1) & \ddots & & \vdots \\ \vdots & & l(p_i, p_i) & \\ l(p_N, p_1) & \cdots & & l(p_N, p_N) \end{bmatrix} R$$

where the adjacency function

$$l(p_i, p_j)$$

is 0 if page pj does not link to pi, and normalized such that for each j, the equation is

$$\sum_{i=1}^{N} l(p_i, p_j) = 1,$$

That is, the elements of each column sum up to 1.

This is a variant of the eigenvector centrality measure used commonly in network analysis.

The values of the PageRank eigenvector are fast to approximate (only a few iterations are needed), and in practice it gives good results.

As a result of Markov theory, it can be shown that the PageRank of a page is the probability of being at that page after a lot of clicks. This happens to equal t ? 1 where t is the expectation of the number of clicks (or random jumps) required to get from the page back to itself.

The main disadvantage is that it favors older pages, because a new page, even a very good one, will not have many links unless it is part of an existing site (a site being a densely connected set

continued

continued

of pages, such as Wikipedia). Google Directory (itself a derivative of the Open Directory Project) enables users to see results sorted by PageRank within categories. Google Directory is the only service offered by Google for which PageRank directly determines display order. In Google's other search services (such as its primary Web search), PageRank is used to weight the relevance scores of pages shown in search results.

Several strategies have been proposed to accelerate the computation of PageRank. Various strategies to manipulate PageRank have been employed in concerted efforts to improve search results rankings and monetize advertising links. These strategies have severely impacted the reliability of the PageRank concept, which seeks to determine which documents are actually highly valued by the Web community.

Google is known to actively penalize link farms and other schemes designed to artificially inflate PageRank. How Google identifies link farms and other PageRank manipulation tools is among Google's trade secrets.

To say that links are an important part of SEO for your web site is probably an understatement. If you want your site to be found, you must have links into it from other sites. Without those links, you may as well be an island in the middle of an ocean full of other web sites.

Incoming links aren't the only ones that matter, either. Links that lead to other web pages and links that enable visitors to surf from page to page within your site are also important. It takes a carefully balanced combination of the three to rank well (in this category) with search crawlers.

How Links and Linking Work

You've seen how important links are to your SEO strategy, and you've seen how links affect your Google PageRank, but how, really, do links work for improving your SEO? As you've already seen, a link *to* your site is a vote for the relevance of your site. Therefore, if you're linking *out* to other sites, then you're voting for them; and internal links ensure that a search engine crawler can find the various pages in your site. A *dangling link* is a link that leads into a page that has no links leading out of it.

Each of these different types of links affects site ranking differently for search engines that take linking architectures into consideration. For example, a dangling link could be ignored entirely by a search engine, or the page to which the link points could score lower on the linking metrics because all the links are coming into the page, but none are going out.

Where a link comes from is as important as having a link (or multiple links). Suppose several links lead to your page from web sites having nothing to do with the topic of your site. This is *Google bombing* in its classic form. The links could affect your search engine ranking, though probably not as much as having no links at all will.

That's part of what makes linking such a tricky business. You need to know how the links on your site will affect the amount of traffic the site has, and you need to know how to have links without going overboard, meaning the crawler labels your site as a *link farm*.

Snagging inbound links

Nearly every web site has links that lead out to other web sites. It's rare to find a site that doesn't link to another site somewhere on the Web. That's how communities are built around specific industries and topics. The links that leave your site are important, but they're not nearly as important as the links that lead to your site. Links that lead to your site — called *inbound links* — as you've already discovered are viewed by search engines as votes for your site within a particular community of sites.

Anytime you're being voted for, you want to have as many votes as possible. Inbound links are no different. You want to have a large number of links that lead to your site. You can achieve those links in a variety of ways, some more effective than others:

- ■ **Requesting links:** The oldest method of gaining inbound links is to request them. This requires that you study your market to find out who the players involved in the market are. Then you contact each one of the sites that you discover and ask it to link to your site. In most cases, the person you contact receives your request, but providing links to other sites is the least of that person's worries, so you may not even get a response. If you do, it can sometimes be months later. In other words, you've put a lot of time into requesting links from other sites for a relatively small return on your efforts.

- ■ **Writing articles:** One of the most effective methods of gaining inbound links is to offer an article for other companies to freely use as long as they include information at the bottom that credits you and provide a link back to your site. This method of gaining inbound links works well, because web sites are always looking for good content to include on their pages. The catch here is that the article you write must be well written, accurate, and useful to other sites in your industry. Once you've produced an article that meets these requirements, you can begin to let others know that you have content available for them to use without cost. Just remember to require a link back to your site in return for the freedom to use your article on their site.

- ■ **Blogs:** Another way to get links back to your site is from bloggers. What started as a strange phenomenon that was mostly personal has now become a powerful business tool, and many businesses rely on links back to their sites from the various industry bloggers out there. In most cases, though, bloggers aren't just going to stumble onto your web site. It's far better for you to contact the blogger with information about your organization, some product that you offer, or news that would interest them. This information then gives the blogger something to use in his or her regular posts. Keep in mind, however, that you can't control what a blogger might say, so it's possible that the review you get from the blogger won't be favorable.

- ■ **Press releases:** Press releases are one of the mainstays of any marketing program. These can be so effective that many organizations hire companies to do nothing but distribute their press releases as widely as possible. What's so powerful about a press release? It's just the facts, including benefits, and it's sent out to publications and organizations that might publish all or part of the press release. Use press releases to send out new items of all types, and send them as widely as you can. News organizations, publications, newsletters, and even some forums, will post press releases. When you write the release, be sure to include a link back to your site.

- **Affiliate programs:** *Affiliate programs* are a type of paid advertising. Amazon's affiliate program is one of the best-known programs of this type. You provide a link to people who want to link back to your web site. They place the link on their site and then when someone clicks through that link to your site and makes a purchase (or converts any other goal you have arranged), the affiliate — the person who placed your link on their site — is paid a small percentage. Usually, the payment for affiliate programs is very low ($.01 to $.05 per click or a small percentage of the sale). Nonetheless, some people make a good living being affiliates, and many organizations receive additional traffic because of their affiliate programs.

    Note that there are some ethical considerations associated with affiliate programs. Many people believe that because you're paying for the link back to your site, it is less valid than if you were to land organic links. However, most search engines see affiliate programs as an acceptable business practice and they won't reduce your rankings because you use affiliate programs. The trick with affiliate programs is to not rely on them as your sole source of incoming links. In addition, most affiliate programs utilize some click-tracking software, which by definition negates the value of the link, because the link on the affiliate's page is going from that page, to the ad server, to your site. Therefore, the link is from the ad server, rather than the affiliate site.

- **PPC and paid links:** Pay-per-click advertisements (which are covered in Chapters 6 through 11) are an acceptable business practice. There is no problem with using PPC advertisements to achieve inbound links to your site. Remember that, like affiliate links, PPC links are not direct links to your site. Paid links, conversely, are different from affiliate links — you pay to have a direct, or *flat link*, placed on a page. Some search engines frown on the practice of using these types of links. Using paid links (especially those that land on *link farms*) is a practice that carries some business risk.

- **Links to yourself:** Linking to yourself is a technique that sits right on the line between ethical and unethical. Linking to yourself from other sites that you might own is an acceptable practice, but if you set up other sites with the sole purpose of being able to link back to your main site and create the illusion of popularity, you're going to do more damage than it's probably worth to you. If you are linking to yourself and you suspect that you might be doing something that would adversely affect your search engine ranking, then you shouldn't do it. There are plenty of links to be had without linking back to your own web sites; you just have to work a little harder for the higher-quality links.

- **Create a gadget or mini-app:** Gadgets and mini-apps (small applications) are a phenomenon much like social media. You create a small program or application that users can find value in and post it on your web site for free download. Then you spread the word on blogs, in articles, and with press releases. Users will download and use the gadget or mini-app, and if they like it, then they'll recommend it to others. A good example of this was the tax calculators that circled around the Web during the 2008 presidential election. It works with media files such as podcasts and videos, or other great content, too. Some call it *link bait*. Others call it smart marketing.

Inbound links are such an important part of a linking strategy that some organizations find themselves caught up in the process of learning who is linking back to them. It's not a bad thing to want to know where your links are coming from, and one of the places you can gather that information is from your web analytics application. Some analytics programs will show you at least the top-performing links to your site. These reports are usually part of the marketing element of the application.

You can also perform a search at Google for the term "link:*yourwebsite*.com." This returns search results for all the web sites that Google considers relevant links to your web site, as shown in Figure 15-1. A similar search on Yahoo! will result in a more complete list of incoming links. This is a good way to figure out who's linking to you, unless there are hundreds of links. If there are more than a dozen or so, you could find yourself surfing the results of this search for far more time than you have to spend examining your inbound links.

FIGURE 15-1

Results of a link query on Google for the ZDnet.com web site.

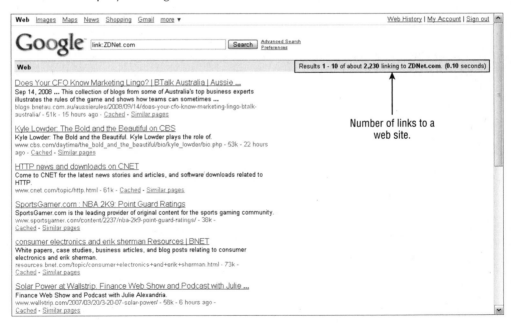

> **NOTE** Some search crawlers also look at the length of time that an incoming link to your site has been in place. Long-standing incoming links show that another site has found your content to be valuable over time, which is another (strong) vote of confidence for your web site.

That's why there's also link-management software that will track your links for you. LinkMachine is one such link-management software (www.linkmachine.net). Link-management software enables you to track and manage your links and linking strategies. It eliminates some of the time-consuming manual tracking tasks you would otherwise perform, such as creating and maintaining a list of incoming and outbound links.

Creating outbound links

If controversy were an SEO strategy, then everyone would be at the top of the SEO game. Unfortunately, it's not. All controversy does is muddy the waters, and that's exactly what the controversy over whether or not you should have outbound links on your site is good for — making life difficult.

The subject of outbound links has often been debated. There are some who worry about *leaking PageRank* — what (supposedly) happens when you link out to other sites. The fear behind leaking is twofold: When you lead people away from your site, they may not come back (hence your visitors *leak* away), and when you link out to other pages, you're reducing the value of each vote because the value of an outbound link is divided by the total number of outbound links.

No one knows for sure exactly what mix of elements is considered when your page is ranked by a search engine. However, it's safe to say that if you have only inbound links and no outbound links, it can't look good for your site — especially these days when social marketing is becoming more and more of a factor for search engine results. The best plan of action is to have a balanced mix of inbound and outbound links. Your site visitors will expect to see some links leading to other sites on the Web, whether those links are simple resources to help them find what they need or something else.

Outbound links also help to establish your expertise in a particular area. Yes, inbound links help with that as well, but it's not enough just to have people pointing to you. You should also have some favorites out there that you find helpful and that you think others will find helpful. When your visitors click through these links and find that you do know what they're looking for, the loyalty points will be awarded to you.

This is how you build relationships with your visitors. And relationships are the ultimate reason to create a web site at all. As long as relationships are your main priority, all the other elements of link building should fall right into place.

When you're creating your outbound links, keep the following guidelines in mind to appease search engine crawlers, because even though the main target for your links should be your site visitors, search engines will pay attention to your links, and your search ranking could be affected by them:

- **Keep your links relevant:** That doesn't mean that you can link only to pages that are in the same industry as your own; but if you do link outside your industry, make sure there is some logical reason for sending your visitors in that direction. Search crawlers examine the content of links closely, both in the links that are created within text and in the actual URL of a link, as much as in the content of pages that are linked together.

- **Don't overuse links:** There's nothing more frustrating for site users than to find that every few words in an article are linked. A good rule of thumb is no more than two or three links per article or blog post on your site. Other links, such as ads for other services, can be added in addition to these text links, but keep them to a minimum.

- **Use keyword anchor text as often as possible when creating your links:** Using the phrase *click here* won't gain you any leverage with a search engine crawler. Using a link that reads *gourmet ingredients,* when that phrase is one of your key phrases will help improve your search engine ranking as long as the link leads to a page that truly is about gourmet ingredients.

- **Be careful whom you link to:** You may have heard the phrase: "Don't link to bad neighborhoods." What it means is that you don't want to link to low-quality sites, because some search engines will penalize you for that. For example, if you link to a spam site or a link farm, search engines are not going to look favorably on that link. If, however, you link to high-ranking sites, you'll gain even more traction with search engines. Remember that although you may not be penalized for sites that link to you, the outbound links on your site are under your control.

- **Don't create pages that contain only links:** This common practice from the early days of the Internet is no longer useful. When search engines see pages that contain nothing but links they read them as spam pages. If you must use a resources page, be sure to include descriptions of each link that you include on the page. Better yet, avoid this practice altogether if there's any way you can.

- **Monitor links and update broken ones:** A broken link is worse than not having a link at all. When you link to a page and don't check back on the links periodically, things could change — companies go out of business, web sites change or disappear altogether. Then, when the search engine crawler follows the links on your page and finds a broken link, this reflects badly on your site. If the broken link is there for a long time, the search engine could reduce your ranking because it appears that you're not maintaining your site properly.

Outbound links aren't the beginning and end of your search engine linking strategy, but there's also no reason to avoid them completely. Use outbound links where they are relevant and useful to your site visitors and not one time more. When you do use them, take the time to ensure that your links are accurate and connect to the correct page.

Taking advantage of cross-linking

Like many other topics we've covered in link strategies, *cross-linking* is one of those practices that isn't black or white but more accurately has dozens of subtle shades of gray. Cross-linking is the practice of linking several sites together, usually sites that are owned by the same company or individual, although that isn't always the case. They can just be random sites (usually related by topic) that have agreed to exchange links. A group of six sites connected by a cross-linking scheme might look something like the diagram shown in Figure 15-2.

Notice how the cross-linked sites are connected and that every site has the same number of links coming into and leaving the page. This is a pattern that search engines look for to determine whether web sites are using linking schemes simply to increase their search engine results rankings — a practice that you now know search engines frown upon. Additionally, cross-linking happens most often with people or companies who own multiple web sites, which also gives the search engine reason to doubt the validity of the links.

FIGURE 15-2

Cross-linked sites create a circular linking scheme that can be read by search engines as a trick to increase rankings.

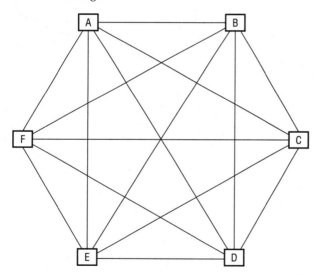

How do search engines know when one person owns all the sites that are cross-linked? The structure of a set of cross-linked sites is the first clue. A group of sites that have naturally occurring links might look more like the asymmetrical diagram shown in Figure 15-3.

Other factors that may help a search engine decide that all the sites are owned by the same person are the IP address of the site and the *WHOIS information*. The IP address is unique to each different web site. Two sites that are owned by the same company are usually hosted on the same server, so the IP address of those sites would be the same. WHOIS information is the record of domain ownership. You're required to provide this information when you purchase a web site.

When sites owned by the same company or individual are cross-linked, search engines look very closely to ensure that the sites are relevant to each other. If they are, then there are no issues with the cross-linking. For sites that are not related, however, search engines look down upon the practice of cross-linking, and your site (or sites) could be penalized for search engine spamming.

FIGURE 15-3

A natural linking between web sites is not as symmetrical or organized as a cross-linking scheme.

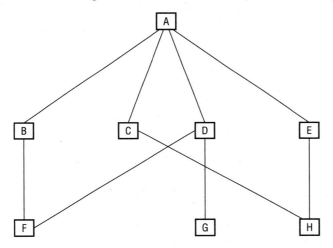

Cross-linking hundreds or even thousands of sites is also likely to raise a red flag. When this occurs, the only real configuration that makes sense is a *link farm* or a set of link farms — and search engines don't like link farms at all. If you want to get your sites completely delisted from the search engine, then set up and take part in a link farm. It will just be a matter of time before your sites are bounced into oblivion.

Still, cross-linking isn't always a bad thing. Sometimes it works nicely, and the main requirement is that sites have something in common so that the links would have occurred naturally anyway. Another thing that helps to keep cross-linking a legitimate linking strategy is for every site to have unique content. If you've created a handful of different sites with exactly the same content on all of them, search engines are going to take notice and your sites will be penalized.

One more way to ensure that cross linking isn't flagged as a "spam-like" practice is to ensure that the cross-linked sites aren't all on the same server. Crawlers examine cross links closely, and having all the web sites on the same server cross-linked together will be noticed. Alone it may not be enough to get your site delisted, but use it in combination with any other activity that looks like it could be spam and you could find your site in never-never land instead of in search results.

As long as you use cross-linking in a legitimate way, there's no reason you should avoid it completely; but like all the other linking strategies, use it wrong and you'll pay the price.

The skinny on link farms

Have you ever seen a large farm from the air? From a few thousand feet up, farms look like orderly divisions of land. Each little square looks perfectly proportioned and perfectly laid out.

That's exactly how link farms look. If you've ever landed on a page with links ordered neatly around the page, and with little or no text explaining all of the various links, then you've landed on a link farm. That's all they are, too — collections of links that lead to other web sites, or sometimes to other link farms.

You'll hear this term often in SEO because link farms are *not* a good strategy for improving your search engine rankings. Search engines don't like link farms because they offer no information that's of any value to the people who perform searches. For that reason, link farms are usually delisted as soon as they're discovered.

It's easy for you to get pulled into a link farm, thinking it's a legitimate link to your site. You'll usually receive some type of solicitation to place a link to one of these sites in return for a link to your site; it's even possible that you'll hear of an SEO firm that uses link farms in an attempt to artificially produce results that help them to charge you more.

That's why it's wise to check closely the places where your links will be placed. If you receive a request for a *reciprocal link,* make sure that the page that will be displaying your link actually is a relevant web page that has some association with the topic of your page. If you check it out and find that you're just being added to a collection of links on a page, many of which are unrelated, don't allow your link to be displayed there.

You may not be the person who created the link farm, but your site can be delisted just as fast as the page for the link farm if you provide a link back to the link farm. All the crawlers care about is that someone is spamming the crawler, trying to make it believe something that's not true.

Knowing what constitutes a link farm is easy. In addition to the site characteristics that have already been mentioned, there are some other indicators that a site might not be legitimate. It's your responsibility to ensure that the pages with which your site is linked are real pages, designed for site visitors, not for crawlers. Here are some other indications of a link farm:

- Link farms have no connection at all to your site, either in topic or in actual relation to the content that's on your site.
- Link farms have long, complex URLs, and links are often stored in deep directories so that it's harder for search engine crawlers to find them.
- Link farms will usually accept any link that is sent to them, so it's not unusual for links to be unrelated. If someone wants to add your link to a site that isn't even remotely related to yours, don't accept.

■ Link farm owners will sometimes send you an e-mail stating they have linked to you and would like a link to their page in return. Again, be cautious of whom you link to or whom you allow to link back to you.

The Basics of Link Building

Building a great linking structure for your web site is not something that happens in the time it takes to throw a web page together. Building a successful link structure takes months, and sometimes longer.

When you begin creating your link structure, you'll probably have mostly outgoing links. Those are links that lead to other pages — popular pages if you can manage it — that will help to bring traffic back to your site. Over time, however, you should be building your links to include not only links back into your site, but other useful links that aren't damaging to your search engine results rankings.

One of the most important things to remember as you're building your link structure is that quantity isn't nearly as important as quality. Your linking strategy will be far more successful if you create links (both inbound and outbound) that are high quality. Link to great sites that are more popular than your own and try to gain links from those sites to yours too.

Of course, getting those inbound links won't be nearly as easy as creating outbound links to other web sites. Gaining links to your site is a business process. It takes time and a lot of consistent effort on your part. As mentioned earlier, one strategy for gaining inbound links is to send letters to prospective sites requesting a link, but don't send out 10,000 generic letters, generated by some mail-merge program that doesn't customize them in any way to the particular site that you're targeting.

Your link request will be most effective if you can give potential linking partners a good reason for them to support you. Perhaps you can show their customers why they should purchase more of that site's products. Whatever the reason, try to give the site you're requesting a link from some motivation to take the time to add your site to their linking system.

Also keep in mind that link building is a time-consuming process. You're not going to populate the Web with links to your site in one week or even one month. Once your site is built and ready for customers, link building will be an ongoing process that you'll work at for the lifetime of the web sites.

Using Internal Links

One linking strategy that's often overlooked is *internal linking*. Internal links are those that lead people from one page to another within your web site. This is different from the navigational structure. Internal links are more natural links that occur in the text on your web pages.

Without a good internal linking strategy, you run the risk of not having your site properly spidered. It's not enough simply to have a navigational structure or a site map (though site maps help considerably). You should also have links that lead from one element (such as a blog post) to other important elements (such as an archived article or news clipping on your site), so site visitors find that moving through the information they're examining on your site is a natural process that takes place without too much difficulty or thought.

The most effective methods of internal linking are as follows:

- Text links
- Links within the footers of your pages
- Inline text links

Text links are those with which you can use anchor tags and keywords. These links most often appear in the text of a page, though they can also appear in other places within your page, as long as the text links are relevant to the content of the page.

Links within the footers of pages are a common practice now. Figure 15-4 shows how some web pages use links within the footers of pages.

Finally, inline links are those links most often contained within the body of some element of your site content, such as articles and blogs. These links can be either proper names or descriptors that are relevant to the pages being linked to.

FIGURE 15-4

Footer links are a common linking strategy that usually take visitors to some element of the site's administrative functions.

Whatever you do with the navigational structure of your web site, *always* avoid using back and forward buttons. Not only are these buttons frustrating for users who want more options than just forward and back, they're also a red flag for search crawlers that your site may not be user-friendly. Take the time to build a navigational structure that gives your visitors the options they want for moving around your page and finding the information they need.

Internal linking is a practice that most companies use to help ease the navigational structure of their sites, and to create links based on important or keyword text. Plan to use internal linking on your site, but don't allow it to have so much power over your SEO strategy that you don't include other elements of SEO.

Judging the Effectiveness of Your Links

After all the time that you'll put into creating a link strategy and a link structure that you hope will increase the traffic flow to your site, you should still take some actions to ensure that you have the most effective links possible.

Don't ignore the importance of monitoring your links for successful linking. Remember to avoid broken links, and actively maintain or change links when your content changes. Manual monitoring can be a pain and very time-consuming, yet it's important to keep up with your links. This is usually done through a *link analysis* program. You can use link analysis software, such as NetMap (`www.netmap.com`). Link analysis programs, once set up properly, can handle everything from inserting new links to monitoring the links that you already have in place. It simply requires you to set up the software and then allow some time for the application to work on your links in the ways covered by this chapter.

Build that time into normal workflow and SEO efforts. Links are too important and carry too much weight with search engines to allow them to languish. Besides, once you have built a great link structure that works, you don't want bad links or badly placed links to reduce the effectiveness of your efforts.

Part III

Optimizing Search Strategies

You can (and should) use more than one search strategy to optimize your site for search engines. You've seen how keywords and PPC programs work, but there are many other ways to get your site in front of potential site visitors and customers.

Part III explains the different types of search strategies you should be considering as you're developing the SEO for your site. In addition to search engines, there are indexes and directories to keep in mind. You can also use pay-for-inclusion services, which are different from the PPC services that you've already explored.

You should understand robots, spiders, and crawlers in order to target these different types of search strategies; and, of course, you don't want to harm your rankings, so there's also a chapter about SEO spam in this section. Finally, you'll find information about social-media optimization, mobile SEO, monetizing your SEO strategy, using SEO plug-ins, and automated optimization.

All of these elements come together to make your SEO strategies a richer, more effective method of drawing site visitors, and converting those visitors to paying customers.

Chapter 16

Adding Your Site to Directories

Very often, search engines and *search directories* are lumped into the same category. After all, you type in a search term and click a button and the results for that search are returned to you, right? That's right, but the data collected by directories and search engines, and the way those search results are returned, are very different. In fact, directories and search engines differ in three fundamental ways:

- How they collect data
- The search results
- How those search results are ranked

IN THIS CHAPTER

Search directories vs. search engines

Geo-targeting and other strategies

Using submission tools

Yahoo! is one of the most well-known search directories on the Internet. It was one of the first names in search, and it remains one of the stronger players in the search market. However, there are dozens of other directories available online, and, like search engines, these search directories can be very specialized, so that entries cover a single topic or a related group of topics. Search directories can also be implemented within an organization, so that you can list and find all the important documentation your company owns.

The advantage of these highly targeted search directories is not traffic volume of the sort you would receive from a search engine or a general search directory; what's important here is the *quality* of the traffic you receive. Specific search directories attract specific users who are searching for specific items. This means that their chances of reaching a goal conversion on your site (assuming your site is targeted correctly) are much higher than those of visitors who come from search engines.

What Are Directories?

Search directories offer a way of collecting and categorizing links to other web sites. They are *not* search engines and behave nothing like search engines. For example, whereas a search engine collects entries using a search crawler or a robot, search directories are populated by people. You or someone else enters your web site into a directory. In some cases, once you've entered it, the entry is reviewed by a real person before the site is included in directory listings.

Examples of human-edited directories include Mahalo (www.mahalo.com) and Pharos-Search (www.pharos-search.com). For both of these search directories you can submit your site to the directory, but it won't be included until a real person reviews it and compares it to your entry to be sure it's accurate. Only when the site has been verified will it be included in search results for the directory.

> **NOTE** Another way your site might end up in one of these human-powered directories is for someone else to submit it. Sometimes that person is a fan of your site; sometimes it's an employee of the directory who finds your site in some other way and thinks it is worthy of inclusion.

The way in which your site is added to a search directory is not the only difference between search engines and search directories. Several additional differences are illustrated in Table 16-1.

TABLE 16-1

Directory vs. Search Engine Comparison

Feature	Directories	Search Engines
How are entires collected?	Manually. Usually individuals or groups of individuals add the web sites that are included in directories.	Search engine crawlers, spiders, and robots collect entries, and people never review the resulting indexes until a site is returned in search results.
How are web sites categorized?	Whole web sites are categorized as single entities.	Each page in a web site is categorized according to the keywords included on that page.
How are results sorted?	By categories and subcategories	By keywords and in some cases web site popularity
Are there inclusion limits?	In some cases, yes. Some directories allow sites to be entered into only one or two search categories.	No. Web sites can be included in as many keyword categories as the sites are optimized for.
One differentiator?	Directories are browsable by subject or categories and subcategories.	Search engines search the full text of a web page, making the results much more comprehensive.

Categorization is likely to be more accurate with a monitored directory, because someone actually checks the site to ensure a proper listing. Sometimes fees are associated with monitored directories.

The most closely monitored directories are human-edited ones. These have a very strict structure, and to get your web site included in the listings, you must accurately provide all requested information. Additionally, human-edited directories reserve the right to edit or change your entry in any manner that they believe is more suitable to the directory with which you're registering (and therefore more reliable for users expecting certain results). Human-edited directories may also charge a fee in order for you to be listed in them. The fees associated with these types of directories can be very steep, because a person or group of people must always be monitoring the directory.

> **NOTE** There is also a fourth kind of directory: a *hybrid directory*. A hybrid directory is actually a combination of a directory and a search engine. Yahoo! and AOL both operate hybrid directories.

The more directories your site is listed in, the better you'll perform in search results. Most search engines crawl directories, and some even use directory listings to supplement their search results. Just be aware that directories can be outdated, so make time to check your directory listing to ensure that it stays fresh. If you notice that the directory doesn't seem to be updated regularly, you may want to remove your listing, because being included in the directory could reflect poorly on your site.

Submitting to directories

By now you've figured out that directories work differently than search engines. Not only must you complete the submission process in order to have your site included in most directories, even when you're submitting the information on your site there's an art to doing it.

How you list your site can mean the difference between the site being included in the directory or not. Before you even begin to create your listing, it's usually a good idea to navigate through the directory to which you're submitting your site. Look at other listings and take note of what works in them.

Keywords are of little importance when you're creating your directory listing. Instead, what will make the difference is the content on your web site. Therefore, if you're faced with listing in a directory that's strict about reviewing sites before they are listed, make sure you have fresh content on your site. It's also a good practice to keep that content fresh by updating it regularly, because your site may be regularly reviewed after it has been accepted into the directory.

Links can also be important when your site is being reviewed for inclusion in a directory, so be sure you keep your links updated. Broken links are typically detrimental to your site, and links that lead to unrelated pages won't reflect well either.

Other elements of your listing that editors evaluate include the following:

- Appropriate categorization
- Accurate titles and descriptions
- Title and descriptions relevant to the subject of the web site
- Domain names that match site titles
- Secure ordering capabilities on e-commerce sites
- Contact information that's easily accessible
- Links to privacy policies, return policies, and product or service guarantees
- Working and appropriate links to other sites and resources
- Images that display properly in the most common browser formats
- JavaScript that is free of errors

NOTE Increasingly, both search engines and directories are taking the actual code used to build the site into consideration when determining search results. It's always a good idea to run your code through an *HTML validator* to ensure that it is free of errors and unnecessary elements. Clean code simply renders better and makes it easier for crawlers to navigate your web site.

In addition to these requirements, most directories have a long list of criteria that are reviewed before a site is actually added to the directory. That's why it can sometimes take weeks or months for your site to be listed. Depending on the volume of submissions to the directory, it can be a slow process for editors to review each web site.

When you're ready to submit your web site to a directory, take the time to completely read the directions provided by the directory. If you don't follow these directions closely, it's far more likely that your site will be rejected from the listings.

One other important submission guideline to remember is to submit only your site's main page. Because directories include sites that have been reviewed, they usually list the whole site as a single entity, rather than list each page separately, as search engines do.

One of the most well-known directories on the Internet is the *Open Directory Project (ODP)* managed by dmoz.org. This general directory is edited by a team of volunteers, and it's representative of the various types of directories that are available for you to list your site with. Although there might be some slight differences, the directions for listing your site with ODP are very similar to those you would find when listing with other directories.

To list your web site in the ODP directory, take these steps:

1. Open the Open Directory Project web site (www.dmoz.org).
2. Navigate to the category and subcategory where it would be appropriate for your site to appear. Then, in the top-right corner of the page, click Suggest URL.

3. You are taken to the submission site. Read all the instructions carefully and fill in the submission form completely.

4. When you're finished filling out the form, click the Submit button. You're taken to a thank-you page, and your submission process is complete.

5. Now you just have to wait for the editorial committee to complete its review. When the review is complete, you should receive notification indicating whether or not the site has been accepted and listed.

It seems like a simple enough process to suggest your site for inclusion in a directory, and for the most part it is, although depending on the requirements, it could be time-consuming to provide all the requested information. What's difficult is adding your site to all the directories that are appropriate for it. This can also be time-consuming, so plan to consistently spend some time on it each day until you've submitted to all the sites you've selected.

Once the submission process is finished, that time you allocated can be used to ensure that your sites are updated to reflect any changes you've made. Changes for which you may want to send an update to a directory include the following:

- Changes to the site's URL

- Correction of grammatical or spelling errors in the title or description of your site

- Changes to the title or description of your site if the scope of the site changes

- Suggestions for a new category if the scope of your site changes

Major online directories

Like search engines, there are hundreds of different directories online. Some are general directories, whereas others are very specific and associated with only one industry or organization. When you're selecting the directories to which you'd like to submit your site, be choosy. Don't try to list your site in a directory that's inappropriate. You'll just be wasting time and collecting rejection slips.

Some of the most well-known directories on the Web are as follows:

- Yahoo! Directory (dir.yahoo.com): The Yahoo! Directory is one of the oldest online directories, but when you go to www.yahoo.com you actually won't be taken to it. Instead, you'll be taken to a search engine, because Yahoo! changed its format not too long ago. However, you can still access the directory by going to the web site just listed. Yahoo! Directory is a general directory.

- GoGuides.Org (www.goguides.org): This directory's purpose is to be completely spam free. It's a comprehensive search directory that even has image-searching capabilities.

- Open Directory Project (www.dmoz.org): The Open Directory Project is one of the most widely accessed directories on the Web. Users submit sites, and volunteer editors review them. ODP is also an open-source technology, so many other directories use this technology as a basis for their own offerings.

- Google Directory (directory.google.com): Google Directory is one of those directories built on the ODP platform. Google is most well known for its search capabilities, but adding a directory takes advantage of the desire of Internet users to dig deeper into very specific search results.

- SearchSight (www.searchsight.com): Another general directory, SearchSight is one of the lesser-known directories, but it's quickly gaining traction in the search market.

One reason why search directories are still hanging on in an age of search engines is the social nature of those directories. Internet users like to participate in organizing the Web (which you learn more about in Chapter 20). Socially monitored sites also seem to have more validity with Internet users. People trust other users who have the same needs and desires they do much more than they trust robots, crawlers, and spiders.

Paid vs. free directories

The free versus paid debate is one that has hit every aspect of the Internet and Internet technologies at one time or another. There was worry about free web site hosting versus paid web hosting, and fret over free e-mail versus paid. In both cases, whether free or paid is better for you turns out to depend on your specific needs.

The same is true of the debate over free versus paid directory listings. Many experts will argue that free directory listings have nothing of value listed in them. This is simply not true. Some free directories are actually very strict about the listings that are included in their results. Similarly, most users believe that paid directories automatically equate to better-quality sites. Again, not true. Paid directories can be just as lax about the review process as any other directory.

The Skinny on Meta Search Engines

Search engines, search directories, and hybrids of the two are not the only search game on the Internet. Another search tool that many people like to use is the *meta search engine*. Meta search engines are search engines that search other search engines.

One of the better known meta search engines on the Web is DogPile (www.dogpile.com). If you conduct a search on DogPile, you'll receive results for that search from more than half a dozen different search engines. Nifty, no?

But how do you apply that to your SEO efforts? One of the criteria that meta search engines use when searching other search engines is the meta data that's included in your site. Keywords and many other aspects that you'll optimize for are also criteria that meta search engines use. Therefore, if you're optimizing for search engines, you should automatically be optimizing for meta search engines.

continued

---

continued
Meta search engines do not behave like regular search engines. These search engines do not include a database of possible results; rather, a meta search engine pulls the results together from other search engines — effectively aggregating them — and then returns only the top search results. The theory is that collecting the top results from many different search engines will help users find the results they're looking for much faster.

Don't discount the impact that meta search engines can have on your site traffic. Although meta search engines are not as popular as some algorithm-based or even human-edited search engines and directories, many people use them, and they have the potential to drive significant amounts of traffic to your web site.

In short, whether you use paid or free directory listings shouldn't depend on cost alone. What matters when you're selecting a directory in which to list your site is how relevant the directory is to your site. After relevance, the next consideration is the quality of the sites that are listed in the directory. If a directory you've selected is full of outdated sites, spam sites, or miscategorized sites, it's clearly not the best place to list your web site.

One more element to consider when choosing directories is the audience that's most likely to use the directory. The company should be able to provide a typical audience profile for you if you can't tell by looking at the types of sites listed in the directory. Going back to a principle you've heard often in this book, your site should be created with the user in mind. The same is true for listing your site. It will be pointless to list your site in a directory of law-based web sites if your site is about home and family topics and products. Audience first. After that, everything will fall into place.

Geo-Targeting SEO Strategies

Creating an SEO strategy for your web site requires more than just choosing what search engines and directories it should appear in. Another consideration is where and how your site should be listed geographically. *Geo-targeting* is a method of targeting specific traffic for your web site based on the geographical location of your business.

As more and more web users take advantage of the Internet as a purchasing and research tool, those same users are integrating local searches into their behaviors and habits. For example, people in the market to buy a plasma television are likely to spend time on the Internet searching for facts and information about plasma TVs. In the beginning, this information can be generic in nature. It doesn't matter where it comes from, so long as it answers the customer's questions.

As they work through the phases of the buying process, eventually users will begin pricing the television, a process that will also take place online. Geography is now becoming more important, but it's not until the user is actually ready to buy that geography becomes essential. Because many users first research on the Internet and then purchase in a local store (or research and purchase on the Internet and pick up the merchandise in the store), those customers may look online for local stores that offer the brand and price they're looking for. If your site isn't listed in some kind of local directory or categorized on at least one level by location, you'll miss out on those sales.

Broadband-enabled cell phones have also become a major reason to think about optimizing your site for location search. The widespread adoption of the iPhone and iPhone-like devices makes it possible for users to search for information — including actual locations — on the fly. These devices have become so prevalent (there are more than 200 different Internet-enabled devices to choose from in the U.S. alone) that some users are dropping their PC- and laptop-based Internet connections and relying solely on their handheld devices for Internet service. This makes geo-targeting even more important.

NOTE You'll find more information about optimizing your web site for mobile search in Chapter 21.

Catering to site users based on their location is smart SEO. Many search engines and directories offer some type of geo-targeting capabilities. Usually, these require that either your physical location be included on your web site or you list your site in the right section of a directory.

You've probably heard it said that the most important factor affecting the success of a business is *location, location, location*. Well, location is just as important on the Internet as it is in the real world, so don't skip the geo-targeting aspect of optimizing your web site. Give search engines and directories the extra information they need to ensure that your site shows up in local searches.

Using Submission Tools

You may have figured out by now that getting your site included in search engines and directories is no easy task. It can take a lot of time, and if you don't follow all the directions to the letter, you risk the chance of being refused for listing. To help ease the process, a class of software tools, called *submission tools*, has emerged for the SEO market.

Submission tools are automated software programs and applications that remember the repetitive information that must be provided in order to get your web site listed in a search engine or directory. They sound like a great idea. Some are, but not all of them.

Many submission tools try to scam web site owners by promising to submit their site to thousands of search engines and directories for one low fee. The problem with that claim is that most of those search engines are either nonexistent or mostly worthless to your site.

Therefore, when considering web site submission tools, look closely at the claims the programs make. Then apply that well-known rule: *If it sounds too good to be true, it probably is.* You can ask for a list of the search engines and directories to which the program will submit your site. After requesting this list, take the time to research the sites before you invest in the tool.

Submission tools can take two forms: *deep submission tools* and *multisubmission tools*. Most web sites are dozens and even hundreds of pages deep. *Deep* means those pages are several levels down in the structure of the site — and often those pages are missed by search engine crawlers, or they're not considered important, but that's not always the case.

Deep submission tools will submit those deep pages to search engines and directories. The process is automated, and the submission tools can be more successful at submitting the deep pages than you might be, only because it takes time to submit pages and the deeper you go, the longer the process.

Multisubmission tools submit your site to multiple different search engines and directories. These tools also help ease the burden of getting your site listed. Rather than having to go repeatedly through the discovery, research, and submission process, you can let the multisubmission tools do the work for you.

Unfortunately, it's hard to know whether the submission tool you select will be the right one, so it is always the best practice to manually submit your site and URLs to directories. Take the time to consult with other program users. If a company that's providing the submission tools refuses to provide a list of references, move on. There are more submission tool providers out there. The right one will meet your expectations and provide the references you need in order to be comfortable using the application.

Chapter 17

Pay-for-Inclusion Services

Search engine marketing is composed of two very different elements. Search engine optimization (SEO), strictly speaking, is about improving your *natural* search engine rankings through tweaking your web site. Pay-per-click (PPC) programs, conversely, are based on the ability to pay for placement. Even Google separates the two in its search results, with natural search results appearing on the left side and paid search results appearing on the right.

When you're fighting today's competition to improve your web site ranking, you need to use every weapon (i.e., tool) in your arsenal. One of those tools is *paid inclusion*, but there's a lot of confusion around paid inclusion and when it should be used. Very often, paid inclusion is confused with *paid placement*. They're very different strategies.

Similarly, when you hear about paid inclusion, you may well hear it called *pay for inclusion (PFI)* or *pay per inclusion (PPI)*. Again, these are not the same animal. Pay for inclusion is a strategy whereby you pay a fee simply to be included in a search index. This fee doesn't guarantee your rank in the index. It's a simple flat fee that's usually paid annually.

Pay per inclusion is also a strategy in which you pay a fee to be included in a search index, but the fee that you pay in PPI is based on the number of clicks you receive as a result of that inclusion. Like PFI, PPI does not guarantee your rank in the search engine. Your only guarantee is that you will be included. Moreover, that per-click fee can often be comparatively high, in the range of $.30 per click.

The service that guarantees your rank in a search index is paid placement, which is also called *pay for placement (PFP)*. When you pay for placement, you are guaranteed that your site will not only be listed, but also will place in a specific rank consistently as long as you're willing to pay the fee for that rank.

There are some other *pay-for* strategies that you might consider. *Paid directory review (PDR)* services guarantee that a review for a directory will take place in a specified amount of time (usually much faster than it would otherwise), but, again, this is no guarantee of inclusion or placement. *XML inclusion* is another story. This is a strategy to ensure that the dynamic content on your site is included in search results. Because some sites have constantly changing content, XML inclusion may be a requirement for them.

The different types of inclusion and what your payments will buy you can be confusing. Table 17-1 summarizes some of the differences among the types of inclusion.

NOTE Over time, Yahoo! has gobbled up a number of other search properties, so you may still see their names — including Inktomi, AlltheWeb, AltaVista, and FastSearch — but they all exist under the Yahoo! umbrella. When you're weighing factors for the search engines to select, keep in mind that all of these are actually just one.

When to Use Pay-for-Inclusion Services

Pay for inclusion, pay-per-click, and all other types of fee-based services are widely debated in SEO circles; but of all of them, pay-for-inclusion services are probably the most controversial. Pay for inclusion is considered by some to be just this side of unethical, and it's only *just this side* because it is such a widely practiced strategy. However, there is a time for paid-inclusion services.

The thing to remember with paid inclusion is that unless you're using it properly, you're just wasting money. Because paid-inclusion services don't guarantee your rank in search results, it's not a strategy that you will want to use for all your search engine optimization. In truth, using paid inclusion for even *most* of your pages will result mostly in a loss of budget that would be better spent on more effective (or at least better guaranteed) SEO efforts.

The exception to this is when you're using paid inclusion as a method of testing the placement of a web page based on your SEO efforts. For example, if you have a page on your web site for which you would like to improve the traffic, and you need to do it quickly, you could register for a paid-inclusion service. This would get your site listed very quickly in search results, and you can use this capability to view the effectiveness of your SEO efforts. Then, if you find that your SEO efforts aren't effective, you can tweak the page you're paying to include until it reaches the level of search-result rankings that you need. Once you're at that level, you'll know how to optimize other pages on your site for the same results.

Paid-inclusion services are generally inexpensive in relative terms. That makes them ideal services for helping you develop a winning SEO strategy through testing. However, to use paid

TABLE 17-1

Fee-Based Inclusion Services

Strategy	Description	Examples	Cost
Paid Inclusion (fee-based)	A strategy that requires you to pay a search engine to include your site in its index rankings — where in those rankings is not guaranteed.	AskJeeves, AlltheWeb, Yahoo!, EntireWeb	$25–$50 per year and up, for inclusion (PFI) depending on the service
Pay-per-Inclusion (PPI); pay for inclusion per click	A strategy that requires you to pay a search engine to include your site in its index and rankings. Your placement in those rankings is not guaranteed.	LookSmart, Yahoo!	Flat-rate setup fee, and then $.20–$.50 per click
Paid Directory Review	With this option, you pay a directory to review your web site listing faster than it would ordinarily be reviewed. The review usually happens in 2–4 days; it does not guarantee your inclusion or placement.	Yahoo!, AlltheWeb	Flat fee, usually $30–$75 but can be higher depending on the directory
Pay for Placement, Paid Placement, Pay per Click (PPC)	This strategy requires that you pay for the placement of your web page in search results. This guarantees that you appear at a certain spot in the results.	AltaVista, Yahoo!, AOL Search, Windows Live Search, Google, FindWhat	Some search engines charge a flat fee for setup. After the setup fee, there is usually a per-click fee ranging from $.05–$.50 or more per–click, depending on the topic and position.
XML Inclusion, Trusted Feed	Used for large sites (usually with 500 pages or more), this strategy enables RSS content feeds to search engines so that regularly changing content is indexed.	AltaVista, AlltheWeb, Kanoodle, Google, Yahoo!	Usually requires a flat fee for setup and then a per-click fee of $.25–$.50. Google doesn't charge a fee.

inclusion for multiple pages on your site, you'd probably have to spend a lot of money that would be better spent on more effective strategies (such as pay-per-click advertising).

Understanding the Business Model

Another reason many paid services have a bad name in SEO is the number of scams that exist to take advantage of webmasters who use the services. It's not at all unusual to see an advertisement that claims your site will be added to "thousands" of search engines for "one low fee" (which is usually well over $300).

The problem with such a claim is that there are not "thousands" of search engines to which a site can be added. A few dozen would likely be the limit for most organizations, and that's if you include all the highly specialized search engines to which a site could be added.

What happens, then, is that the organization signs a contract with you, you pay their fee, and then you may or may not ever be submitted to any sites, much less to the sites that are appropriate for your web pages. In most cases, your own SEO efforts will achieve some search results rankings for you before these services will.

That's not to say there are not legitimate companies out there that will help you gain better placement for your web site, and some services may actually submit your site to search engines and directories using paid-placement or paid-submission capabilities; but unless these services are coupled with other SEO services, you could probably do much better without spending the extra money. The one consideration that can cut the other way, though, is the time factor. It will take many hours to research and submit to search engines on your own.

If you do find a services that looks as if it offers the features you need — reporting capabilities, URL monitoring capabilities, web metrics, and so on — and you have the budget to invest in it, take a preliminary step or two. Before you hire a company, take the time to learn about the features that it is promising. Are they realistic? If a company promises that it can make your site rank number one in all the different search engines the company works with, you can bet this won't happen. The number-one spot is very tough to achieve. Moreover, how can a company offer the same guarantee to all of its customers? Clearly, not everyone can be number one.

Likewise, if a company you're considering claims that it can increase clicks to your site by dozens, hundreds, or even thousands of visitors, think carefully before you commit. Clicks are just clicks. The company isn't guaranteeing conversions, and without conversions you're not making any money. Clicks can be collected in many ways, but that doesn't make them useful or even relevant. Be sure you completely understand what a submission firm (or even a general SEO firm) is offering and how that translates into your bottom line. If what it offers doesn't equal increased sales for your site, it's probably not worth the investment.

Take the time to confirm a company's claims to ensure it has a legitimate business model. If it claims it will submit your site to 1,000 search engines (or even 100), ask for a list of those search engines. Look up each search engine and ensure that your site is appropriate for those engines. Most of the time, a company will claim to *submit* your site to that huge number of search engines and directories, but submission is *not* inclusion or even paid placement. There's no guarantee that the company can make your site appear in the index, much less in the search results.

Finally, if you're considering hiring a company to submit your site to a variety of search engines, ask for customer referrals. Of course, the company is only going to provide names of customers who have demonstrated a willingness to speak well of it, but you can still call those references and ask very specific questions.

Ultimately, hiring a company to submit your site to search engines should be a decision based on your specific needs. If you have time, then you can do all the necessary search engine submissions yourself. It may take longer for you to submit to all those sites, but the money you save by doing it yourself can be applied to other, more-efficient marketing and SEO tactics.

Managing Paid Services

When you choose to use paid services such as PFI or PPC, you may find that managing the different services quickly becomes as difficult a task as working without them. You need strategies to manage all of them as efficiently as possible.

One huge help when trying to manage your SEO, paid services, and everything that goes along with them is to find a software solution that enables you to manage as many facets of your SEO strategy as possible from one location. You won't find a single service or software application that manages everything, but it's possible to find one that enables you to more easily monitor and manage your PPC, PFI, and some of your other marketing efforts at the same time.

When selecting a software management program, look for something that has a trial period so you can try it out before you sink a lot of your budget into it. User interfaces, the capabilities of the program, and several other factors can work against you and leave you hating the solution that you've selected.

Another strategy for managing your paid services effectively is to devote a block of time each day to staying on top of the management process. That might be as little as 20 minutes or as much as two hours, depending on how much you need to monitor, but scheduling that into your day ensures that it will happen. That's essential, because falling behind on your management tasks can seriously affect your SEO campaigns (not to mention make it much harder to catch up).

Finally, when you're managing your paid services, stay within your budget. If your strategies require more than is available in your budget, two things can happen. One, your SEO strategies can lose effectiveness because they're not funded. Two, eventually they can fail altogether because the funds that make the strategies possible won't be forthcoming.

Hiring the Right Professionals

One thing is absolutely certain about SEO, whether or not you're using paid services: It's going to be a time-consuming process. Cutting corners is not an option, because the wrong SEO practices are far more detrimental to your site than doing nothing at all. When time isn't on your side, hiring an SEO professional is an option to consider.

It's not at all unusual to hear about a company or web site owner that's been scammed by a supposed SEO consultant who guaranteed them top placement in hundreds of search engines. Again, it's just not possible for anyone, even an SEO expert, to guarantee that your site will appear at the top of search engine rankings. Nonetheless, many people claiming to be SEO experts will tell you they can do just that. Don't believe them.

Only a few accreditation programs exist for people who claim to be SEO experts. In most cases, what happens is this: A web site designer or owner who has had to create a site for SEO decides he or she can implement SEO for others for a profit. However, just because these people have done SEO on their own sites doesn't mean they can plan SEO on your site in the most effective manner possible.

Two accreditation programs *are* offered, by SEMPO (www.sempo.org) and Bruce Clay, Inc (www.bruceclay.com). Therefore, if the individual or firm that you're looking at to help with your SEO efforts claims to be an expert, ask if they have been accredited. In most cases, the answer will be no. You can contact both SEMPO and Bruce Clay and request a reference for an accredited SEO consultant.

In most cases, it will take a team of people to perform proper SEO techniques for your site. That team might include someone to submit your site to directories and search engines, someone to create and submit articles to other sources that will link back to your site, someone to design or supplement the design of your site to make it attractive to search engines, and someone to manage the whole SEO program from beginning to end, including reporting to you, the web site owner.

Contract Considerations

If you want someone to help with SEO on your web site, here are some guidelines:

- Ask for references and look at those references for previous customers who rank well in searches in their industry. The most successful SEO firms can provide references and case studies that prove those companies are worth your SEO budget investment.

- Ask about the practices that the firm under consideration considers unethical. Many unethical SEO tactics can get your site removed from search rankings entirely, so you could find yourself with a big bill and a site that doesn't appear in search results at all. If possible, have a list of unethical practices, labeled as such, included in the contract, along with penalties for use of those tactics.

- No legitimate SEO professional or firm will guarantee results. If the professional or firm you are considering is guaranteeing specific results, move on. A good SEO firm will not guarantee anything that's not completely under its control (search engine rankings are not under its control, because no one knows the specifics surrounding any search engine's ranking algorithm).

When you find an SEO firm that offers the services that you need, you can expect to receive certain specific services from them. The services vary from firm to firm, but here's a list that you can use as a good rule of thumb:

- A professional SEO audit. The audit should thoroughly examine your site and your existing SEO efforts to determine what works and what needs to be improved or started.
- Keyword and competitor research
- On-page SEO. This indicates how each page of your web site is optimized. On-page SEO includes elements such as HTML tags, keywords, and content.
- Optimization of internal site navigation. Your internal navigation can have a serious effect on how your site performs in search results, so a good SEO will examine and optimize that navigation structure.
- Link building
- Progress monitoring
- Staff training. SEO requires ongoing efforts. Your staff will need to be trained in the most successful methods for maintaining optimization.

Professional SEO firms can offer a lot of benefits to your web site. After all, your core business is likely not SEO, but an SEO firm's is. The good ones can properly optimize your site, and your services, in less time than you can. That reason alone should be enough to make you consider hiring an SEO firm, whether or not you end up doing so.

When the Relationship Isn't Working

Despite all of your best efforts, factors can combine to make a relationship between your organization and an SEO firm not work. The problem can be in the relationship, in the SEO strategies, or in some other aspect of the situation. The question is, what do you do if you find that your SEO firm (or an individual SEO professional) is just not what you expected?

There's no easy answer to that question unless you address it at the very beginning of the relationship. If you address it early, you can include a clause in your contract outlining the various scenarios that would enable either party to terminate the relationship.

If you don't address the possibility early, however, you may find yourself stuck with an SEO firm or professional that's doing nothing for you except running up a big bill. Do whatever you can to protect yourself. Know your contact at the SEO firm and how to reach that person when you need to ask questions or find out why something is (or isn't) happening.

Your relationship with your SEO firm should operate within the same parameters as a relationship with any other provider. Don't assume that because SEO is different from using a hosted technology or dealing with a service vendor, it should be governed by less-stringent requirements. SEO is a service for you, and the relationship is like that with any other vendor. As such, just as much attention should be given to it.

Chapter 18

Robots, Spiders, and Crawlers

You're getting well along in the book, so you should have a pretty good handle on what exactly robots, spiders, and crawlers are, right? No doubt you do, but did you know that there is much more to these Internet creatures than just the fact that they crawl from one web site to another?

Spiders, robots, crawlers, or whatever else you choose to call them can determine how well you rank in search engines, so it's best to make friends with them as quickly as possible. Certain strategies will help you find favor with these crawlers (which is the name we'll use to lump them all together), whereas other strategies, unfortunately, will help you find your way right out of search engine rankings.

A sad fact about crawlers is that sometimes you'll be treated unfairly when you've done absolutely nothing wrong. Some of the strategies that you may want to use to improve the optimization of your site can look suspicious to crawlers. When they see those strategies they will automatically penalize you for trying to spam the search engine, even when you're not.

That's what makes it so important for you to understand not only the intimate details about how crawlers work, but also about what makes them happy and what makes them move on without looking back.

What Are Robots, Spiders, and Crawlers?

You should already have a general understanding that a robot, spider, or crawler is a piece of software that is programmed to *crawl* from one web page to another based on the links on those pages. As this crawler makes it way around the Internet, it collects content (such as text and links) from web sites and saves those in a database that is indexed and ranked according to the search engine algorithm.

When a crawler is first released on the Web, it's usually *seeded* with a few web sites and it begins on one of those sites. The first thing it does on that first site is to take note of the links on the page. Then it *reads* the text and begins to follow the links that it collected previously. This network of links is called the *crawl frontier*; it's the territory that the crawler is exploring in a very systematic way.

The links in a crawl frontier will sometimes take the crawler to other pages on the same web site, and sometimes they will take it away from the site completely. The crawler will follow the links until it hits a dead end and then backtrack and begin the process again until every link on a page has been followed. Figure 18-1 illustrates the path that a crawler might take.

FIGURE 18-1

The crawler starts with a seed URL and works its way outward on the Web.

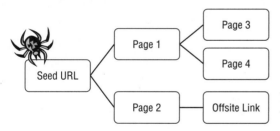

As to what actually happens when a crawler begins reviewing a site, it's a little more complicated than simply saying that it *reads* the site. The crawler sends a request to the web server where the web site resides, requesting pages to be delivered to it in the same manner that your web browser requests pages that you review. The difference between what your browser sees and what the crawler sees is that the crawler is viewing the pages in a text-only interface. No graphics or other types of media files are displayed. It's all text, and it's encoded in HTML, so to you it might look like gibberish.

The crawler can request as many or as few pages as it is programmed to request at any given time. This can sometimes cause problems with web sites that aren't prepared to serve up dozens of pages of content at once. The requests will overload the site and cause it to crash, or it can slow down traffic to a web site considerably, and it's even possible that the requests will just be fulfilled too slowly and the crawler will give up and go away.

As you can see, the crawler is programmed to have the same tolerance and patience that site visitors have. Therefore, if your site visitors are willing to wait three seconds for a page to load — and that's considered a very patient visitor on most sites — then the crawler will likely only wait that long as well. After that time, the crawler will move on to something more responsive.

If the crawler does go away, it will eventually return to try the task again; and it might try several times before it gives up entirely. However, if the site doesn't eventually begin to cooperate with the crawler, then it is penalized and your site's search engine ranking will fall.

What does this mean to you? If you have pages on your site that are very graphic intensive and are slow to load, or if you have pages that are slow to load for any other reason, you may need a way to keep crawlers off those pages. You'll learn shortly how you can redirect a crawler, but first consider a few other reasons you may not want a crawler indexing a page on your site:

- **Your page is under construction:** If you can avoid it, you don't want a crawler to index your site while this is happening. If you can't avoid it, however, be sure that any pages that are being changed or worked on are excluded from the crawler's territory. Later, when your page is ready, you can allow the page to be indexed again.

- **Pages of links:** Having links leading to and away from your site is an essential way to ensure that crawlers find you. However, pages of links seem suspicious to a search crawler, and it may classify your site as a spam site. Instead of having pages that are all links, break links up with descriptions and text. If that's not possible, block the link pages from being indexed by crawlers.

- **Pages of old content:** Old content, like blog archives, doesn't necessarily harm your search engine rankings, but nor does it help them much. One worrisome issue with archives, however, is the number of times that archived content appears on your page. With a blog, for example, you may have the blog appear on the page where it was originally displayed, and also have it displayed in archives, and possibly have it linked from some other area of your site. Although this is all legitimate, crawlers may mistake multiple instances of the same content for spam. Instead of risking it, remove some of those instances of content (such as from the main page) or make your archives off limits to crawlers. (Technically, both options are the best choice in this situation.)

- **Private information:** It really makes better sense not to have private information (or proprietary information) on a web site, but if you have a compelling reason that dictates you *must* have it on your site, then definitely block crawlers from access to it. Better yet, password-protect the information so that no one can stumble on it accidently.

There are many more reasons why you may not want to allow a crawler to visit some of your web pages. These are just a few of the most common ones. It's a little like allowing visitors into your home. You don't mind if they see the living room, dining room, den, and maybe the kitchen, but you don't want them in your bedroom without good reason. Crawlers are the guests in your Internet house. Be sure they understand the guidelines under which they are welcome.

What's the Robot Exclusion Standard?

Because crawlers do have the potential to wreak havoc on a web site, there are in fact some guidelines to control their behavior. Those guidelines are called the *Robot Exclusion Standard*, the *Robots Exclusion Protocol*, or *robots.txt*.

The file `robots.txt` is the actual element that you'll work with. It's a text-based document that should be included in the root of your domain, and it essentially contains instructions to any crawler that comes to your site about what they are and are not allowed to index.

To communicate with the crawler, you need a specific syntax that it can understand. In its most basic form, the text might look something like this:

```
User-agent: *
Disallow: /
```

These two parts of the text are essential. The first part, `User-agent:`, tells a crawler what *user agent*, or crawler, you're commanding. The asterisk (*) indicates that all crawlers are covered, but you can specify a single crawler or even multiple crawlers.

The second part, `Disallow:`, tells the crawler what it is not allowed to access. The slash (/) indicates *all directories*. Therefore, in the preceding code example, the `robots.txt` file is essentially saying that *all crawlers are to ignore all directories*.

When you're writing `robots.txt`, remember to include the colon (:) after the `User-agent` indicator and after the `Disallow` indicator. The colon indicates that important information follows to which the crawler should pay attention.

You won't usually want to tell all crawlers to ignore all directories. Instead, you can tell all crawlers to ignore your temporary directories by writing the text like this:

```
User-agent: *
Disallow: /tmp/
```

You can also take it one step further and tell all crawlers to ignore multiple directories:

```
User-agent: *
Disallow: /tmp/
Disallow: /private/
Disallow: /links/listing.html
```

That piece of text tells the crawler to ignore temporary directories, private directories, and the web page (title Listing) that contains links — the crawler won't be able to follow those links.

One thing to keep in mind about crawlers is that they read the `robots.txt` file from top to bottom, and as soon as they find a guideline that applies to them they stop reading and begin crawling your site. Therefore, if you're commanding multiple crawlers with your `robots.txt` file, you want to be careful how you write it.

This is the wrong way:

```
User-agent: *
Disallow: /tmp/

User-agent: CrawlerName
Disallow: /tmp/
Disallow: /links/listing.html
```

This bit of text tells crawlers first that *all* crawlers should ignore the temporary directories. That means every crawler reading that file will automatically ignore the temporary files; but you've also told a specific crawler (indicated by `CrawlerName`) to disallow both temporary directories and the links on the Listing page. The problem is that the specified crawler will never get that message because it has already read that all crawlers should ignore the temporary directories and has gone off to read the rest of your site without ever getting to the specifics you set forth for that one crawler.

If you want to command multiple crawlers, you need to first begin by naming the crawlers you want to control. Only after they've been named should you leave your instructions for all crawlers. Written properly, the text from the preceding code should look like this:

```
User-agent: CrawlerName
Disallow: /tmp/
Disallow: /links/listing.html

User-agent: *
Disallow: /tmp/
```

> **NOTE** If you have certain pages or links that you want the crawler to ignore, you can accomplish this without causing the crawler to ignore a whole site or a whole directory or having to put a specific meta tag on each page.

Each search engine crawler goes by a different name, and if you look at your web server log, you'll probably see that name. Here's a quick list of some of the crawler names you're likely to see in that web server log:

- Google: Googlebot
- MSN: MSNbot
- Yahoo! Web Search: Yahoo SLURP or just SLURP
- Ask: Teoma
- AltaVista: Scooter
- LookSmart: MantraAgent
- WebCrawler: WebCrawler
- SearchHippo: Fluffy the Spider

These are just a few of the search engine crawlers that might crawl across your site. You can find a complete list, along with the text of the Robot Exclusion Standard document on the Web Robots Pages (www.robotstxt.org). Take the time to read the Robot Exclusion Standard document. It's not terribly long, and reading it will help you understand how search crawlers interact with your web site. That understanding can also help you learn how to control crawlers better when they come to visit.

It pays to know which crawler belongs to what search engine, because there are some *spambots* and other malicious crawlers out there that are interested in crawling your site for less-than-ethical reasons. If you know the names of these crawlers, you can keep them off of your site and keep your users' information safe. Spambots, in particular, are troublesome, because they crawl along the Web searching out and collecting anything that appears to be an e-mail address. These addresses are then collected and sold to marketers or even people who are not interested in legitimate business opportunities. Most spambots will ignore your robots.txt file.

> **TIP**   You can view the robots.txt file for any web site that has one by adding the robots.txt extension to the base URL of the site. For example, www.sampleaddress.com/robots.txt will display a page that shows you the text file guiding robots for that site. If you use that extension on a URL and it doesn't pull up the robots.txt file, then the web site does not have one.

If you don't have a robots.txt file, you can create one in any text editor. Keep in mind that not everyone wants or needs to use the robots.txt file. If you don't care who is crawling your site, then don't even create the file. Whatever you do, though, don't use a blank robots.txt file. Crawlers automatically assume an empty file means you don't want your site to be crawled, so using a blank file is a good way to keep yourself out of search engine results.

Robots Meta Tag

Not all site owners have access to their web servers, but they still want to have control over how crawlers behave on their web sites. If you're in this category, you can still control the crawlers that come to your site. Instead of using the robots.txt file, you can use a *robots meta tag* to make your preferences known to the crawlers.

The robots meta tag is a small piece of HTML code that is inserted into the <HEAD> tag of your web page. It works generally in the same manner as the robots.txt file. You include your instructions for crawlers inside the tags. The following example shows what your robots meta tag might look like:

```
<html>
<head>
<meta name="robots" content="noindex, nofollow">
<meta name="description" content="page description.">
<title>
Web Site Title
</title>
```

```
</head>
<body>
```

This bit of HTML tells crawlers not to index the content on the site and not to follow the links on the site. Of course, that might not be exactly what you had in mind. You can also use several other robots meta tags for combinations of following, not following, indexing, and not indexing:

```
<meta name="robots" content="index,follow">
<meta name="robots" content="noindex,follow">
<meta name="robots" content="index,nofollow">
<meta name="robots" content="noindex,nofollow">
```

The major difference between `robots.txt` and robots meta tags is that with the meta tags you cannot specify which crawlers you're targeting. It's an all-or-nothing tag, so you either command all the crawlers to behave in a certain way or you command none of them. It's not as precise as `robots.txt`, but if you don't have access to your web server, it's a good alternative.

NOTE Unfortunately, not all search engines recognize the `robots.txt` file or the robots meta tags, so in some cases you have no control at all over what the crawler examines on your site. However, more search engines seem to be allowing these commands, to help classify the Web more efficiently.

Search engine crawlers can help your site be indexed so that it appears in search results, but they can also cause problems with your site if they don't follow the guidelines outlined in the Robot Exclusion Standard or if your site is not stable enough to support the way the crawler examines it.

Knowing how to control the way that search engines crawl your site can help to ensure that your site is always at its shiny best (or at least appears to the search crawler to be). It won't necessarily give you complete control of all the crawlers on the Web, but it will help with some of them.

Inclusion with XML Site Mapping

You may remember from Chapter 4 a brief mention of XML site mapping. It's time to revisit XML site mapping so that you understand how it can help your web site.

XML site mapping is actually the companion to the Robot Exclusion Protocol. It's an *inclusion protocol* — a method by which you can tell crawlers what is available for them to index. In its most basic form, an XML site map is a file that lists all the URLs for a web site. This file enables webmasters to include additional information about each URL, such as the date the URL was last updated, how often the URL changes, and how important the URL is in relation to the other pages on the site.

The XML site map is used to ensure that crawlers can find certain pages on your web site, such as dynamic pages. The site-map file can be placed in the `robots.txt` file or you can submit it directly to a search engine. Doing either of these, however, is not guaranteed to get your site indexed by the search engine, nor will it cause the search engine to index your site any sooner.

Nor does an XML site map guarantee that all the pages on your site will be indexed. It's simply a guide that the crawler can use to find pages that it might otherwise miss.

Creating an XML site map is the first step to including it in your `robots.txt` file or submitting it to a search engine. There are many sites on the Internet offering applications that will help you create your site map. For example, Google offers a site-map generator that will help you create your site map after you have downloaded and installed the required software. But Google isn't the only game in town. Dozens of other site-map generators work just as well.

Creating your own XML site map

The alternative is to write your own XML site map. The site-map protocol extends requirements for writing a site map that's fully functional. The top two requirements of that protocol are as follows:

- Your site map must consist of XML tags.

- Your site map should be *UTF-8 encoded*. UTF-8 encoding stands for *8-bit UCS/Unicode Transformation Format* and is a type of code that's consistent with ASCII.

Another requirement for your XML site map is that data values within the site map must be *entity escaped*, which means that special characters indicating alternative interpretations must be used. Entity escape codes you can use in your XML site map include those listed in Table 18-1.

TABLE 18-1

Entity Escape Characters

Character		Escape Code
Ampersand	&	&
Single Quote	'	'
Double Quote	"	"
Greater Than	>	>
Less Than	<	<

These escape characters are used in URLs to replace the characters indicated. Therefore, the URL

    http://www.example.com/product.html&q=name

would look like the following after the escape codes are included:

    http://www.example.com/product.html&q=name

In addition to entity escaping, you must also use a set of XML tags. The ones you'll use most frequently are shown in Table 18-2.

NOTE The code snippets used in this chapter are examples of how site maps should be written specifically for Google. For the most part, these snippets will be the same across the various search engines, but before you begin writing your site-map code, review the guidelines set forth by the search engine you're targeting. Luckily, Google, Yahoo!, and MSN have all agreed to follow the same site-map standard.

TABLE 18-2

XML Tags Used for Site Mapping

Tag	When Used	Description
`<urlset>`	Always required	This tag encapsulates the file and references the current protocol standard.
`<url>`	Always required	This is the parent tag for each URL entry. The remaining tags are children of this tag.
`<loc>`	Always required	This is the URL of the page. This URL must begin with the http protocol (`http://`) and end with a trailing slash, if your web server requires it. The length of the URL must be less than 2,048 characters.
`<lastmod>`	Optional, only when needed	The date of last modification of the file. This date should be in W3C DateTime format (see `www.w3.org/TR/NOTE-datetime`). This format enables you to omit the time portion, if desired, and use YYYY-MM-DD.
`<changefreq>`	Optional, only when needed	This is considered a hint and not a command. Even though search engine crawlers consider this information when making decisions, they may crawl pages marked "hourly" less frequently than that, and they may crawl pages marked "yearly" more frequently. It is also likely that crawlers will periodically crawl pages marked "never" so that they can handle unexpected changes to those pages.
`<priority>`	The default priority of a page is 0.5.	Please note that the priority you assign to a page has no influence on the position of your URLs in a search engine's result pages. Search engines use this information when selecting between URLs on the same site, so you can use this tag to increase the likelihood that your more important pages are present in a search index. Also, note that assigning a high priority to all the URLs on your site will not help you. Because the priority is relative, it is used only to select between URLs on your site; the priority of your pages will not be compared to the priority of pages on other sites.

If you're using all the tags in Table 18-2 in your XML site map, it may look something like the following site map. This site map includes only a few URLs, each with a different set of optional parameters. Notice that the escape characters are used in the URLs, too:

```
<?xml version="1.0" encoding="UTF-8"?>
<urlset xmlns="http://www.sitemaps.org/schemas/sitemap/0.9">

   <url>
      <loc>http://www.example.com/</loc>
      <lastmod>2005-01-01</lastmod>
      <changefreq>monthly</changefreq>
      <priority>0.8</priority>
   </url>
   <url>
<loc>http://www.example.com/catalog?item=12&amp;desc=vacation_
hawaii</loc>
      <changefreq>weekly</changefreq>
   </url>
   <url>
<loc>http://www.example.com/catalog?item=73&amp;desc=vacation_
new_zealand</loc>
      <lastmod>2004-12-23</lastmod>
      <changefreq>weekly</changefreq>
   </url>
   <url>
<loc>http://www.example.com/catalog?item=74&amp;desc=vacation_
newfoundland</loc>
      <lastmod>2004-12-23T18:00:15+00:00</lastmod>
      <priority>0.3</priority>
   </url>
   <url>
<loc>http://www.example.com/catalog?item=83&amp;desc=vacation_
usa</loc>
      <lastmod>2004-11-23</lastmod>
   </url>
</urlset>
```

The URLs that you can include in your XML site map are determined by the location of your site map. For example, if you place your site map on the page http://www.example.com/catalog/sitemap.xml, any URLs that begin with http://www.example.com/catalog can be included in the site map. However, if you have a URL http://www.example.com/images/, it won't be included in the site map because it doesn't fall into the catalog category. You can solve this problem by creating another site map or by using only the base URL for your site (http://www.example.com/).

Once you've created your site map (or had one generated by a site-map generator), you need to insert it into your robots.txt file. The site-map directive is independent of the user-agent directive, so it's not important where in the robots.txt file you place it. All that's important is that you use the site-map directive, `<sitemap_location>`, replacing "location" with the URL where your site is located. For example, a site-map directive might look like this:

```
Sitemap: <sitemap_http://www.example.com/sitemap.xml>
```

You can have more than one site map for your site, but if you do, you need to create a site-map index that crawlers will read to learn where your site maps are located. The site-map index looks similar to the site map but includes a few different directives. Those directives include the following:

- `<sitemap>`: This tag encapsulates information about the individual site map.
- `<sitemapindex>`: This tag encapsulates information about all the site maps in a file.

In addition to these tags, you'll also see the `<loc>` and `<lastmod>` tags in the site-map index. Following is an example of what that index file should look like:

```
<?xml version="1.0" encoding="UTF-8"?>
    <sitemapindex
xmlns="http://www.sitemaps.org/schemas/sitemap/0.9">
    <sitemap>
        <loc>http://www.example.com/sitemap1.xml.gz</loc>
        <lastmod>2004-10-01T18:23:17+00:00</lastmod>
    </sitemap>
    <sitemap>
        <loc>http://www.example.com/sitemap2.xml.gz</loc>
        <lastmod>2005-01-01</lastmod>
    </sitemap>
    </sitemapindex>
```

The index file contains a list of locations for your XML site maps. It's not uncommon to have multiple site maps, and in some cases it's advisable to have multiples. For example, if your site is divided into several different categories, you may want to have a separate site map for each category. This enables you to separate and differentiate the links within a category, giving a different weight to each according to its function on your site.

You should be aware of one limitation to site maps: They are limited to no more than 50,000 URLs and 10MB per map — and if you're using multiple maps listed in a site-map index, there can be no more than 1,000 site maps. This is a pretty large allowance, so you may not ever have to worry about the limits, but you should still know what they are.

Submitting your site map

After you've created your site map, you have two alternatives. You can leave the directive for the site map in your `robots.txt` file and wait until a crawler comes along and finds it, or you can go ahead and submit it to the search engines that you're targeting.

How you submit your site map to search engines may vary widely. For example, if you want to submit your site map to Google, you need to create a Google account and link it to the Webmaster Tools section of Google. Once you've created an account, you can submit your site map from that interface. With Yahoo!, you'll have to go through a similar process. With other search engines, the process will also be similar, though some of the details differ.

Submitting your site map to one of the search engines won't guarantee that all the pages on your site will be crawled, or that they will be included in SERPs. However, the site map gives the crawler some direction, so it will help improve the crawling that your site receives. This is no guarantee of where your site will rank, but at least you'll know that it has been reviewed as thoroughly as it can be, given the control that the crawler has in the situation.

Chapter 19

The Truth About SEO Spam

S pam is the Internet's version of the telemarketers who call you during dinner and won't take no for an answer. It pops up where it's least wanted, it's more prolific than pine trees in Mississippi, and the only purpose it really serves is to generate money for the spammers, who keep at it because they assume that the law of averages is on their side — send out enough spam and someone will respond.

IN THIS CHAPTER

What constitutes SEO spam?

Why SEO spam is a bad idea

Avoiding SEO spam

Spam in SEO operates under the same principle, except SEO spam fills the search engine results pages with results that have little or no value to the searcher. If you do something that a search engine sees as spamming it, your search rankings will be penalized. It's even likely that you'll be removed from search rankings entirely.

Some SEO is a clear-cut case of spam, which is usually classified as *black-hat SEO*, but there are also cases of spam that aren't necessarily as obvious. These fall into a gray area in which the practices used may or may not be considered spam, depending on how you handle them.

To make spam even more difficult to define, search engines change their definitions of spam regularly. What works and is acceptable today may well be classified as spam tomorrow, so if you don't know that a change has been made or is coming, you may look at your rankings one day and find that you're above the fold on the first page, but look at the same rankings the next day to find you've been relegated to page 10 of the results.

Only the search engines know what constitutes spam from one day to the next, which makes it very difficult for you to stay off the spammers' lists if you're doing any SEO activities that are borderline spam. Sure, you can monitor the search engine algorithms (see the following note) and try to keep up with the changes that are made, but that's no guarantee that you won't get caught up in the changes. It's also a reactive way to manage your SEO campaign.

> **NOTE** The easiest way to monitor search engine algorithms is to keep up with what's happening in SEO. Some of the best places online to learn about what's changing are ISEdb—Internet Search Engine Database (www.isedb.com), High Rankings Advisor (www.highrankings.com), and SEONews.com. Of course, if you're specifically interested in what's happening at Google, the official Google Webmaster Central blog (http://googlewebmastercentral.blogspot.com/) is the best way to keep up.

What Constitutes SEO Spam?

If SEO spam is so hard to define, then how do you know whether what you're doing is right or wrong? Good question. Unfortunately, the answer is that you don't always know, but there are some guidelines that you can follow that will help you stay out of the spam category. Basic, good web-design practices are your best defense. If you're handling your web site search marketing using the guidelines provided by the various search engines you'll target, you should be in a position not to worry about being classified as a spammer:

- **Don't do anything that makes you worry that you're doing something wrong:** If you're doing something on your web site that you have to worry is going to get you banned from a search engine, you probably shouldn't be doing it. This includes strategies such as using hidden text on your web pages, using doorway pages or cloaking your pages, and creating false link structures. Even if you don't know that these strategies are banned by search engines, when you consider the sneakiness of the strategy, you'll be able to tell that it's probably one that you shouldn't be using.

- **Don't make your web site appear to be something that it's not:** It's easy to put a spin on something to make it appear more attractive than it really is. People do it all the time where products and services are concerned, but using that same strategy on your web site may get you delisted. Creating false link structures is one way you might make your site appear more popular than it really is. The problem with using that strategy is that it won't take a crawler long to figure out that all those sites are interconnected.

- **Don't trust someone who says that a certain practice is acceptable if you even suspect that it's not:** Some unethical SEO people will tell you that it's okay for you to use certain obvious spam techniques as long as you use them correctly. Wrong. Spam is spam. It doesn't matter how you use it; the search crawler will still see it as spam and you'll still suffer the consequences, while the unethical SEO consultant will take the money and leave you in the crawler's bad graces.

SEO spam is also called *spamdexing* (because you're spamming indexes), and it appears in all shapes and sizes. Some techniques are obviously spam. Some aren't clearly spam, but you should avoid them anyway. The list of spamming techniques is huge, but a dozen or so items on that list are always present:

- **Transparent links:** These are links that are included in the page, but that users can't see because they're the same color as the background.

- **Hidden links:** These links are on the page but are hidden behind elements such as graphics. They don't turn the graphic into a hyperlink, but a search engine can find them and follow them, even when visitors can't.

- **Misleading links:** Misleading links are those that appear to lead to one place but actually lead to another. If you click on www.onewebsite.com but are actually taken to www.differentwebsite.com, then you've been misled.

- **Inconspicuous links:** These links appear on a page but they're usually unnoticeable because they're represented as graphics that are 1×1 pixels in size.

- **Keyword stuffing:** This is loading the content or the meta tags of a web site with keywords that are repeated over and over.

- **Meta tag stuffing:** This is stuffing meta tags with keywords that are repeated over and over.

- **Doorway pages (or gateway pages):** These pages are designed specifically to draw search crawlers but are essentially useless to visitors. Often, a doorway page will have only the visible text *click here to enter.*

- **Scraper sites:** These are web sites that *scrape,* or copy, their content from other pages on the Web. Search engines don't like scraper sites because they're not original and because they usually direct visitors to another site that's less relevant to their search terms. Scraper sites are also often used by phishers and other Internet criminals as a way to steal people's credit card information, bank account information, or even their identities.

- **Machine-generated pages:** These are web pages put together by a program that grabs the content from other web sites. The content that's grabbed could be from within the current site or from sites belonging to other people. Usually these pages are considered spam because they are of no value to web site users.

- **Links in punctuation:** This is a clever scheme. Some unethical SEOs create a hyperlink that's contained in a piece of punctuation. It's done by using the following tag:

```
<a href=link> </a>Include real words here</a>
<a href=link>.</a>
```

That little snippet of code will leave the words in the link (and you can replace link with the web site address of your choice) in plain text, but the period at the end of the link will contain the link. Because it's so small, most people won't notice it, but the link is there, so search engines will find it.

- **Cloaking:** This technique is used to make a highly optimized version of your page appear to search engines, but a more user-friendly page appear to site visitors.

- **Excessive cross-linking:** Excessive cross-linking can be a sign that a company has created multiple domains strictly for the purpose of building a false linking structure with a single web site.

- **Hidden text:** This text is the same color as the background of a web page so that users can't see it. Search engines can, however, and the text is usually an incomprehensible collection of keywords and phrases.

- **Duplicate content:** Duplicate content on a web site is construed as being a ploy to trick a search crawler into thinking the site is more relevant than it actually is.

- **Link-only pages:** These pages contain only links and should be avoided. The one exception to this rule is the site map that you make available to visitors so they can quickly find their way around your site.

- **Redirect pages:** Redirect pages are usually coded for SEO, but they're useless to site visitors. When site visitors land on this page, they're asked to wait while they are redirected to another web site. Search engines look down on this practice because very often the web page that is redirecting is optimized for SEO but not for people.

Use Caution with Link-Trading Strategies

If content is the most important element of a web site, links are probably the next. Most search engines now look at links to a web site — both those that lead to the site and those that lead away from the site.

In an effort to take advantage of the authority that links give a web site, many web site owners have banded together to create link-trading, or reciprocal linking, strategies — *you link to me and I'll link to you.*

For a long time, those strategies worked pretty well. You could send out an e-mail to a company and suggest that two sites create links, each to the other's site. Obviously, by doing that each site gained a link into and out of its site.

Then some people began taking advantage of the strategy, and rather than exchange links with other relevant web sites, some web site owners began to exchange links with anyone who would allow it. Then those same unethical people began building dozens, hundreds, and in some cases even thousands of web sites with the specific intent of cross-linking with the one page whose ranking they were trying to artificially raise.

That's when search engines began to take note that people were manipulating link-trading schemes to boost their search ranking, and some search engines have now added reciprocal linking and link-trading strategies to their list of unacceptable practices. Therefore, be aware that if you use these strategies, you could be dropped from the search results.

continued

continued

Does that mean you can never link to a page that's going to link back to you? No. It means that search engines are now paying more attention to the *places* to which you link. They're looking at the sites to which you're linking to ensure that they're relevant and have something of value to offer to users who might click through the links.

If your links do meet those requirements, you won't be penalized for them; but if they appear to be links just for the sake of linking, your site will be penalized and in some cases even delisted from a search engine. If you plan to exchange links with other web sites, make sure those sites are relevant to the topic of your web site or the web page on which the link appears.

- **Link farms:** Link farms are simply pages of links that are created just to artificially boost a linking strategy in an effort to speed the appearance of the web site in the top search ranking positions.

- **Spamblogs:** These are machine-generated blogs and their only purpose is to draw search engine rankings.

- **Page hijacking:** Page hijacking is accomplished by copying a very popular page on the Web and using it to represent your site to search engines. When users see your page in search results, they click through the link only to be taken to your actual page.

- **Sybil attacks:** Sybil attacks are created when a spammer creates multiple web sites that are all interlinked for the purpose of creating a false link structure. (These are termed Sybil attacks in reference to a famous case of multiple personalities in which a woman named Sybil was thought to have as many as 17 different personalities. The case later became the basis for a popular film. Sybil attacks are like multiple personalities for a web site.)

- **Wiki spam:** This involves using the open editability of wiki sites to add links to a spam site in the wiki listing. Because this practice became so frequently used at one point, especially on Wikipedia, the `nofollow` tag has been added to most wiki additions to prevent spamming search engines.

The list is long, and many other items could be included. Moreover, as soon as the search engine algorithms change a little, even more will be added to the list.

Why SEO Spam Is a Bad Idea

Using any of the SEO techniques that are considered spam can result in your site being penalized or even completely banned. That's reason enough not to use them, but there are other reasons to avoid SEO spam.

People — site visitors, your customers — don't like spam. They don't like spam in their e-mail boxes, and they don't want to be directed to web pages that are spam. Therefore, even though SEO spam may offer one short-term benefit — your site will temporarily rank high in search engine results — the pitfall outweighs that benefit, because when visitors click onto your site, they'll leave almost immediately.

Spam on the Internet just doesn't make sense. When it's so easy for a person to move from one web site to another, or one company to another, why would you want to run them off as fast as they land on your site? A much more logical approach is to build your web site with the intent of both drawing *and keeping* the user on your site. That means providing useful information in a user-friendly format.

When visitors come to your site and realize that you've tricked them to get them there, they're going to be annoyed. They'll click right back off your page, and they're more likely to remember your web site negatively. If you're trying to build a business, making a bad first impression isn't the way to do it.

Another reason to avoid SEO spam is that it can give you a black eye professionally. Although SEO spam can temporarily raise your site's visibility in search results, just as site visitors will see what you've done, so will your competition — and they'll be secure in the knowledge that your rise to the top will be short-lived. It won't be long before your site is delisted from the search results and your competitors will be back in the positions from which you bumped them. What's the point? The only company that suffers is your own.

Clearly, if you've considered using SEO spam techniques, you should think again. If you've talked to SEO consultants who tell you SEO spam techniques are okay, or that you won't get caught because search engines don't pay attention to this or that detail, ignore them. SEO spam can be costly — both in terms of the money that you lose implementing SEO only to be delisted from the search results and in terms of the sales and loyalty that you'll lose from irritated visitors and customers.

Avoiding SEO Spam

So spamming a search engine isn't the best idea in the world. When you are caught spamming one, the penalties differ according to the search engine, but most will delist you from search results. Being delisted isn't the worst thing in the world that could happen to your site. In most cases, you can get your site reincluded.

It may require explaining to the search engine the tactic you employed, why you employed it, and how you corrected it, followed by resubmission to the index. Then it could take a couple of months (or longer) to be reincluded. Then you have to work your way back to the top of the results. The whole process could take six months to a year or longer.

Time is a valuable commodity when you're talking about the Internet and the possibilities that it brings to your revenues. Time lost on the Internet is easily just as expensive as having a bricks-and-mortar store that you failed to open on one of the busiest days of the week.

What's at stake makes it especially worrisome that you could possibly spam a search engine and not know it. It wouldn't be intentional, but the results would be the same, so how do you avoid this? How do you rank well without falling into the black hole that leads to search engine spam?

That's actually an easy question to answer. There's only one way to avoid being labeled as a spammer, whether accidentally or intentionally: *Build your web site for your audience and not for a search engine.* Really, it's that simple.

Here's why: The purpose of a search engine is to find, index, and serve content to people who use the search engine to find something. The search engine's target audience is those people. In an effort to do the best job possible for those people, the search engine is going to look at every page it indexes in the scope of what's best for the searcher.

Therefore, if you approach creating your web site in the same manner that a search engine approaches serving content to its users, your goals will automatically align. It's that natural alignment that will keep you out of trouble with search engines.

Smart site design

You should already know how to design your web site with the user in mind, but the following guidelines will help ensure that search engines can see that your site is exactly what searchers are looking for:

- **Provide users with unique, relevant content:** The most important element of your site is probably the content that you put on it. Provide the information that users need to help them understand, compare, or make decisions. If you make it useful, then users (and crawlers) will love you.

- **Use links appropriately:** You want a good balance of links into and out of your site. You can't necessarily control all the links that come into your site, but you can influence them by participating in your industry. In addition, when you build links that lead away from your page, make sure they take users to other sites that are also relevant and useful.

- **Keep your site user-friendly:** Think in terms of the design elements that users like and don't like. If you don't know what those are, do some research, because plenty of studies have been done. Among design elements that aren't likely to gain you any love from your users are Flash pages, frames, and difficult or changing navigational structures. Crawlers don't like these any more than users do. When you're designing your site, consider using a focus group to help you design the site in a way that users will be comfortable with. If users are comfortable with it, crawlers probably will be, too.

- **Don't obsess over where your page ranks in search results:** Yes, you want to have your web site featured as high as possible in search engine rankings, but not at the expense of everything else you should do to get your site in front of the right customers. Obsessing over your rank leads to investing too much time and money into making a search engine happy. It's a much better practice to obsess over giving your users what they need and building loyalty.

Spam of any kind is bad, and no one wants to be labeled a spammer. Being labeled as SEO spam is probably one of the most detrimental blows that your web site can suffer, so instead of focusing on how you can make search engines like your site, focus on how you can make users like your site, and search engines will naturally follow the users.

Chapter 20

Adding Social-Media Optimization

A sk any child over the age of 10 what MySpace is and you'll likely get a pretty good description. During the conversation, you'll also probably hear about other sites such as Flickr, Facebook, Shout-Life, YouTube, Twitter, and Jaiku. These are all examples of the different *social networks* that have become an Internet phenomenon over the past few years.

Social networks are groups of people who are linked by some type of connection. MySpace is a social network where friends — people who know each other — connect. New friends come into the mix. Friends' friends come into the mix, and eventually you have a network of people (as shown in Figure 20-1) who may not know each other in the real world but are connected via the Internet.

What is phenomenal about this social network is how quickly people have adopted it. Using the connections made available by social networking, the category of *social media* has grown nearly as quickly.

Social media refers to the content generated by social networking. The publishing mode for social media is many-to-many publishing. What this means is that a group of people publish a work or works that are distributed to another group, or several groups, of people.

Literally defined, social media are the technologies and practices that people use to share content, opinions, insights, experiences, perspectives, and multimedia. These technologies and practices can be translated into all different kinds of social networking. Table 20-1 provides a short list of some of the types of social media and social networking available.

IN THIS CHAPTER

What is social-media optimization?

The value of social media

Social-media strategies

Measuring social-media optimization

317

FIGURE 20-1

A social network is a group of people connected by a common interest.

 Individual

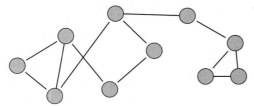

TABLE 20-1

Types of Social Media and Networks

Type of Social Media/Network	Description	Examples
Wikis	These are collaborative web sites. The concept behind wikis is that anyone who has access to the site is able to add to or change any page on the site.	Wikipedia
Social networks	A group of people tied together by some common interest, be it online gaming, antiques, gourmet cooking, or any other subject imaginable.	MySpace, Facebook, Villij
Presence	Presence applications are like miniature blogs. These sites enable users to communicate back and forth using their services. Conversations range from mundane to important on these web sites.	Twitter, Jaiku, Pownce
Video sharing	Have a great vacation video you want to share? YouTube takes "America's Funniest Home Videos" to a whole new level. If you have a digital video camera and some time, you can create and share any kind of video.	YouTube
Virtual reality	This interesting social-networking category is like living in a fantasy world. You create everything about your life: your looks, your personality, and all of your surroundings. But don't think this is just a game. Living a virtual life can be more than just fun; it can also provide a viable income for some people.	Second Life

continued

TABLE 20-1 *(continued)*

Type of Social Media/Network	Description	Examples
Events	Events networks connect people according to the events that they are attending or want to attend. If you want to know who's going to be at that TobyMac concert Thursday night, check out one of the social-events networks.	Upcoming
News aggregation	These social networks are connected by current and past news. If you find a news story that you think is good enough to be shared with people whose interests are similar to yours, you can add it to your network for them to view.	Digg, Reddit
Photo sharing	Everyone wants to share their photos. Photo-sharing networks enable you to share your pictures with anyone that you want. Most of these services also allow online photo storage.	Flickr, PhotoBucket, Zooomr
Livecasting	Livecasting is literally live webcasting. A community is built around the webcasts, including everything from blogs to chat rooms.	Justin.tv
Episodic online	These social-networking sites are built around online videos, but the difference here is that each person tells a specific story in a series of episodes. The social network is built around your favorite episodes.	YourTruman-Show
Media sharing	If you want to create a network of people with whom you can share all kinds of media files, these are the services to use. Connect to as many or as few friends as you like when sending e-mails, videos, audio files, and more.	ShareNow, Share
Music sharing	Not music file-sharing, but creating community around music. Most of these sites allow for integration with iTunes or other media players to keep track of the music you listen to, and make recommendations based on your tastes and the tastes of your network.	last.fm, pocketfuzz

continued

TABLE 20-1	*(continued)*	
Type of Social Media/Network	**Description**	**Examples**
Social bookmarking	Social bookmarking is one of the most widely used social-media techniques. These services allow you to tag news stories, blogs, videos, audio files, web sites, and other Internet-based services to share with friends. Tagged sites are then ranked (and searchable) according to the number of tags received.	del.icio.us, ma.gnolia.com
Social network aggregators	Social networks have become so pervasive that, much like meta search aggregator engines, social network aggregators have begun to arise. The concept is to log in to one place and see all your updates from various social networks, photo sharing, and presence applications.	socialthing!, profilactic

Social media, then, are services that enable you to publish or distribute content to a core group of people who are connected according to some central interest. If you've ever heard the term *Web 2.0*, then you've heard someone talking about technologies such as social media.

The concept of Web 2.0 is that the next generation of Web-based services will be structured differently from those in the past. It's not about new technologies, however. Instead, Web 2.0 is about the way that people will interact with the Web.

In the past, it was pretty straightforward. You went to a web site, saw what there was to see, and then if you liked it you talked to your friends or sent them an e-mail that included a link. Web 2.0 is about streamlining that process and taking advantage of the connections that the Internet enables. Specifically, Web 2.0 is about using the Web as an application. This means that many social-media sites are considered Web 2.0 sites, but not all Web 2.0 sites are social networks.

Now, when you find something you like online, sure, you can send your friends an e-mail, but you can also distribute it using one of the social-networking services. This enables you to stay connected with your friends, it streamlines the connection to those friends, it adds new friends to the network, and it makes it possible for you to receive items of interest from them as well.

In short, social networking and social media are all about one thing: communicating with your friends about common interests. People want to organize and classify the Web according to their personal preferences. These technologies enable them to do just that, rather than depend on someone else's classification, and possibly someone who doesn't see the world the way they do.

What Is Social-Media Optimization?

When you understand what social media are, it's not a long leap from there to *social-media optimization*, which is using social media to spread the news about your web site. Instead of tweaking the elements of your web site, when you practice social-media optimization you are participating in social networks and tweaking the content that you share within those networks.

It's through that participation and optimization that your site is distributed, and that's what brings traffic to it. There are also a couple of added benefits to social-media optimization. First, it's free in terms of monetary investment. There is no cost to participate in these networks except your time. However, make no mistake about it, you will have to invest a chunk of front-end time into this type of optimization. You must become familiar with the communities and participate long enough to establish a name for yourself before anyone will take serious notice of you.

The other benefit of social-media optimization is that it's really a *viral marketing* strategy. Nearly everyone is familiar with a virus. It's that nasty little bug that multiplies exponentially and makes you believe death would be an improvement. Viral marketing is neat, not nasty, but it works in a somewhat similar way.

When you can tap viral marketing for your online presence, word of your brand spreads like a virus — it spreads exponentially (faster and faster) as the *buzz* increases, and there doesn't seem to be any way to stop it, which in this case is good. If your marketing message has become viral, then you can expect to see a serious increase in the number of visitors to your site — and, by extension, the number of goal conversions that are reached.

Viral marketing is a *good* thing; and when you've optimized your social-media participating, you can almost guarantee that your marketing will soon have that viral quality you're seeking.

What's different about social-media optimization?

In short, everything. Social-media optimization is not at all like web site optimization, though it should be part of your overall optimization strategy. Instead of adding keywords in the right places, tweaking your meta tags, and digging up the right balance of links, you're doing something different — creating relationships, generating content, and tagging the Web. Don't sell it short. The value of social media has already been proven by many organizations on the Web.

One thing to keep in mind as you're considering social-media optimization is that it's not as simple as throwing a few crumbs at a social network and waiting for people to come along and share those crumbs with their friends. They won't.

If you approach social media in that manner, you'll end up wasting your time, and by the time you wise up, the people who populate the social-networking communities you tried it on won't be as easy to win over. People don't forget when a faker tries to jump in their midst for purely marketing purposes. It's the fastest way to send you right to the bottom of the social-media pond.

Social-media optimization is about first joining communities and creating relationships. It's only by going through the process of becoming part of the community that your brand will begin to be recognized by other community members, and that's when your efforts will begin to pay off.

When you're optimizing for social media, you don't focus on adding keywords to your content or tweaking your meta tags. Instead, you focus on providing something that the members of your chosen social network need. It may be an article, it may be tagging news stories that are especially relevant to your industry, or it may be adding your expertise to a forum. However you participate in the community, it is that participation that will be your best optimization tool.

The Value of Social Media

It's obvious that social-media optimization has value. Sites such as MySpace, YouTube, and Facebook are all sites that no one thought would amount to anything, but they did. As social animals, people love being part of a community, and that includes an online community. The generation that has just entered the workforce and those growing up right now are Internet pros, and their parents are pretty proficient with it, too.

All of these people are involved in all kinds of activities online, from shopping and downloading music to participating in social networks. The kids are networking socially for different reasons than the parents, but both are participating.

The question then is not whether social media has value, but how much value it has. If you look at an experiment done by *Marketing Experiments Journal* (www.marketingexperiments.com), you can quickly appreciate that social media might be more valuable than you thought.

The experiment compared the cost and effectiveness of social-media marketing against pay-per-click advertising over the span of one year. The results? Social-media marketing cost a company $3,600 — the salary ($10 an hour) for an employee to become a part of and market to social networks. That investment drew 93,207 visitors to the site over the course of the year (which works out to be just under $.04 per visitor).

The PPC application was a little faster. Instead of having to wait weeks or months to get involved in a community, the PPC ads could be started almost immediately. The company spent $1,250 on PPC ads over the course of the year, and those ads drew 2,057 visitors to the site for a total cost of almost $.61 per visitor.

Social media had much more impact, and ultimately cost the company less money on a per-visit basis. In fact, the social-media optimization yielded a 1,578 percent better return on investment than the PPC ads did!

The value of social media is undeniable, but so are the difficulties that you may face as you try to implement a social-media-optimization effort. For example, you can't rush headlong into a new social network and expect to be able to post your ads anywhere you want. That will get you banned from the community fairly quickly. It will also create animosity between you and the very people you're trying to reach.

Again, you have to participate in the communities; and you can't fake your participation. Social networkers will recognize your efforts as being disingenuous and will treat you accordingly. The only way to be effective with social-media optimization is to become a *real* part of the social network. If you can accomplish that, then the rewards will be better than any marketing plan you've used to date.

Social-Media Strategies

We've established that using social media as a marketing technique requires a different approach than some of the more traditional marketing that you've probably done to this point. It's also very different from the tasks that you'll complete as part of your SEO efforts.

Social-media optimization is a term coined by Rohit Bhargava. When he came up with it, he also outlined five strategies to help others accomplish optimization of their social-media efforts. Over the next few months, several other industry experts added to the list, which now contains 16 guidelines that will help you optimize your social-media efforts:

- **Increase your linkability:** The linkability of your site is determined by the amount of content that you have available to users who might come from social networks. Old, stale, and rarely changing content will not help with your social-media optimization, so begin by updating your content and your content strategy to ensure that it is interesting for visitors who might come from your social network.

- **Make tagging and bookmarking easy:** Don't make users try to figure out how to add your blog or site to their content feed. Instead, make it easy with a function that generates the necessary URL or code for visitors to add you to their important links. There are tools available to help with this, including the RSS Button Maker at www.toprankblog.com/tools/rss-buttons/.

- **Reward inbound links:** People who link to you want something in return. If you can provide a link to them in your blog, *blogroll*, or some other area of your web site, people and companies will be much more likely to link to you. Just remember to keep the links into and out of your site directly related to the topic of the site.

- **Help your content travel:** Traveling content means having content that can be accessed from another site easily. If you have content that many people will be interested in saving, consider making that content available in PDF format or as an audio or video file. That way, when users want to spread your content, it will be easy for them to do so.

- **Encourage the *mashup*:** A mashup is a web application that combines data from more than one source into an integrated experience for your site users. For example, if you make it possible for others to embed your content in their blog or web site in exchange for a link back to you, your popularity will climb faster than if you don't enable them to move your content from one place to another.

■ **Be a user resource, even if it doesn't help you:** Today's Internet users, and especially those users who participate in social media and social networking, expect you to provide information that is useful to them. If you're not providing that information, they'll go to someone who is. Be a *good resource ambassador* — try to help people without expecting anything in return. You will be rewarded anyway, because your actions prove your site's worth.

■ **Reward helpful and valuable users:** Helpful and valuable users will be your greatest asset as you're creating your social-media optimization. Find a way to reward those users so they will continue to be helpful.

■ **Participate:** If you don't participate, your thoughts and opinions will not be welcome in a social-media network for long. In order to leverage the power of social media, you have to be willing to participate.

■ **Know how to target your audience:** Audiences can be tough. If you approach the wrong audience with the wrong message, you'll be slaughtered in the court of opinion. Before you make that kind of mistake, take the time to learn with whom you will be participating in the community.

■ **Create content:** Content is key to social-media marketing. If you make it a point to create fresh, unique content regularly, visitors will come to you because they know they can find the current information they need.

■ **Be real:** Social networkers can spot a fake nearly as quickly as they could spot a three-dollar bill. Don't try to con your audiences. Eventually, they'll catch on and annihilate you. Be who you are. That will get you much further than being what you think others want you to be.

■ **Don't forget your roots, be humble:** When you participate regularly in social media, you may find yourself in the position of being considered an expert. Many people let this distinction go straight to their head. Remember that someone else was on top yesterday and will be tomorrow, so treat the people around you as you would like to be treated when you're not the talking head of the moment.

■ **Don't be afraid to try new things, stay fresh:** One of the greatest benefits of social media is the ability to use your creativity to do something different. In social-media optimization, creativity is often rewarded with better traffic and higher interest.

■ **Develop a social-media optimization strategy:** As in any SEO effort, you don't want to be wandering in circles as you try to optimize your social-media presence. Develop a strategy that keeps you on track and helps you target the social networks that are most closely related to your topic.

■ **Choose your social-media optimization tactics wisely:** As great a marketing tool as social media can be, it can also be the most detrimental practice you institute. If you use the wrong tactics in a social-media forum, you can expect to find your efforts worthless. You can also expect that it will be very hard to rebuild the trust that you destroy.

■ **Make social-media optimization part of your processes and best practices:** Social-media networks require constant participation. That means ongoing efforts — daily. Integrate your social-media optimization strategies into your daily SEO workflow.

Bhargava and the other social-media experts who put this list together are people in the front line of SEO and SMO (social-media optimization) every day. These guidelines will help you begin your optimization process. If you follow them, then you'll be well on your way to gaining all the value available from social networks and social media.

In addition to the preceding guidelines, the following suggestions should also be helpful as you create your social-media strategy. Some are technical in nature, and others are simply a matter of etiquette:

■ Spend some time listening to your audience before you join the conversation. This time enables you to gain an understanding of the language, the tone, and the expectations of the conversation participants.

■ As you begin to participate in social networks, monitor what effect your participation is having. Note carefully how you're received, and track your site metrics at the same time. Sudden jumps or dips in your metrics can point to participation that is effective or ineffective.

■ Use what you learn to craft your social-media optimization strategy. You have to have one. Use the information that you gather as you're watching and listening on a social network to ensure that your strategy is targeted properly.

■ Deliver content that adds to the conversation. If your content doesn't add anything, the other participants will either ignore you or roast you faster than you can burn a marshmallow at a bonfire.

■ Use RSS feeds to enable your content. RSS feeds instantly update anyone who is watching your content, and that's good for you. It means that your links will spread faster than anything else you could have done to share them.

■ Social media is all about relationships. Engage and encourage participation, build relationships, and think of it from the perspective of "What can I give?" instead of "What can I get?"

■ Choose a theme related to your core content that is actively being discussed online and stay within that theme. Include articles, webcasts, videos, or whatever else works well with your theme, and try to look at the theme from different angles. That's the key to opening discussion, dialogue, back links, and all the things that go into making someone want to pass on what you've got to offer. If you offer something no one is talking about, you won't have any results.

- Approach social-media optimization as an individual. You can't approach others in a social network as a company. A business will automatically garner suspicion ("I know you're here only because you want to sell me something").

- Develop content that will appeal to the networks in which you participate, both from an audience perspective and from an information perspective. If you are trying to market to a 30-something soccer mom, having a 55-year-old male CEO try to get her attention isn't going to work. Why not hire a 30-something soccer mom with a similar perspective?

- Consider hiring bloggers or other social-media participants. If it makes sense to use social-media marketing for your organization, you may have to devote a large chunk of time to it each week. If you don't have the time to commit to that, consider hiring someone to do it for you. At ComputerWorld (www.computerworld.com), a full staff of freelance bloggers helps to keep news current and relatable to the industries in which it appears. If they can do it, you can, too. Hiring a blogger isn't usually as expensive as you might think. Typically, you can expect to pay anywhere from $10 to $50 per post, depending on the industry.

Measuring Social-Media Optimization

If you're participating in social media, you're going to want to know how it's working. But before you even begin to measure your success, you need to know what you're measuring it against. Define concrete goals for your efforts. Those might be to increase your web site traffic by a certain amount each month, to increase conversion values, or to reach some other goal. Whatever the goals, use them as a guide as you're planning your social-media optimization efforts.

Once you've decided what you want from social-media optimization, you can measure the results that you're gaining from your efforts. The most obvious indicator is web-site traffic. If your traffic begins to climb, it's a pretty good bet that your social-media efforts are working.

If you don't want to rely solely on site traffic as an indication of your success, there are several other elements you can look at to determine the effectiveness of your social-media optimization efforts.

You should first have a blog, and then track who is reading it. There are many good web analytics packages that will track the most popular content on your site. You can probably also see where those site visitors are coming from and how much time they're spending on your page. This information will help you determine what blog entries are most successful and who is sending the most traffic to your blog, so that you can capitalize on that information.

Next, you can monitor the number of visitors who are actually interacting with your content by checking your guest book, forums, or comment capabilities. Guest books aren't nearly as popular as they once were, but if you're participating in a social network and you don't have forums or comment capabilities on your blog, you're missing a large part of the value of social media.

Also pay attention to how often you're added to social-bookmarking sites. Sites such as del.icio.us and StumbledUpon are a couple of the social-bookmarking sites that can help boost your site traffic. The easiest way to monitor your site in social-bookmarking networks is to create an account with them and then use the account to search for your URLs. In other words, who is actually adding your site/article/blog posts to sites?

Measure how many readers are actually subscribing to your RSS feeds. The number of subscribers you have on your RSS feeds will be a good indicator of how well you're doing in your SMO efforts. The more subscribers you have, the more popular your site will be.

Another way to measure your success with social bookmarking is to watch who is linking to you. If you have a good analytics program, it will probably provide you with a report that shows where incoming links originated. If your analytics program doesn't provide this information, you can still figure out who's linking to you using that old standby: a web search. To find out who is linking to your site, use the following search string, replacing *yourwebsite* with the actual URL of the pages you want to track: `link:http://www.`*`yourwebsite`*`.com`.

One last way to gauge your success in the social-media space is to monitor how many people are connected to you. In MySpace and Facebook, that might mean how many friends you have. In LinkedIn, it would be how many colleagues you are connected to, and on Digg the measurement you're looking for is the number of times your content is tagged.

These are all indications that you're being followed by someone. And the more people with whom you can build a relationship, obviously the better your success will be. That's probably the most important rule of all to remember about social-media networking and social-media optimization: *Build the relationship first and the rest will fall into place.*

Chapter 21

Mobile Search Engine Optimization

I f the social media that we covered in the last chapter are important to search engine optimization, then mobile SEO is essential. The mobile Internet is a phenomenon that seems to have caught "experts" off guard. No one thought that people would be interested in surfing the Web on their phone. The screen is too small, and the Internet loads slowly in comparison to broadband. Generally speaking, it's not the same experience that Internet users are accustomed to.

The experts were wrong. On Christmas morning in 2007, hundreds of thousands of people unwrapped new iPhones, set them up, and immediately got online. In fact, Google's mobile search statistics for the iPhone platform that morning were higher than searches for all other mobile platforms combined.

What was this? People actually wanted to surf the Web on their phone? Well, maybe not as much on those tiny 1-by-1-inch screens, but when the form factor for devices changed, suddenly everyone wanted in. The iPhone and other cell phones like it now offer slightly larger screens and better controls that are more conducive to using the mobile Internet. There are roughly 200 different models of cell phones available in the U.S. market, about a third of which are well designed for mobile surfing

A new giant is born, although it's not quite giant-size just yet. As with all children, though, it's getting there quickly. Mobile Internet usage may be in its infancy, but it will soon be mature.

For you, this means being cognizant of the changes that are coming. It also means that now is the time for you to begin to understand how mobile Internet users behave, because that behavior is going to change the way you look at SEO.

The Mobile User Experience

Understanding the importance of mobility to your SEO platform begins with understanding the mobile user experience — and that experience begins with one simple truth: The mobile user experience is not monolithic. It differs in the capabilities of the mobile networks that are used to access the Internet, in the way that the devices are used, and in the way that visitors use the Web. To be successful with a mobile-enabled web site, you must keep these three differences in mind as you develop your mobile strategy.

Mobile networks

The one issue that held mobility back was the availability of mobile networks that were actually useful. Until recently, surfing the Internet on your mobile phone (all other things aside) was like surfing on a dial-up connection or worse. Currently, there are two available mobile data networks: 2G (also called the *Edge network*) and 3G.

The 2G network transfers data at about 360 Kbps or less. That's not terrible, but for web sites that are built for broadband and large displays, it does create a slower — sometimes maddening — experience. Still, even a 2G network is tolerable on a mobile platform when working with web sites that are designed for mobile surfing.

The 3G network can be considerably faster. In some areas, the data transfer rate can be as much as 7.2 Mbps, and most of the major wireless carriers now offer 3G network speeds, which reduces much of the irritation that users experienced in the past with mobile Internet access.

Increased network speeds also mean that you can offer your mobile users a richer mobile experience. However, keep in mind that mobile is still not the same as broadband, and the richness of the mobile Internet experience is derived from better features and functionality, not flashier graphics and bandwidth-eating applications.

Mobile devices

Clearly, one of the main factors affecting the mobile user experience is the device with which the user accesses the mobile Web. As mentioned earlier, there are more than 200 different devices available on the cell phone market. Not all of them are even Internet-enabled, but of those that are, many still have screens that are only 1 inch by 1 inch. A few offer screens that are a bit bigger, but not big enough to make the mobile user experience appreciably better.

What has changed the way people connect on the Internet using a mobile device are devices designed much like the iPhone. These devices are all screen, though some have a slide-out keyboard or a digital keyboard on the screen. That overcomes some of the difficulties that users had in the past with entering URLs and information into web forms.

Devices today are also set up to switch seamlessly between mobile network web surfing (meaning surfing the Web on the wireless carrier's network signal) and Wi-Fi network capabilities (meaning the user can connect to a wireless network, such as the one that's probably used in your home or office). This switching capability makes it possible for users to access faster download speeds, making the user experience less frustrating.

It also helps preserve the battery life of the device, lack of which is another complaint you'll often hear from users about surfing the Internet on a mobile device — it eats battery the way a fire consumes dry brush. A Wi-Fi network still consumes a great deal of battery life, but it uses slightly less battery power than what's required for the carrier's network.

In general, until more recent generations of wireless devices, none has been specifically designed for surfing the Internet. That's changing rapidly. The iPhone's release led to an avalanche of devices that are mostly screen, with increasingly improved methods of input. Now all that remains is building a mobile Web that intersects with visitors' needs — and that's the biggest difference between mobile Internet users and those who use a desktop or laptop computer.

How mobile users use the Web

You want to reach your web site visitors no matter where they happen to be, both physically and in the buying cycle; but there's not much you can do about the wireless networks that mobile users are using to connect to your site or about the devices that enable them to make that connection. What you can have an impact on, however, is how you meet mobile users as they surf the Web.

It's a tried-and-true sales tactic, really — meet the users where they are. It's the reason why there are still so many traveling salespeople flying from one place to another to seal a deal. Busy people don't have time to come to you — they want you to come to them, especially if they want something that you're offering. For you, that means understanding just where the user is, and then moving forward to occupy that space in time.

Perhaps the most important thing to understand about mobile users is *why* they use their mobile devices to access the Web. The two main reasons are to find information (where have you heard that before?) and to pass the time while waiting in line, on the subway, or at appointments. Each of those reasons drives very different behavior.

When users pick up their devices to find something on the Web, they want to locate whatever it is they're looking for — answers, information, or products — very quickly. Entering text, whether web site addresses or URLs, on a mobile device isn't easy. The average search string on a mobile search engine is 30 characters, but it takes about 40 characters and nearly a full minute for the average user (not a 14-year-old) to enter that search string.

Devices without full QWERTY keyboards usually require the user to press a key multiple times to reach the desired letter when spelling out words; and even devices that do have full keyboards are harder to use than their full-size counterparts. The keys are small and can be hard to press, especially for a person with large hands.

More important, users aren't willing to spend a lot of time looking for whatever it is they want. The best you can hope for is that a user will search through two pages of results to find the answer he or she seeks. In most cases, mobile search results have only 6 to 10 results per page, so if your web site doesn't show up in the first 12 to 20 results returned, you don't stand a chance of drawing mobile users to your site.

The other reason mobile users use their devices to access the Internet is to fill idle time. Time spent waiting in line, in movie theaters, between classes, in cab rides, on the subway, or while waiting at appointments can be used to accomplish something productive or be entertained. That means you must offer something either productive or entertaining to potential mobile web site users.

For example, e-mail and calendar applications are the most frequently used applications on a mobile device such as the iPhone or the Android G1 phone. Streaming music and video come in at a close second, and games and other productivity applications follow. Therefore, in order for your web site to be truly useful to mobile users, it must offer something that enriches them either through productivity or entertainment.

A good example of how that might work is a product web site that includes tutorials. Mobile users might come to your site initially through a laptop or desktop computer. Then, later, after they've ordered a product from you, the ride into work is a good time to learn more of the tips and tricks that make using whatever device they bought from you easier to use, so they access your web site on their mobile device.

If your mobile site is well designed, users can find written tutorials that provide the information they seek. You might even consider including a link to a YouTube video that shows users how to perform a specific task or accomplish a specific goal. The key, however, is that it has to be short and to the point. Mobile users don't want to waste time wading through advertisements and information that has no bearing at all on the problem they're trying to solve. Be direct and keep any marketing pitches you might want to share to a bare minimum.

One last thing you should understand about mobile users is that they tend to access their phone with only a short chunk of time available (a couple of minutes to about 10 minutes). If your mobile web site offers useful information, tools, or entertainment to help them fill that small amount of dead time, then they're more likely to come back to you in the future or to reach whatever goal conversion you've set up for your mobile web site.

Mobile Web Site Design

Understanding that most mobile devices just aren't designed to surf the Web, and that most mobile Internet users are result-oriented, goes a long way toward helping you design a mobile web site that visitors will want to use. The technology to build a mobile web site is not much different from the technology you use to build a regular web site. The major difference is that your mobile web site should be coded in XHTML and be compliant with the World Wide Web Consortium's design guidelines.

The major differences in web site design are in the way you design a page. Because the capabilities of the mobile Web are not the same as those of the Internet, you'll need to make some adjustments to how you design a web page.

NOTE In reading this, you might get the impression that there are two Internets — a regular one and a mobile one. Of course, there is technically only one Web, but different versions of the pages are presented to viewers depending on whether they are seeing them through a regular browser or through a mobile web browser. Mobile web pages — those that are truly created for the mobile Web — are written differently than web pages written for the regular Web. You can have a single web site that automatically renders differently for a mobile browser, but often the functionality is messy. Moreover, many web sites don't take mobile web browsers into consideration, which means that in some cases these won't display at all. Web sites that work well on mobile browsers usually maintain two versions of web site — one for the regular browser and one for the mobile browser. Technically, both of those pages exist on the same Web.

Before we get too far into the details of designing a mobile web page, there are a couple of things that you should know about mobile web site addresses. As you've already seen, mobile devices aren't the easiest devices on which to enter a URL or other text. The long URLs that you're accustomed to seeing on the Web aren't too appealing to mobile web users. Instead, you should keep your URL as short as possible.

It's also important to realize that a mobile web site is not just a copy of your regular web site. It will render differently on a mobile device, so the best thing you can do is to take a hint from some of the larger companies that have mobile alternatives to their own web site. That means using a mobile extension for the web site address (such as .mobi) or even just using some other designation that differentiates the mobile site from the regular site. Google uses the URL http://m.google.com/.

Once you've figured out the URL for your mobile web site, you should keep numerous other guidelines in mind:

- **Keep the navigation simple**: Users don't want to be overwhelmed by links and they don't want to be lost in web-site-loop hell. Offer the links users need in order to move a page or two deeper into the site at a time, and always remember to keep the *home* link easy to find. One last note on links: Try to make text links large enough for users with touch screens to touch them without hitting other links accidentally.

- **Use images sparingly**: If you must use an image, make the resolution on it only as high as necessary.

- **Don't use Flash, pop-ups, JavaScript, or frames**: No exceptions. Just don't do it. Mobile devices aren't equipped to display these technologies. Using them will result in mobile web pages that don't display well, or at all.

- **Keep the most important content at the top of the page**: The controls on most mobile devices make scrolling difficult, so users don't tend to scroll all the way to the bottom of the page. If you want users to see something, the closer it is to the top of the page, the more likely it is to be seen.

- **Use formatting tags like <h> and <b> to ensure that mobile web crawlers understand the page layout**: These tags are more important on mobile web pages than regular pages because they provide clues to crawlers about the content of the pages. (Mobile web pages tend to be more text based, meaning text tags have more weight with crawlers.)

■ **Use a `robots.txt` file to ensure that your site is crawled quickly and appropriately**: The guidelines for the `robots.txt` file for mobile web sites are the same as the guidelines for the `robots.txt` file that you use on your regular web site (discussed in Chapter 18).

One last note about designing mobile web sites with SEO in mind: Mobile web browsers are notoriously unforgiving when it comes to improper XHTML coding. Improper coding can cause your web site to display strangely or not at all, so be sure that your site is well coded.

If you're in doubt about how something will display on a mobile phone, you can always use a mobile preview application such as Skweezer (`www.skweezer.com`), Opera Mini (`www.operamini.com/demo`), or Google's mobile simulator (`www.google.com/gwt.n`). These simulation applications show how your web site will appear on a mobile device, as shown in Figure 21-1.

FIGURE 21-1

The Google-Geek.com web site displayed on the Internet and on the Skweezer mobile Internet simulator.

To use any of these three preview applications, all you have to do is go to the URL, type your web site address into the form provided, and then click Display. The web site address that you entered will be displayed on the page. This enables you to quickly see how your page will display in a mobile format. It is slightly off, because you're still using a full-sized browser to display the page, but you can quickly determine whether something is amiss: formatting, whether images will display, and how text and links will appear on the page.

Mobile SEO

Just as the form and factor of the mobile Web is different from those sites you'll find on the regular Web, so is SEO. The general principles that apply to SEO — most notably that you should design your site with users in mind — still apply, but some details are very different.

For example, the plan that you have for SEO on your mobile web site should be a little different than your SEO plan for your regular web site. In general, you should create goals for your mobile web site that are not more than three clicks away from the landing page on which mobile users come to your site. Users aren't as likely to click dozens of pages on a web browser running on a mobile device.

Another area where your SEO plan will likely differ is in the number of keywords that you plan to use on your web site. Your mobile web site should be well optimized for one to two keywords, not the dozens you'll probably use for regular web sites. Right now, there isn't as much competition on the mobile Web, reducing the need for dozens of different keywords, but those keywords also bloat the back end of your mobile web site and can affect the way it downloads and displays.

Link strategies for your regular web site will also be slightly different for your mobile web site. Make your link strategies very specific, with the intention of reaching whatever goal conversions you've set up for your mobile site. And all of that needs to be done within the context of keeping your link strategy simple, as you learned earlier in this chapter.

An element that you might not have considered adding to your mobile web site is the social element that you learned about in Chapter 20. It also applies here, especially on the mobile Web, whose main adopters are still younger users who tend to be social-media fanatics.

When possible, include bookmarking and tagging tools on your mobile web site; and include "Send this page" links to make it easy for web site visitors to e-mail the page link to themselves or others who might be interested. Another way to help your site visitors stay connected is to make any phone numbers included on your site clickable. Mobile device users appreciate the ability to click-to-call, and creating clickable phone numbers is easy. You use the same HTML code that you would use for a link, except that instead of using a URL, you add the phone number, as shown here:

```
<a href="tel:12345667891">123-456-7891</a>
```

The last element of SEO for your mobile web site is getting the site noticed. It starts with submitting to mobile and local directories. Mobile directories, such as Cantoni.mobi and Mobicious.com, are an obvious choice. Submitting your mobile web site to local directories, however, might not be so obvious, but it makes sense.

One of the ways people use their mobile devices is to find local information when they're on the move — movies, restaurants, directions, phone numbers, and so on. The best way to ensure that you show up in those local searches (and increase your web site visitors, as well as your local visitors) is to list your web site in local directories (such as CitySearch.com or Local.Yahoo.com).

In addition to adding your site to the directories that are appropriate, you should also be thinking about how you can build buzz for your web site. Fortunately, building buzz for a mobile web site is a little easier than building it for a regular site, because mobile capabilities are still newsworthy. For example, one large pharmaceutical company recently made national news with press releases about a mobile application that it released to help users learn flu facts in the area where they reside.

Press releases carry much more weight with consumers when you're advertising or creating buzz for mobile web sites because everyone's focus is currently on mobility. Mobile SEO *is* different from traditional SEO on many levels, but in some ways it's still the same old SEO monster that you've been wrestling for ages. In the end, however, it's the site visitor who matters. If your site, whether a traditional web site or a mobile one, is designed for the user, everything else will follow. It may take a while, but ultimately the visitor has the deciding vote on how well your web site performs.

The Rapid Evolution of Mobility

As I write this, Google and T-Mobile have just released the new HTC G1 mobile device based on the Android platform; and the iPhone is officially the most popular and most sought-after device on the market. Copycat devices seem to appear daily — with touch screens and mobile Internet and media capabilities that were only imagined in the past.

Each of these new releases is followed fairly closely by an announcement of yet another phone (coming soon) that does more, does it better, and is more affordable. Industry researchers have already discovered that lower-income users are buying these mobile Internet-enabled devices as replacements for laptops and desktops. Why invest in a computer when you can invest a little more in a phone that does it all?

It is this interest in mobility, mobile devices, and the mobile Internet that's going to drive rapid change in the industry. Over the next few years we'll see dramatic developments in devices, capabilities, and probably even the services that are available on mobile devices. Of course, that doesn't mean that it's too soon for you to become involved in the mobile Internet.

In fact, now is the perfect time to get involved, because longevity will count in a few years. Right now, having a mobile-enabled web site positions you in a place that's not overcrowded or hard to get noticed. The time you invest in your mobile-enabled web site will have benefits now and in the future.

Just understand as you're getting your mobile web site up and running that, as with SEO for the Internet, SEO for the mobile Web will change rapidly. More and more companies will adopt mobile technologies and some will exploit current SEO ratings to rocket their sites to the top. Search engines will catch on, and ranking factors will change.

If you get involved in the mobile Web, just be prepared to move quickly. Monitor and test on an ongoing basis, and always be prepared to change your strategy at a moment's notice. It will pay off in the long run, even though it's certain to be a lot of work.

Chapter 22

Monetizing Traffic as an SEO Strategy

You may have heard about web site monetization strategies in your travels through the SEO world. Basically, a web site monetization strategy is a method by which you can begin earning money through your web site, even if you're not offering any products or services of your own.

For example, have you ever been on a purely content site that runs ads on the right-hand side of the page or at the top or bottom of the page? If you have, those ads are probably part of that web site's monetization strategy. People visit the site for the content, find something interesting in the ads, and click through them. Depending on the ad and the company that provides it, web site owners are paid either per click or a percentage of the purchase that the site visitor makes based on the ad.

In other words, web site monetization is how you begin earning money from your site very quickly. It may not be a ton of money, but some revenue stream is better than nothing, right? But wait. What does earning money from (or monetizing) your web site have to do with SEO? Well, that's a somewhat complicated answer.

You would think that putting advertisements or affiliate applications or products on your site wouldn't have anything at all to do with SEO, but in fact it can help your SEO rankings perform better. These monetization strategies have you linked to other web sites, and when done well, these links are relevant to the content on your site. You already know what that means with search engines, right? Good links help you build good rankings.

Moreover, being a part of a monetization strategy sometimes means that your web site is a feature of the site to which you're linking. It doesn't always happen, but some affiliate programs have a "Vendor of the Month" or "Highlighted Partner" application that features one of their affiliates each month (or week, or day, depending on how it's set up). So, while you might not be generating a ton of traffic in the beginning, being featured on a well-established web site can help to steer more traffic to your site faster than straight SEO alone.

The boost in traffic, in turn, can be enough to be impressive to search crawlers, boosting your SEO rankings so that your site appears higher in search rankings. Getting the picture? Affiliate marketing and other types of placement advertising services can have some unexpected benefits. But beware. Not all monetization opportunities are created equal.

Understanding Ad Placement Services

Before we get too far into the different types of monetization programs that you can apply to your web site, allow me to address the most popular: ad placement services. You're probably already somewhat familiar with ad placement services, especially if you've ever used Google's AdSense or Yahoo!'s Publisher Network. Ad placement services are just that. They are services that place ads on web sites with available space. The companies that perform this service try to match ads as closely as possible to the web sites on which they'll be displayed. This ensures that you don't find ads for Barbie dolls on a martial arts web site. They're not foolproof, though. Sometimes ads that aren't quite related end up on the same site.

Usually, however, they won't be totally off; and in return for displaying the ad, the owner of the site on which the ads are displayed is paid each time a site visitor clicks the ad. The amount of that payment depends on a lot of different things:

- **How much the advertiser is paying per keyword click:** Usually these ads are based on keywords, and advertisers bid for placement based on the popularity of the keyword. The more they pay, the better placement the ad will get. That usually means a lot of money to land on very well-known sites; however, less-known sites (like your own, for now) will be much cheaper. The advertisers can advertise for less, but you're not going to make a ton of money, either.

- **Popularity of the keyword upon which the ad is based:** Think AdWords. It is programs like AdWords that advertisers use to find available ad space on the Web that matches the keywords they want to advertise with. Obviously, less popular (and more niche) keywords are less expensive, whereas more popular (and broader) keywords are more expensive. For you, this means that if your site is well optimized for niche keywords, advertisers can afford to place their ads on your site. Again, you might not get paid as much as if your site were well optimized for broad keywords, but the principle that some income is better than none applies also in this situation.

- **How much space you have in which to advertise:** Certain types of advertisements work better than others. For example, some text-only ads don't typically perform quite as well as graphical ads; but some graphical ads scream *advertisement,* while others blend well into your site and become just another element of the content that you're offering. It's these ads that blend well that you want to include on your site, because they'll perform far better than ads that stand out as ads.

To make this type of monetization work for you, you need to have some blank space on your web site in which you can place ads, and you need to have a little time to devote to making the ads blend with your site as much as possible (without violating program policies, which differ from company to company). Then, it's just a matter of testing different types of ads to see which seem to get the most clicks. This is done by placing ads on your site for a predetermined amount of time, and then switching them with different types of ads after that time is up. After waiting for the same amount of time to elapse, you can then compare the click-through rates for each type of ad to see which one seems to draw the most attention from your site visitors.

Using these programs, you can begin to see a slow stream of revenue trickle in for your web site, even before you've built the server-slaughtering traffic volumes that you dream about. And because you're linked to other sites that are presumably more popular than your own, you're building your rankings in search engines.

Ad placement services aren't the only game in town, however. There are other methods of web site monetization that might work better for you than ad placements.

Monetization Service Overviews

The two most well-known monetization services for your web site are Google AdSense and Yahoo! Publisher Network. These are basic ad placement services that enable you to place ads, which are paid for by advertisers, on your site. There's nothing more to it; you just place the ads and then get paid when your web site visitors click through them.

There are other ways to make a little money (and improve your SEO), too. Some programs enable you to offer products for sale. In these programs, you're paid a percentage of the sale each time someone clicks through your web site to the store. Amazon.com is probably the best known for this type of affiliate program. Amazon allows anyone with a web site to be an affiliate. On your personal web site, you place ads — that you build using Amazon's software — for products that you think your site visitors will be interested in. Then when someone clicks through the ads and makes a purchase, you're paid a small percentage for that sale.

It's not a bad deal if there are specific products you'd like to offer to your site visitors. These can be any products that are available on the Amazon.com web site, including your own if you have products available at Amazon. Like other monetization programs, the link between your sites is noticeable to search crawlers. Amazon also allows you to take part in activities that can increase traffic to your web site (such as blogging-type services and reviews).

In addition to services such as Amazon.com, there are many more that you can use to monetize your web site:

- **Commission Junction:** This company enables the publisher, or affiliate, to sell products or provide special offers to their customers from advertisers such as Best Buy and 6PM.com. The company has been in business for more than 10 years and offers a wide array of products and services for almost any niche you can think of.

- **LinkShare:** With this service, you link to advertisers' products and services using links built with the LinkShare application. Then, each time a visitor on your site clicks through the link, you're compensated for it. This is another company that offers a wide variety of products and services that reach all manner of niche markets.

- **ClickBank:** If you're more interested in offering digital products (such as ebooks and other downloads) then ClickBank might be the right company to help you monetize your web site. ClickBank specializes in digital products and offers more than 10,000 items in nine product areas.

- **Azoogle Ads:** Azoogle Ads is a cost-per-action company. That means you place Azoogle ads on your web site and each time one of your site visitors performs an action (signing up for an offer of some type, usually), you get paid for it. This company has been operating for about nine years, and has offers listed by Fortune 1000 and Fortune 500 companies.

- **Hydra Network:** Hydra Network is another cost-per-action company that enables you to list offers from other companies on your web site. Each time a visitor on your site takes advantage of one of the offers, you get paid.

- **ReviewMe:** Do you like to review products and services online? If you do, then ReviewMe might be the right company for you. This company pays you to review products and services, based on the product owner choosing your blog from others in the same category. Blogs are picked based on the number of readers and past reviews (if there are any).

- **Text-Link-Ads.com:** This site sells only text-link ads from advertisers to publisher. Then, based on the number of clicks that you receive on the ads, you're compensated at an agreed-upon rate. Much like keyword advertising, the rate varies according to the text links that are published.

- **TextLinkBrokers.com:** This is another text-link service. The requirements for this service are at least 20,000 page views per month, so a brand-new web site might not be able to take advantage of this method to build a revenue stream. It is something to keep in mind for future monetization, however, as quality links build search engine rankings.

There are a variety of ways in which you can monetize your web site. You just have to choose the one that's right for you. Keep in mind that if your site is brand-new, it may take some time to build a revenue stream with these programs. However, with the right number and type of monetization strategies integrated into your web site, you should be able to build search engine rankings — and that all starts with a good monetization plan.

Monetization Strategies for SEO

As with any SEO strategy, the first thing you need to do when you begin considering a monetization strategy is to come up with a plan that's tailored to your web site. That means not only planning what type of monetization program (or programs) you intend to use, but also deciding how that program fits in with your web site as a whole and in your SEO strategy.

In order to determine how all these elements fit together, you need to know exactly what you want to accomplish with your site and what you hope your SEO plan will do to help you accomplish that, and then determine how monetization can push all those goals forward. This means you need to have a solid understanding of your business before you even begin to choose the type of monetization plan that will work best for your site.

Choosing the right monetization strategy

Once you understand what your goals are and determine that your efforts will help you attain those goals, you can begin to decide on the type of strategy that will likely work best for you. Keep several things in mind as you look at the various monetization options available:

■ **What will your visitors expect to see on your web site?** Most web site visitors are tired of, and even numb to, most ads. They don't see them most of the time, and if they do, it's only because they're looking for something specific. Therefore, what's that specific thing your site visitors might be looking for? If you're running a geo-caching web site, then visitors might expect to see product ads for GPS systems, or if you're running a home-schooling web site, they might expect to see advertisements for educational products or services that help improve teaching. Spend a little time looking at your site through your visitors' eyes to gain some insight into what they might want to find on your site. Then find a company that offers that and monetize your web site accordingly.

■ **What fits into the style of your web site?** If your site is a blog, then graphic ads might not be the best option. Text ads might be more appropriate for the site. Conversely, if you can include product ads that are relevant to the posts that you're publishing, then those might work, too. Another option for a blog web site might be sponsored blog posts. Just be sure they're not too "salesy." Most web surfers today don't have patience for the hard sell.

■ **Which of the available monetization strategies will help your SEO efforts?** SEO efforts are boosted by incoming links from popular web sites. They're boosted by traffic and relevant content. As you're looking at the various monetization services available, consider how the service might provide additional weight to your SEO efforts — and make sure that whatever method of monetization you choose is consistent with any optimization that you've already done on your site.

> **CAUTION** Beware of the possibility that monetizing your web site could *reduce* your PageRank score. Search crawlers in general (and Google specifically) watch web sites to see whether links are purchased or paid for. If they are, your PageRank score could be affected. That doesn't mean, however, that your actual search engine ranking will be affected — only the PageRank number that's generated in your toolbar. If you use PageRank as a method of monitoring your web site success, though, you'll want to know that adding monetization to your site can affect that ranking number.

Adding monetization to your web site

After you've determined what type of monetization will work best for your site and how you should implement it, then all that's left to do is actually add the monetization to the site. Generally speaking, the technology for adding a monetization strategy is determined by the company that you use. With Google AdSense, for example, all you have to do is add a snippet of code to your web site where you want an AdSense ad to appear, and then publish (or republish) your web page. Simple enough.

Not all monetization strategies are created equal, however, and some might not be that simple. Others might be even simpler. Once you've determined which monetization service you want to use, you should be able to obtain a detailed explanation from that service.

Placement: deciding where ads appear on the page

The next question on your mind might be where to put the ads on your page. A lot of time and effort has gone into determining how web site visitors view web pages and blogs, and how that affects the ads that appear on those pages. For example, if you have a blog that you're trying to monetize, the ad placement (according to Google) should look something like what's shown in Figure 22-1. Each area in which an ad can be placed has been carefully studied to determine whether it is a location likely to draw attention from the blog reader.

On a regular web page (non-blog), Google suggests ad placement as shown in Figure 22-2. On this *heat map,* the darker spots represent the best-performing locations for ads, while the lighter spots reflect locations that don't perform as well. Keep in mind, however, that these placement suggestions are specific to AdSense. If you're looking at other monetization programs, check with the company that offers the program for the best layout options based on the type of monetization strategy offered.

Monitoring success with monetization

The final thing you'll want to do with whatever monetization strategy you choose is to ensure that your efforts are actually successful, both in terms of monetization and boosting your SEO. Obviously, whether or not you receive payments from the monetization company is going to be a sure sign as to whether your strategy is actually working for you or not.

How do you know how monetization affects your SEO efforts? You need to use some type of analytics program. We'll talk more about analytics programs in Chapter 26, but for now you

FIGURE 22-1

Google suggests these ad placements for ads on blog pages.

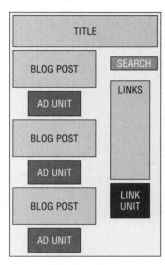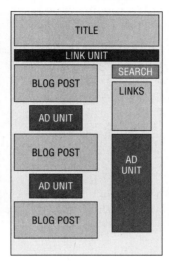

FIGURE 22-2

The Google AdSense *heat map* shows the best placement for AdSense-type ads on your web page.

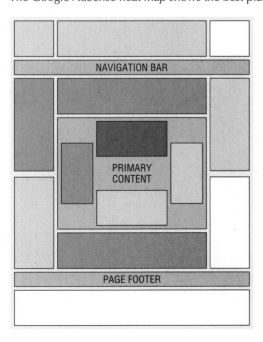

need to know that some programs, such as Google Analytics, can help you track how these monetization strategies affect your SEO. Google Analytics, particularly, offers reports that look closely at your content and established goals for your site and how those things affect your site visitors. Once you set up a monetization strategy, you can add customized reports to Google Analytics that will help you track that monetization strategy.

As with any other SEO strategy you implement, you may have to experiment with and test different monetization strategies to find one that works well on your site, provides a regular income stream, and helps to boost your SEO. You're probably not going to find the right combination the first time you put ads or products on your page. Indeed, it might take months to find the right combination; but with some attention to detail and regular monitoring, you will find that right combination.

Remember that ultimately your efforts are aimed at providing your visitors with the content, products, and services they want. As long as you keep the value to your visitor in mind, eventually you'll land on a combination that works for those visitors. When you do, you should see increased revenues from your site, improved search engine rankings, and a steady climb in the amount of traffic that moves through your site each week. It's a winning combination. You just have to tweak it until it works for you.

Chapter 23

Plugging In to SEO

IN THIS CHAPTER

Understanding plug-ins

Choosing the right plug-ins

There is no debate about one aspect of SEO: You must have it. Most of the traffic to your web site will come from search engines, and the effort that you put into SEO will be reflected by your search engine rankings. The problem is that it's hard to know what you're doing right and what you're doing wrong with your SEO efforts.

It's a bit of a guessing game even with the best tools made for monitoring SEO success. However, there are a few tools that you can use to help you monitor some elements of SEO. These tools, called *plug-ins*, can't tell you everything there is to know about your SEO, but they will give you some numbers that help you to understand where you're succeeding and where you need to concentrate your efforts. Some SEO plug-ins also give you details about other web sites, so you can learn what works for them as well.

How does that help you? Understanding what elements work on your web site helps you focus on the elements that aren't working; and understanding what elements work on other web sites gives you something to compare against your own efforts. For example, if your web site has been in search rankings the same amount of time as Web Site B, but Web Site B is ranked in the first five search engine results while yours is ranked below number 10, then you can learn something useful by looking at what Web Site B is doing. Maybe it has more social-bookmarking links than you do, or perhaps its PageRank is higher than yours. SEO plug-ins can help you zero in on the reasons.

Understand that these SEO plug-ins won't tell you everything there is to know about all the elements of your SEO or that of your competitors. Plug-ins provide insight, not simple answers.

Understanding Plug-Ins

Before we get too deep into what plug-ins you might find useful for SEO purposes, you should understand exactly what a plug-in is. In its simplest form, a plug-in is a mini-application that performs a specific function once it is installed as a part of a larger program. For example, many of the plug-ins that you use for SEO purposes *plug in* to the browser that you're using. Then, when you're on a web site you can click on the plug-in icon to find information about that site. With many plug-ins, you don't even need to click an icon; the information is displayed as part of a toolbar automatically.

To use these plug-ins, you must first download and install them. They're designed to install into the browser without any coding from you. Most SEO plug-ins are designed to work with the Firefox browser, as that's the browser of choice for most people in charge of SEO. Internet Explorer is generally considered to be a poor second choice; and if you use it, you'll learn very quickly that it's mostly useless for SEO. There are a couple of SEO plug-ins for Internet Explorer, though, so you're not completely out in the cold if you're a die-hard Microsoft user.

Your main concern with Internet Explorer should be that your pages display well in it. Otherwise, Firefox has the most functionality from an SEO standpoint, largely because it's tweakable, meaning if you have the expertise, then you can make it do just about anything you want. If you don't have that knowledge, it's a pretty good bet that someone else does and has already come up with a plug-in that will work for your purposes.

If you were an early adopter of Chrome, you'll find that it's not yet compatible with very many of these browser plug-ins. There is one industrious soul at ChromePlugIns.org who has spent some time creating SEO tools for use in Chrome that you might find handy. They're not quite plug-ins, but they work in a similar way, so a brief discussion of these tools is included later in this chapter.

Another set of plug-ins that you'll come across are those used with WordPress blogs. There are dozens of WordPress plug-ins that help you SEO your blog better, but these plug-ins work only with WordPress blogs, and some of them only with specific blog templates.

Another difference between the browser SEO plug-ins and the WordPress plug-ins is that the browser plug-ins give you data about web sites — information about links, keywords, PageRank, or Alexa Ranks, among other things — whereas the WordPress plug-ins give you the ability to use meta tags on your blog posts and add keyword descriptions and other SEO elements that you can already add to web pages that don't have plug-ins.

Choosing the Right Plug-In

Dozens, if not hundreds, of SEO plug-ins are available. Many of them do pretty much the same thing, while many others perform completely different tasks. Which ones are right for you? The answer to that question (as with so many others) is that it depends on what you need.

Many web site owners use multiple SEO plug-ins. Few plug-ins monitor more than one element of SEO, so in order to have multiple facets of your SEO strategy measured, you need multiple plug-ins. The key is determining what you need.

The first decision, of course, is whether you need WordPress plug-ins or standard plug-ins for your web site. That's easy enough to determine, as you know what type of site you're working on. For our purposes here, we're going to assume that you're looking for plug-ins for a general web site to use in your web browser. If you need more information about WordPress plug-ins, a quick Internet search should turn up all the information you need about what plug-ins are available.

For web sites, you can choose among several different plug-ins, each usually monitoring something different. Some monitor links, while others monitor PageRank or keyword density, and still others monitor several elements. The selection process, then, begins with understanding what's available and what you can do with it.

Google Toolbar

Google Toolbar, offered by Google, is a plug-in for Firefox that enables you to add different functionality. The basic toolbar, shown in Figure 23-1, has capabilities that enable regular users to look at functionality such as PageRank, or to add quick links to different types of searches or to spell-checking and translation services.

FIGURE 23-1

The Google Toolbar installs directly into Firefox and can be altered to meet your needs.

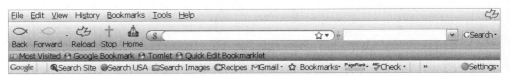

What makes the toolbar particularly useful for SEO is that you can add and remove buttons to suit your needs. To add SEO-specific buttons to the Google Toolbar, all you have to do (once the toolbar is installed in your Firefox browser) is click the Settings button on the right side of the toolbar and then select Options. Click the Buttons tab and then click Add. You're taken to the Google Button Gallery, where you can search for "SEO."

That search turns up 36 different buttons that you can add to the toolbar, including the following:

- Keyword Suggestions for Google
- SEOBook Competitive and Keyword Research Tool
- seomanagement
- Google vs Yahoo Search Results
- SEO Search Engine
- Toolurl.com
- Multiple Datacenter Link Popularity Check
- SEO Tip of the Day
- SEOBook Link Research Tool
- SEOLens
- SEONews
- Website Traffic
- Code to Text Ratio
- Page Size Lookup

As you can see from this list, there are a variety of different tools that you can plug in to the Google toolbar. Everything from keyword research tools to SEO news and blogs is available. All you have to do is decide which ones are most useful for you.

NOTE There are also Google Toolbar buttons for Internet Explorer, but the catch is that you must use Google Toolbar 4.0. At the time of this writing, Google Toolbar 4.0 is the standard offer, but Google Toolbar 5.0 is in beta testing, so unless these buttons are updated, you may not be able to use them as you're reading this. To learn more about the buttons (which are being offered by SEOBook), check out http://tools.seobook.com/buttons/.

Alexa Toolbar

The Alexa Toolbar, shown in Figure 23-2, is tied into Alexa's web-traffic statistics, so the numbers that you'll find when you use this toolbar are a little skewed. Still, Alexa provides enough information to make the toolbar useful.

FIGURE 23-2

The Alexa Toolbar has two parts: the actual toolbar at the bottom of the page and the related links at the top of the page.

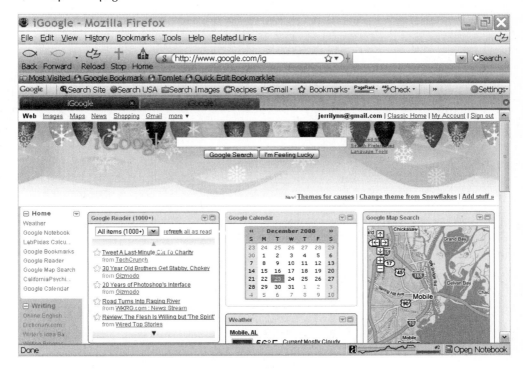

This toolbar looks quite a bit different from the Google Toolbar, but it offers some good information. The menu at the top shows you pages similar to the one shown in Figure 23-3. You can click any of those links to be taken to a similar page, so if you want to see what pages are ranked like your own, start on your page, and then click through the similar links to learn more about those pages.

The graphics at the bottom of the page provide a quick indication of the site's popularity over a four-month period (that's the lowercase *a*, followed by the black line), and the overall popularity of the site (that's the shaded bar with the number above it). The thing to keep in mind about these stats is that they're skewed to Alexa's ranking criteria specifically, so they're not necessarily indicative of how the site ranks at Google, Yahoo!, or MSN (or any other search engine).

FIGURE 23-3

Click the Related Links menu to see other pages related to the one you're on.

In addition to this information, if you right-click on the graphics at the bottom of the page, another menu is available to you. This menu, shown in Figure 23-4, takes you to Alexa's web site, where you can learn who owns the page, how fast it loads, how many other sites link to the page, and additional details about the traffic levels for the site.

FIGURE 23-4

Additional information about the page you're looking at can be found on the Alexa web site.

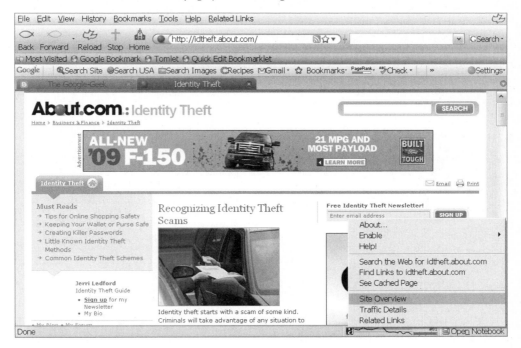

SEOQuake

The SEOQuake Toolbar offers a wealth of information about any web site that you visit online. This toolbar, shown in Figure 23-5, lists numerous statistics, including the following:

- PageRank
- Google Rank
- Yahoo! Rank
- Alexa Rank

- PageAge
- Whois Information
- Keyword Density
- Number of Links (to and from the page)

FIGURE 23-5

The SEOQuake Toolbar puts useful information about a web site as close as a click away.

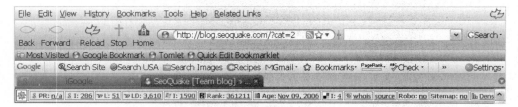

You can add plenty of other plug-ins, too, including plug-ins that provide information about social-bookmarking and networking applications.

When you click any of the blue links in the SEOQuake Toolbar, you're taken to a page on the SEOQuake web site that provides additional information about that specific statistic. For example, if you click the Density link, you're taken to the SEOQuake page that lists the density of keywords used on the page, including the words and the number of times they are used. This can help you quickly determine which of your keywords are ranking well, according to the metrics that SEOQuake uses.

One more important note about SEOQuake: It is available for Internet Explorer if that's your browser of choice.

SEO for Firefox

The SEO for Firefox plug-in, shown in Figure 23-6, is much different in appearance than any of the other plug-ins shown so far. As you can see, it's not really a toolbar per se, but an icon that indicates whether the plug-in is active or not. If the icon is in color, then SEO for Firefox is active. If it's black and white, then the plug-in is turned off.

FIGURE 23-6

SEO for Firefox provides plenty of information about a given web page, but it's not visible until you select it.

To access the information provided by the SEO for Firefox plug-in, you actually have to right-click the web page. Once you right-click on the page, a new menu appears. Hover your pointer over the SEO for Firefox option and a submenu appears. That submenu offers four options:

■ **Options**: Enables you to change the options for SEO for Firefox. You can add and remove statistics about a page that you do or do not want to see.

■ **Look up this page**: This option opens a pop-out window (see Figure 23-7) that shows various statistics for the page, including PageRank, Google cache date, traffic value, page age, social-bookmarking data, and more.

FIGURE 23-7

"Look up this page" provides statistical information about the page that you're viewing.

Name	Data
PR	6
Google Cache Date	Dec 23 2008
Traffic Value	82,892,170
Age	12-1998
del.icio.us	4,113
del.icio.us Page Bookmarks	5
Diggs	0
Digg's Popular Stories	58
Stumbleupon	-
Twitter	100
Y! Links	4,570,000
Y! .edu Links	130,000
Y! .gov Links	2,980
Y! Page Links	476
Y! .edu Page Links	1
Technorati	-
Alexa	81
Compete.com Rank	18
Compete.com Uniques	37,619,245
Cached	6,120,000
dmoz	4,330
Bloglines	3,158
Page blog links	40
wikipedia	-
dir.yahoo.com	2,004
Botw	435,027

- **Sort Results**: This option enables you to sort the SEO for Firefox results for the page that you're on.
- **SEO XRay**: Overlays information about a page on top of the actual page, as shown in Figure 23-8. This information is somewhat different from the information that you see when you select the "Look up this page" option. Among the differences, you'll see the page meta description and keywords in the XRay view.

FIGURE 23-8

The SEO XRay overlays information about the page with data that helps you to see what SEO elements are used.

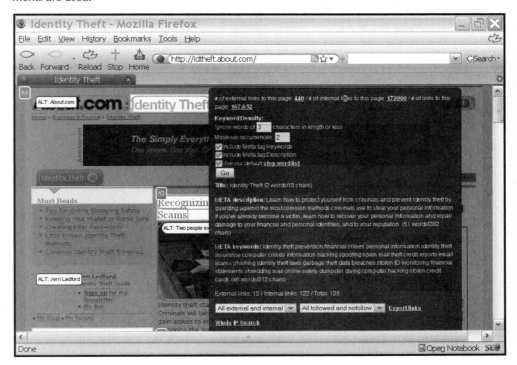

SEO tools for the Chrome browser

Google Chrome is the newest browser addition to the browser war, the ongoing competition between Microsoft and everyone else to create the most desired and most useful browser on the Web. Currently, Chrome accounts for only 2 to 5 percent of the browser installations on the Web, but that percentage is growing, and it's very popular among technological types who appreciate a browser that doesn't crash often and provides some very good security features.

If you're one of those people, you've probably been frustrated by the lack of SEO plug-ins for Chrome. Fortunately, the good folks over at ChromePlugIns.org have come up with a solution for many of those issues.

Not exactly plug-ins, these mini-applications act more like (and are installed like) bookmarks, but you can still find some useful information with them. Among the many mini-apps that you can install are the following:

- Google Cache
- Google Links
- Search for URL
- Google Images from Site
- Google Info
- Related Sites/Pages
- Pages Indexed in Yahoo!
- Pages Indexed in MSN
- Yahoo! Directory
- Alexa Rank
- Compete.com Details
- Archive.org
- Delicious Bookmarks
- Show Domain's Robots.txt
- Number of Links on a Page

You can find the code for these and other functions at `www.chromeplugins.org/google/ chrome-tips-tricks/google-toolbar-chrome-50.html`. All you have to do is copy the code and add a bookmark in the Chrome browser. Once you've installed it, from the page you want to learn more about, just click the bookmark that you created. You'll be taken to a page that shows you the requested information.

It's not the best solution to adding SEO capabilities to the Chrome browser, but for now it's the only option you have. The creators at ChromePlugIns.org monitor the message boards where this information is located pretty closely, so if you experience difficulties, you can post a question and someone will usually respond quickly.

Keep in mind that there are hundreds of different plug-ins available out there. I've simply outlined a small handful of the most frequently used ones. If you don't find what you're looking for here, look around online. You'll find everything that you're looking for and more.

Chapter 24

Automated Optimization

Pay attention in just about any technology industry and eventually you're going to hear the term *automation*. That's because so much technology consists of repetitive actions that are best suited to automation.

Therefore, when you hear the term automation associated with SEO, you may be thinking, "Wow, optimization automation! How cool is that?" It would be super cool. After all, there are a lot of repetitive tasks in search engine optimization.

Using keywords on your pages is one area where you might be able to automate the optimization. A good content-generation system would make it easy for you to quickly generate keyword-optimized content that you could change out on your site regularly. Even tagging your site might be an option for automation. It would seem to be an easy task to create a piece of software that would add your chosen keywords to the correct tags.

Of course, not all automation is created equal — and when you're working on your SEO strategies, there are some things that software programs just can't do.

Being creative is one of those things. You can tell a piece of software what to do, but the software can't look at a problem from several angles and find a creative way to solve it. If the solution isn't provided by an algorithm in the program, you are stuck without an answer.

Automation has its good and bad points. Some elements of SEO lend themselves to optimization; others do not.

Should You Automate?

Although some form of automation has been around since the time of the ancient Greeks, automation is a concept most often associated with the industrial age. There was a time when humans were responsible for every step in manufacturing a product of any type. When people realized that it would be much faster (and cheaper) to have a machine do some of the menial, repetitive tasks, automation was born.

Since those first glimmers of inspiration, automation has been applied to numerous different products, strategies, and processes — even on the Internet. Nearly as soon as computer and web applications were developed, someone started trying to automate them.

As useful as automation is, it doesn't work for everything. Customer service is a good example. While you can automate some aspects of customer service, such as those annoying menus from which you must select an option when you call your bank or local utility company, when it comes to dealing with real people, you have to have real people do the job. Machines just don't understand how people operate.

SEO is one of those technologies that fall into the category of "you can automate some aspects, but there has to be human interaction, too." A computer program can carry out a predefined set of activities based on guidelines that are also predefined, but when you have dynamic (changing) parameters, as you do in SEO, there are limits to what you can automate.

Automating keyword research is an example. There are plenty of programs available on the Web that will help you with some aspects of keyword research. You can find programs that generate keywords for you, or that look at your competition's site to see what keywords it is using and how it is using them. A piece of software can also monitor keywords that you're using in PPC programs to help you know when your bid is too low. But a program doesn't possess the nuances of human reasoning and understanding that are part of determining which of those keywords will work for your particular web site.

Creativity is one reason not to automate. A second reason is that many search engines look down on automated SEO strategies. There are bits of SEO that you can automate without being penalized. We've talked about keywords, but you can also automate some of your management functions such as analytics and rank monitoring.

Tasks that you never want to automate include site generation, automatic link programs, and content generation. It will be obvious to search engines that you've automated these tasks, and the result of that automation won't be better rankings, as you might hope. More likely, the result will be having your site delisted from search engine results, at least temporarily.

When you're considering taking the automation route, stick with the automation of functions that aren't critical to providing customers and site visitors with the information and capabilities that they need. Don't automate content or linking, and certainly don't automate the creation of your web site. Use your creativity to make those elements of your site as appealing to site visitors as possible, and leave the automation for the mundane administrative functions that have no impact on your customers.

It's Not Always a Penalty

If you read the information on the Internet, you'll find that many people disagree about whether or not search engines should penalize companies that don't follow their guidelines. You'll also find that the search engines won't admit publicly to penalties that reduce your ranking, only to penalties that get you delisted from the search engine. Nonetheless, both things can happen, but not always for the same reason.

There are many reasons why a search engine might delist you from its index. Cloaking, keyword stuffing, linking schemes, even overoptimization — these are all general spamdexing tactics that will cause a search engine to delist your site.

Once you're delisted, you can get relisted. All you have to do is correct the problem and then give the search engine time to recrawl your site. When the offending strategies have been removed, you'll be added back to the index — but it could take as much as six months!

More often than not, however, you're not delisted, your rank just falls suddenly. This is probably not the result of a penalty from the search engine. Instead, it's more likely that your site ranking drops because there's a problem with your site or your web server. Some of the reasons that you may find your rank falling include the following:

- **A search engine algorithm change**: Search engine designers are constantly tweaking their algorithms, so it's not at all unusual to find that your site position drops because of a subtle change to the way the crawler indexes your site. This is why it's always good to stay abreast of changes at the various search engines.

- **Server and hosting issues**: If your server is down, or if it's running slowly, a crawler might have a difficult time crawling the site. If so, it's likely to give up and move on to another site. In some cases, your web host might ban a search engine from crawling your site because other clients have complained or because the crawler is creating problems with the hosting services provided. Any of these problems will cause your site ranking to drop.

- **A poorly written robots.txt file**: A `robots.txt` file is a useful tool to have on your site, but if the file is written incorrectly it may cause crawlers to not crawl your site completely, or even at all. Make sure that file is written properly so your ranks don't drop dramatically.

- **Broken or spammy links**: Your links don't have to be actual spam in order to be perceived as such. If they appear to be spammy, a crawler might abandon the indexing of your site. Broken links will also stop a crawler. Crawlers don't like anything that forces them to back up and start over again.

continued

continued

■ **Another site becomes more relevant than yours**: A new or redesigned site may surpass your site. It happens. There is no such thing as perfection in SEO. Other sites are working hard to improve their site rankings too, and sometimes their efforts will be more successful than yours. All you can do is try to stay on top of the SEO game, creating new content and keeping your site as useful as possible for site visitors.

If your site ranking drops for no apparent reason, start investigating. Find the problem and fix it immediately if possible. If not, stay on top of the people who can. If you're delisted, well, fix the problem as soon as possible, and don't make the same mistake again. It's an expensive lesson to have to learn, but after a month or so without any search ranking at all, you will understand how important it is to always stay on a search engine's good side.

Automation Tools

Automating certain SEO tasks is one way to make the best use of your time. Of course, you want to avoid automation strategies that put you on a search engine's blacklist, but there are plenty of places you can use automation and many different kinds of automation tools.

One thing you won't find is an all-in-one solution. Some great SEO tools out there will help with many aspects of SEO, but they will still leave one or two areas untouched. For example, Web Optimization Easy 4.5 (www.websitepromotionsoft.com/search-engine-optimization.html) will help with 45 ranking factors, but it doesn't cover them all. And although it can help you to understand why the top 10 web sites in your area rank well, it won't help you manage keyword bids.

When you can find a program that does most of the automation you need, and you're comfortable with the tool's interface, then by all means try it; and use other tools to supplement any areas the single tool doesn't cover.

It would be nice if there were standards in place that made it easy to monitor all your SEO efforts from a single dashboard. There are not — but you can piece together the tool solution that reduces the amount of time you put into repetitive SEO work, which enables you to focus your creative energies on those aspects of SEO that will truly improve your search rankings.

You have to be careful about choosing solutions, though. Some of the automation tools available on the Web are not worth the time it takes to install them. Many of these tools are buggy, they don't perform as well as they should, and they can cause your system to crash — or worse, they can create problems with your web site.

When you're looking for automation tools for your SEO efforts, begin by looking at the areas that you need to automate. Are you spending hours and hours on keyword research when what you should be doing is generating unique copy for your web site? If so, then a keyword research automation tool such as WordTracker (www.wordtracker.com) will help free up the time you need to work on your content.

Are you obsessed with your rank and how your competition measures up? You shouldn't be. Let an automated monitoring tool such as Rank Tracker (www.download32.com/rank-tracker-seo-tool-i37132.html) obsess for you while you spend that time doing something useful about your current rank.

In order to choose your tool(s), evaluate your needs and then look for tools that meet those needs. Try to find tools that can accommodate business growth. Your automation needs will change over time as your site matures, as your SEO efforts mature, and as SEO as a strategy changes. You want a tool that's scalable as your site grows and evolves.

In addition, keep in mind that price isn't always the best indication of which tools are better than others. Some free tools on the Web are excellent. Those that aren't free can cost anywhere from under $100 to well over $1,000, and they can also be as excellent or as lousy as some of the free tools. To ensure that you're getting a tool that will provide what you need within your budget, try finding tools that offer a free trial period. These tools usually allow you to try their software for 30 days without cost. The full functionality of the tool may not be available to you, but you should be able to tell from the trial period whether the interface is comfortable and the tool provides the metrics and solutions that you need.

One more way to find a good tool is to ask around. Chances are good that you know other people who are in SEO or who own a web site and have done their own SEO. These people may have already been through the trial process with various tools and can therefore offer some advice, thereby reducing how much time you need to spend researching the best tools for you.

Automation works best when it is applied to the right aspects of your SEO campaign. If you limit your automation to administrative functions and use tools that suit your needs, you'll have ample time to devote to far more important activities, such as providing your customers with exactly what they're looking for, and on their terms.

Part IV

Maintaining SEO

One of the grievous mistakes that many web designers (or whoever is in charge of SEO) make is to assume that SEO is a one-time activity. Of course, as you know by how, it is an ongoing process that must be monitored and maintained in order to be truly effective.

In this part, Chapter 25 explains some of the most important elements of monitoring and maintaining your SEO efforts. Then, in Chapter 26, you will learn how to analyze your SEO strategies, including the techniques, conversions, and even other types of logs that are associated with SEO. These techniques will help you maintain SEO and continue to gain value from your SEO efforts.

Chapter 25

SEO Beyond the Launch

t's done. You've spent weeks or months optimizing your web site, integrating yourself into social networks as an expert, testing the right keywords, and digging for all the right links. Now you're number one for your keywords and the traffic coming to your site surpasses anything that you've had in the past. It's time to sit back and put your feet up on the desk. A nice nap, a long lunch. Now that you're not working on SEO all the time, you're free to do some of the more interesting things that are allowed (or not) during working hours.

Stop. That's a nice dream, but it's not the way SEO works. You've achieved a top rank? So what? Tomorrow you could be buried three pages deep in search engine results or worse, because a search engine changed its algorithm and you weren't on top of it. Or maybe you just got knocked down below the fold of the first page because other web sites added some features that made them more popular than yours. Below the fold is not terrible, but it's also not above the fold, right where users can see your listing without having to scroll — and it's not the top position that you held yesterday.

It's Not Over

In order to maintain that great rank that you've finally reached, you have to stay on top of your SEO efforts. You've read it more than once in this book already — SEO is an ongoing process. Once you're where you want to be, a lot of work must be done to keep you there. Even a short time away from your efforts could lead to a drop in your position.

With that in mind, a good practice is to include an outline in your original SEO plan for the actions you need to take regularly and the amount of time you'll need for them. On average, you'll need to devote at least a couple of hours a day to your ongoing SEO efforts, and at times more than that will be required.

Monitoring your position

There are plenty of things to do in the time that you allot for ongoing SEO efforts, but it should all start with some form of position monitoring. Position monitoring can usually be accomplished with a software application but be careful — Google specifically calls the use of automated rank checkers a violation of its terms of service and may disable your ability to connect to and do searches on Google.com. Moderate use of such software probably won't be a problem. Many people use these tools to track their position, so if you can't take time out of your schedule every day to check the rank of your web site by keyword in every search engine you're targeting, an application to handle it could provide the position information you need.

Monitoring web analytics

Monitoring your web analytics is also an important part of your ongoing SEO, because this is where you'll find information about where your site visitors are coming from, how long they're staying on your site, and what pages they visit while they're there. An analytics program should also tell you how many people are *bouncing* — coming to your site and leaving immediately. A bounce is an indication that your site is not optimized properly, especially if the bounces happen on landing pages that are designed to greet visitors who click on advertisements or marketing URLs. Visitors who bounce from your site are not finding what they thought they would find, based on the search engine results or advertisements they clicked through.

Monitoring keywords and links

You may also want to monitor other portions of your SEO strategy. For example, monitoring keywords and links is always a good idea. Keywords can change. The popular term for something in your industry could be one thing today and something completely different tomorrow. You have to stay on top of trends in order to take advantage of them.

Monitoring your links is a matter of making sure they lead exactly where you expect them to lead. You may also want to keep an eye on where links to your site are coming *from*. Incoming links can be damaging to you if they're coming from unrelated web sites, or if the sites they're coming from have been determined by search engines to be *bad neighborhoods*. A bad neighborhood is an unethical site or group of sites.

As with monitoring your search rankings, monitoring links and keywords is also a task that lends itself to automation. A good software application can keep track of these elements of your SEO plan and let you know when you need to pay attention to and improve your SEO efforts in one area or another.

In addition to monitoring your links, you'll also want to add to links and to content over time. If you add hundreds of links to your site overnight, search engine crawlers will likely not be impressed. Instead, they'll look at those links with suspicion and might even assume that you're spamming the search engine. If that happens, you'll be delisted from search rankings until you fix what you've done wrong.

It's far better to add links to your site a few at a time. You can add a few every day or every week, depending on how many people want to link to your site. Avoid adding all your links on a single day, as it won't look good for you.

Keeping content fresh

Content is also an element of SEO that needs to be maintained over time. Your content should change regularly. In some cases, that means every day; in others it means once a week or once a month. Even more important than the schedule with which you change your content is the content itself. Over time you should be adding to your collection of relevant, useful content. If what you have on the site isn't relevant or useful, then replace it — and don't put any piece of content on your site that doesn't give your visitors something useful.

In the same category as content is adding new pages to your web site. If you have an active site, over time it should grow. Search engines take note of the number of pages included in your site each time you're crawled. Landing pages, articles, blogs, newsletter archives, and site maps are types of pages that will cause your site to grow, so if you're maintaining your SEO, site growth will be a natural extension of that.

When adding new pages, you should also be adding internal page links. Link every page on your web site, and use an easy linking structure. The main links for your site — to pages such as your home page, the contact page, or category overview pages — should appear on the top or side of your page in your main navigational structure and be repeated at the bottom of every page.

In addition, if you're using PPC ads that lead to landing pages, then the landing pages should be added to your navigational structure as well. Users don't like to be dropped in the center of a jungle and left to figure out how to get where they want to go. Anticipate and then provide a clear path for any direction your visitors might like to take.

Finally, if you haven't already done it, now is the time to rename pages and images that don't include keywords. Using the default titles created by your web site design software won't win you any points with search engines. Instead, change those page names to reflect the keywords that you've chosen. Ideally, the page name will be the same as the page title; if possible, it will also contain relevant keywords.

Your images may also need to be retagged. There are image-specific search engines that index your images for display. For example, if you run a custom stationery company, including pictures of your stationery that are labeled with keyword-rich names may help you rank better in both image searches and general searches. Keep your image alt tags updated, too.

If you change your relevant keywords, don't forget to also replace meta tag keywords or update meta descriptions as your page changes. It won't do you any good at all to have one set of keywords in your meta tags and another set used on the customer-facing portion of your web pages.

In short, the basic elements that helped you reach the top spot through your SEO efforts need ongoing attention. Even the competitive research that you did back in the beginning needs to be updated regularly. Your competition is also changing. If you don't stay on top of those changes, then you'll find yourself behind the competition and will have to fight your way back to the top again.

Using Content Management Systems

Not very long ago, if you used the terms *content management system (CMS)* and *SEO* in the same sentence, you'd probably draw an audible gasp from any SEO experts. That's because in the past, content management systems had a way of demolishing all the advantages of SEO.

Most of the problem was that content management systems created pages that contained long URLs with multiple variables that blocked search crawlers from crawling the pages. That's not the case today. CMS providers have fixed that problem and increased the usability of those systems for the express purpose of improving or maintaining SEO.

Content is the backbone of the Internet. The Internet was created as a way to share information, so it only makes sense that content is an integral part of the structure of the Web. Using a content management system can help you remain an active part of the Web, because it helps you to generate the content that you need to attract the customers you want.

Content management systems are usually used in a situation where your content is derived from many different sources. For example, if you run a web site that contains a blog to which several people contribute, then adding a content management system can help you maintain control over that group of content providers. It can also help strengthen your web site structure by automatically structuring your links and providing the templates on which your content appears.

One more redefined capability of a CMS is the application's ability to improve your content in terms of SEO. The latest CMS systems can create keyword-rich content and include SEO-appropriate titles, meta tags, and anchor text.

Including a CMS system in your SEO efforts is not a bad idea these days. If you have a site that generates a lot of content by a lot of people, a CMS system might be the application that helps make the content side of your SEO efforts successful.

SEO Problems and Solutions

No matter how smoothly your SEO implementation goes, eventually you'll run into problems. Most of them won't be major, such as having out-of-date keywords or meta tags, but you can also have a few major problems with your SEO implementation.

You've been banned!

Probably the most worrisome of issues you could encounter is being banned from a search engine, Google specifically. If you're delisted from search rankings, you can always fix whatever problem caused the delisting and apply to be relisted. However, once you're banned, that's it. There is no way to have that URL relisted in search results.

If you depend on your search ranking to keep you supplied with customers and sales, being banned from a search engine is a frightening prospect. Even a single day without search engine visibility can cost your company dearly, not only monetarily but also in terms of customer loyalty.

There's good news. Despite the fact that you hear a lot about being banned from search engines, it's really not all that likely to happen — in fact, it's very rare. You have to participate in some pretty offensive tactics (such as page hijacking, keyword stuffing, malware distribution, or other decidedly black-hat SEO techniques) before you will be banned. Of course, there are exceptions to every rule, and even search engines have a bad day now and again.

What do you do if you're in a top-ranking slot one day and the next your site is nowhere to be found in search rankings? Before assuming you've been banned from a search engine, make sure. You can search for your site on Google using the search string site: *www.yoursitename.com*. If your site is included in Google's index, then the pages that are included in the search rankings should appear in the search results. If they do, then you haven't been banned, but you may have been penalized for something. Try to figure out what and fix it.

If you don't see any pages listed for your site, it's still possible that you haven't been banned. The best way to find out is to e-mail the search engine. Be professional when you send the e-mail — you don't want to make matters worse by being rude, especially if you have done something to be banned.

If you have in fact been banned from search rankings, there's probably nothing you can do to get back into the search engine's good graces. Once a site has been banned, it's extremely rare for it to be relisted. Instead, you'll have to start over with an entirely new URL and a few hard lessons learned. Not a fun prospect, as whatever customer base you had before the banning will likely be lost.

The moral of the story is that you should stay in favor with search engine crawlers. Avoid anything that looks sneaky, suspicious, or underhanded. You might find yourself fighting penalties at some point, but you won't be banned from search rankings altogether.

Content scraping

Another major problem that you might encounter in your SEO efforts is having your site content stolen. This is usually accomplished by a *scraper site* that uses a *scraper bot* to copy the content on your site. This can be an SEO problem because the scraper bot will look for an XML site map. Finding that map makes it far easier for the bot to gather content.

Even without an XML site map, a bot can scrape content from your site, but it's much harder. If you are worried that your content is in danger, one thing you can do is not use an XML site map at all. In some cases, this is a viable option. In other cases, an XML site map is essential to having some pages within your site indexed.

If not using an XML site map is out of the question, you could place an XML site map on your site, but remove it after the site has been crawled. The best way to know when your web site has been indexed by a crawler is to look at the server logs. Usually you'll see a request for the robots.txt file in the file log. Around that request you should see the name of the crawler that requested the site map. After the one that you want to have access to your site map has crawled it, you can delete the file. But remember that this only makes it harder for hackers to exploit your site map, not impossible.

The next time the crawler comes around, it should already have the links for the pages that were included in the site map. Of course, that doesn't guarantee those pages will be crawled again. Without the site map, the pages could be removed from the listings. It's a judgment call on your part based on what is most important to you.

Click fraud

Click fraud has been addressed in this book a few times already, but it bears mentioning here — briefly. Click fraud is the most troublesome of SEO problems because it's very hard to control. If you suspect your PPC ads are being targeted for click fraud, report it immediately to your PPC provider.

Any number of problems, including click fraud, can arise with your SEO campaign. Everything from inadvertent SEO spam to the issues listed here can happen at any time. Fortunately, even though the possibility exists, such things don't happen all the time, and in fact probably not as often as all the warnings might lead you to believe.

The best thing you can do to protect yourself from the problems that you can encounter with SEO is to follow the guidelines laid out by the search engine or directory that you're targeting. Avoid black-hat SEO techniques, and in general be professional about how you conduct your SEO efforts.

Chapter 26

Analyzing Success

I f you want to maintain successful SEO efforts, you need to analyze what works and what doesn't, and try to extrapolate why, based on the information that you have. That information can vary, depending on how you gather it.

There are many methods for measuring the success of your SEO efforts. Some people are happy just to see their site traffic and sales rising, but if your SEO strategy is to work toward achieving a more complicated goal, you might need more ways to measure the success or failure of your efforts.

As an example, if you've implemented SEO strategies in an effort to increase the number of visitors to your site as a way of creating or improving brand recognition, you might not be as interested in the sales achieved by your SEO efforts as you are in the creation of returning visitors.

It doesn't matter if your SEO goals are monetarily based. You can create goals, and conversion values, for nonmonetary activities such as newsletter sign-ups, filling out a form, or even requesting additional information. Whatever your goals are, learning which SEO efforts work and which don't is vitally important to ensuring that you're always putting forth your best effort to reach those conversions.

IN THIS CHAPTER

Analyzing SEO success

Analyzing web stats

Competitive analysis

Conversion analysis

Analyzing server logs

Analyzing SEO Successes

You know that search engine rankings for your web site can change from week to week. Those changes can be caused by competition, modifications to search algorithms, and changes to your web site. To maintain your top ranking, you must constantly monitor and make changes to your web site. It's through this monitoring that you'll also be able to see how successful your SEO efforts are, and measuring the success of those efforts is essential to keeping you on the right track.

Managing SEO expectations

Before you can begin to analyze what you're doing right and wrong in SEO, you first need to know what to expect. Realistic expectations will keep your view of your SEO results realistic as well. SEO is not the only answer for your web site, but it can help improve your site traffic and conversions if you are patient and understand how to leverage your SEO expectations.

SEO time line

The first expectation that you'll probably have to rein in is the SEO time line. Many people implement some aspect of SEO and expect to see results overnight. Obviously, paid results are going to be profitable faster than true SEO efforts, and sometimes a minor change or tweak will have an overnight effect. But that's usually a fluke, and within a day or so your ranking will correct itself to be somewhere between the high point and the low point.

Taking the extraordinary out of the equation, SEO can still be a long process. It can take anywhere from a few weeks or months to more than a year to start seeing solid rankings and targeted traffic. You'll have to be patient to be rewarded for your SEO efforts. Of course, the actual time frame for seeing full results will vary according to the keywords you're using and the state of your web site when you begin your optimization process.

Hands-on involvement

Whether you've hired an SEO consulting firm or are doing it in-house, you have to be involved in your SEO efforts from start to finish — and because *finish* never really arrives, you have to be involved on an ongoing basis. Become a champion of SEO and help the others in your organization to understand and value the results that SEO efforts provide.

This applies even if you've hired a company to do the majority of the tasks needed for successful site optimization. You have responsibilities in the client-customer relationship. Your most important responsibility is to communicate what you need from the SEO company and what your goals are for site optimization. You also have a responsibility to stay involved in the SEO process, so that you know where your optimization efforts are now, where they are going, what works, and what needs to be changed, tweaked, or abandoned altogether.

Your participation in your SEO program will ensure that you know what's going on, where you currently stand, and what your SEO company is doing for you. This is also the easiest way to hold an SEO company accountable for its responsibilities to you.

With your expectations in line, you can begin to truly analyze the success or failure of your SEO efforts. There are several methods for analyzing where you stand, all of which are valid. What makes one more useful than another is mainly determined by your needs — you should under-stand exactly what you're trying to achieve and what indicators you're looking for in order to know whether you're actually achieving those goals.

Another factor affecting your method of tracking and analyzing your success is your budget. Some organizations can afford automated tracking tools that tell them basically everything they need to know about the success or failure of their SEO campaigns. Other organizations don't have that kind of budget. Fortunately, there are some methods of analysis that won't consume your entire SEO budget.

Find yourself

If all you really need to know is where your web site appears in search rankings, you can use the search engines and directories that you're targeting to do a keyword search. That keyword search should show you where your site is ranking. It won't show you much more than that, but it does help you to monitor your position so you know whether your efforts are working or not. Just don't base your decision on a single search. Search for your key-words daily over a period of time to ensure that your rank on any given day isn't just an anomaly.

If you're using this method of analyzing your success, you'll need a historical view that shows where your site appeared in search rankings before you began your SEO efforts. With this measurement, you can compare your current rankings to see if your listing is climbing or falling. Without historical data, you should, at the very least, take stock of where your site appears in rankings on the first day of your SEO campaign. This won't tell you the average ranking for your site, but it will give you a good idea of where you should start.

Analyzing Web Stats

Most web site hosting companies now provide some form of web statistics program, but it may be limited to basic measurements such as number of hits, number of unique visitors, search terms used to find your site, IP addresses accessing your site, and locations of people accessing your site. Even this basic information, however, will help you to learn where your visitors are coming from, although you might want to add to those metrics by expanding your web stats package.

If you're looking for a web stats package that's more comprehensive, a few are available online free. Most notably, Google Analytics will provide most of the measurements you'll need, including keyword tracking for AdWords and other PPC applications. You can also buy numerous types of web statistics software, some hosted online and some that are hosted on your own computer. Find the package that's right for your needs, and you'll have all the measurements you require to analyze how successful your SEO efforts are in terms of driving targeted, converting traffic to your site.

Baseline statistics

When you're analyzing your web statistics, there are a few principles you should keep in mind. These principles will help you understand your metrics and how they correlate with your SEO efforts.

Baseline statistics are the measurements that you collect *before* you begin to implement changes to your site, such as the changes you'll make as you're optimizing your web site. Record statistics such as the average number of visitors to your site each day. You can later compare this number to statistics that you collect after your SEO strategies have been implemented, to see the results of your efforts. If your numbers aren't improving as you would expect given the changes you've made, then you may not have done something right, or some other aspect might need to be adjusted. Your baseline measurements will help you to see (over time) where you stand.

Referring web sites

Referring web sites are those sites from which your site visitors come. If you have PPC ads on Google's AdWords network, the referring web site might be one of the search engines those ads are distributed across. If you've written articles and newsletters that have been distributed across the Web, the sites that host those might be the referring web sites.

Most analytics packages will track your referring sites, which are then provided in a report that shows you from where your site visitors are coming. This information enables you to quickly determine whether your SEO efforts are paying off. If you have several types of campaigns that should be leading from one site or another but you don't find one of those sites listed, then you know those efforts are not working. In that case, you need to figure out why.

Referring keywords (paid and organic)

Another useful measurement you'll find in most web statistics packages is keyword tracking. Most web statistics packages will track both paid and organic keywords. Which paid keywords are tracked depends on the stats package you use, but nearly all of them will track organic keywords.

The value of organic keyword tracking is that you can learn how your site is being discovered. The words and phrases that visitors use to find you gives you valuable insight into the way they think about and prioritize the subject of your business. For example, most people won't search for "financial services." It's more likely that they'll search for "money market account," or "savings account," or even "free checking account." A stats package that tracks these words will help you monitor and analyze the keywords that work for your site and help you stay on top of cultural and linguistic shifts that reflect and change the way people think.

Visit duration

One of the statistics that you should watch closely is the measurement for visit duration. This measurement tells you how long your site visitors spend on your site, and it can be an indication of how well your site is targeted to the visitors who are finding it. For example, if a visitor comes to your site through your search ranking for a particular keyword and spends more than a few seconds on the site, it's likely this visitor has found something of interest.

Conversely, visitors who come into your site and then leave immediately (remember, this is called a bounce) are an indication that your site isn't well targeted for the keyword that led the visitor to the site in the first place.

Visit depth

Like visit duration, visit depth can tell you a lot about your site visitors and what they find useful on your web site. Visit depth is a measurement of the number of pages, and which ones, that visitors viewed while they were on your site.

A visitor who comes to your site and views only one page likely didn't find anything interesting on that page. However, visitors who come to your site and view four, nine, or even dozens of pages have found something that interests them. These are valuable visitors to you, because each new page they view is another opportunity for you to reach a goal conversion.

Most analytics applications have a visit depth report, though sometimes it's combined with the visit duration report. Where it appears depends on the analytics application that you're using, but pay particular attention to this report (especially in combination with the other reports that you're viewing) for hints about what leads visitors deeper into your site.

Repeat visits

Another report that you'll find interesting is the repeat visits report. This report tells you how many of your visitors are *not* first-time visitors. A lot of SEO emphasis is put on drawing first-time visitors to your site — sometimes so much so that the importance of repeat visits is forgotten, but make no mistake: Repeat visits are essential.

Repeat visits come from site visitors who found something they needed on your site. When they need that or something similar again, they return to your site. This builds loyalty, which is an essential part of building a relationship with your site visitors and customers.

Visitors who are loyal to your site will often start there, before they look anywhere else. For you, this translates into increased sales or goal conversions.

If your repeat visits report shows a low number of repeat visitors to your site, you know that the site isn't *sticky* enough — it doesn't have enough content that is of value to site visitors. A low number of repeat visitors is a clear indication that you need to focus on meeting the needs of your site visitors and ensuring that the visitors who are coming to your site are a good match with what you're offering.

Additional statistics

You may want to track a few other statistics to gain a clearer picture of the traffic to your site, the behaviors of your site visitors, and how those can be correlated by aspects such as location and technical capabilities. Some of the additional stats that you might want to track include the following:

- Page views
- Unique visitors
- Keywords used by search engine
- Location information
- Technological capabilities (web browsers, operating systems, and so on)

Knowing how you can track your SEO results will help you use all the resources available to you to analyze those results. You can then make changes that can improve your rankings and the accessibility of your web site so that you can increase your sales conversions and profits.

Competitive Analysis

Competitive analysis is a step you should take in the very beginning of your SEO efforts. It should be right at the top of your to-do list, along with keyword analysis and tagging your web site. In fact, you should probably do a competitive analysis even before you begin tagging your site.

Your competitive analysis doesn't end there, however. Like analyzing your web statistics, conversions, and other elements of your web site, your competitive analysis should be ongoing. Competitors will change. They'll learn how to reach a search engine better. They may even change their customer approach just enough to always stay ahead of you. They'll keep you guessing, and the only way to figure out what they're doing that you're not is to spend the time it takes to analyze what they're doing.

As you're going through this analysis process, keep in mind that you're not checking out only your direct competitors. You need to look at those competitors who are ahead of you in search rankings, even if their offerings are different from yours.

Plan to spend a few hours per week on this analysis. You should look at all the sites that are ahead of you, but specifically those sites that rank in the top five to ten positions in the SERPs.

You already know what you should be looking for. Look for the same indications that you examined during your original competitive analysis, which include the following:

- **Site rankings:** Where in the SERPs is the site ranked? Take note, especially, of the top three to five sites.
- **Page saturation:** How many of the competition's pages are indexed? Not every page on a site will be indexed, but if your competition has more or fewer pages ranked, you may have overlooked some aspect of page inclusion and exclusion.

- **Page titles:** Are page titles consistent? What keywords do they contain, if any at all? How your competition uses titles can give you an indication of what you're doing right or wrong with your own.

- **Meta data:** What meta data is your competition including? How is it worded? How does it differ from your own? Remember that you can access the source code of a web site by selecting Source from the View menu of your web browser.

- **Site design:** How is the competition's web site designed? Site architecture and the technology that is used to design and present the site are factors affecting how your site ranks. Learn what the competition is doing and how that differs from what you're doing.

- **A robots.txt file:** The `robots.txt` file is accessible to you, and looking at it could give you some valuable insight into how your competition values and works with search engines.

- **Content quality and quantity:** How much quality content is included on your competitor's site, and is it all original or is it reused from some other forum? If a site is ahead of you in search rankings, its content is probably performing better than yours. Analyze it and find out why.

- **Link quality and quantity:** Your competitors' linking strategies could hold a clue to why they rank well. Look at the link structure. If they're using legitimate linking strategies, what are they? If they're not, don't try to follow suit. Their actions will catch up with them soon enough.

CAUTION Be careful not to copy your competition too closely. Instead, use their success as a way to jump-start your own creative process for improving your web site. Some web site owners fill the internal workings of their site with bogus keywords, tags, or other elements in an effort to keep the competition from catching up to them. If you follow their dubious practices too closely, you could end up doing more harm than good.

Maintain your competitive analysis over time. It should be an ongoing activity that helps you stay abreast of how those companies that rank better than you reach those rankings. Examine them closely, and then spend some time finding creative ways to improve your rankings based on what works for the competition.

Conversion Analysis

If you're driving customers to your site simply to have them visit you, you're wasting your time and effort. Site traffic alone will not build brand recognition today. There must be other elements of supplying your customers or potential customers with what they need. Of course, what you should be supplying them with depends on your line of business, but even accounting for the differing needs of audiences, there's still a way to measure or attach a value to your site visitors.

Your conversions are your ultimate measure of how well your site optimization and design work, and you should constantly be focusing on the conversions that your site drives. Without conversions, you're not making any money. That doesn't mean that conversions all have to be monetarily based, just that they have to fulfill some goal that you have outlined for your web site.

There are two types of conversions: revenue conversions and prerevenue conversions. Revenue conversions are actual sales. A sale is a conversion goal. If you sell anything from your web site, you should have a conversion goal for reaching the end of a sale. That might mean the goal is achieved when a user clicks through to the thank-you page or when the order confirmation is displayed. These conversions require the exchange of money for goods or services.

Another type of conversion is the prerevenue conversion. Prerevenue conversions are all the other steps in the selling cycle — activities that lead up to the final sale. For example, a prerevenue conversion might be something such as having the visitor request additional information about a product or service, or sign up for a newsletter that you are offering. These are valid conversions that should also be tracked.

The types of conversions remain the same across the life cycle of your web site, but the actual conversions may not — and that's the reason you need to conduct regular conversion analysis. In your conversion analysis, you're looking for a number of things, including an increase or decrease in the number or pattern of conversions. Increases and decreases in these trends will help you recognize when something is working or when something needs changing.

When you see a negative trend in your conversion rate, you know it's time to begin trying something different. It may be that your products need to be changed, it may be that your newsletter is no longer appealing, or it could simply be that your competition is funneling your audience away from you.

One way to see these trends in your web analytics is to look at your sales cycle. Ideally, you should know your sales cycle even before you put your web site online. The sales cycle reflects the steps that a user takes to complete a sale. It's usually divided according to the natural progression that visitors make from entering your site to the completed sale.

This natural progression should be trackable with your web metrics program. One report that will be extremely helpful is a *funnel report*, or *sales funnel report*. This type of report enables you to set up a sales funnel on your web site and then track the effectiveness. It also shows where your site visitors might fall off in the process of making a purchase. You can then use that information to change and improve elements of your SEO and your web site that might be causing that fall off.

Conversions are the ultimate goal in all your search marketing efforts. Yes, you want to drive customers to your site, but more than that, you want those customers to *do something*. That something is your conversion — and if you analyze the conversion process, you'll be able to track patterns showing what works and what doesn't.

Analyzing Server Logs

Web server logs are the records that servers keep of who accesses files (in this case, web sites) that are stored on the server. A server log is a long, ugly, and complicated document in which a lot of very usable information is buried, but if you don't know what you're doing, it could take a very long time to figure out what's usable and what's not in that server log.

That's not a huge problem, though. There are all kinds of server log analyzers that you can use to help you decipher the log and find the information that you're looking for. One of the most well-known is AWStats (http://awstats.sourceforge.net/). An example of the Robots/Spider Visitors report is shown in Figure 26-1.

One thing you'll notice about AWStats is that it looks a lot like the web analytics software that you've looked at. That's because it is essentially the same thing. Web analytics software does the same thing that a server log analyzer does. The difference is that server log analyzers sometimes provide more information than basic web analytics applications.

FIGURE 26-1

AWStats reads your server log and provides a graphic representation of the information found there.

Robots/Spiders visitors (Top 10) – Full list – Last visit			
29 different robots*	Hits	Bandwidth	Last visit
MSNBot	4640+865	150.99 MB	21 Aug 2007 - 13:12
Unknown robot (identified by 'bot/' or 'bot-')	2144+4	14.44 MB	06 Aug 2007 - 22:13
Yahoo Slurp	238+122	1.20 MB	21 Aug 2007 - 10:49
Googlebot	172+31	1.51 MB	21 Aug 2007 - 11:55
Speedy Spider	90+25	1.64 MB	20 Aug 2007 - 12:24
MSNBot-media	43+28	867.95 KB	19 Aug 2007 - 18:32
Yahoo! Slurp China	28+28	167.01 KB	20 Aug 2007 - 23:20
Alexa (IA Archiver)	0+51	39.00 KB	18 Aug 2007 - 20:42
Unknown robot (identified by hit on 'robots.txt')	0+31	21.24 KB	21 Aug 2007 - 10:26
Unknown robot (identified by 'crawl')	17+14	621.34 KB	18 Aug 2007 - 01:50
Others	63+97	1.59 MB	

* Robots shown here gave hits or traffic "not viewed" by visitors, so they are not included in other charts. Numbers after + are successful hits on "robots.txt" files.

No matter which solution you choose to use, it's a good idea to use the program to analyze your web site traffic regularly. The reports generated by both types of software will give you insight into what works and what does not work on your web site.

Maintaining the analysis of your site, your competition, traffic, conversions, and server logs is one way you can stay on top of your SEO strategy. What you learn from these metrics is how your SEO and search marketing campaigns are performing, and when you know that you can keep up with any changes that are happening and prepare for future shifts as necessary. In other words, if you're analyzing your successes, you're not left in the dark wondering what happened to your ratings.

Part V

Appendices

Appendix A

Optimization for Major Search Engines

I n general, search engine optimization basics are all the same. Each search engine differs in what it's looking for, however, so what makes you rank well with Google might not make you rank well with Yahoo! or MSN.

This is the conundrum with search engines. Each is based on its own proprietary algorithm, and even if all of the major search engines had the same requirements for ranking (and they don't), those requirements could still be ranked differently.

Therefore, you must first include all the basics of SEO — keyword optimization, meta tag optimization, link optimization, and content optimization. Then, after the basics are complete, you can begin to worry about individual search engines and what it takes to be ranked in each one.

NOTE Remember that a search engine is not your customer. It will lead you to potential customers, so you do need search engine rankings, but you should think first of your own customers and then about your SEO. Be sure your site is what potential or existing customers need, and then you can begin to think about how you can tweak the inner workings of the site to improve your search engine ranking.

IN THIS APPENDIX

Optimization for Google

Optimization for MSN

Optimization for Yahoo!

Optimization for Google

By this point in the book, you should have a pretty good idea of how Google works, including how your sites are indexed and what you should avoid doing. This section provides a bit more detail to help you understand how Google ranks your site. These additional tips will help you to improve your rankings.

The first thing you need to understand about Google is that, given time, if your site is on the Web and has at least one link to it, you will eventually be crawled. For example, I have never done anything with my personal web site in terms of SEO. I haven't checked the code to ensure that it's written with search engines in mind. I haven't used or invested in keywords, and I haven't submitted my site to a search engine. My site is also hopelessly out-of-date right now and the link structure is inactive.

Yet, if you type my name — Jerri L Ledford — into the Google search engine, my personal web site will be on the first page of results returned. I'm ranked high for my name, because (presumably) there is only one of me.

Of course, your site is probably going to be much more diverse than mine, so how do you get Google to take notice? Again, be patient. Google will crawl your site in a short period of time (sometimes it takes less than a week), and once your site has been crawled, you can begin the slow climb through the search results.

On my personal site, it took nearly a year to reach the top-ranking name searching slot for my site, and it's gradually fallen because I haven't had the necessary time to put into maintaining it. I never took specific SEO steps to boost that rank, though. It happened naturally. It's my personal web site, so I don't put a lot of effort into it. In short, it is what it is, without any type of SEO strategy at all.

If your site is topically related to other sites, however, you probably won't be able to throw your site on the Web and wait for it to be indexed at number one; and although you will be indexed automatically, you'll have to compete for top placement.

Google doesn't sell placement, either. There are ads above and to the right side of the search results, but ads are the only placement that's available for purchase. That means that where your site places is based on your SEO and search marketing efforts.

Understanding Google PageRank

Google's proprietary ranking algorithm is what makes it different from the other search engines. An element of that algorithm is Google PageRank.

Google explains PageRank like this:

> *"PageRank relies on the uniquely democratic nature of the Web by using its vast link structure as an indicator of an individual page's value. In essence, Google interprets a link from page A to page B as a vote, by page A, for page B. But, Google looks at considerably more than the sheer volume of votes, or links a page receives; for example, it also analyzes the page that casts the vote. Votes cast by pages that are themselves "important" weigh more heavily and help to make other pages "important." Using these and other factors, Google provides its views on pages' relative importance.*

Of course, important pages mean nothing to you if they don't match your query. So, Google combines PageRank with sophisticated text-matching techniques to find pages that are both important and relevant to your search. Google goes far beyond the number of times a term appears on a page and examines dozens of aspects of the page's content (and the content of the pages linking to it) to determine if it's a good match for your query."

In other words, a PageRank is based on a ballot system that compares your site to all the other pages on the Web that are related. The comparison enables the algorithm to determine which pages are most relevant to a search query based on numerous elements of the page. A hyperlink to a page counts as a vote of support. The PageRank of a page is defined recursively, or in comparison to the other pages that Google is also ranking, and depends on the number and PageRank metric of all pages that link to it. A page that is linked to by many pages with high PageRank receives a high rank itself. If there are no links to a web page, there is no support for that page.

Google assigns a numeric weighting for each web page on the Internet; this PageRank denotes your site's importance according to the PageRank algorithm.

CROSS-REF   For more information on Google's PageRank algorithm, see the sidebar in Chapter 15 titled "Understanding Google's PageRank."

Google Webmaster Tools

If you want to successfully rank on the Google search engine, then you should follow the guidelines that are laid out in Google's Webmaster Central (www.google.com/webmasters/). Also available at Webmaster Central is a set of tools that enables you to analyze and add to your site to help make it more Google-friendly. Those tools include the following:

- **Site Status Wizard:** Use this to determine whether your site is currently being indexed by Google.

- **Webmaster Tools:** This is a set of tools designed to help you improve the indexing and ranking of your site. You can also find the Google Sitemap Generator here.

- **Content Submission Tools:** Use these to submit your site to Google, or to add products to Google Base or content to Google Book Search.

- **Google's Webmaster Blog:** Find tips and strategies for ranking well in Google on this blog. You'll also find changes to the Google algorithm and other information that you'll need to stay on top of your site rankings.

- **Webmaster Discussion Groups:** Talk to others about what they're doing to improve their Google rankings.

- **Webmaster Help Center:** If you don't understand something about Webmaster Central, here's where you'll find an explanation.

Google APIs

One more tool that you might find useful for improving your search engine rankings are the various Google APIs (application programming interfaces) that are available. These programming interfaces enable you to use Google technology to your own benefit.

For example, using the Google Gadgets API, you can create gadgets that are available to iGoogle users. These gadgets (when they're popular) help provide links back to your web site that give you a favorable image in the eyes of the Google crawler — and, of course, because the APIs are provided by Google, there could be some benefits to using them (strictly speaking, however, Google does not take that fact into consideration during the ranking process).

Ideally, use of Google APIs should be limited to creating applications and gadgets that your site visitors find useful. It's when those users' needs are satisfied by your efforts that buzz begins to build and more and more people use the programs you've designed with the API. This in turn improves your search rankings simply on the merits of traffic and usability. That's a great vote for your site and could potentially go equally as far with Google as your other SEO efforts.

Ultimately, if you follow the guidelines laid out earlier in this book and design your pages for people, not search engines, you'll rank well in Google. You may need to tweak some of the inner workings of your site — keywords, links, meta tags — and you'll need to be patient, but given time, your ranking with Google will occur naturally. Then all you have to do is continue improving your offerings for customers and stay on top of maintaining your site, and you should see your ranking climb gradually.

Optimization for MSN

MSN is now powered by Microsoft Live, and although you can go to the MSN.com web page and still access MSN search capabilities, the underlying technology has been rebranded as Microsoft Live. It's still one of the top three search engines, and it's definitely not one that you should ignore. Studies have shown that searchers who enter your site from MSN searches may be fewer in number than those from other search engines, but they routinely have higher conversion rates.

As with other search engines, the basic optimization techniques that you've learned are the best way to get your site listed with MSN search. MSN does not allow paid ranking, so your organic efforts will be the deciding factor for your rankings.

The one difference with MSN is that this search engine puts more emphasis on the freshness of content than other search engines. Specifically, sites that update high-quality, relevant content on a regular basis have a better chance of ranking high with MSN. Therefore, if you have not yet implemented a content strategy and you want to rank well with MSN, you should plan and implement a strategy.

MSN, like Google, indexes pages according to a proprietary algorithm; and like Google, MSN (or more accurately, Microsoft Live) has a set of guidelines that you should follow if you would like your site to rank well. Those guidelines can be found by going to MSN or Microsoft Live and using the search string "Site Owner Help." The guidelines that you're seeking should return as the top search result.

MSN also looks at your meta description tags and the title tags on your pages. So pay close attention to creating the most useful and relevant tags you can. Also include keywords and important information as close to the top of each of your pages as possible.

Over time, it's certain that the MSN brand will be folded into and eventually replaced by Microsoft Live Search. Branding is likely to be the only thing that changes when this happens. MSN had long used Microsoft technology (MSN, after all, *does* stand for Microsoft Network). This means that your SEO efforts will remain viable even as the MSN/Microsoft Live rebranding takes place.

Optimization for Yahoo!

Every search engine differs a little bit from the others, and Yahoo! is no exception. Whereas Google focuses on elements such as relevance of content and links, and MSN focuses on freshness of content and the tags on your site, Yahoo! is more focused on keyword density and keywords in the URL and title tags.

Therefore, if you've used basic SEO techniques, you'll likely be listed with Yahoo! in a matter of time. Your rank on Yahoo! depends on the competition, of course, so you'll need to focus carefully on the keywords that you select if your industry is a highly competitive one. Just be careful, because using a higher density of keywords in order to rank well in Yahoo! could cause you problems with MSN and Google. It could appear to those search engines as though you're stuffing your site with keywords.

The Yahoo! search crawler is called SLURP, and it ranks your page based first on your keyword density. According to Yahoo!, the optimum keyword density breaks down as follows:

- **Title tag:** 15 percent to 20 percent. Yahoo displays the title tag content in its result page. Therefore, write the title as a readable sentence. A catchy title will attract readers to your web site.

- **Body text:** 3 percent. Boldfacing the keywords sometimes boosts the page's ranking, but be careful not to overdo it. Too much boldfaced content irritates readers.

- **Meta tags:** 3 percent. The meta description and keyword tags provide important keywords at the beginning of your web page. However, don't use the keywords repeatedly in the keyword tag, because Yahoo! may consider that practice spam. Write the description tag as a readable sentence.

Yahoo! also looks at the inbound links to your site, and of course there are other factors SLURP considers while it's crawling your site.

Even when you're optimizing for three (or 15) different search engines, a few basic optimization strategies are essential and relevant for all of them. Rather than focus on all the differences and stress yourself out, focus on all the actions that are similar for each search engine, and then consider ways you could change or improve your site so that it will be the most relevant, and the most locatable, for your potential visitors. Put customers and visitors first, and your search engine rankings should follow naturally.

Appendix B

Industry Interviews

The SEO industry, like any other technology arena, is full of people who have differing views on what works and what doesn't. There are always a few things that everyone agrees on, though.

The folks actually working in the field are the ones who know where theory and application diverge to create a workable solution. They can tell you what strategies are sure to be successful and which ones are sure to flop.

If you're working in SEO or search marketing of any form, you probably have questions you'd love to pose to someone who has been working in the industry for a while. The interviews in this section give you that opportunity — with me, Jerri Ledford, acting as your rep.

Here you'll find 16 interviews with people across the SEO industry. These are the people in the trenches, who are faced each day with implementing SEO either for themselves or for other organizations.

They understand your challenges — from budget to manpower — and they've faced the same decisions about SEO that you have. In these interviews, they share their advice with you, and offer their best tips and their opinions about what works, what doesn't, and what's coming.

Eric Bloomfield, Vice President of Client Service & Technology, SendTraffic

Eric Bloomfield has been with SendTraffic for more than three years. During that time, Bloomfield has managed all the technological capabilities surrounding SendTraffic's SEO and SEM offerings.

SendTraffic was founded in 1999. It's an online marketing firm specializing in search engine marketing and optimization, lead generation, and targeted vertical marketing. In addition to SEM and SEO offerings, SendTraffic also provides paid inclusion and feed management, web site analytics, and phone sales analytics.

Jerri: What do you see as the current state of SEO?

Bloomfield: It's always changing, and it requires that you just stay on the top of your game all the time. With the ever-changing algorithms that Google and Yahoo! use, they can change it on a dime. You have to stay on top of it. We hear stories all the time about Google changing their algorithm and then companies lose 80 percent of their business. We try to stay current. You have to stay ahead of the changes, and that's accomplished through best practices.

Jerri: How valuable is vertical SEO?

Bloomfield: I think vertical search is just the way everything needs to go. One of the most effective SEO strategies that you can employ is knowing your vertical and knowing where it's going. For example, we deal with insurance, so I know everything there is to know about insurance. I research the trends and pay attention to the news — but if I knew nothing about these things, then there are SEO strategies that I would do differently. Knowing your vertical very well and knowing what works in the vertical makes it possible for you to do better with your SEO efforts.

It really all starts with the keywords and knowing what keywords work for your industry. Then try to beef up the content and make sure you're included in the right directories in the industry. Then those keywords will pull more weight in a vertical search engine than with other general search engines. Your site is going to get weighted more heavily than if you're in general.

If you're just doing general linking and not doing things within your vertical then you're not doing as well as you could be doing. We also stay on top of it, so we have content that's right for that vertical. And we often make sure that we're pushing the content out to them. But we need to generate it. There are other companies that have the content and just need for us to tell them what to do with it.

Jerri: How is vertical SEO or search marketing different from general SEO?

Bloomfield: I actually haven't dealt with anything that's not vertical SEO. Everyone has to target according to their market. Even in dealing with Yahoo! you're targeting one of the different verticals within Yahoo!. If you're targeting general SEO, you're going to spend a lot of money and you're not going to get much. Almost everything you do is highly targeted and vertical.

I haven't really had a case where someone came to me and said, "I need everything." It's really a case of "Here are my targets, here's what I need, and here's how I'm going to get it."

Jerri: What tips would you give an organization just going into SEO?

Bloomfield: You've got to have control of your web site. One of the big issues is that everyone has good plans but they don't have the ability to carry out those plans. Determine what your approach is. Focus on what you can change and what you can't change.

Know about what pages you're dealing with and what you should change and what you shouldn't. I'll say, "Here are my pages, I'm really concerned with how the search engines see them and how customers see them." Then I just need to have a good strategy for creating and deploying content and then stick with it. I have to have a good plan on how I can continually add these pages and keep my content fresh.

It's so important that you have a plan in place to keep this going because you spend all that money — and if you don't keep up with it you'll have spent that money for nothing.

Jerri: Is there anything else about SEO that you think might be important for my readers to know?

Bloomfield: It's tough. For an SEO it's about staying current, because it's such a changing field. There's always a need to stay on top of search engine trends. It's about staying ahead of that curve and making sure that whatever changes the search engines make, you are able to make changes very quickly, too. It's having the ability to make changes in a continuously changing environment.

Jessica Bowman, SEMPO Board of Directors, In-House SEO Expert

Jessica Bowman is a member of the SEMPO board of directors and does independent consulting. She relishes the human side of SEO, the art of SEO — getting people to do what you need to be done.

Bowman has managed search engine optimization across North America and Europe, in five different languages. Her diverse experience in project management, web site usability, and process analysis has given her unique insight into working with IT to get things accomplished — one of the biggest challenges for in-house search marketers.

Jerri: How does having your search marketing in-house differ from hiring someone to help you with your search marketing strategies?

Bowman: The overarching tactics that need to be executed are the same for both search marketing in-house and outsourced.

The key differences are:

- The innovativeness of your strategy due to differences in experience and knowledge of doing your search marketing. Many in-house search marketers fell into their role and/or are fairly new to the world of search marketing. Their challenge is to compete in the SERPs with competitors who have hired a more experienced search marketing person or agency.

- When bringing search marketing in-house with dedicated resources, you now have someone there 40 hours a week, in the halls and at meetings, who is able to represent and champion search marketing, keep it top-of-mind and high in the priority list. In contrast, when you hire an agency, the selling of search marketing changes is left to someone who has other things on their plate.

Jerri: Is there anything about search marketing that's more difficult when you're doing it in-house?

Bowman: Yes, you're busy in meetings! When you're in-house, there is a lot of networking and schmoozing that has to happen to get and keep search marketing efforts a high priority and not removed from projects. Just because you know what needs to be done to boost your organic rankings does not mean it's easy to implement — there are priorities, politics, and red tape that must be overcome and some people are just resistant to the changes needed for search marketing. It is a challenge to be the person in meetings, networking and schmoozing, and also the person who has to execute the search marketing tactics. It can be done, it is just challenging.

The second thing is that some companies (or even particular individuals/departments within a company) seem to have more trust in what a consultant says versus what an employee says. Any in-house search marketer could give you examples of how they pitched changes again and again and received opposition; however, once a consultant recommended that same change, it suddenly became a wonderful idea that is technically feasible. This is one of the reasons why I recommend that in-house search marketers have an SEO consultant available for outside counsel.

Lastly, when your rankings drop, or traffic decreases, you don't typically have other sites that you can compare with to see if they saw something similar; whereas when you work with an agency, they work with many clients and can compare you with a number of sites to see if there was a big change in the formula that affected many companies, or it is something that specifically affected you.

Jerri: Do you ever work with outsourcers on parts of your search marketing?

Bowman: Yes. I love to outsource portions of a project. I have a short list of preferred vendors for keyword research, directory submissions, troubleshooting, copywriting, site audits, question and answer, code reviews, and there is even one someone I use to keep me up to speed on industry news when I get extra busy.

Jerri: What suggestions would you make for organizations that are considering bringing their search marketing in-house?

Bowman:

- Know what you're getting into. There are many ways to bring search marketing in-house and structure the team, tactics, etc. Search marketing in-house will not likely reach its fullest potential if your in-house search marketer is also allocated on other things. You typically spend about 80 percent of your time selling SEO and 20 percent actually doing SEO work. Also, bear in mind that while the agency you hired only worked 20 hours per week, outside of your billable hours the consultants kept up with trends and news outside of that 20 hours. And they live and breathe search marketing all day, making them far more productive than a typically isolated in-house search marketer. Also, your outside consultant wasn't responsible for getting the changes through the IT department.

- Budget for outside counsel, a more experienced consultant to reach out to when you have questions.

- Make it a priority to attend search marketing conferences, at least two conferences per year. When you're in-house, you tend to lose perspective and put on your "corporate-tinted glasses." Conferences bring you back to the search marketing reality and keep you grounded.

Jerri: Is there anything particular that an organization should avoid if it's managing its search marketing in-house?

Bowman: Don't work in isolation. It's very easy to get so caught up in busywork that you lose touch with changes in the industry. At one time cloaking was accepted; now it can get you banned. Just last year buying links worked; now Google penalizes when they know a site is buying links, and they have asked people to report it.

Don't get so busy that you don't have time to stay abreast of the industry happenings and continuously expand your knowledge. I now have the expectation that I will spend two hours a day reading about the industry — while no one else on my in-house team spends this much time, your most senior search marketer should.

Jerri: What changes do you see coming that will affect the way organizations use search marketing in the future?

Bowman:

- *Brand protection and management* — Search engines are where people go for information about a company, product, service, or an answer to their question. They use search engines like a question-and-answer machine. Search engines display a wide variety of sources of information for users, some of it favorable, and some of it unfavorable. In coming years, companies (e.g., PR departments) will finally catch on that there are things you can do to influence the search results, just as there are things you can do to influence the media in the offline world. You just go about it in a completely different manner, but the goal and results are similar.

- *Videos* — Google now displays highly relevant videos in their regular search results. This means that companies have the opportunity to have a video in front of Google users, displayed as an image — a rare and highly valuable commodity in the Google SERPs. It's an eye-grabber and will give your company far more visibility than any other company on the search results page — even if you aren't listed in position one. We are already starting to see search marketers dabble in videos more than ever before. In the next few years companies will get more involved, offering useful interviews, how-tos, and entertaining videos for their target audiences. The risk for the late adopters is that by the time they join the online video market, online videos will be quite mature and there will be little room for error without receiving public criticism. The benefit of being an early adopter is that everyone is still trying to figure out what is successful; therefore, errors are more acceptable.

Jerri: What kind of changes will these trends require for in-house search marketing?

Bowman: They need to adopt and get involved in new media — social media and online videos for sites like YouTube.com.

It's funny, back in the early days of SEO, large companies weren't on the bandwagon and small businesses could easily overtake larger businesses in the search results. Now larger companies have caught on, and it's now more difficult for the smaller businesses to outrank larger businesses for many search terms. Social media today is like SEO in the early days — large companies aren't on the bandwagon. There are far more risks and challenges that prevent big companies from going in this direction. For large companies, doing nothing seems like less of a risk than diving in and risking a backfire or no ROI. What they don't realize is now is the time to backfire. It's going to be more acceptable to mess up now than it will be in five years, when they're ready to start getting involved.

Jerri: Is there anything else you think might be important for organizations to understand about in-house search marketing?

Bowman:

- My biggest advice is the same for any company. Search marketing is not a project. It is like marketing and public relations — it never ends. Once you get high rankings you need to maintain your high rankings. And in order to continue growing your search marketing traffic you need to go after new opportunities (new niche phrases, video optimization, local search, brand protection, etc.).

- Know the in-house life cycle.

- Understand that just because you build the team, it does not mean high rankings and traffic increases will come. Your in-house search marketer needs to work with many people and several departments to get search marketing changes out the door and they are competing with many other high-profile projects for resources and priority. If the changes don't launch, you are not going to meet your goals. I find that management is on-board with SEO; it is the lower-level managers and technical leads that have opposition and cause delays in launching changes.

- Just because you bring search marketing in-house, it does *not* mean your outsourcing days are over. Search marketing in-house is like an on-staff corporate attorney — there are times when you will need to reach to outside counsel for sound advice.

FIGURE B-1

The in-house SEO life cycle as defined by Jessica Bowman.

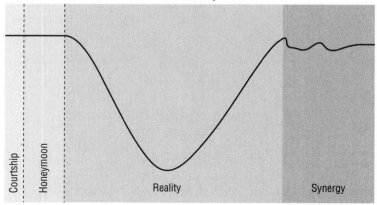

In-house SEO Life Cycle

Courtship
Honeymoon
Reality
Synergy

Source: SEMinhouse.com

Brian Combs, Founder and Senior VP, Apogee Search

As an online marketing expert and Internet pioneer, Brian Combs specializes in bringing measurability to marketing. Before founding Apogee Search with William Leake in 2002, Combs was director of marketing and business development for Journyx, the leading provider of web-based time- and expense-management solutions. At Journyx he oversaw all marketing and strategic partnership activities.

Since 2004, Apogee has grown to become one of the 20 largest SEO/PPC firms in the country, with clients in the hundreds. The company has achieved top Google rankings for clients on horrendously competitive keywords with high search volumes in areas such as consumer and auto finance, home security, consumer-packaged software, online education, and insurance-type products.

Jerri: Where do you see the current state/importance of SEO?

Combs: The industry is still in the "Wild West" stage, but beginning to mature. As the ROI of SEO is difficult to track (although not impossible), many SEO firms (and individual SEOs) are able to get away with providing the appearance of value, while providing very little actual value.

SEO, of course, can be a very effective marketing technique, but like all marketing, efforts must be made to track the results so that improvements can be made.

Jerri: What can organizations do right now to improve their SEO?

Combs:

- Install a tracking system. Find out what actually works.
- Run a PPC campaign for 30 days to prove which keywords matter. Optimizing for keywords with no search volume will not provide any benefit.
- Put those keywords as the *first* thing in their title tags.
- Start link building.

Jerri: What should they be focusing on for future improvements?

Combs:

- Better content.
- Create compelling link bait.
- Continue link building.
- Invest more in a keyword selection testing campaign (PPC).

- If you're trying to master hundreds to thousands of keywords, work with the content management system to programmatically automate much of the content-driven SEO (for example, dynamically populating title tags with database-provided keywords).
- Stay on top of, and take advantage of, emerging trends in social media.

Jerri: Are there any strategies that organizations might know about but are not implementing that might help with SEO results if they did?

Combs: So many organizations believe that the content part of SEO means generating page after page of keyword-stuffed copy. People should focus on creating copy for a web site's visitors, not the search engines. Use one's keywords in the copy, but use them naturally.

Concentrate on regularly creating new, quality content for your web site. This will help both with SEO, and with building the traffic of your site.

Jerri: What is one facet of SEO that most small and mid-size business don't do well, and how can they improve that?

Combs: There are two facets:

- How they choose keywords. (Don't do it on visibility metrics, don't do it based on industry-speak.)
- Lack of link building. (SMBs typically have even less in the way of trust rank or link infrastructure with which to work than the big dogs; therefore, link building is even more important to them.)

Jerri: What changes in SEO are coming as the result of the growth of social media?

Combs: Social media provide a tremendous extension of the ability to create and rapidly promote link bait, including new sources of links. These new link sources can also be great sources of native traffic and potentially cause huge changes in the *way we search*, and thus a potential threat to the Google hegemony.

Jerri: Are there any other coming changes that will affect SEO?

Combs:

- Mobile and local advertising.
- Video content.
- Google's never-ending thirst for new revenues, and dislike of the SEO industry (a change agent).

Jerri: Is there anything I haven't touched on that might be important for small to mid-size organizations to know about SEO?

Combs: Most "SEO experts" are no more SEO experts than the organization they work for. Much can be self-achieved with proper research. This industry is enough of a snake pit of vipers that it really does pay to do a bunch of research yourself (and even potentially some of the work yourself) before you buy from a vendor. Bad SEO can really, really hurt you, and cause you to lose multiple years of marketplace momentum.

Lastly, make sure you focus on the real results. Rankings alone don't pay the bills. In most cases, neither does web traffic. Track and analyze the results of your SEO efforts, making sure that you are increasing leads and/or sales.

Rhea Drysdale, SEO and Social Media Coordinator, We Build Pages

Rhea Drysdale is the SEO and Social Media Coordinator at We Build Pages. She's also an associate editor for Loren Baker's *Search Engine Journal*, and the co-founder of a local SEM association.

We Build Pages is an Internet marketing service based out of Troy, NY. At We Build Pages, Rhea manages client relationships and contributes to organic search and social media strategies.

Jerri: What do you see as the current state of SEO?

Drysdale: I think that SEO is experiencing a major evolution with the recent universal search update on Google and new Ask.com user interface changes. However, it's still in its infancy compared to other forms of marketing. With that in mind, I think marketers are still trying to figure out what they can do with it. And, unfortunately, the "rules" for SEO change on a daily basis, which makes it difficult to keep up with those changes and provide formal education in a classroom setting.

As search engines evolve, I'm really interested in seeing how search behavior changes accordingly. I think users are going to get smarter about how they search, which will challenge marketers to be more savvy in the methods they use to reach those users.

Jerri: What are companies doing well in SEO?

Drysdale: At this moment, I think the experienced companies are doing an excellent job of tracking results and justifying the SEO return, something that hasn't been easy in the past. As an in-house SEO, my biggest challenge is educating companies on an invisible marketing technique. Even if the return is less, most companies would prefer to spend their ad budgets on a banner ad than SEO. There's something sticky about visuals, whereas SEO feels a bit like smoke and mirrors to those that aren't intimately familiar with it. So companies that are able to translate results and track return are rising to the top, while the more money-hungry spammers are crumbling. This is great for both the SEO reputation and companies seeking quality campaigns.

Jerri: What are some of your challenges and successes in SEO?

Drysdale: With my background in e-commerce, the biggest personal challenge has been tracking leads, which requires human interaction to document return. Previously, I could tie my efforts to specific dollars, but now the source is much more difficult to discern.

A lot of companies like the concept of SEO, but they don't have the infrastructure to support it and it fizzles out over time. You have to have a unique approach with every company or client to see phenomenal success. Some will do better with a certain strategy than others, since certain target markets just aren't going to be receptive to different techniques. It's a matter of understanding your customers — how they search and how they think, what words do they use when they search. What phase of the buying or information-gathering cycle are they in when they get to your site? Once you understand the customer, it's much easier to reach them.

Jerri: What kind of changes do you think social media are going to have on SEO?

Drysdale: With recent updates on Google and Ask, I think it's more apparent than ever before that certain industries need to make a concerted effort to be everywhere! This means developing videos, blogs, generating news articles, and having a presence on social networks. When we talk about social media, most people think about MySpace and Facebook, but there are hundreds of specific niche networks that are worth marketers' attention. For example, Café Mom and Stylehive are terrific networks for the beauty and fashion industry. Would you rather spend thousands on poorly targeted MySpace ads or hundreds on a highly targeted presence that will generate much greater conversions?

If marketers can start a conversation on those networks, beyond ads, the return is even greater. They will naturally build a following, which will in turn produce qualified backlinks and content. The SEO implications are huge if social media campaigns can be successfully implemented and maintained.

Jerri: How important will vertical markets be in the future?

Drysdale: I don't see them going anywhere, if that's what you mean. Verticals offer a more targeted method of finding information. So I think people will use them and they will continue to grow. I know that Google is trying to organize all of the world's information, but ultimately, if users can narrow their search right from the start, they will, and verticals make that possible.

A quick side note: Google's reliance on backlinks for rankings limits them when it comes to highly relevant, recent web content. The universal search update should allow for postings of recent news and blog articles, but if I'm looking for something specific that's just a few weeks old, more often than not I have to resort to creative search behavior or verticals to find the information. So, until Google or the other engines can account for new content, I see verticals maintaining or increasing in popularity.

Jerri: What other trends do you think will affect SEO over the next 18 to 24 months?

Drysdale: I'm a little concerned about personalized search but not immensely so. I think it's still in its infancy and the search engines are dabbling in it to see what they can do. It's a little disconcerting as a marketer, because I can't tell how the search results differ for a user in Montpelier, Vermont, versus San Jose, California, or even in my own city if they have radically different search behavior from other users. From an SEO standpoint, you can't tell where traffic comes from and how it reaches you, which makes it difficult to track changes. I'm all about the numbers, and if I can't see the numbers I feel like I'm flying blind, which is never a good thing.

As for universal search and the compartmentalized UI at Ask.com, I'm very interested in how this will affect search behavior and interaction with the results pages. I was really amazed by a recent eye-tracking study from Gord Hotchkiss of Enquiro who found that the "golden triangle" is broken as images are introduced. This sounds somewhat obvious, but the implications on paid search and emphasis of top position natural rankings might be less intense as marketers discover where users are clicking.

I'm also interested in seeing the evolution of link bait and bloggers. I think the time and knowledge involved in implementing a high-quality viral marketing campaign will leave many marketers scratching their heads. As for bloggers, their credibility is often called into question, but more important, the amount of noise on the Web is unbearable. I'm hoping that over time we see a decline in the number of bloggers and an increase in their quality.

With both bloggers and viral marketing, I think that companies that embrace these campaigns early on will do much better in the long run than those that wait for a proven return and "safe" approach.

Paul Dyer, Director of New and Interactive Media, CarryOn Communications

Paul Dyer is an expert in SEO and other advanced Web technologies. As director of new and interactive media at CarryOn, Dyer brings a breadth of technical knowledge and field experience in social media, search engine optimization, web design, and Web 2.0 product development. He is a frequent speaker on SEO and public relations for social media, having presented at *Bulldog Reporter*'s PR University, the Los Angeles chapter of PRSA, a national PRSA teleseminar, the University of Southern California Annenberg School for Communication, the PR Online Convergence Conference, and as part of a professional development series for several top-100 PR firms.

CarryOn is a leading national mid-size consumer brand public relations and brand communication agency with offices in Los Angeles, New York, and Chicago. The agency's specialty is offering fresh perspective and tailored solutions that accommodate the unique needs of significant consumer brands.

Jerri: How are social media changing the way organizations reach their customers on the Web?

Dyer: In the Web 1.0 world, organizations built a web page that had information about themselves, their purpose, their product, or whatever information they wanted to convey to their customers. For the savvier organizations, there was a halfway point between Web 1.0 and Web 2.0 in which search engine optimization of the organization's main web page took priority for reaching their customers online. Now in Web 2.0, with social media, organizations have a plethora of online forums where they can reach their customers. Places like YouTube, MySpace, Flickr, Digg, and Facebook are carrying the flag for social media, but niche communities and social sites are popping up almost daily. These sites are dramatically changing online communications from being primarily "pull" communications (trying to pull your customers through the search engines) to a push/pull combination that previously never existed. Organizations can now push their message through these communities, as well as pull their customers who are conducting keyword and tag-based searches. In the search engines, organizations are also finding that these social media sites do half the SEO work for them. Sites like YouTube and MySpace have such high volume of traffic and backward links, they can achieve strong search rankings — normally much stronger than small or startup companies with little resources. All companies have to do is target their content in these communities for the keywords they want a search engine presence for.

Jerri: How will that shift in communication affect SEO?

Dyer: Traditional SEO focuses on driving search engine traffic to a corporate page. With social media, SEO can apply to any number of other sites, but the purpose is to build not just a web site, but a web *presence*. This is accomplished by syndicating content in a plethora of web destinations — blogs, social networks, social bookmarks, image and video galleries, and more. By syndicating keyword-rich content in these destinations, organizations can cast a much wider net with their message and maybe even spark that ever-elusive dialogue with their key audiences.

Jerri: What aspects of SEO should small and medium-size businesses focus on most closely at this time?

Dyer: First things first. Small companies need to be strategic about the keywords they go after. With SEO and online advertising budgets creeping ever higher, few small companies have the resources to compete for keywords that have monthly search volume in the millions. Instead, small companies should focus their efforts on a few highly specific search terms for which users will definitely be interested in their company's content. At that point, organic SEO for these key terms becomes critical, and SEO releases are a great first line of attack. SEO releases have been available for several years now, but still remain one of the strongest ways for small companies to receive valuable and highly ranked links from pages on which they control the content.

Jerri: What upcoming SEO technologies and strategies should these organizations begin to focus on?

Dyer: There are a number of up-and-coming technologies, but I will focus specifically on SEO releases, as that is where my real expertise lies. A properly conceived SEO release can be a powerful tool for driving traffic to your site and increasing your site's search ranking. The best strategy is to craft a release for every key term that is central to your business. This release should be written specifically for that key term and include it in positions of prominence like the headline, meta tags, and first paragraph. It should also use the term in a high keyword density — 2 percent or higher. This term can then be hyperlinked to a key-term-specific landing page on the company's web site — for instance, linking Product A as a key term to the landing page for Product A. Doing this alone will increase the backward links and the keyword relevance of your site for this term.

To take the campaign to the next level, companies can then distribute a second release that is targeted for the very same key term. For this release, in addition to linking the term to a specific landing page, it can also be linked to the original press release at the distributor's web site (on Marketwire.com, for instance). Doing so will drive the original press release up the search rankings for that term as well as your company site and enable you to hold down more than one position in the search engines.

Jerri: What's the most frequently missed aspect of SEO for social media?

Dyer: The most frequently missed aspect is strategy. Many companies are dipping their toe into the social-media pool, but few are doing so strategically. Instead, companies are doing what I like to call "throwing Hail Marys." They are posting videos into YouTube, building MySpace pages, uploading image galleries to Flickr, and getting involved in the blogosphere, but they are doing so blindly and without any continuity. Success in social media and the way to achieve strong search results comes through regularly updating content and creating a web of information. If you have keyword-rich content in social sites, you will achieve strong search results by networking (linking) that content together. There has to be a strategic and continuous connection between all of your company's social efforts.

Jerri: What's the most important aspect of SEO for social media?

Dyer: The most important aspect of SEO for social media is syndication. This means making sure all of the regularly updated content on your corporate site, as well as the social sites you participate in, is available via RSS and linked together to form an online network that encompasses your organization's total web presence. Not only will this build readership and relationships in these communities, the RSS feeds will have a positive impact on the search rankings of all your various locations with content.

Jerri: Do you have any specific message for readers about social media and how they will affect SEO now and in the future?

Dyer: The most important thing for people to realize is that social media represent a fundamental shift in the way people meet, communicate, and interact. It is not a passing trend or a "here today, gone tomorrow" fad. Like e-mail and the mobile phone before it, social media is a new conduit through which people communicate.

Miki Dzugan, President, Rapport Online, Inc.

Miki Dzugan believes that online marketing efforts should produce positive bottom-line results. That comes from many years of general management experience. Dzugan brings more than 30 years of experience in the fields of manufacturing, software development, computer hardware marketing and sales, computer software consulting, property management, education, and hospitality management into her position as president at Rapport. Her varied background enables her to quickly grasp the management goals of companies, and then define ways for them to integrate the use of the Internet into their marketing communications functions.

Rapport Online, Inc., was founded as an outgrowth of many years of Internet marketing and web site development experience. Building rapport aptly describes the power that Internet communications tools bring to doing business.

Rapport encompasses branding and believes that branding online is not achieved through advertising, but rather through experience and buzz. Rapport stresses direct communication and harmony in its environment, and strives to provide these to its customers.

Jerri: What do you see as the current state of SEO?

Dzugan: For many SEO experts, the SEO/search engine relationship is a game of chess, us versus them. They try to game the search engine to get their client to the top of the heap by taking advantage of what they can understand of the search engine algorithms. This may be done without respect to whether the site really belongs at the top of results. In other words, the search engine has the objective to produce the most useful result for the searcher and the SEO is working to push his or her client in the searcher's face.

SEOs that work against the best interest of the search engine are killing the golden goose. If the search engine does not produce good results, it will not be used.

Working with the best interest of search engines and searchers as well as our clients produces lasting results. Sites that are optimized to rank high in results where they provide the best value are not as vulnerable to changes in search algorithms. Clients that were optimized years ago still retain a high position in results even for quite competitive search terms.

You will find SEO divided into black hat and white hat, with a big gray area that the experts debate. My thought is that if you are helping search engines to serve the searchers well, you are behaving ethically and effectively in the long term.

Jerri: What do you mean by helping the search engine serve searchers well? Are there specific activities that organizations should be doing?

Dzugan: The worst case of *not* serving the searchers well is to optimize a porn site to come up on top for a search for "candy land" for example. This kind of abuse is really hard to get past search engines now. It is easier to identify activities that organizations should not be doing — there is a whole list of spamming activities that can still sometimes succeed, temporarily. Organizations should stake out their keywords carefully and aim for those that are realistically achievable. For example, a web site selling shoes has a better chance of achieving top results on a phrase, such as "women's narrow shoes" or "child sport shoes" than if they go after "shoe" and "shoes."

As part of this method of SEO, I stumbled upon the concept of branding through search results. I'm beginning to hear more of this idea in industry discussions. I think this will be the next big thing in SEO.

Jerri: Explain how branding through search results works.

Dzugan: We use the kind of narrowing of keywords described above to reinforce our client's brand. For example, my own company, Rapport Online, is very small, and how do you compete on keywords like "search engine optimization" without a staff member to work on that full time? We are staking out the concept of building rapport as the online marketing approach. Our site ranks on the first page of Google results for "keyword ad calculator" and other more specific phrases that relate to a cost-per-customer-acquired approach to online marketing.

Jerri: What strategies should companies be using to create their brand in search results?

Dzugan:

- Stake out the desired keywords.
- Use pay-per-click advertising to get your sales pitch across.
- Optimize top-level pages for the desired brand keywords.
- Get linked in to the most popular and industry-related directories, using the brand concepts in the description.

Jerri: And are there some branding opportunities that are better than others?

Dzugan: Certainly, less competitive brand concepts and more differentiating concepts are better. Our client Powder Technology, Inc., produces test dust for testing of engines, filters, etc. We have staked out the keyword "test dust" (not as easy as it sounds) and if you search on that keyword in Google you see that they pretty much own the top of the first page of results.

Niche brand concepts are easier opportunities than more general concepts, such as "best shoes" but, if you can pull it off, the more general concept will get much more traffic because more people will be using it in search. Just remember that if you are promoting your product as the "best" and it is inferior, you undermine consumer confidence in your company and the search engine that was used.

Jerri: What are the coming trends that you see affecting search engines over the next few months?

Dzugan: Ask Google. People have been waiting for mobile search to take off and maybe that will finally happen. It is hard with the small screen to effectively browse the Net — it's a whole different animal.

Google is working on personalized search, but I'm not keen on that concept because I don't really think the desired search result can be effectively predicted on past searches — not if you use search for a variety of reasons.

Jerri: Is there anything else you think is important for readers to understand about SEO?

Dzugan: SEO is still a "buyer beware" industry. When considering SEO assistance, don't fall for the slick presentation or guarantee. Get references. And never buy from a company that approaches you through unsolicited e-mail.

Rand Fishkin, CEO and Co-Founder, SEOmoz

Rand Fishkin has been involved with Internet technologies for almost 15 years. He began working with a company called Marketlink International and eventually moved to a web-development startup firm with Gillian (who happens to be his mother). Since coming together, Gillian and Rand have changed the model of their business to arrive at the current iteration of SEOmoz.

SEOmoz provides companies around the world with consulting, Internet marketing, and search engine optimization services. Some of its clients include AllBusiness, Benchmark Capital, Drivl, National Public Radio, and Shoe-Store.net. Rand and SEOmoz are well-respected names in the SEO industry. You may have seen Rand at an SEO conference if you've attended one in the last few years. Even if you didn't know his face, you should be able to pick him out. He's the one wearing yellow Pumas.

Jerri: What do you see as the state of the SEO industry today?

Fishkin: That pretty broad. From a growth standpoint, I think the industry is positive. It continues to grow at a steady pace.

From a maturity standing, I think we still have a long way to go. There's been a lot of bad press, bad companies, and snake-oil salesmen that need to be dealt with. And a lot of companies get caught up in bad contracts. The industry is still very young, and we have a long way to go before it becomes mature.

Jerri: What's the difference between SEO and search marketing?

Fishkin: Technically speaking, SEO always leans toward the organic side of search marketing — it doesn't include paid services. Search marketing as a whole is anything that you do to market your web sites through search.

Jerri: So how is social media marketing different from SEO?

Fishkin: Social media marketing refers to a couple of big techniques. The first is viral-content creation and promotion. There has always been some form of viral content, but the appearance of portals like NetScape, Spin, and others has enabled social media to spread like never before.

An example of how this has changed would be the linking structure of a blog. A blog post goes out, people link to it, those links are spread, and before you know, the post is linking to thousands of other web sites. It's one of the ways that you can grow a link structure very quickly.

The second side of social media marketing is social network marketing and reputation management. There are more ways available now for companies to grow their reputation. You need to have a presence on sites like Facebook, LinkedIn, and MySpace. It's brand marketing — you can build and share your brand over the Web.

415

Jerri: How can organizations use social media to improve their business?

Fishkin: First, you have to have a great deal of familiarity with the space. You have to have a deep understanding of the community and you have to become part of the community — sharing content, creating content, tagging content, and interacting with other people in the community. If you aren't familiar with this space or you don't participate in the space, you won't be successful.

How much time is spent participating in this space depends on your specific needs as an organization. Some organizations only need to devote a few hours a week. Three or four, because social media isn't that important to their organization. There are companies, though, like AllBusiness, where social marketing is more important and it's nothing for them to spend 80 hours a week participating in social marketing. It's all determined by your business and what your business needs are.

Jerri: What do you see as trends in the SEO space?

Fishkin: It would be foolish to ignore what Google calls "universal search" and we call "vertical search." It's in vertical search that companies find highly qualified traffic, and there's going to be a significant amount of traffic in these areas. Vertical search can include:

- Local search
- Product search
- Instant answers (like Ask.com), which is a rapidly growing area of search
- Image search
- News search
- Travel search

And there are many more. All of those are vertical that can lead you closer to the customer that you want to reach.

Jerri: What are your thoughts on what's being called "human-powered search"?

Fishkin: Basically, I think it's a joke — less than useless. A waste of time. It doesn't scale, results are of considerably worse quality than an algorithmic search, and there is very little hope that it would take off in the next few years. I could be wrong, too, but in my opinion it will never achieve results that have the quality which engineers can put into algorithmic results.

Jerri: Where do you see that organizations are performing poorly in search marketing?

Fishkin: That's really a story of two different worlds. Less than 10 percent of small and medium-size businesses in the U.S., and less around the world, have paid any attention to search marketing and are deriving any value from it at all. And they don't really care. Many small and micro business owners don't know how the Internet can impact their business, and they don't care.

But then there are a very small number of tiny Web-based businesses that have come to it over time that have seen phenomenal results. Etsy.com is an example. But mostly smaller businesses have no interest in search marketing.

It's in the larger companies where we generally tend to see great hunger for knowledge from users. And even then, a great number of larger businesses have still not begun to focus on search marketing. These companies usually do one thing, like pay-per-click marketing, and nothing else.

Jerri: Is there anything else about search marketing that you think might be important to mention?

Fishkin: There are thousands of topics we haven't touched on, and there are lots of tips that I could give you. But if I had to choose one, I would say that companies should look at widget strategies, and try to design and deploy a high-demand widget that can be plugged into a blog or browser. When done successfully, widgets are really great. You can get phenomenal amounts from traffic and links to your site when you have a good, high-demand widget.

We're also fond of link-baiting strategies and content strategies as a means of providing relevant information to site visitors.

Duane Forrester, Founding Co-Chair for the In-house SEM Committee with SEMPO

Duane Forrester is an in-house search marketer for a sports media company in Canada. He's also a private search marketing consultant; and for SEMPO (Search Engine Marketing Professional Organization), a professional organization for search marketers, he is a co-chair for the In-house SEM Committee and a board member.

SEMPO is a global non-profit organization serving the search engine marketing industry and the marketing professionals engaged in it. Its purpose is to provide a foundation for industry growth through building stronger relationships, fostering awareness, providing education, promoting the industry, generating research, and creating a better understanding of search and its role in marketing.

Jerri: Does being an in-house search marketer change the way that you approach SEO and search marketing?

Forrester: Being in-house doesn't change it, my perspective does. And my perspective is that I treat my company as if they are my client and I am their consultant. I am a consultant, but when I start getting into the nuts and bolts of search marketing, it's no different than if I were at an agency. I would approach search marketing the same way, I just wouldn't know the client as well as I know the client that I'm an in-house marketer for.

There are some differences worth noting between smaller and larger companies, however. Smaller businesses usually have fewer stakeholders in a given project, making it much easier to be heard at the table and ensure the right bits get "baked into" the search optimization pie from the very beginning.

Because our organization isn't large, I can sit down with a product manager and say, "Here's what I need and here's why I need it." They can then build the product around those needs, making the entire process more efficient.

So one benefit is that it's much easier, since I'm in-house, to get exactly what we need integrated very early in the development cycle.

Jerri: What would you consider the state of search marketing today?

Forrester: There's a lot of offshore growth in search marketing and a proliferation of search engine software. Lots of seemingly knowledgeable search marketing experts take a software application and spin it to make it appear to meet more needs than it does. It's a very lucrative business.

But if I were going to hire a search marketing company and planned to spend $7,500 to $10,000 a month for that service, I would expect the effort to be based around knowledge, not just a software tool. There should be some level of personal experience and interaction as well.

It is so expensive to hire a search marketing company now that I would shy away from any consultant or business that relies on a software program to guide them. For the same budget, there are some great search marketers who have a lot of experience — experience makes the difference, not software.

Many search marketing consultants are expensive and they rely on diagnostic software to do the job that should really be done by an experienced person. Using the software, they will do a basic examination of the site and give you a report on their findings.

Then, based on their understanding of your site, your needs, and where you are currently, they will provide a series of recommendations that may or may not be accurate. The state of search marketing when the software was built and the state of search marketing when the software is used often changes — subtly and dramatically. There can be a large discrepancy there.

So what happens is companies hire these search marketing organizations and it's just money out the door. The money is spent and the company finds that they get little or no value from the investment — no usable return. So they're out the money and they still don't have the help that they need.

Relatively few people have a large amount of experience in search marketing. For the handful that do have considerable experience (more than three or four years, which is often the minimum requirement when an organization is hiring a search marketing consultant), trying to recover from the damage done by these services becomes an image protection mechanism.

I want the industry to look good. If it doesn't, I suffer because my potential customers still remember when they got burned. I have to come up against the bad stuff and try to overcome it. This is part of the reason why I take on so few clients.

So I would say that when you're looking at search marketing capabilities, you need to know what questions to ask. If you don't know what questions to ask you're going to find yourself in the position of spending money and never receiving results. You're going to get a lot of pitches from people who don't know what they're doing. Asking the right questions will help you know if they're experienced or just someone who thinks they can handle search marketing because they bought some software.

Jerri: What should organizations be focusing on to improve search marketing?

Forrester: Training is one area that is still being developed in this industry. I'm a bit biased, but I think the SEMPO curriculum is one of the best available today. It's not an endorsement of a person's capabilities. When they finish a course, they receive only a certificate of completion. Other programs offer a "certification," which can lead potential clients to feel the person is not only knowledgeable, but ethical, too. But no program could ever hope to certify an individual's ethics. It comes down to perception and presentation. If someone says they are "certified" and you don't understand exactly what that certification entails, it's easy to assign more credit to an individual than they deserve.

There are other training options besides SEMPO. I tend to gravitate toward the broader theory-based components of education as opposed to the "here's a tool and here's how to use it" method. But some people work better with theory and others work better with tools. Personally, I don't use tools in search marketing, or I use them as little as possible, and if I do have to use a tool, I only use it for specific tasks. Keyword research and link management are two areas that come to mind. I use specific tools to help me manage workloads in those areas, but I'd never put my trust in software that claims to "optimize my site" for me — software like that is only as good as the programmer who built it, and only as current as the last update. Miss an update and you may be in dangerous territory.

The search marketing industry is still very young. There are not a lot of experienced SEMs with seven-plus years of experience, and those who do have it are expensive to employ or contract with — though their experience leads them to be able to perform, so many are easily worth it.

Those seeking to build in-house teams of SEMs in their own businesses tend to seek a lower number of years of experience. Typically, in other industries, to reach the management level or the director's level and above, five to seven-plus years of experience are required. I see lots of search marketing management jobs posted each week where management-level positions are seeking only two to three years of experience.

Most smaller companies cannot afford to hire a six-figure SEM to get the best. They need to strike a balance, so less experience is often acceptable. This is not a reflection on a company's level of professionalism, but rather a statement of the relative youth of our industry. There just aren't that many deeply experienced SEMs floating around — and those there are command higher salaries. The critical point for companies to remember is this: While learning the basics of search marketing can be compressed into a short period of time, and a person can be theoretically competent, it's often the better network that the more experienced person has that makes a difference.

Jerri: How are organizations budgeting for search marketing?

Forrester: The budget for search marketing has continued to grow over the last two or three years, but no additional funds have been added to cover that budget. Instead, companies take that budget from other areas like e-mail marketing and pay-per-click advertising. Organizations are already worried about marketing strategies like PPC because of click fraud. That's a serious concern, because it's very real and hard to control.

So what we see is organic SEM budgets that are growing at the expense of other areas of marketing. Many companies feel organic search offers the best ROI — it's a long-term investment that can be comparatively low-cost. Large PPC campaigns can easily run into the millions of dollars each year. By comparison to a PPC campaign that requires a constant influx of money to perform, organic search marketing needs are often met after a number of months of work, effectively moving a web site to a new baseline level of inbound traffic. This type of effort will continue to perform long after the last bill to an effective SEM consultant is paid.

Jerri: If organizations are taking away from their e-mail and PPC marketing budgets, then what are they doing to ensure that potential customers are seeing them?

Forrester: There are two models for the marketing that companies are doing: organic and paid. In paid, money is being shuffled around so that organizations are bringing their search marketing in-house or they are hiring third-party vendors to manage their search marketing efforts.

On average, the overall marketing budgets are not growing. Companies are looking for what are profit centers, so they need to allocate existing budgets differently. The money has to come from somewhere, and it usually comes from other marketing efforts.

For example, if a company's marketing budget for PPC has been $100,000 a year in the past, and they begin to use a consultant or vendor that requires $10,000 a month for six months, that leaves just $40,000 a year for PPC marketing. And that's one area where budgets are being shuffled. Companies understand that an agency will likely help them get better converting traffic for their investment, either by providing better converting traffic or by reducing the cost of existing search marketing campaigns. And most search marketing agencies are very good at what they do. Many larger agencies do not practice "churn and burn" tactics. They know if they perform for a client, the client will come back. Short-changing a client for the sake of immediate profits is always a poor business model, yet is sadly still popular with many of today's "instant experts" who use software to manage everything and claim to understand what they're doing.

We are also slowly beginning to see some of the older, larger advertising agencies toying with the idea of doing search marketing now. As traditional advertising spending has dropped consistently, these larger organizations are beginning to realize that their customers want more options for marketing, and the online channel brings good results for less investment. So the larger agencies have begun to realize that they could be holding onto a portion of their clients' spending if they are offering the search marketing capabilities that those clients want. But these older companies are kind of behind the eight ball now, because search marketing companies have already been established and they're good at what they do, so these more traditional agencies will have a hard time breaking into this space.

Jerri: What tips would you give an organization looking to hire a search marketing consultant or firm?

Forrester: First, get a list of past clients, and not just anyone in the organization. Request the contact name and number for the person who was responsible for the SEM agency relationship. Then meet with them and ask them the hard questions. Ask how the relationship went. Ask if and how quickly the company responded to their requests. And the most important question to ask is, "If you needed work done again, would you still hire this company?"

The agency's job is to make you look like a hero, but if they are overloaded, you end up in a situation where you're just left hanging. So, if a reference says they would prefer to do their search marketing in-house or would not hire the company again for any reason, then you should reconsider whether you want to hire the company. It's a telltale sign when a previous customer won't hire the company again, but if they say they would, then that's a good endorsement for the company.

In the end, it's a leap of faith — at some point you'll need to pony up the cash to get the program up and running. Just make sure that whoever is handling the agency relationship in-house understands enough of the various facets being worked on to know if the agency is getting the job done properly. If you are a marketing manager tapped to manage this effort, get cracking on learning about organic search and paid search marketing yourself. Even a basic level of understanding can be enough to spot problems and get this sorted properly for you.

Jerri: If you find that your relationship with a search marketing organization isn't working, how do you get out of that relationship?

Forrester: Contracts, contracts, contracts. Make absolutely certain there are performance clauses in the contracts before you sign them. And because search is a long-term investment, clarify how long it will take to reach the results that you're being promised by the search marketing firm. Then you can incorporate a provision to pay a percentage of the fee up front and the balance of the fee when the performance goals are reached. If the organization is doing a good job with meeting their promised performance goals, then they should have no problem allowing this type of clause in the contract that they ask you to sign.

The most important part of hiring a search marketing firm is vetting them as a vendor. Ask for at least three references and then speak to them. If for some reason you can't reach one of the references, then go back to the vendor and request another one. Successful agencies should have plenty of customers waiting to tell others how good they are and, in fact, larger agencies have a list that's as long as your arm of people who have praise for them.

One final thought: If an agency or consultant *ever* promises you they can get you ranked as number one for any organic efforts, run, don't walk, away from them. No one can guarantee results in the world of organic search results. We don't know the actual algorithms the engines use to rank sites, so making guarantees such as number one is just a sales tactic, nothing more.

Results should be measured on actual metrics — inbound traffic from each search engine, conversion on the site, those types of things.

Stephen Harris, Managing Director, SPH Associates

Stephen Harris has been involved in the Internet marketing space since the late 1990s — initially as director of e-business technology at ADP, creating the first e-business platform for small business payroll services. Since then, Harris has designed and managed affiliate marketing programs and worked at DigitalGrit, an online marketing agency. For DigitalGrit he devised and provided project management processes to search marketing for large-scale, big-brand companies.

Harris's hands-on experience with SEO and online marketing has been as a consultant for the firm he started — SPH Associates. The firm is focused on small businesses, and this venue has led to his beliefs about conversion-based thinking for SEO.

Jerri: Where do you see the current state/importance of SEO?

Harris: SEO is very important ...   at least that is what business owners think. I receive calls where they say they need SEO — but in truth we learn that they need more effective web design and even paid-click programs. This does not mean to dispel the value of a top ranking — for credibility and indeed traffic — as per the EyeTool/Did-It study. [You can find this study at www.eyetools.com/inpage/research_google_eyetracking_heatmap.htm.]

I also see a ton of snake-oil salespeople, or people who simply give the client what they asked for without actually listening to what they need. There are people who claim they will submit your web site to the top 200 search engines. There are some that say they guarantee top listing on a few of the top 200 search engines but would never make such a claim for Yahoo!, Google, or MSN [companies that represent around 98 percent of all searches]. These snake-oil salespeople make it hard for legitimate SEO professionals to earn trust in the small and mid-size business space.

However, it is clear that the top three or four search engines are so ingrained into our way of life — we use Google as a verb — that it is important for businesses to design their web sites not only for effectiveness and usability, but also to get long-tail benefits.

Jerri: Could you please explain what you mean by long-tail benefits?

Harris: It just means that well-written, readable, and relevant content will help the site appear highly ranked on obtuse or lesser used search terms. But in accumulation, all these "little used" terms can add up big-time. I think that natural, well-written content that speaks to the reader will allow for long tail — rather than content that is gamed (or abused) for the top keyword that the SEO specialist is trying to achieve results for.

Jerri: What can organizations do right now to improve their SEO?

Harris: Work backwards — examine your web site and make sure your house is in order. Make sure your content is quick and tight yet readable — and do the SEO basics — title tags, image

425

tags, and the like. This all by itself will help your site to be relevant, and relevancy is key to Google success and, of course, conversions.

I am more of an on-site optimizer. I find some off-site linking to be dubious. I think the winds may be changing, causing highly linked sites not to be as relevant unless the links are truly relevant.

I provide suggestions to my clients on how to get effective links, and provide them with linking code to give to their peers and customers. I do employ someone that does linking since it still works, even though I don't fully agree with pursuing linking strategies.

Just create a relevant and compelling site. Make me want to be there and everything else will work out.

Jerri: What should web site owners be focusing on for future improvements?

Harris: From an SEO standpoint [web site owners should] become thought leaders in their space, using blogs, writing articles, and posting on the Web. [You should also] create a Web 2.0 stickiness to your site. Give people a reason for being there and wanting to come back. This in itself is not an SEO play, but by having strong content that is frequently updated and extended, you give the robot spiders plenty of reason to want to come back time and again.

Jerri: Are there any strategies that organizations might know about but are not implementing that might help with SEO results if they did?

Harris: I have been trying to figure this out, [looking for] some technology that enhances SEO beyond what we all know already. Unfortunately, some of these [technologies] tend to come back as black hat, which I am not a party to. The only black hat area I think should be *carefully* allowed is creating a clone for heavily Flashed sites, but that is a tough one to call.

The key is Web 2.0 — social integration; updated, frequent, and relevant content; and thought leadership. This all goes back to Google's principles on relevancy! Make it relevant and they will come ... and come again.

Jerri: What do you consider a strong, viable web site and how does that impact SEO?

Harris: Well, I am such a content purist sometimes — I believe that one should have a brief but good strong content strategy that tells me who you are, what makes you great or special, why should I be here, and how do I learn more (which falls under permission marketing). I can live without a lot of Flash and images. But I always lose that argument and concede the need for aesthetics.

Seriously, a good balance of content and attractiveness will rule the SEO day. Too much Flash and gee-whiz does not help conversions or relevancy except in some unique cases. A well-designed, well-written web site will do well from all perspectives.

Jerri: What changes in SEO are coming as the result of the growth of social media?

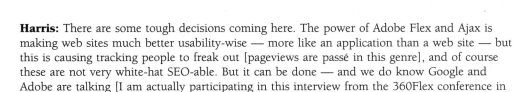

Harris: There are some tough decisions coming here. The power of Adobe Flex and Ajax is making web sites much better usability-wise — more like an application than a web site — but this is causing tracking people to freak out [pageviews are passé in this genre], and of course these are not very white-hat SEO-able. But it can be done — and we do know Google and Adobe are talking [I am actually participating in this interview from the 360Flex conference in Seattle].

I think the biggest changes are, again, that balancing act between the visual and the content, and how to balance them effectively. But here is a radical thought: SEO may not be as important for a strong social site, whereas word of mouth and viral marketing will be what delivers the visitation. Could social sites be able to thumb their nose at the search engines?

Jerri: Are there any other coming changes that will affect SEO?

Harris: Well, we think that Flex and other tools will become SEO-friendly. We hope people get it — and write their sites to focus on the visitors, not the robot spiders. To my knowledge, no sales have come from the spider . . . but they do come from the visitors.

We also are well aware of strong vertical search engines, and this may be an area where the rank-and-file SEO specialist is not focusing — to optimize for vertical search engines that are within the space of the client web site.

Jerri: Is there anything I haven't touched on that might be important for small to mid-size organizations to know about SEO?

Harris: Cost . . . cost is a huge issue. Education is another. I spend so much time discussing maintenance programs and the need to keep doing SEO monthly. It is not a one-time thing. And of course educating people that you do not need to pay people to submit your web site, and that no one can guarantee a top position on the top three search engines.

Again, back to cost. Small businesses have been educated that they need SEO, but they find they cannot easily afford it. Even mid-size businesses feel this way. The issue is that SEO is still mystical — whereas they know paid-click programs work, or if it doesn't work they can stop it quickly. The snake-oil people aren't helping.

My approach recently has been more commonsense–based, as discussed earlier. When someone asks me about SEO, I immediately ask them about their web site. Is it working for them? Then I look to see if it is effective and usable. I also try to manage their expectations. I had someone ask me to get them top-ranked for the word "diamonds," and they ended up not hiring me because I said they should consider more realistic targets like "quality diamond earrings" or something similar. Of course, for $100,000 maybe I could have gotten them top rankings [for such a broad term] but they only wanted to spend $5,000.

I am coming up with a product called SEO Lite, which provides basic usability and web effectiveness, along with SEO best practices and education about what web site owners can do on their own for optimization.

I do hear of major companies that have stopped their SEO initiatives. It's all about results and costs.

Jerri: In what circumstances would a company stop their SEO initiatives?

Harris: When they feel or perceive that they are not getting any real results from their ranking versus the cost of the maintenance fee. I think that this is often a perception, that maintenance fees bleed site owners dry, especially where it takes a long time to achieve high ranking for a top keyword. I think showing the long-tail increase may help stem this kind of maintenance remorse. It also may be a lack of clear communications with the client, or it could be specialists that get lazy and then the client does not feel there is any real effort occurring.

Jerri: If they are not focusing on SEO, what are they focusing on to improve site visits and conversions?

Harris: Site usability, implementation of Web 2.0, paid-click programs. And I think these are, or could be, even more important for clients initially, as they can achieve an immediate kick in visits and establishment of retention and loyalty. If the site is built using SEO standards, then over time the long-tail effect and time can naturally lift the site. I have not done any meaningful changes to my own site (www.stephen-harris.com) in many months, yet it is top-ranked! And in some very competitive keywords!

Ryan Hoppe, Director of Marketing, ATG

Ryan Hoppe serves as director of marketing for the Art Technology Group (ATG). Prior to his appointment at ATG, Hoppe was senior marketing director for FAST Search and Transfer. Before joining FAST, Hoppe managed product marketing for Microsoft Office Enterprise 2007 as part of Microsoft's Information Worker Division. Hoppe has also held product marketing and marketing communications positions at Groove Networks, Bose Corporation, and the communications consultancy Brodeur Worldwide. Hoppe holds a bachelor of science degree in communications from Cornell University.

ATG delivers innovative software to help high-end consumer-facing companies create a richer, more adaptive interactive and guided experience for their customers and partners online and via other channels. ATG's customers include: A&E Television, Aetna Services, Alcatel, American Airlines, Barclays Global Investors, Best Buy, BMG Direct, Eastman Kodak, Ford Motor Credit, HSBC, Hyatt, J. Crew, Merrill Lynch, Newell Rubbermaid, Target, U.S. Army, Walgreen Company and Wells Fargo.

Jerri: Could you give me an overview of what you're calling site search?

Hoppe: SEO is about driving traffic to destination sites on the Web; but when someone arrives at a destination site and wants to explore its content, that's where site search kicks in. Providing additional, relevant content helps build loyalty and keeps people on the site, which in turn helps boost search engine rankings.

There was an interesting study done by Susan Feldman at IDC. It indicated that up to 70 percent of searches on the Internet occur at destination sites. That means that only about 30 percent of all search goes through general web search engines like Google or Yahoo!. That gives you a sense of how large site search is.

Jerri: Does site search fall into the category of vertical search?

Hoppe: Not necessarily. Vertical search is still a web search engine; it's just crawling vertical-specific content and then using a tuned relevancy model to highlight relevant content in that vertical. The knock against Google and Yahoo! is that their web search relevancy model is too broad and is not really tuned to niche content. Vertical search engines better understand your context and tune their relevancy models appropriately.

For example, if you're looking for financial data on "bonds" using a vertical search engine, and you search for the word "bond," you would receive information (in the vertical) about financial bonds. But if you typed that same search into Google you might get James Bond very near the top of the results. The web search engine had no idea that you were looking for financial bonds, whereas the vertical search engine understood your context.

Jerri: Is there any value in SEO for site search?

Hoppe: Site search does some bad things and good things related to SEO. I'll give you the bad first.

Site search provides users with a truly dynamic experience versus static web pages that are pre-programmed. Landing pages and category pages, for example, traditionally have static content that is chosen by a marketer or merchandiser. Web crawlers are much better at crawling these types of pages with static content and keyword-friendly URLs. A search engine results page, on the other hand, is truly dynamic. It didn't "exist" before you typed in the search query and hit Return. The page — and its content — is rendered on the fly. Web search crawlers sometimes have a hard time indexing dynamic pages because they are not part of the site map; they are created at the moment of need.

Now the good. First, [you] can rewrite the URLs of search results pages to make them easier to crawl, inserting search keywords into the URLs. Second, [you can] create *topics pages* — landing pages focused on a specific topic that use search to draw in the most recent, relevant content on that topic. Topics pages help boost SEO because they are part of the standard site map, yet have dynamic, rich content that should help generate significant link activity.

Jerri: What's a tag cloud?

Hoppe: Tag clouds are usually boxes on a web page that help users explore other content related to a topic. Typically, the words in the cloud all have different sizes and formatting, so some words would have more emphasis than others, based on their relevancy or weight to the original topic.

Jerri: Is there anything we haven't touched on that would be important for people to understand?

Hoppe: SEO and site search are very distinct. However, one thing we haven't discussed is how site search can boost SEO purely by creating a better user experience. A web site that has advanced site search helps build a loyal community of visitors by enabling people to easily find what they are looking for on the site, and helping them explore and discover related content. It also helps recommend content to users as it gets to know them, based on their previous search and site interaction habits. By having a loyal base of users who come back to the site more and more, a web site should increase its inbound links, which in turn will drive up SEO. Though this is an indirect benefit, it is important to point out how search is becoming less of a "utility" for users and more of a way to create rich, dynamic site experiences that keep people coming back.

Diane Kuehn, President & CEO, VisionPoint Marketing

Diane Kuehn founded VisionPoint Marketing after holding numerous executive sales and marketing positions with, among others, Cox Communications, SourceLink, High Speed Net Solutions, and ADVO — the largest direct marketing firm in the U.S. Today, she's what the company calls the "lead brainiac."

VisionPoint Marketing is a marketing solutions agency providing integrated programs — interactive and/or traditional tactics — for mid-size organizations in a variety of industries including higher education, health care, biotech/life sciences, pharmaceutical, high tech, and business services.

Jerri: What's the big deal about SEO? Why is it suddenly the "must have" strategy for web sites?

Kuehn: I really think this is not new. I think that it's just a matter of people figuring out the Web. There are a lot of organizations that are just beginning to realize there has been a paradigm shift in the last 12–18 months.

I'm not sure the "must have" is a recent focus. I think that a lot of organizations have spent the last five to ten years figuring out what to do with their web site first. Now, as most are considering how the Web has changed, especially over the past few years, and they need to do a redesign, organizations realize that if they want to optimize their sites for the search engines, they need to start that process when they are redesigning and building their site.

This is the time to start the SEO process. I think SEO hasn't been something that they've focused on in the past as much, because they haven't focused on web site redesign. A lot of things are happening now that are causing people to refocus at this time.

The cost of search is zero. Since search is free, we are no longer basing our decisions on Yellow Pages. And search is even faster than word of mouth. Google search result pages are better than having perfect retail space on Main Street or a perfect billboard, so by optimizing your web site you can really do so much more, and you can get better results and it doesn't cost as much as it has in the past. Before, you had to spend a lot of money on all those other marketing outlets. Now, if you can be good at organic SEO, you have a jump-start on getting people to your site.

Rather than marketing — intrusive marketing — at your customer, prime customers (those who are ready to buy and are specific to your niche), you need to make sure they find you. Using search marketing you can meet their needs, rather than hit them with intrusive marketing. And if you are ranking well organically, there is an assumed authority that you are a leader in a specific field.

The last research I saw is that conversion from organic click versus paid click is three to one overpaid. And B2B [business-to-business] clients do know the difference. They're savvy enough in general to know the difference.

Jerri: What are some of the most frequently ignored strategies for implementing SEO? How does ignoring those strategies hurt organizations and how could improving them help?

Kuehn: A company or organization really needs to understand that ranking well in search engines is not about paying an agency to just do it. They have to build content. It truly is about building valuable content on your web site or out in the community.

It comes down to content versus search. People are finding things faster; they search for stuff and find it, and then when they get there, they're interacting more. So sites are built for the search engine — search engines are getting smarter so they recognize when a site isn't built for people. Then, when the people come to the site and see it's built for a search engine, they won't stay. Focusing on building for search engines doesn't work. You have to provide the audience with the content that they want.

Some companies don't understand that they need to build content. I just saw some research yesterday that talks about how time spent on content as an activity on the Web has increased by 37 percent, while search as an activity has decreased by 35 percent, over the past four years. Focusing on simply getting top results in rankings on the engines isn't going to get you new customers. You need to build content that helps you get top rankings on the engines *and* positions your organization as a thought leader or provides your audience with the content that they want.

Blogs, tutorials, high-quality tips and tricks . . . companies need to have the mindset that giving away info that is truly valuable is the best strategy. When you have good content that's linkworthy, then people are going to link to it.

Another thing that companies need to think about is navigation: how pages on your site interlink, and how the site works when you are dropped in the middle of it. If you're doing it right, people are coming into your site from all different places. Your design needs to be such that they know where they are in the site and they know how to get around. I have found that a lot of organizations think that the old standbys, such as pages that are about us, or contact pages and the like, are sufficient. They're not thinking about "when I land in the middle of the site, I still want to know how to get around." It's just assumed that I'm coming in from the home page and that's not always what happens.

Jerri: Are there other aspects of SEO that organizations could improve upon?

Kuehn: The biggest strategy that we find is undervalued or ignored — that not only helps SEO but also makes a site more user-friendly — is its information architecture. Planning out your site's navigation in such a way as to allow someone who drops right into the middle of the site from a search engine results page to still know where they are, how to find additional information, and motivates them to take the call to action, is extremely important. Once again, it's not about getting top rankings on the search engine results page; it's about getting the right people to your site and then engaging them.

Jerri: In what areas is SEO being handled well?

Kuehn: People are starting work in modern coding standards and that is good for SEO. We build all of our sites in xHTML. That means that it can work extremely well for the user in all of the different browsers, but also it's read the best by spiders, and mobile devices display it just like it's supposed to be displayed. Now I'm starting to see customers who are starting to recognize that this is an important thing. And other firms that are also starting to code that way.

Jerri: What's coming for the future of SEO and how can organizations begin to prepare for those coming changes now?

Kuehn: I think that what's happening with the Web . . . if you think of the evolution of search engines and the search engine algorithms, they have to stay a couple of steps ahead of the search engine spammers. So we're starting to see search results or weighting a site more by using a human editor. For example, there is some indication that Google may begin weighing Digg results into the authority given to a web site.

We are also going to see more and more content that is built specifically for SEO being removed from search engine result pages. Social search — Mahalo is a good example — wikis of search results, and other methods of human-filtered content are becoming popular. And it will work especially well if you can develop a way to use other search tools like Google and Yahoo! and filter out all the useless information.

Google is best suited to figure this out. So while there are sites out there like Digg and you're using them to vote as to whether a site is good or not, I think that Google could start to figure out how to weigh human input into their algorithm, and then that's essentially what's going to happen. The future is going to be more about "let's not focus so much on the search engine, let's focus on what's valuable content."

It's like the saying, "If you build it they will come." I think humans, as opposed to a machine, might think about your site and how valuable your site is, and that's going to be much more important than anything else that you can do. So if you can get people to drink the Kool-Aid on that — if you build it, they will come.

Jerri: How do you see vertical SEO going?

Kuehn: I think we're a little bit far off from that right now . . . that being where you want to spend a lot of time. Of course, it depends on how niche your business focus is. Let's use real estate as an example. If you're in real estate, you're going to want to focus on major search engines because that's where your audience is. Your audience isn't going to be something niche.

It depends. There are sites like Knowledge Storm where you see a lot of tech things and you can pay to be on there. That can be very effective from the marketing perspective of participating on that, but right now the money and focus should be on where people are going, and right now they're still on the major search engines. I think it's a ways off before people are going to their own niche area.

If Google can figure out how to deliver me good results (in specific vertical or niche areas), why would you try something else? Why would you split your searches up into different areas?

Matt Naeger, Executive VP, Operations, IMPAQT

Matt Naeger graduated from Duquesne University Law School and applies his legal training and expertise to the search industry in a multitude of ways — specifically as they relate to online client branding, as well as trademark and copyright issues. He spent six years managing large-scale direct marketing analysis projects for Fortune 500 clients before the start-up of IMPAQT in 1999. Naeger is also recognized as a true "thought leader" in search, frequently speaking at leading industry events and summits, as well as being considered a go-to source for search analysts and media.

IMPAQT was founded in 1999. The company redefined search marketing and stays at the forefront of the industry with a combination of innovation, strategy, expert staff, and analytics. IMPAQT's offerings include search engine optimization services, paid-search management, search education services, agency partnerships, search analytics, strategic consulting, customized reporting, and online/offline data integration. The company currently services Fortune 1000 corporations with data-intensive search marketing needs in the B2B, finance, insurance, pharmaceutical, retail, and travel industries.

Jerri: What do you see as the current state of SEO?

Naeger: People are starting to look at how organic optimization works with paid-search marketing strategies. In the beginning, there was a more siloed [compartmentalized] approach to search engine optimization and search engine marketing. Many organizations saw it as two different programs, and it was either one or the other. But now people are beginning to realize they have to do both together. When both are implemented, we have seen that they support each other and each becomes significantly more successful than when they operate independently.

Jerri: How does SEO fit into overall search marketing?

Naeger: To begin with, users still don't necessarily understand that a sponsored link is paid for. Even a lot of marketers don't understand. We find that many organizations are doing either one or the other, but they don't do both, but SEO should be a core component of any online marketing strategy. The opportunity to capture a very large audience at what is comparatively a small cost is something that should never be overlooked by a marketer in today's world.

SEO should also be utilized as a means of growing the depth of understanding of what users are wanting from your site and your company. By optimizing your web site to appear within organic search results, you can then evaluate the relevant terms associated with your site for potential purchases in engines where your placement may be lacking. As you evolve your online marketing strategies, SEO and SEM should both be looked at not only as a way to capture customers, but also as a way to understand them, and by extension a way to understand the effects of your total brand marketing efforts.

Jerri: What are organizations not doing that would improve their SEO if they did do it?

Naeger: Organizations are not educating people internally enough to allow them to understand what effect SEO and SEM can have on the marketing of their brand. This education should be done across the entire organization and not just within the marketing group that is responsible for the effort. To implement SEO effectively and successfully, multiple departments and third-party agencies must be involved, educated, and completely aligned.

They should educate the content team that "this is why the content should be done a different way," and show them how content can affect SEO.

They should educate the public relations department that a press release is not just a single document. It should be linked to the corresponding page on your web site.

Organizations should also look at SEO and SEM in order to build a web site that doesn't have to have changes made to it to keep up with any marketing changes that are made. That's where content management systems can help to integrate content into the site in a way that's relevant. They should build the site within the content management system, so that it can automatically integrate that press release or piece of content into the site in a quick and efficient manner.

One more thing is that people are turning a blind eye to other types of media. Search is a channel that is dramatically affected by both online and offline marketing. Companies should consider their overall media mix, and measure the results of that media by both online and offline effects.

Something that some organizations don't understand is that just because you're placing an ad on a search engine doesn't mean that ad has to be a click-to-sale effort. It's also a method that you can use to look at the data provided through search. The data collected during search can help uncover the intent of the customer, based on how they search and what they searched for. This is where the industry will turn next: complex data analysis and leveraging all of its intellectual value across all ad media.

Finally, a third capability that search marketing gives you is the ability to see how your competitors' advertising, both online and offline, can drive the awareness of the category and therefore may affect your marketing efforts as well. As you enhance the sophistication of the way you utilize online and offline tracking data, you will be able to react to and take advantage of the efforts of your competitors in ways that have not been possible in the past. As an example, using your search marketing results, you can learn what specific feature-interests consumers developed out of a new product launch, and using this information you can gain insight into the consumer mindset, which can then be utilized to build how you market your product in the future.

Jerri: What about social media marketing? How will it change SEO?

Naeger: Social media marketing helps you to build brand advocacy and lets you learn how consumers feel about your marketing efforts.

We will continue to see some big numbers on the growth of social media marketing until it reaches a maturity level. But it's not mature yet, and more and more people are finding it's useful. Social media change the way in which people find information. They don't want to spend as much time searching anymore. Social media give consumers the ability to find the information that they need based on recommendations from their friends and colleagues, as opposed to the message that the marketer is trying to send to them through their advertising.

The big question in the industry is, how can social media marketing affect search engine results pages? Until recently, social media haven't shown up in search engine results, but now we're starting to see more and more social media sites showing up under general research-based search terms. This is the reason that the search engine marketing industry began to take notice of social media.

The next evolution of the question right now is, how can we as search marketers understand and influence what is driving the inclusion of these results with the search landscape? Marketers want to understand how pages are showing up on their brand and what those pages are saying about them. A good example of a site that is driving a lot of search visibility for brands is Wikipedia. Wikipedia consistently ranks well in Google searches, and in particular for those searches relative to brand information. So marketers are trying to figure out how to use social media to rank well, and how to control social media search results algorithmically in order to help control the view of the brand that a searcher is presented with inside of organic search results.

Jerri: How long will it be before we see this algorithmic control and ranking of the influences that social media have on web sites?

Naeger: We probably won't ever see ultimate control, but I think people will find a way to influence search results with social media. There's also a lot more talk about vertical search, and even in social media marketing I think the search world will become more verticalized.

Verticalized search is where people are finding other places they want to search. I think the next evolution of search is of a person telling a search engine how, where, and what to be told and then utilizing the engine to deliver on that request. What this means is that people are starting to utilize different search engines for different types of content, and in the future this will also extend to using different search engines for different categories of information as well.

If you ask users to tell you what they want you to tell them, they will. Especially as it applies to organic SEO, consumers are saying they want information that's not necessarily of the brand, yet is specific to a particular type of content area or format. If vertical engines can deliver on this request in a fashion that is easy to use, then they will have the advantage over the personalized search features of the major search engines.

Jerri: Is there anything else that I haven't touched on that you think is important?

Naeger: The big thing is that the data and learning that you derive from what people do inside a search engine has an effect that we can't even fathom yet. There are ways to look at, track, and understand that data that are still in development. And when we figure out how to do that, we'll have the ability to provide users with the information they need through not only customized search programs, but also through the customization of all marketing efforts.

There's an adage used in the search space that goes, "He who has the most data wins." But that's only effective if you can look at the data, understand what it is telling you, and apply that understanding to your campaign. And I think that's where improvements for the future need to, and will, be focused.

Simon Otter, Technical Manager, thebigword

Simon Otter is the group technology manager at thebigword, with overall responsibility for the technology and associated processes used in creating integrated, efficient translation services.

Much of Otter's role involves working with customers to understand their technical and process requirements and then adapting technology to fit their needs. An early starter in IT, Otter began programming at the age of eight, and after graduating in software engineering, held several IT positions with the Ford Motor Company, creating localized public-facing software solutions, among many other projects. He is a chartered IT professional, a member of the British Computer Society, and a chartered engineer.

Thebigword is one of the largest translation companies in the world. Its web site is translated into nine different languages, and the company offers translation services to more than 3,000 clients in 77 languages.

Jerri: Tell me about your perspective on SEO localization.

Otter: We have been thinking about and developing how we should handle SEO for clients asking us to localize their web sites. It's quite a dark art, and everyone thinks differently about SEO. For some, it's just keywords and meta tags, and those customers want them translated, but there's much more to it. There are many different inputs that go into the mix of how to choose one keyword or another.

Typically, SEOs try to expand their keyword lists to other related keywords and compound phrases or terms and then build the needed content around these. And when you're doing it in one language, there's an almost subliminal process that goes into finding synonyms and related keywords, because it's your language and you recognize the keywords and phrases that will work for less money. There is a lot of careful selection and discarding of keywords.

When you're working with a multi-lingual site, it isn't that easy. When you go into another language, you immediately have a language barrier. What we propose to do is find the people who are enabled to translate but are also able to interpret the results once they're translated to see what words are still relevant.

As it stands, if an English-based company were to translate their site into German, the keywords could be translated, but the company wouldn't know what the words were. They could see the metrics for them, but they can't read the words, so it's difficult to tell if they're the right keywords.

Once you translate something to another language, there is usually a choice of words. Some of those words will have the same meaning as the English keywords, but others will not. And you don't want to use the keywords that don't translate into your message.

We propose to work within an SEO environment in a multi-lingual environment. We could translate the keywords into another language and then an SEO coordinator could review that translation and discard the words that are not relevant. Once you've translated the words and expanded your [second language] keyword list, then you must see if the words are still relevant, and if they are back translated — translated back to English — are they also still relevant?

Our thinking is around liberating the SEO environment. Once translated, then we could build a glossary that whenever you translate one word, this is what you should use for this word in this language. Then you could write all of the content around those keywords. And it would be based on the keywords that have already been examined and carefully chosen.

Jerri: Does the localized way people think affect how they consider SEO localization?

Otter: The way people think does play a role in localization. I think it does. An American might not think of localization as much as people in other countries do, but that's changing. A lot of education is required to help people understand the need to present localized web sites, but I would say it varies by corporate culture.

We suggest that you find an SEO partner when you're localizing your web site. We don't recommend hiring an individual, because in our experience, individuals aren't equipped to handle localization. Find a partner that specializes in translation because a company like that has more resources and can return a translation to you that's been validated or approved.

Once you've decided what keywords you want, you can build a glossary of those terms so the next time a word comes up, the proper translation for that word is already decided upon. Another tool you can use is a translation memory.

A translation memory allows you to analyze your pages against the translation memory to leverage existing translations. This is a method that's often used in translation to speed the process and keep the content consistent. Translators come and go. But you need consistency and you need to achieve the correct translations as quickly as possible.

We also work with our clients to understand their link structure. Links are important in SEO, but translating a link is a little more difficult than translating a word or phrase. So we work with clients to understand their link structure. We do essentially a translation of the links on a page to make it possible to contain a link hierarchy.

Sarah Skerik, VP Distribution Services, PR Newswire

Sarah Skerik is the vice president of distribution services for PR Newswire. In this role, she is responsible for managing the core wire product, content syndication, media relations, customer reporting, and targeted distribution products. PR Newswire Association LLC (www.prnewswire.com) provides electronic distribution, targeting, measurement, and broadcast/multimedia services on behalf of tens of thousands of corporate, government, association, labor, non-profit, and other customers worldwide.

Using PR Newswire, these organizations reach a variety of critical audiences, including the news media, the investment community, government decision-makers, and the general public, with up-to-the-minute, full-text news developments. Established in 1954, PR Newswire has offices in 11 countries and routinely sends its customers' news to outlets in 135 countries, in 40 languages.

Jerri: What are some of the misconceptions about public relations from an SEO perspective?

Skerik: First, let me put a finer point on my perspective. Public relations is not separate from SEO, it is a component of SEO. I'm thinking about all of PR Newswire's clients, which range from large to tiny. The large companies do SEO really well, and the small companies do SEO really well. Where the missed opportunity lies is in those mid-range companies that are large enough to have silos between the marketing and public relations departments.

Today, companies are spending a lot of time optimizing their sites. And in doing that, there are so many opportunities to really leverage press releases. But it requires a little shift in thinking. For example, about a month ago I was talking to a customer about SEO, and I was trying to understand their different departments and services. And what I found is that each person focuses on a different aspect of the company, but no one owned or took responsibility for the public.

Traditionally, press releases have been focused on delivering a message, not on how that message can be connected to search as part of their marketing campaign. And for that to take place, what really needs to happen is for organizations to develop an understanding of SEO across the organization. What keywords are relevant? What landing pages are relevant? All of this should be applied to press releases.

These are more involved than just what sits in the marketing department, because at the end of the day, the message is across the organization. Search engines put a lot of emphasis on content, so it's important to look at press releases not just as press releases, but as content.

For most organizations, content is a problem. That's one of the reasons that social media has become so popular. Blogs are a power indicator that there's fresh content here; and if a search engine sees that you've got regularly updated, fresh content, then they'll return to index your site more often.

My favorite advice to tell our customers is to stand back and really get a good understanding of how customers talk about your company and products. Then try to reach your customers using the way they speak and think. You can't change human behavior. Instead, you need to change the content to reach the people.

I would suggest that you march right over to the person in charge of SEO about any keyword research they have done. This helps you determine what keywords your customers are using, and then you can integrate those into your press releases.

Jerri: In integrating your press releases with the rest of your search marketing efforts, should you include links in them?

Skerik: Yes. You have to think of press releases as part of your content, not separate entities. It's absolutely fabulous to include the keywords that have been identified as productive for what you're marketing. And you can add extra emphasis to those keywords by linking them to corresponding pages on your web site.

The best practice is to link your press release to a page on your web site that's related to the keyword. The search engine then infers that the keywords, press releases, and links are all related and relevant.

Be careful, though, because you can dilute your efforts if the keyword is linked to a page on the site that doesn't contain that keyword. For example, if your keyword is "hot dog" and you decide to link it to a section on your page about hamburgers, reasoning that people who like one would be interested in the other, you actually risk diminishing your audience. Linking to a page that doesn't strongly support your message is a mistake, because search engines won't make the connection, and your ratings can suffer as a result. The search engine will see the press release, see the link, and follow that to the web page to see that there's nothing related to the keyword. If the search engine doesn't see something related, then that page won't get a powerful reciprocal connection.

This is where press releases can be really powerful. You send out a press release with links back to your site and it's widely distributed. The results will be links back and forth to your site, so the search engines will see the connection and it lends credibility to your site. Web sites that have the highest visibility are those that have hundreds of links back and forth. Here, again, this is an opportunity to strengthen your SEO because linking helps to build the overall authority of your site.

Jerri: You said there had to be a shift in the way that organizations think about using press releases. Does there also need to be a shift in the way companies think about using SEO as a means of gaining visibility for the message?

Skerik: Yes. Writing a press release is where some difference in thinking comes into play. Headlines are one area where you can gain a lot of mileage for SEO. Headlines are so important that

The New York Times is training their writers in SEO techniques so they know how to write headlines that are search engine friendly. Instead of the catchy headlines that most media organizations use, the practice now is to use contextual headlines that are relevant to the subject of the press release and that contain keywords.

Search engines read from the top down just like people do, and information at the top of a press release has the most importance. If you don't use keywords in your headlines, then you can lose really important real estate.

Clear writing, writing from the top down, including important information at the top of the press release, and writing in a natural style are all important to search engines, too. These are the same strategies that work to make content both people friendly and search engine friendly.

One more mistake that some people make is to try to write a press release to appeal to everyone, and that just doesn't work. It's not search engine friendly and so is not meaningful to SEO. Focusing your message is the better practice, from both the SEO and news writing standpoints.

Andrew Wetzler, President, MoreVisibility

Andrew Wetzler co-founded MoreVisibility ten years ago. Today, the company, which started with three people, has grown to more than 40 and has been named to the Inc. 500 list two years in a row. MoreVisibility targets small and mid-size businesses in niche markets, helping them create strategies for SEO and SEM. Some of their clients include the Metropolitan Museum of Art, Sony Disk Manufacturing, Clemson University, GarageTek, and Hagerty Insurance.

Wetzler is a member of MSN's Search Advisory Council and is the membership chair of the Direct Marketing Association's Search Engine Marketing Council.

Prior to MoreVisibility, his background includes 10 years of direct-marketing consulting, during which he taught organizations how to better utilize multiple channels to improve campaign performance. Andrew serves on the board of directors for Jambase.com. He holds a B.A. in economics from Tulane University.

Jerri: What do you see that organizations are doing well in search engine optimization today?

Wetzler: I think the first line in the sand is where in the process SEO comes into the mix. There are several categories: those companies that already have a web site and know they need SEO and also those companies that are about to invest in a major redesign and want to integrate SEO into the redesign. The second category is companies that have it in their head that they want SEO in the future, and they are planning their site around SEO principles.

Organizations are trying to create a balance between the search engine experience and the human experience — they're trying to decide which is most valuable and on which they should focus more of their attention.

I say they are both valuable. Organizations need to build a web site that first accomplishes the objectives, but you ought to have an understanding of the elements of SEO and how to use those to improve your search engine ranking.

Jerri: In what aspects of SEO are organizations not doing so well?

Wetzler: There are a couple of areas. Content is one area because organizations see content for search engines differently than content in general.

We try to get our clients to narrow the scope of their content on a page so there are not too many ideas on a page. This focus makes content more valuable and more relevant. And more focused content means that you continually have fresh material on your site, which is better because search engines see the content change more often and will revisit the site more often.

Jerri: What trends do you see that organizations should focus on now which will have impact in the future?

Wetzler: Again, I think that organizations need a careful balance of the bells and whistles with the notion of what a search engine needs to see.

Also, organizations should be thinking about making a web site that is easy for search engines to navigate but is also appealing to the user. And as new technologies evolve and begin to be implemented, organizations should carefully research and understand the impact those technologies will have on SEO.

Going back to the previous question for a minute, another situation where things get tripped up is when a smaller organization is part of a larger organization, but a separate entity. Often we see that a satellite office has a clear picture of what they want from SEO, but they are often without the ability to achieve that picture because their hands are tied by the corporate organization.

For example, we talked with a small local office of a large non-profit organization. They wanted to incorporate better SEO into their site, but when we looked at their site we found there was a lot of duplicate content across the web site. But fixing that has to come from the top down, so our hands were tied. Because the larger organization wouldn't change the way they did things, the duplicate content couldn't be removed.

If the SEO goals of the larger organization don't fit with the SEO goals of the smaller organization, there are limits to what can be done.

Jerri: Is there anything else that you think is important for organizations to understand about SEO?

Wetzler: There is one thing that I think some organizations miss. The organization should not look at SEO as the whole picture. SEM should be part of the bigger picture. Small to mid-size businesses are looking for a solution that gets their ranking up naturally, but it takes more than just organic SEO. SEO efforts should be combined with marketing efforts in order to achieve the best possible exposure.

There are also some companies that have incredible natural search engine results that want to know why they should invest in a paid program like pay-per-click. The combination of SEO and SEM is more effective than either of them alone.

Jill Whalen, Founder and CEO, High Rankings

In the early 1990s, Jill Whalen was a housewife and mom who discovered a passion for the Internet and building social media and social communities on the Web. Twelve years later, she's involved in SEO daily and is a well-known SEO expert at her consultancy, High Rankings.

Whalen prides herself on providing close, personal care to her clients through High Rankings. Through her SEO strategies, Whalen helps clients such as Geico, Breeders.net, Proctor & Gamble, the Log Homes Council, and the Discovery Channel reach better search rankings.

Jerri: What usually brings a client to you?

Whalen: Being a pioneer in the search marketing industry for 12 years and having a newsletter subscription base of 25,000+ subscribers has built a lot of credibility and trust around the High Rankings brand. Many of our clients have been newsletter subscribers for many years, and they want confirmation that what they've been doing on their own is sufficient. Often our first contact is with the Internet marketing manager of a small to mid-size B2B company who simply doesn't have the time to keep up with everything in the SEO space.

Jerri: What do you see as some of the least successful practices in SEO?

Whalen: There are a number of things in SEO that people believe are necessary, but which in reality have little to no actual effect on bringing highly targeted search engine traffic. For instance, submitting your web site to the search engines has no effect on whether your site will be indexed or ranked well. Putting keywords into the meta keyword tag is not needed if you are concerned with Google. Optimizing for keyword phrases that nobody actually searches for in the engines is another common SEO practice that yields no results.

Jerri: What are some of the most successful practices?

Whalen: Successful practices include carefully researching keyword phrases and systematically choosing the pages of the site in which they should be targeted. Then it's simply a matter of working them into the pages in a natural way.

Jerri: Are there any strategies that small and mid-size business know they should be using but don't? Why?

Whalen: We often find that the actual architecture of a site should be changed for best results in the search engines. But since this can often mean a fundamental redesign of the entire web site, it's not something that can always be done, and "workarounds" have to be found instead.

Jerri: What guidelines would you give a small or mid-size business that is just beginning to implement SEO strategies?

Whalen: I'd highly suggest thinking about their SEO at the very beginning of their web site development, or at least while they're in the process of a redesign. If they do that, they can get things right from the very start. Many small to mid-size companies spend tens of thousands on a redesign, and then they try to hire a company such as High Rankings for SEO. At that point, it can sometimes be too late, or certainly not as cost effective as it could have been had they consulted with an SEO firm during the redesign process.

Jerri: What changes have you seen in search engine optimization and search engine marketing over the last few years?

Whalen: The greatest changes have been in how companies measure the success of their SEO campaigns as well as the advent of social media marketing as a link-building tool.

For measuring success, it used to be done via search engine rankings; however, as rankings have become far less static, it's actually an impossible measurement. Search engines are no longer showing the same thing to everyone anymore. Most search results are personalized as well as geo-targeted. Today's measurement for success is in search engine traffic, conversions, and sales.

With social media marketing, web sites such as Digg and del.icio.us, as well as numerous other popular online communities enable savvy search marketers to get their clients' products and services noticed in a completely new way. Since having numerous high-quality links pointing to your web site is a big factor in getting found in the search engines, "link baiting" has become a popular new form of viral marketing that can really help an SEO campaign get off the ground.

Jerri: Will SEO even be possible as social media grows? If so, how will it change the way that SEO is achieved?

Whalen: Yes, as in the previous answer, it has already changed things to a certain extent. However, social media alone are not going to be half as effective if you have a "broken" web site. At High Rankings, we like to say that we "fix" web sites to be the best they can be for the users as well as the search engines. You'd be surprised how much good usability goes hand-in-hand with good on-page SEO. Very often, the things that make a web site better for its users also make it better for the search engines. After all, Google wants to find the best web sites for their users — the searchers.

Jerri: Any other changes that companies considering or even already using SEO should be aware of? How are those changes likely to affect SEO in the future?

Whalen: I'm of the SEO school of thought that the more things change, the more they stay the same. The same fundamental principles I've written and talked about since the early 2000s are still often the same ones we talk about today. The search engines want the same things they've always wanted — the most relevant web site for the search query at hand. The trick, if you will, is making your site actually be the best, and then getting the word out to others about it.

Jerri: Is there anything I haven't touched on that you think is important for small and mid-size businesses to understand about SEO?

Whalen: The greatest difference we see today is that you can't fake being the best anymore. There is simply too much competition out there. The best way to set yourself apart from all the others is to truly be creative and unique. If you're just going to offer the same product or service as everyone else, you don't stand a chance of making it in the search engines anymore.

Appendix C

SEO Software, Tools, and Resources

When you begin working with your SEO strategies, you'll find you need all kinds of resources. Most of those will be available on the Web, but it might take some searching to find them.

Rather than send you off to use a search engine, this appendix provides the URLs for dozens of tools that will help you optimize for search engines. You'll find everything from search engines and directories to keyword tools and other resources, which can be used to either improve your SEO in some way or submit your site when you're ready.

Some of the tools included in these pages are free, and the fees for the others vary dramatically — from very low (under $.05 per click) to very high (over $10,000 for the application). Obviously, all of the tools won't be for you, but if you're looking for something specific, these links should at least give you a place to start looking.

This listing of resources is by no means exhaustive, of course. Many other services and applications are available, and you are encouraged to check them out.

IN THIS APPENDIX

Major search engines and directories

Secondary search engines

Meta search engines

Keyword tools

Content resources

RSS feeds and applications

Search engine marketing resources and articles

Registration services and programs

Link resources and software

Pay-per-click

Major Search Engines and Directories

There aren't tons of major search engines any more. Since all of the consolidation in the industry, there are only a handful of really large search engines and directories, but there are hundreds of smaller ones that range from very general to very specific in nature. The following list covers the primary search engines. Secondary search engines are listed in the next section.

Google: www.google.com

Yahoo! Directory: http://dir.yahoo.com

Yahoo! Search Engine: www.yahoo.com

Open Directory Project: www.dmoz.org

Microsoft: www.microsoft.com

Ask: www.ask.com

Secondary Search Engines

The listings allowed in secondary search engines and directories can be general or specific. This list doesn't differentiate the search engines from the directories, and they aren't separated by types of listings, but there's still a pretty comprehensive list here, so you should be able to find enough places to list your site to keep you busy for quite some time.

AlltheWeb: www.alltheweb.com (same index as Yahoo)

AltaVista: www.altavista.com (same index as Yahoo!)

Simpli: www.simpli.com

Slider: www.slider.com

Miva: www.miva.com/us

Search123: www.search123.com

All the Internet: www.alltheinternet.com

Windows Live Search: www.live.com

MySearch: www.mysearch.com

Alexa: www.alexa.com

HotBot: www.hotbot.com

Netscape: www.netscape.com

Wisenut: www.wisenut.com

Lycos: www.lycos.com

Findtarget: www.findtarget.com

Towersearch: www.towersearch.com

Entireweb: www.entireweb.com

LiveSearching.com: www.livesearching.com

Scrub the Web: www.scrubtheweb.com

SearchHippo: www.searchhippo.com

ExactSeek.com: www.exactseek.com

Information.com: www.information.com

123World: www.123world.com

Jayde: www.jayde.com

LinkMaster: www.linkmaster.com

Qango: www.qango.com

Xoron: http://xoron.com

ZenSearch: www.zensearch.com

1800Miti.com: www.1800miti.com

Aesop: www.aesop.com

AXXASEARCH: www.axxasearch.com

Claymont: www.claymont.com

Cozy Cabin: www.cozycabin.com

Infotiger: www.infotiger.com

WhatUSeek: www.whatuseek.com

Where2Go: www.where2go.com

Genius Find: www.geniusfind.com

01 Web Directory: www.01webdirectory.com

Yeandi: www.yeandi.com

So Much: www.somuch.com

Wow Directory: www.wowdirectory.com

Business.com: www.business.com

Gimpsy: www.gimpsy.com

Go Guides: www.goguides.org

JoeAnt: www.joeant.com

Skaffe: www.skaffe.com

Web-Beacon: www.web-beacon.com

Beaucoup!: www.beaucoup.com

Complete Planet: http://aip.completeplanet.com

AlltheBizz.com: www.allthebizz.com

Find Hound: www.findhound.com

BizWeb: www.bizweb.com

Directory Archives: www.directoryarchives.com

Mavicanet: www.mavicanet.com

Re-QUEST dot Net™: www.re-quest.net

SuperSeek: www.superseek.org

Web World Index: www.webworldindex.com

Bigall.com: www.bigall.com

International Business Directory: www.internationalbusinessdirectory.com

Cipinet: http://directory.cipinet.com

America's Best: www.americasbest.com

LCN2000.com: www.lcn2000.com

At Home Business Portal: www.athomebusinessportal.com

BizWeb.com: www.bizweb.com

BamInfo.com: www.baminfo.com

Christ Engine: http://christengine.com

Among Stars: http://amongstars.com

Family Friendly Sites: http://familyfriendlysites.com

InCrawler: www.incrawler.com

SplashDirectory: www.splashdirectory.com

Kahuki: www.kahuki.com

Greenstalk www.greenstalk.com

Clush: www.clush.com

ALS Links: www.alslinks.com

Octopedia: www.octopedia.com

InfoListings Direct www.info-listings.com

Zorg-Directory: www.zorg-directory.com

DMOZ Zilla Direc www.dmozzilla.com

MostPopularSites.www.mostpopularsites.net

World Site Index: www.worldsiteindex.com

DataSpear: www.dataspear.com

Top Web Director www.twd.in

Meta Search Engines

Meta search engines are those that search search engines. This listing of meta search engines will point you in the direction of the most frequently used ones. You can't submit your site to most meta search engines. Instead, in order for your site to appear in these rankings, it must appear in the top listings in several other search engines.

DogPile: www.dogpile.com

MetaCrawler: www.metacrawler.com/info.metac

Kanoodle: www.kanoodle.com

7MetaSearch: http://7metasearch.com

Ixquick: www.ixquick.com

iZito.com: www.izito.com

Vivisimo: http://vivisimo.com

kartOO: www.kartoo.com

Mamma: www.mamma.com

SurfWax: www.surfwax.com

Clusty: http://clusty.com

CurryGuide.com: http://web.curryguide.com

Excite: www.excite.com

Fazzle: www.fazzle.com

Gimenei: http://gimenei.com

IceRocket: www.icerocket.com

Info.com: www.info.com

InfoGrid: www.infogrid.com

Jux2: www.jux2.com

metaEureka: www.metaeureka.com

Turbo10: http://turbo10.com

WebCrawler: www.webcrawler.com

Cuil: http://www.cuil.com

Mahalo: www.mahalo.com

Zuula Search: www.zuula.com

Keyword Tools

You could spend half your life and most of your budget trying to figure out which keywords will work best for your site, for your content, and for your search engine rankings. Tools, like the ones listed here, will make optimizing those keywords at least a little easier.

Google Keyword Tool: `https://adwords.google.com/select/KeywordToolExternal`

Google Search-Based Keyword Tool: `www.google.com/sktool/#`

WordTracker: `http://freekeywords.wordtracker.com`

SEO Book Keyword Suggestion Tool: `http://tools.seobook.com/general/keyword`

Submit Express Keyword Suggestion Tool: `www.submitexpress.com/keytracker.php`

Global Promoter Keyword Suggestion Tool: `www.globalpromoter.com/seo-tools/keyword-suggestion-tool.cfm`

BRL Keyword Suggestion Tool: `www.build-reciprocal-links.com/keyword-suggestion`

Trellian: Search Word Suggestion Tool: `www.keyworddiscovery.com/search.html`

Microsoft adCenter Labs Keyword Research Tools: `http://adlab.msn.com/Keyword-Research.aspx`

Keyword Intelligence: `www.keywordintelligence.com`

The Permutator: `www.boxersoftware.com/thepermutator.htm`

Keyword Typo Generator: `http://tools.seobook.com/spelling/keywords-typos.cgi`

SEMPhonic: `http://semphonic.com`

Digital Point Solution Search Engine Ranking Tools: `www.digitalpoint.com/tools/keywords`

Keyword Density Analyzer: `www.keyworddensity.com`

Search Engine Ranking Report: `www.top25web.com/cgi-bin/report.cgi`

Web Site Keyword Suggestions: `www.webconfs.com/website-keyword-suggestions.php`

Keyword Discovery: `www.keyworddiscovery.com`

SEO Research Labs: `www.seoresearchlabs.com`

SEM Rush: `www.semrush.com`

Keyword Density: `http://tools.davidnaylor.co.uk/keyworddensity`

Content Resources

Because content is such an important part of your web site (and your web site optimization), you'll need to know where to find it. The links in this section not only take you to content providers, but also to content syndicators and other content tools that will have the text on your page working overtime to keep visitors on your site.

ArticleDashboard: www.articledashboard.com

Creative Commons: http://creativecommons.org

Ezine Articles: http://ezinearticles.com

FreeSticky: www.freesticky.com/stickyweb

GoArticles.com: www.goarticles.com

IdeaMarketers.com: www.ideamarketers.com

World Wide Information Outlet: http://certificate.net

AbleStable Syndication: http://www.ablestable.com/resources/library/articles.html

FeatureWell.com: www.featurewell.com

MagPortal: www.magportal.com

Moreover: www.moreover.com

OSKAR Consulting: www.electroniccontent.com

Pages: www.pagesmag.com

Uclick: http://content.uclick.com

YellowBrix: www.yellowbrix.com

Hot Product News: www.hotproductnews.com

Internet News Bureau: www.internetnewsbureau.com

M2 Communications: www.m2.com/m2/web/page.php/home

OnlinePressReleases.com: www.onlinepressreleases.com/onlinepr/index.shtml

PR Newswire: http://prnewswire.com

PR Web: www.prweb.com

USANews: www.usanews.net

Google Knol: http://knol.google.com

CopyScape: www.copyscape.com

DupeCop: www.dupecop.com

RSS Feeds and Applications

In today's world of constantly changing content, RSS feeds and applications can contribute to your site optimization by keeping your content in front of prospective customers at all times. The content resources included here will help you set up all of the RSS options that your site needs.

Feedster: www.feedster.com

Lockergnome: www.lockergnome.com

NewsGator: www.newsgator.com

NewsKnowledge.com: www.newsknowledge.com/home.html

Syndic8: www.syndic8.com

Freshmeat: http://freshmeat.net

SourceForge.net: http://sourceforge.net

Technorati: http://technorati.com

BlogDigger: www.blogdigger.com

IceRocket: www.icerocket.com

Google Reader: www.reader.google.com

BlogPulse: www.blogpulse.com

Bloglines: www.bloglines.com

Sphere: www.sphere.com

Search Engine Marketing Resources and Articles

We could talk about SEO and SEM for hours and still not cover all there is to know about it. That's why it's good for you to immerse yourself in the culture of SEO. That way, you can keep up with what's going on in the industry and changes that might be made to the way SEO and SEM are achieved most effectively.

Search Engine Watch: http://searchenginewatch.com

Pandia: www.pandia.com

HighRankings.com: www.highrankings.com

Search Engine Spider Simulator: www.webconfs.com/search-engine-spider-simulator.php

WebCEO: www.webceo.com

Search Engine Simulator: www.delorie.com/web/ses.cgi

Measuring Up: www.measuring-up.com/seo-reference/seo-resources.html

ClickTracks: www.clicktracks.com

Similar Page Checker: www.webconfs.com/similar-page-checker.php

Search Engine Saturation Tool: www.marketleap.com/siteindex/default.htm

Internet Marketing Tools: www.webuildpages.com/tools/internet-marketing-page.htm

Meta Keyword Tool: www.apogee-web-consulting.com/tools/keyword_tool.php

Advanced Meta Tag Generator: www.optimization-services.com/meta.asp?id=4

Meta Tag Generator: www.searchbliss.com/free_scripts_metatag.htm

Search Engine Spider Simulator: www.webconfs.com/search-engine-spider-simulator.php

Webmaster World: www.webmasterworld.com

SEO Roundtable: www.seroundtable.com

SEO for Firefox: http://tools.seobook.com/firefox/seo-for-firefox.html

SpyFu: www.spyfu.com

Compete.com: www.compete.com

Caphyon Advanced Web Ranking: www.advancedwebranking.com

SoloSEO: www.soloseo.com

SEM Check: http://semcheck.com

SEO Digger: http://seodigger.com

SEO Quake: www.seoquake.com

SEO Automatic: www.seoautomatic.com/app

Google Webmaster Tools: www.google.com/webmasters

Latitude: www.latitudegroup.com

Registration Services and Programs

After looking at that huge list of search engines and directories at the beginning of this appendix, submitting your site to all of them might seem like an overwhelming task. If it does, the links in this section will take you to services and programs that can help automate your submission and registration processes.

AddPro: www.addpro.com

Ineedhits: www.ineedhits.com

Dynamic Submission: www.dynamicsubmission.com

Web Position: www.webposition.com

Submit Wolf: www.submitwolf.net

Directory Submission Tool: www.123promotion.co.uk/directorymanager

URL Rewriting Tool: www.webconfs.com/url-rewriting-tool.php

Link Resources and Software

Links are nearly as important as the content on your site, so you'll need some additional tools to help you stay connected with your linking strategies, and to help you gather links to your site or push links out from your site.

LinkPopularity.com: www.linkpopularity.com

MarketLeap: www.marketleap.com/publinkpop/default.htm

AntsSoft Link Popularity Checker: www.antssoft.com/linksurvey/index.htm

Xenu's Link Sleuth: http://home.snafu.de/tilman/xenulink.html

Link Alarm: www.linkalarm.com

Backlink Anchor Text Checker: www.webconfs.com/anchor-text-analysis.php

Backlink Builder: www.webconfs.com/backlink-builder.php

Backlink Summary Tool: www.webconfs.com/backlink-summary.php

Reciprocal Link Checker: www.webconfs.com/reciprocal-link-checker.php

Broken Link Checker: www.dead-links.com

Reciprocal Link Spider: www.recip-links.com

Site Link Analyzer: www.seochat.com/seo-tools/site-link-analyzer

Link Appeal: www.webmaster-toolkit.com/link-appeal.shtml

Link Popularity Check: http://uptimebot.com/sql/one.php

Robots Txt Generator: www.mcanerin.com/en/search-engine/robots-txt.asp

Robots.txt Syntax Checker: www.sxw.org.uk/computing/robots/check.html

Link Harvester: http://tools.seobook.com/link-harvester

Backlink Watch: www.backlinkwatch.com

SEO Link Analysis: http://yoast.com/seo-tools/link-analysis

LinkScape: www.seomoz.org/linkscape

Pay-per-Click

Pay-per-click (PPC) will likely be a large part of your marketing efforts for your site. PPC goes hand in hand with SEO, so the links in this section should help you find all of the PPC tools that you need. There are even some PPC services included in these listings.

Miva: www.miva.com

Enhance Interactive: www.enhance.com

EPilot: www.epilot.com

PayPerClickSearchEngines.com: www.payperclicksearchengines.com

7Search: http://7search.com

SearchFeed: www.searchfeed.com

Yahoo! Search Marketing: http://sem.smallbusiness.yahoo.com/searchenginemarketing

Google AdWords: https://adwords.google.com

Social-Media Tools

Social media is the next major shift in SEO that's happening right now. Web 2.0 is all about the social nature of the Internet, and if you don't tap into that social aspect, the SEO on your site will quickly be out of date. Using social-media tools, however, you can get a jump-start on your social-media strategy.

Social Tagging Tool: www.topsemtips.com/tools/sociable

Del.icio.us: http://del.icio.us

Digg: www.digg.com

Furl: www.furl.net

Twitter: www.twitter.com

MySpace: www.myspace.com

Facebook: www.facebook.com

LinkedIn: www.linkedin.com

Propeller: www.propeller.com

StumbleUpon: www.stumbleupon.com

Reddit: www.reddit.com

Newsvine: www.newsvine.com

Fark: www.fark.com

Clipmarks: http://clipmarks.com

Shoutwire: http://shoutwire.com

Social Bookmark Wordpress Plug-In: www.twistermc.com/blog/social-bookmark-plugin

Smogger Social Media Blog: http://smogger.wordpress.com

Micro Persuasion: www.micropersuasion.com

Social Media Optimization: http://social-media-optimization.com

SMO Mashup: www.smomashup.com

Mobile Optimization Tools

Right in line with social-media optimization is optimizing your web site for the mobile Web. With iPhones the current mobile phone of choice, and in many cases the Internet device of choice, reaching visitors through the mobile Web is becoming more and more important in your SEO efforts. These resources will help you start or improve your Mobile SEO efforts.

Google Mobile Proxy: www.google.com/gwt/n

Mobile Search Marketing Guide: www.mobilesearchmarketing.com/guide.php

Palm OS Emulator: www.tucows.com/preview/261443

Windows Mobile 2003 Pocket PC Development: www.microsoft.com/Downloads/details .aspx?familyid=57265402-47A8-4CE4-9AA7-5FE85B95DE72

Windows Mobile 2003 Smartphone Emulator: www.microsoft.com/downloads/details .aspx?familyid=8fe677fa7-3a6a-4265-b8eb-61a628ecd462

Google Mobile: www.google.com/xhtml

Yahoo! Mobile: http://mobile.yahoo.com/onesearch

Technorati Mobile: http://m.technorati.com

Google Mobile Sitemaps: www.google.com/support/webmasters/bin/ topic.py?topic=8493&hl=en

Yahoo! Submit a Mobile Site: http://siteexplorer.search.yahoo.com/mobilesubmit

Website Accessibility Initiative: www.w3.org/wai

Appendix D

Worksheets

SEO Plan

Goals and Strategies	Notes
Primary goal	
Secondary goal	
Secondary goal	
Secondary goal	
Description of marketing strategy	
Who are your best customers and why?	
Who is your competition? (Include URLs)	
What's the geographic scope of your marketing?	
Web Site Design	
Corporate history, news, PR, or current events?	
Executive bios?	
Product and service information?	
Customer support/live help?	
Online requests for information or contact forms?	
Membership-only content?	
Contact information?	
Forums?	
Educational materials?	
Links or resources?	
Archived content?	
Unique title tags on each page?	
Meta keyword tags?	
Meta description tags?	
Headers?	
Alt tags?	
Anchor text?	
Links and linking strategies?	
Keyword density? (Suggested 3–7 percent)	
Keyword Considerations	
Keyword brainstorming	
Initial keyword list	
Keyword research	
Pay-per-click strategies	

SEO Plan *(continued)*

Goals and Strategies	Notes
Content Considerations	
Well written and reader friendly?	
Keywords included in body text?	
Keywords included in titles?	
Keywords included in directories?	
Keywords included in file names?	
Keywords contained in images? (Should be avoided)	
Keyword variation?	

SEO Checklist

Current State

Check your rank in the major search engines.

Don't overuse or misuse rank-checking automation.

If it works, don't "fix" it unless the fix will improve your SEO efforts.

Keep your site fresh and persuasive.

Keyword Research

Use your visitors' words, not just your own.

Focus on phrases.

What key phrases are most popular?

What relevant key phrases have less competition?

Web Site Design

Is your site visually attractive?

Is your site's topic apparent at first glance?

Are your filenames based on relevant keywords?

Try to avoid frames. If you can't or don't want to, use appropriate workarounds.

Include a site-map page.

Include a `robots.txt` file.

Avoid delays and dead ends.

Write Clean Code

Put your indexable content as early as possible in the source code.

Put heavy JavaScript and CSS code in external files.

Include spider-friendly navigation.

Make Use of Tags and Attributes

Title tag

Description meta tag

Keywords meta tag

Alt tags

Headlines and headers

Keyword-based links

Table summary tags

SEO-Approved Content

Create unique content.

Make content as effective as possible.

Examine and adjust keyword density.

Avoid invisible text.

Avoid very tiny text.

Optimize your entire site.

Optimize your interior pages.

Give each page its own focus.

Manual Submissions

Submit to search engines and directories.

Know what your submission software does before you begin to use it.

Do not oversubmit.

Do you have a site map?

Linking Strategies

Cultivate quality links.

Avoid garbage links.

Offer accurate, enticing descriptions.

Ask for key-phrase or keyword discount.

Allow return links sparingly.

Links from third parties?

Conversions

Improved sales conversion often outweighs improved SEO performance.

Four Phases of the Buying Process Worksheet

This worksheet enables you to track your users through each step of the buying phase. With this information, you can then correctly apply SEO techniques to target and reach your site visitors where they are.

Prep Work

What is the profile of your target audience? Describe your audience completely as you understand them to be, including all phases of the buying process.

Phase 1: Curiosity

Describe your understanding of what your web site visitor is seeking in this particular stage.

List the content you have available to visitors in this stage of the buying process. Be sure to rank these items in order of importance, with 1 being the highest.

What content is missing? Again, rank the missing content in order of importance, with 1 being the highest.

Marketing activities currently employed to reach potential visitors in this stage. (Check all that apply and include a brief description of what the marketing activity includes.)

- ☐ Print
- ☐ TV
- ☐ Radio
- ☐ Direct mail
- ☐ Trade shows
- ☐ Seminars
- ☐ E-mail
- ☐ Permission marketing
- ☐ Affiliate programs
- ☐ Banner ads
- ☐ Word of mouth
- ☐ Other (please describe):

Phase 2: Deeper Curiosity

Describe your understanding of what your web site visitor is seeking in this particular stage.

List the content you have available to visitors in this stage of the buying process. Be sure to rank these items in order of importance, with 1 being the highest.

What content is missing? Again, rank the missing content in order of importance, with 1 being the highest.

Marketing activities currently employed to reach potential visitors in this stage. (Check all that apply and include a brief description of what the marketing activity includes.)

- ☐ Print
- ☐ TV
- ☐ Radio
- ☐ Direct mail
- ☐ Trade shows
- ☐ Seminars
- ☐ E-mail
- ☐ Permission marketing
- ☐ Affiliate programs
- ☐ Banner ads
- ☐ Word of mouth
- ☐ Other (please describe):

Phase 3: Justification and Value

Describe your understanding of what your web site visitor is seeking in this particular stage.

List the content you have available to visitors in this stage of the buying process. Be sure to rank these items in order of importance, with 1 being the highest.

What content is missing? Again, rank the missing content in order of importance, with 1 being the highest.

Marketing activities currently employed to reach potential visitors in this stage. (Check all that apply and include a brief description of what the marketing activity includes.)

- ☐ Print
- ☐ TV

- ☐ Radio
- ☐ Direct mail
- ☐ Trade shows
- ☐ Seminars
- ☐ E-mail
- ☐ Permission marketing
- ☐ Affiliate programs
- ☐ Banner ads
- ☐ Word of mouth
- ☐ Other (please describe):

Phase 4: Purchasing and Owning

Describe your understanding of what your web site visitor is seeking in this particular stage.

List the content you have available to visitors in this stage of the buying process. Be sure to rank these items in order of importance, with 1 being the highest.

What content is missing? Again, rank the missing content in order of importance, with 1 being the highest.

Marketing activities currently employed to reach potential visitors in this stage. (Check all that apply and include a brief description of what the marketing activity includes.)

- ☐ Print
- ☐ TV
- ☐ Radio
- ☐ Direct mail
- ☐ Trade shows
- ☐ Seminars
- ☐ E-mail
- ☐ Permission marketing
- ☐ Affiliate programs
- ☐ Banner ads
- ☐ Word of mouth
- ☐ Other (please describe):

Keyword Worksheet

Keyword or Phrase	Number of Impressions	Search Popularity	Estimated Click-Through Rate	Estimated Conversion Rate	Cost per Conversion	Landing-Page URL

PPC Keyword Worksheet

Keyword or Phrase	Category	Bid	Estimated Click-Through Rate	Estimated Cost	Estimated Conversion Rate	Landing-Page URL	Ad Title	Ad Description	Notes

Keyword Checklist

Brainstorming? (Enter preliminary keyword list here.)

Review competitors' sites? (Look specifically for HTML tags such as the title tag and meta tags.)

Check multiple keyword suggestion tools? (Enter the suggested terms below.)

List final keywords below.

Keyword tagging throughout web site?

Keyword testing? (Describe testing and methods used.)

Keyword Performance Worksheet

Keyword or Phrase	Cost per Click	Cost per Sale	Brand Awareness	Lifetime Keyword (Yes or No)	Products per Customer Value	Customer Loyalty Index	Notes

A/B Testing Worksheet

Factor/Attribute Tested	Control PPC Ad	Testing PPC Ad	Notes About Testing
Item number/description			
Goal page			
Completed goals			
Percent completed			
Percent change			
Paid (ads)			
Paid conversions			
Conversions and percent change			
Income from keywords			
Percent changed			
Average cost per conversion			
Testing results			

PPC Competition Worksheet

	URL	Competitor 1* Visible Keywords Links	Number of Inbound Page Rank (in more than one search engine)
Main page			
Page 2			
Page 3			
Page 4			
Notes about web site			
SERPs rank			
PPC sponsorship assessment			
Notes			

*Repeat this information for each competitor.

Link-Tracking Worksheet

URL	Requested Landing Page	Contact: E-mail and Web Site	Date Requested	Link Received	Landing Page	Notes

Rank-Tracking Worksheet

URL	Baseline	Month 1	Month 2	Month 3	Month 4

Glossary

8-bit UCS/Unicode Transformation Format
A variable-length character encoding for Unicode. It is able to represent any character in the Unicode standard, yet the initial encoding of byte codes and character assignments for UTF-8 is consistent with ASCII.

A/B testing   A method of advertising testing by which a baseline control sample is compared to a variety of single-variable test samples.

Ad groups   A group of ads that target one set of keywords or sites.

Adversarial search   A search algorithm that looks for all possible solutions to a problem, much like finding all the possible solutions in a game.

Affiliate programs   A method of promoting web businesses in which an affiliate is rewarded for every visitor, subscriber, customer, and/or sale provided through his or her efforts.

alt attributes   HTML tags that provide text as an alternative to the graphics on a web page.

alt tags   See alt attributes.

Alternative tags   See alt attributes.

Analytics   Measurement of web site statistics such as the number of visitors, where they arrived from, and how much time they spent on a web site.

Anchor tags   Text used to create links to other pages. Text is displayed as a link instead of the URL for the link being displayed. An anchor tag can point users to another web page, a file on the Web, or even an image or sound file. You're probably most familiar with the anchor tags used to create links to other web sites.

Anchor text   See anchor tags.

Anonymous FTP   A file transfer protocol that enables a user to retrieve documents, files, programs, and other archived data from anywhere on the Internet without having to establish a user id and password. By using the special user id of "anonymous," the network user bypasses local security checks and has access to publicly accessible files on the remote system.

Application programming interface (API)   A programming interface that enables other programs to interact with web browsers and web servers for the purposes of creating functionality between a program running in the browser or on the web server and the application.

Automated bid management   A process that uses software to monitor and manage the amount bid on a keyword or key phrase.

Bait and switch   A deceptive method of drawing users to a web site by providing the search engine with a highly optimized web page, but serving the user a different page.

Behavioral targeting   A technique used by online publishers and advertisers to increase the effectiveness of their campaigns. The idea is to observe a user's online behavior anonymously and then serve the most relevant advertisement based on that behavior.

Bid jamming   Placing a keyword bid that is just one penny below the highest bidder in an effort to force the advertiser to consistently pay a higher amount for the keyword.

Bid management   A method of monitoring used to control the amount spent on keyword bidding in pay-per-click and other paid-use keyword programs.

Black-hat SEO   Unethical SEO strategies.

Blog   A web site where entries are written in chronological order and commonly displayed in reverse chronological order.

Blogroll   A list of links to other blogs or web sites that the author of the blog regularly likes to read.

Body text   The text that makes up the body, or main section, of a web page.

Boolean search techniques   Search techniques formed by joining simple terms with *and*, *or*, and *not* for the purpose of limiting or qualifying the search.

Bounce   The term used to describe a web site visitor landing on a web page and immediately clicking away from it.

Brand keywords   Keywords that are associated with a well-known brand.

Bread-crumb trail   A text-based navigation strategy that shows where in the site hierarchy the currently viewed web page is located and your location within the site, while providing shortcuts to instantly jump higher up the site hierarchy.

Broad Head keywords   Generally, broad keywords that are in high demand and often cost considerable sums to use in pay-per-click and other paid keyword advertising.

Broken links   URLs or text-based links that do not lead to the expected page.

Buying process   A process that potential customers go through, consisting of four phases, from hearing about a product to purchasing that product.

Buzz   The talk that is going around the Internet about a product or service.

Call to action   A statement that entices a potential customer to make a purchase, sign up for a newsletter, or take some other desired action (e.g., "Buy now while supplies last!")

Cascading style sheet (CSS)   CSS is a style-sheet language used to describe the presentation of a document written in a markup language. Its most common application is to style web pages written in HTML and XHTML, but the language can be applied to any kind of XML document.

Category words   Broad keywords usually used by potential customers during the early part of the buying process. Category words include those that encompass a large range of topics, products, or services.

Clickbots   Software applications that run automated tasks over the Internet. Typically, bots perform tasks that are both simple and structurally repetitive, at a much higher rate than would be possible for a human editor alone.

Click fraud   A type of Internet crime that occurs in pay-per-click online advertising when a person, automated script, or computer program imitates a legitimate user of a web browser by clicking on an ad for the purpose of generating a cost-per-click without having actual interest in the target of the ad's link.

Click-through rate (CTR)   A way of measuring the success of an online advertising campaign. A CTR is obtained by dividing the number of users who clicked on an ad on a web page by the number of times the ad was delivered.

Click-throughs   See click-through rate.

Closing tag   An HTML tag indicating that a previously executed command should stop.

Code jockey   A person who is highly trained in computer languages and writes programming code full-time.

Constraint satisfaction search   The process of finding a solution to a set of constraints. Such constraints express allowed values for variables. A solution is therefore an evaluation of these variables that satisfies all constraints.

Container tags   A set of HTML tags that *contains* a full command. Usually indicated by the opening and closing tags (e.g., Bold).

Content cloaking   Content hidden by creating web site code that can detect and differentiate a search engine crawler from a site user. When the crawler enters the site, it is redirected to another web site that has been optimized for high search engine results.

Content management systems   A software system used for content management. Content management systems are deployed primarily for interactive use by a potentially large number of contributors.

Content-rich doorways   Doorway pages that contain a lot of heavily keyword-optimized content.

Content scraping   A technique whereby a computer program extracts data from the display output of another program.

Contextual targeting   The term applied to advertisements appearing on web sites or other media, such as content displayed on mobile phones, whereby the advertisements are selected and served by automated systems based on the content displayed by the user.

Cookies   Parcels of text sent by a server to a web browser and then sent back unchanged by the browser each time it accesses that server.

Copyright infringement   The unauthorized use of material covered by copyright law in a manner that violates one of the original copyright owner's exclusive rights, such as the right to reproduce or perform the copyrighted work, or to create derivative works that build upon it.

Core keywords   The broad keywords around which your web site is based.

Cost-per-action   See pay-per-click.

Cost-per-acquisition (CPA)   The amount it costs for a web site to acquire a new visitor or customer.

Cost-per-click (CPC)   A bid, placed on a keyword advertisement, that is charged each time a visitor clicks the advertisement.

Cost-per-conversion   The average cost of acquiring a conversion, or goal.

Crawl frontier   The URLs that a crawler can follow from a given point.

Crawlers   Search engine programs that *crawl* from one site to another, following the links given to them or included in the page they are examining.

Cross-channel tracking   A feature that enables PPC users to track their PPC programs on different computers and with different cookies.

Cross-linking　The practice of linking several sites together — usually sites that are owned by the same company or individual, although they don't have to be owned by the same company. They can also be random sites, related by topic, that have agreed to exchange links.

Dangling link　A link to a page that contains no other links.

Database　A collection of information stored in a computer in a systematic way such that a computer program can consult it to answer questions.

Dayparting　The practice of dividing the day into several parts, during each of which a different type of radio programming or television programming appropriate for that time is aired.

Deep submission tool　A tool that submits even the deep-level pages of your site to a directory or search engine.

Demographic targeting　Targeting a specific group of people for advertisements based on a particular demographic trait.

Deprecated tags　Older HTML tags and attributes that have been superseded by other, more functional or flexible alternatives.

Directory　A way of organizing files and other directories.

Domain cloaking　A strategy that enables you to redirect users to your existing web page while maintaining your URL in the browser's address bar.

Doorway pages　Web pages created for spamdexing — that is, spamming the index of a search engine by inserting results for particular phrases with the purpose of sending users to a different page. They are also known as bridge pages, portal pages, zebra pages, jump pages, gateway pages, and entry pages.

Drop shipping　An arrangement whereby merchants sell products from their catalogs or web sites and the products are shipped directly from the manufacturer or distributor, enabling the merchant to avoid incurring any costs for warehousing, packaging, or shipping.

Dynamic ASP　A method of creating dynamic forms and pages using the ASP.NET programming language.

Dynamic content　Content that changes regularly — usually news, blog content, or other types of easily renewable content resources.

Dynamic parameters　Refers to the changing part of a URL that provides data to a database so the proper records can be retrieved. Dynamic parameters are usually written on the fly when a particular document is requested.

Dynamic URLs　URLs that change according to variables such as content date or location. These URLs are usually written as the particular content is requested. Most often seen on product web sites where the product offerings change frequently.

Dynamic web pages　Web pages that deliver custom content created on the fly in response to specific input from the user.

Edge network　The second-generation (2G) wireless network used to transfer data to cell phones and other mobile devices.

Edited directories　Directories that are monitored and edited by humans.

Emo   A slang term used to describe people who have been labeled as emotional in nature.

Entity escape   Characters used to replace symbols when the search crawler is stopped by a specific character.

Error 302   A web site error that appears when a specific web page or web site has been moved temporarily.

Error 404   A web site error that appears when a specific URL cannot be found and no other indicator that the web site exists is apparent.

External navigation   A navigational structure that leads users off your web site.

Externalize   To run software from an external location, such as a file on a web server.

False Internet   When traffic is redirected to another web site that looks and feels the same as the intended site, but is actually designed and created as a method of redirecting traffic for criminal reasons.

Feed   See RSS feed.

Flash   A popular authoring software, developed by Macromedia, used to create vector graphics–based animation programs with full-screen navigation interfaces, graphic illustrations, and simple interactivity in an anti-aliased, resizable file format that's small enough to stream across a normal modem connection.

Flat link   A link that leads directly from a search engine or directory listing to a specific page on a web site, rather than to the main page of the web site.

Forbidden search terms   Words used in search that are censored by search engines.

Frameset   An HTML file that defines the layout of a Web page that is composed of other, separate HTML files.

FTP (File Transfer Protocol)   A common method of moving files between two computers over the Internet.

Gadgets   Small applications designed to run on a desktop or toolbar. The applications can be any useful *gadget*, from a clock to a note-taking application.

Generic keywords   Keywords that are broad in nature.

Geo-targeting   Serving of ads to a particular geographical area or population segment.

Goal conversion   Achieving a preset goal. In SEO, a goal conversion occurs when a site visitor completes a task you have defined.

Google Analytics   A web site statistics measurement program.

Google bombing   An attempt to influence the ranking of a given site in results returned by the Google search engine.

Header tag   The HTML tag that denotes the header of a web page.

Heat map   A graphical representation of data pertaining to how visitors use web sites. Some heat maps show how the eye travels across a web page, while others show how users click certain elements of a page.

Heuristics   Rules of thumb, or techniques, that people follow in order to make judgments quickly and efficiently.

Hidden pages   Article pages that are outside the standard navigational structure.

HTML tags   Code elements in a web page that identify different parts of the web page so the web browser will know how to display it. In some cases, HTML tags represent elements that are not displayed for users but are used by search engine crawlers for the purpose of indexing the web page.

Hybrid directory   A directory that uses both directory listings and search engine listings.

img tags   An HTML tag used to define alternative text in place of a graphic in the event that the graphic cannot be displayed.

Impressions   The number of times that people see a web page or advertisement.

Inbound links   Links to your web site from someone else's site.

Inclusion protocol   A protocol that tells search engines what they should include in their indexes for your site.

Indexing   A method by which web pages are classified in search engine databases. Each search engine uses a different algorithm to determine where in the index the web page should appear.

Informed search   Search that applies to a regular search using directing properties.

Internal linking   The links that lead from one page to another within the structure of a single web site.

Internal navigation   See internal linking.

Invisible keyword stuffing   Creating keywords on a page that are formatted in the same color as the web page's background in order to make them invisible to people but detectable to search crawlers.

JavaScript   A system of programming codes, created by Netscape, that can be embedded into the HTML of a web page to add functionality. JavaScript should not be confused with the Java programming language. In general, script languages such as JavaScript are easier and faster to code than more structured languages such as Java and C++.

Key performance indicators (KPIs)   Metrics by which the performance of a software application or other piece of software is measured. These indicators are usually determined by the software vendor or the customer who uses the software.

Keyword advertising   Advertising that is linked to specific keywords or key phrases. Usually, keyword advertising refers to pay-per-click advertisements, but it can take other forms as well.

Keyword density   The frequency with which chosen keywords or phrases appear on a web page compared to the other text on the page.

Keyword marketing   Marketing strategies built around the keywords that potential visitors use to find your web site. Keyword marketing usually refers to marketing efforts that require no monetary investment.

Keyword performance indicators   Elements of keyword performance that are used to weigh the effectiveness of a given keyword.

Keyword poison   Keywords that reduce the effectiveness of the keywords with which you have chosen to market your web site.

Keyword spamming   The practice of overusing keywords in an attempt to trick search engines into ranking a web site higher in search results.

Keyword stuffing   Adding more keywords to a web page, either in text or in HTML tags, than is appropriate.

Keyword suggestion tool   A software application that can suggest keywords based on the content of a web site or that can define various combinations of preselected keywords.

Keyword testing   A method of testing individual keywords to learn which words are the most effective for your marketing efforts.

Landing page   The web page to which visitors are directed when they click through an advertisement.

Leaking PageRank   The theory that linking to other web pages can reduce the PageRank of your web page. There is no proof that PageRank can be leaked, but nor is there proof that it cannot.

Link analysis   An examination of the links leading to and away from a web site to determine whether the links are quality links. A link analysis often also includes an examination of how successful the links are at providing customers with the correct information or at bringing new traffic to a web site.

Link bait   Downloadable files or content that's placed on a web page with the specific intent of building the number of links to a web page. The link bait strategy is often used with gadgets or high-demand content that visitors will find useful.

Link bombing   See Google bombing.

Link farms   Web pages that contain only links to other pages in an attempt to draw search crawler attention.

Link strategy   A method of defining what links a web site needs and where those links should lead to or from. The link strategy often also includes a strategy for receiving the desired incoming links.

Link tag   An HTML tag that defines a hyperlink within a document. The HTML code used is as follows: `<a href="URL HERE">Link text here</a>`.

List search   The ability to search for multiple terms by separating each term with a comma.

Long Tail   The Long Tail is a phrase coined by Chris Anderson in an October 2004 article in *Wired* magazine describing how a small portion of very popular products generate a sizable income, while a large portion of semipopular products generate small amounts of income that when added together can be equal to or larger than the income generated by the very popular products.

Long Tail search   Highly targeted, niche keywords.

Manual bid management   The practice of managing your keyword bids on your own, without the assistance of software.

Mashup   A web application that combines data from more than one source.

Match types   The conditions under which you prefer that your PPC ad be shown. These can be conditions such as the topic of the site on which the ad is shown, the placement or size of the ad, and even the exact pages that are allowed for the ad.

Matures   People who fall between the ages of 61–75 years old.

Meta refresh   An HTML meta element used to specify a time interval (in seconds) after which a web browser should automatically refresh the current web page.

Meta tagging   HTML elements used to provide structured metadata about a web page.

Millennials   People who fall between the ages of 18–25 years old.

Monitored directories Directories in which the submissions are read by human editors but rarely changed by those editors.

Multisubmission tool A submission tool that will submit your web site to multiple search engines.

Natural language A language that is spoken, written, or signed by humans for general-purpose communication, as distinguished from formal languages such as computer programming languages.

Natural language capabilities The ability of a search engine to retrieve web pages based on search terms that are written in natural language, as opposed to those that use Boolean operators.

Natural language search See natural language capabilities.

Negative keyword tool A keyword tool that highlights keywords you would *not* want included with the key phrases you are searching for.

nofollow tag An HTML tag that tells search engine crawlers that they should not follow a specific link or set of links on a web page.

noframes tag An HTML tag that indicates the content of a framed web site but ignores the frames.

Open directory project A directory that is populated by volunteers.

Opening tag An HTML tag indicating that a command is coming. The opening tag usually takes the following form: <b>.

Operators Special characters that are used when creating search queries (and in some programming languages) to better define the desired result.

Organic keywords Keywords that appear naturally on web pages and draw decent search engine rankings. These are usually keywords for which no paid keyword advertising programs or other paid advertising efforts are involved.

Organic SEO Strictly speaking, SEO efforts that are integrated with web site design and do not require a monetary investment.

Page-jacking A way of spamming the index of a search engine. It is achieved by using a popular web site to create a rogue copy displaying content similar to the original to a web crawler, but redirecting web surfers to unrelated or malicious web sites.

Page saturation The number of pages that a search engine recognizes for your web site.

PageRank A method by which web pages are ranked in Google search results.

Paid directory review (PDR) A fee-based service in which a web site is reviewed for a directory more quickly than others. A paid review does not guarantee inclusion or rank.

Paid inclusion (PI) service A service that connects search directories to consumers who will pay to have their web site added to that directory.

Paid placement A method of improving search engine ranking. The web site owner pays a fee to have a site listed in a search engine or directory, but that fee does not guarantee the search engine ranking for that site.

Pareto's Principle Also known as the 80/20 Rule, this principle holds that for any given event, 80 percent of the results come from 20 percent of the activity.

Path The route (or order of pages) that a visitor travels through your web site while visiting.

Pay-for-inclusion (PFI)   A strategy whereby you pay a fee simply to be included in a search index. This fee doesn't guarantee your rank in the index. It's a simple flat fee that's usually paid annually.

Pay-for-placement (PFP)   The service that guarantees your rank in a search index, which is also called *paid placement*.

Pay-per-click (PPC)   A keyword advertising program in which your ad is placed on other web sites by keyword match. In PPC programs, you're charged each time a web site visitor clicks your ad.

Pay-per-inclusion   A strategy in which you pay a fee to be included in a search index, but the fee that you pay in PPI is based on the number of clicks you receive as a result of that inclusion. Pay-per-inclusion still doesn't guarantee your rank in the search engine. You are only guaranteed inclusion.

PHP   A programming language that enables server-executable scripts to be inserted into web pages to increase the level of functionality that is available to web site visitors.

Placement targeting   A method by which you target your keyword advertisements to a specific web site or even to a certain location on a web site because that's where you believe you'll get the best response to those ads.

Plug-ins   A mini-application that performs a specific function after it is installed as a part of a larger program.

Poison words   See stop words.

Post-search ads   Advertisements that are served to web site users upon their exit from a web site, based on the pages they looked at while navigating through that site.

Primary search engine   One of the major search engines that are more general in nature.

Product words   Specific keywords that people usually use for searches when they're in the purchasing stage of the buying process.

Qualified traffic   Those visitors who are more likely to reach a conversion goal you've established for your web site.

Qualified visitors   See qualified traffic.

Reciprocal Link   When two web sites link to each other. Usually a consensual linking relationship, though reciprocal linking can also occur naturally for web sites in the same topic area.

Reference landing   Refers to the state visitors are in when they land on your web page during the early stages of the buying process.

Return on investment (ROI)   A mathematical calculation showing how much profit is returned for the investment that was made.

Reverse Bar   The bar at the top of a web page that shows the title given to the page. Usually, this bar is colored and the lettering in the bar is white.

Robots   Computer programs that visit a web site based on links and other criteria set out by the search engine algorithm.

Robot Exclusion Standard   See Robots Exclusion Protocol.

Robots Exclusion Protocol   A file that tells robots, or web crawlers, what not to look at while they are on your site.

Robots meta tag   A simple mechanism to indicate to visiting web robots whether a page should be indexed, or if links on the page should be followed.

robots.txt The file that is used to tell robots and crawlers what not to crawl on your site.

RSS feed A syndication feed that grabs news, blogs, or other activities and presents the reader with up-to-date content.

Scraper bot Software that crawls the Internet looking for content to steal.

Scraper site The web site where scraper content is collected.

Scraping Copying web site materials from another web site in an effort to create a false web.

Search algorithm A mathematical equation used to define what words or phrases someone is looking for and how the collected results should be returned to them.

Search directory A listing of the different web pages available on the Internet, divided by category and subcategory.

Search engine An application that indexes and serves content to an Internet user who is looking for something specific.

Search engine optimization (SEO) Improving a web site in order to attract search engine crawlers.

Search engine results pages (SERPs) The pages of results that are returned after an Internet user searches for a specific word or topic.

Search engine spam The process by which some people try to artificially influence the search engine into indexing their site and ranking it higher in the results.

Search marketing strategy A marketing strategy that applies specifically to achieving high rankings within search engine results pages.

Search profiling A method by which marketers can use the behaviors and actions of Internet users to target other users with similar interests and preferences.

Search query The string of words and characters used to perform a search engine search.

Secondary search engines Search engines that are more targeted in nature than primary search engines. These search engines are also smaller than primary search engines.

Seeding The process of loading a search crawler with URLs to examine.

Server side include (SSI) An easy server-side scripting language used almost exclusively for the Web. As its name implies, its primary use is including the contents of one file in another, via a web server.

Server-side redirection A method of URL redirection using an HTTP status code issued by a web server in response to a request for a particular URL. The result redirects a user's web browser to another web page with a different URL.

Simple directory A basic web directory that usually enables users to perform a search.

Site map A document that outlines where every link leads. Also a document that's included in the HTML code for a web page that directs crawlers where to go.

Site mirroring Including an exact duplicate of a web site in another location, usually stored on another server.

Snippet A brief portion of a larger piece of content.

Social bookmarking A way for Internet users to store, classify, share, and search Internet bookmarks.

Social media   A group of web-based applications that enable people with like interests to share that interest and other parts of their lives through participation in an online community.

Social-media optimization   A set of methods for generating publicity through social media, online communities, and community web sites.

Social network   A social structure made of nodes (which are generally individuals or organizations) that are connected by one or more specific type of relationship, e.g., values, visions, ideas, financial exchanges, friends, kinship, preferences, problems, trade, web links, sexual relations, travel, and so on.

Source code   The basic code around which a program or application is designed.

Spambots   Like crawlers, applications that crawl the Web searching out and collecting anything that appears to be an e-mail address. These addresses are then aggregated and sold to marketers, or even people who are not interested in legitimate business opportunities, for the purpose of sending out bulk e-mails.

Spamdexing   The process of spamming a search effort.

Spiders   Web crawlers that examine and index web pages.

SQL search   An alternative search module that offers an advanced search operand; searching by taxonomy term, user, and date; filtering within results; and an advanced search page.

Static URLs   URLs that do not change, but instead remain constant over time.

Static web pages   Web pages that stay the same all the time.

Stemming   The growth of one related word from another, using prefixes and suffixes, e.g., "game," "gamer," "gaming," "endgame."

Stop words   Forbidden words that will cause a search engine to stop crawling your web site.

Submission tools   Software applications that automatically submit a web site to search engines and directories.

Subset (data)   A small portion of an overall group of data.

Syntax   The rules governing the construction of search expressions in search engines and directories.

Table summary tags   HTML tags that provide a summary for a table in the event that it cannot be tagged properly.

Targeted search engines   Search engines that are targeted to a specific audience.

Text-delimited Excel files   Excel files that retain data formatting.

Throw-away domains   Domains that are purchased specifically for the purpose of having a referring domain. When these domains are discovered, they are deleted.

Title tags   HTML tags that define the title of a web page.

Total cost of ownership (TCO)   The total amount that ownership of a piece of software or application costs, based on not only the cost of the software, but also any other costs required to make that software work as expected.

Transactional landings   These are the entries that web site visitors make onto your site, based on keywords used to find the site during the purchasing phase of the buying process.

Tree searching   The process of searching data in a very logical way.

URL rewriting   A method for rewriting dynamic URLs based on the request received by the web server defining exactly what the visitor is seeking.

User agent   The client application used with a particular network protocol; the phrase is most commonly used in reference to those that access the Web.

UTF–encoded   See 8-bit UCS/Unicode Transformation Format.

Viral content   Shared content that quickly spreads online through a self-replication viral-type process. Viral content can be intentional or spontaneous.

Viral marketing   Marketing techniques that use pre-existing social networks to produce increases in brand awareness, through self-replicating viral processes, analogous to the spread of pathological and computer viruses.

Virtual include   See server side include.

Web 2.0   A perceived second generation of web-based communities and hosted services, such as social-networking sites, wikis, and folksonomies, which aim to facilitate collaboration and sharing between users.

Web directory   See search directory.

Webmaster   A person who designs and maintains web sites.

WHOIS Information   A database of information that lists who owns what domain name on the web.

XML inclusion   XML tags that tell a search crawler what should be included in the crawler's index for that URL.

XML site map   A file that lists all the URLs for a web site. This file is usually not seen by site visitors, only by the crawlers that index your site.

Zipf's Law   Developed by the linguist George Kingsley Zipf, this is a principle essentially stating that the specificity of any word is inversely proportional to its rank on a frequency table.

Index

Numbers

The books you read to succeed.

Get the most out of the latest software and leading-edge technologies
with a Wiley Bible—your one-stop reference.

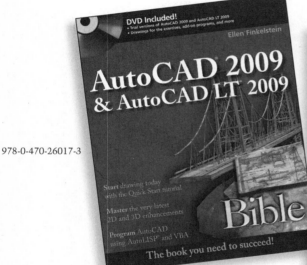

978-0-470-26017-3

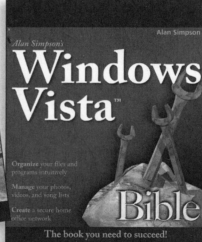

978-0-470-04030-0

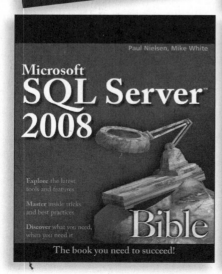

978-0-470-25704-3

978-0-470-37918-9